# *Applied* **BASIC** *Programming*

ROY AGELOFF
*University of Rhode Island*

RICHARD MOJENA
*University of Rhode Island*

**WADSWORTH PUBLISHING COMPANY**
Belmont, California
A division of Wadsworth, Inc.

82 9029 2

**Library of Congress Cataloging in Publication Data**

Ageloff, Roy, 1943–
  Applied BASIC programming.

  Includes index.
  1. Basic (Computer program language)
I. Mojena, Richard, 1943–      joint author.
II. Title.
QA76.73.B3A36       001.6'424       79-21142
ISBN 0-534-00808-9

Editorial production services by Cobb/Dunlop Publisher Services, Inc.

*About the Cover:* The cover of this book began as a black and white photograph of plastic daisy printwheels. The color was computer-generated through a high-resolution video camera, and the resulting image was converted to a 35mm transparency. Photograph courtesy of AGT Computer Products, Inc., 914 Westwood Blvd., Los Angeles, California 90024.

Printed in the United States of America

  4  5  6  7  8  9  10——84  83  82  81

*To the best part of us*
SHANA *and* YARA
*with love*

# *Preface*

This textbook is designed for a first course in BASIC programming. No prerequisites are required, other than fundamentals of first year algebra.

The combination of features described below distinguishes this book from others in the field.

**Topical coverage.** In Part I of the book, Chapter 1 provides a comprehensive overview of the field, while Chapter 2 introduces a four-step program design procedure and illustrates the process of running programs. Part II, Chapters 3 through 9, presents **minimal BASIC** essentially as specified by the proposed ANSI standard (*see pages 39–292, front cover*). Part III treats selected concepts in **enhanced BASIC,** including formatted output statements, data files and matrix commands (*see pages 293–352*). Part IV presents debugging concepts and techniques (Module A); an introduction to pseudocode, top down design, modular programming, structured programming, and other elements of programming style (Module B); and selected case studies (Module C).

The book can be used by itself in a course that emphasizes programming, in which case Chapters 1–11, Chapter 12 (optional), Module A, Module B, and a case in Module C can be covered in the equivalent of one semester.

Alternatively, the book can be used in conjunction with a nonprogramming book in a course that also emphasizes hardware, data processing, management information systems, social issues, and other topics. In this case Chapters 1–6, Module A, and optional material in other chapters can be assigned.

We might note that the PRINT USING statement (Chapter 10) can be assigned any time after Section 3.5 or Section 4.5; data files (Chapter 11) can be assigned any time after Section 5.3 (FOR/NEXT loops); assignment of debugging (Module A) is strongly recommended before the exercises at the end of Chapter 3 are attempted; and pseudocode, top down design, and structured programming (Module B) can be assigned any time after Chapter 5.

**Emphasis on meaningful applications and uses of the computer.** Applications include those relating to information processing and those relating to mathematical modeling.

*TABLE 0.1   Page References for Applications Programs*

## Information Processing

tuition revenue 19, 28, 49, 55, 64, 73, 75, 78, 90, 101

depreciation 70, 101, 289, 306

psychological self-analysis 86

sales commissions 107, 117, 119, 127, 149, 158, 304

finding minimum value 123

property tax assessment 137, 218, 283

personnel benefits budget 139, 284

affirmative action search 140, 321

computerized matching—a file search 141, 247

credit billing 142, 284, 306, 322

student fee bill 144, 285, 306

traffic court fines 162, 164, B-23

interactive price quotations 165, 218, 283

mailing list 175, 247

telephone company billing 176, 284

aging customer accounts 177, 306

checking account report 181, 285, 306

analysis of bank deposits 188

table look-up 205, B-23

direct access to array element—SAT scores 209

sorting 212

crime data summary 218, 247, 285

revenue sharing 220, 306

alphanumeric distribution 221

exam grading 222, 286

financial report 238, 337

income tax 241, B-23

interactive airline reservation system 247

personnel salary budget 250, 286

Fortune 500 sort 251

questionnaire analysis 253, 286

cross tabulations 254

electric bill 287, 306, 322, B-24

class grades 315

computerized inventory control system 317

payroll 322

student billing B-7

automated repair and maintenance system C-4

## Mathematical Modeling

costing 51, 68, 99, 135

microeconomics 52, 69, 99, 135

temperature conversion 53, 68, 98, 134

automobile financing 66

blood-bank inventory 69, 100, 136, 322

forecasting population growth 70, 100

bank savings account 91

revised tuition revenue 101, 172

retirement contribution 102, 172

bank drive-in queuing system 102, 173

factorials 138

quadratic roots 139

police car replacement 145

inflation curse 152

sales forecasts 178

installment loans 180, 285, 306

crew selection—a combination problem 183

bracket search algorithm 185, B-26

mean and standard deviation 203

support facility for oil drilling platform 219

polynomial root search 223

Poisson-distributed electronic failures 249

state lottery numbers 260

mathematical functions 264

polynomial plot 270

automobile rental decision 275, 283, B-23

craps simulation 286

statistical analyses 290

brand switching 338

solving systems of simultaneous linear equations 343

stock portfolio valuation 347

faculty flow model 348

multiple linear regression analysis 349

replacement model C-1

inventory simulation C-11

They are described in a wide variety of contexts, including areas in business, economics, mathematics, statistics and emerging areas in the public sector (e.g., health care delivery, emergency response systems, allocation of public resources, etc.).

Table 0.1 summarizes and references the applications described in the book through examples and exercises. This table clearly illustrates our philosophy that problems should be presented in an *evolutionary* context. As new material is learned, many examples and exercises improve upon previous versions of the same problem. This approach not only is pedagogically sound but also is consistent with (but not identical to) the evolutionary nature of program design in the "real world."

Module C describes three extensive applications using the *case method* of study popularized by graduate programs in business administration. These cases are designed as capstone programming assignments using a proven technique that simulates reality more effectively than end-of-chapter programming assignments.

**Extensive examples and exercises.** The learning of BASIC is greatly facilitated by numerous and carefully designed examples and exercises. More than forty *complete* programs are illustrated within the book; about half of these are accompanied by program flowcharts. Exercises are found both within chapters (Follow-up Exercises) and at the end of chapters (Additional Exercises). The book has more than 300 exercises, many with multiple parts. The chapters on minimal BASIC programming (Chapters 3–9) average 34 exercises per chapter.

Follow-up exercises serve to reinforce, integrate, and extend preceding material. This feature gives the book a "programmed learning" flavor without the regimentation of such an approach. Additionally, we have found that they create an excellent basis for planning many classroom lectures. Answers to selected follow-up exercises are provided at the end of the textbook. Answers to those follow-up exercises marked with either a single (*) or double asterisk (**) are given in the *Instructor's Manual.*

The chapter-end exercises offer opportunities for review and the development of new programming problems. All programming problems include test data. Examples and exercises are generally framed in business, economic, and public sector scenarios to interest and motivate the student. Exercises are ordered from least to most difficult. The more difficult exercises are designed to challenge the good student, and are identified by a double asterisk (**).

The histogram in Figure 0.1 summarizes the breakdown of space devoted to textual matter, examples, and exercises within Chapters 3–12. This further highlights the strong emphasis (75%) placed on examples and exercises within the primary programming chapters.

**Evolutionary approach.** Coverage of programming proceeds from simple to difficult, with students running complete programs by the end of Chapter 3. By design, the pace of chapters builds slowly, to encourage confidence and to develop a sound foundation. Necessarily, this approach discards the complete treatment of a topic in one place. For example, transfer of control is broken up into Chapters 5 and 6, and I/O is specifically discussed in Chapters 3, 4, 7, 8, 10, 11, and 12.

In addition, many sample programs and exercises are introduced early, and then improved and expanded in later chapters as new features of the BASIC language are presented.

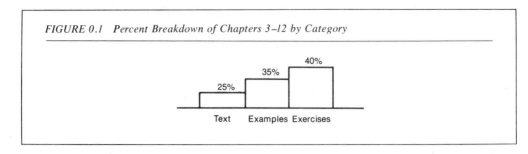

FIGURE 0.1   *Percent Breakdown of Chapters 3–12 by Category*

**Common errors.** The necessary process of debugging is time consuming, frustrating, and difficult to master by beginning programmers. In our experience, students commit certain programming errors more commonly than others. Accordingly, the book features sections on debugging procedures and common errors in *each* programming chapter, beginning with Chapter 4 and ending with Chapter 12.

**Top down design and structured programming.** The topics pseudocode, top down design, and structured programming in *Module B can be assigned anytime after Chapter 5* by those instructors who wish their students to design and write programs using these techniques. The assignment of Module B before Chapter 7 would serve to review style issues and to consolidate design philosophy at a receptive point in time.

The early assignment of structured programming is especially desirable if the local system supports structured BASIC statements. It is less desirable if minimal BASIC statements are used to simulate control structures to the letter, since forcing an inherently unstructured language (minimal BASIC) into pure structure requires "sleight of hand."

Our personal preference is to live with the unstructured faults of minimal BASIC while keeping in mind the spirit of structured programming (for example, top down execution and minimal use of GO TOs). This tradeoff will remain, of course, until the ANSI committee and the industry see fit to standardize a set of structured BASIC statements, a development we strongly endorse.

**A book on programming and problem solving, not a programming manual.** We believe that a BASIC course should be much more than just a course that teaches the BASIC language. It should teach the *process* of programming as a creative activity, from conceptualization of the problem to implementation of the computer program.

Our emphasis on applications, examples, and exercises is in keeping with this belief. Additionally, we give structure to the programming process by introducing a four-step procedure in Chapter 2 that facilitates the design and documentation of programs.

A programming course also should broaden a student's perspective. Accordingly, Chapter 1 overviews the field more thoroughly than the typical introductory chapter, and Module B discusses style issues of keen topical interest.

## Acknowledgments

We wish to express our deep appreciation to many who have contributed to this project: to Mike Snell and Jon Thompson, our editors, for unflagging encouragement, support, and expert advice; to Jenny Sill and Paula Delucchi, for liaison par excellence; to Warren Rogers, Chairman, and Richard R. Weeks, Dean, both of the University of Rhode Island, for consistent administrative help; to Diane Marcotte, for overseeing the preparation of hundreds of copies of the manuscript for class teaching; to our students, who suffered through "ditto" copies of the manuscript, yet managed to teach us something about teaching; to our reviewers, Larry Cook, Auburn University, Dennis Coleman, University of Hawaii, Henry Etlinger, Rochester Institute of Technology, Myron Goldberg, Pace University, Richard Hatch, San Diego State University, Richard Lott, Bentley College, R. Waldo Roth, Taylor University, and Clinton Smullen, University of Tennessee, who provided invaluable corrections and suggestions for subsequent revisions; to Fred Wild, for help with the manuscript and "grunt" work on the *Instructor's Manual;* to Fran Mojena, for her skill, patience, and steadiness in typing through several drafts of the manuscript, while claiming that she actually learned something; and to our immediate families, who remained cheerfully supportive in spite of our frequent absence.

*January, 1980*                                                                   ROY AGELOFF
*Kingston, Rhode Island*                                              RICHARD MOJENA

# Contents

## PART III   ENHANCED BASIC

# PART IV   MODULES

## PART I

# *Foundations*

# CHAPTER 1

# *Orientation*

The electronic computer is one of humankind's foremost technological inventions; for good or for bad, its presence affects each of us, and its future holds even more potential to affect our lives.

    This chapter is an orientation to the course you are about to take. We first define the computer and discuss its impact. Thereafter we provide a relatively complete, nontechnical overview of what makes up a computer system and a preview of how to communicate with the computer. Finally, we outline how you will benefit from this course.

If you are warm-blooded and living in the twentieth century, then we suspect that you are curious about the computer. Hopefully, by the time this course is over, we (together with your instructor) will have helped you translate that curiosity into a continuing, productive, and rewarding experience.

## *1.1*
## *WHAT IS A COMPUTER?*

A **computer** can be defined most generally as *a device which is capable of manipulating data to achieve some task.* Given this definition, adding machines, cash registers, gasoline pumps, and electronic calculators all qualify as simple computers. The machine we usually think of as a computer, however, can be identified by four significant characteristics:

1. Electronic
2. Speed
3. Storage capability
4. Ability to execute stored instructions

### *Characteristics of Electronic Computers*

The great speed of today's computers is a direct result of miniaturization in solid-state electronics. To give you a rough idea of the speed capabilities of large electronic computers, consider the following estimates. One minute of computer time is equivalent to approximately 6700 hours of skilled labor by a person using a calculator. In other words, a person using a calculator would take one hour to accomplish what a computer can accomplish in less than one hundredth of a second. In fact, the electronic transfers within computers are so fast that computer designers use a basic unit of time equal to one billionth of a second (called a *nanosecond*)—quite a feat when you consider that the basic unit of time for us mortals is one second.

A second significant characteristic of electronic computers is their capacity to store large amounts of data and instructions for later recall. In other words, much like the human brain, the computer has "memory." For example, computers at most universities can store several million characters of data in primary storage and hundreds of millions of characters in secondary storage.

Finally, an electronic computer is differentiated from most other computing devices by its ability to store instructions in memory. By this we mean that the computer can execute a set of instructions without interference from human beings. This characteristic makes the computer efficient: it can do its thing automatically while we do something else. Of course, the computer cannot completely do without us, but more about that later.

### *Computer Classifications*

To further narrow the definition of an electronic computer, we make the following distinctions: analog versus digital computers and special-purpose versus general-purpose computers.

The **analog computer** manipulates data represented by continuous physical processes such as temperature, pressure, and voltage. The fuel injection system of an automobile, for example, deals with physical processes as it regulates the fuel/air ratio in the carburetor based on engine speed, temperature, and pressure; the gasoline pump converts the flow of fuel into price (dollar and cents) and volume (gallons to the nearest tenth). Not surprisingly, therefore, analog computers are used primarily to control such processes. For example, analog computers now control the production of products such as steel and gasoline, provide on-board guidance for aircraft and spacecraft, regulate the peak energy demands of large office buildings or factories, and monitor the vital life signs of patients in critical condition.

As a strict computational device, however, the analog computer lacks the precision one needs with counting. Place yourself in the role of a computer which has the task of adding the numbers 1 and 2. Your props are a ruler, pencil, paper, and a jar of beads. You might proceed with your task as follows: first, you take out one bead from the jar and place it on the paper; next, you take out two beads from the jar and place them on the paper; finally, you count the number of beads you have on the paper. *Exactly* three, right? Now, be an analog computer. With pencil, paper, and ruler, draw a line one inch in length; next, draw a two-inch line at the end of the one-inch line you drew earlier; now measure the length of this overall line. Is your line exactly three inches long? Not really, only *approximately three,* for the accuracy of your answer depends on the precision of the scale on the ruler, the steadiness of your hand, the acuteness of your eyesight, and the sharpness of your pencil point. When it comes to calculating, the counting approach based on beads is more accurate than the approach based on measurement.

You will be using the **digital computer,** which operates by counting digits. This type of computer manipulates data (numbers in our decimal system, letters in our alphabet, and special characters) by counting *binary (two-state or 0-1) digits.* Hybrid computers which combine the features of digital and analog computers have been designed for certain types of applications, such as the analysis of aircraft designs which are tested in wind tunnel experiments.

We have been classifying computers by how they process data, but we can also classify them according to their function. **Special-purpose computers** are designed to accomplish a single task, whereas **general-purpose computers** are designed to accept programs of instruction for carrying out different tasks. For example, one special-purpose computer has been designed strictly to do navigational calculations for ships and aircraft. The instructions for carrying out this task are built into the electronic circuitry of the machine so that the navigator simply keys in data and receives the answer. Other special-purpose computers include those used in color television sets to improve color reception; those used in personal business exchange (PBX) telephones to perform various functions, such as automatic placement of a call at a preset time and simplified dialing of frequently used phone numbers; and those used in automobiles to calculate items such as "miles of fuel left" and "time of destination," and to monitor and read out instantaneously the status of oil level, gasoline level, engine temperature, breakline wear, and other operating conditions.

In contrast, a general-purpose computer used by a corporation might accomplish tasks relating to the preparation of payrolls and production schedules and the analyses of financial, marketing, and engineering data all in one day. Similarly, the academic computer you are about to use might run a management simulation one minute and analyze the results of a psychology experiment the next minute, or it might even accomplish both of these tasks (and more) concurrently.

In general, compared to the special-purpose computer, the general-purpose computer has the flexibility of satisfying the needs of a variety of users, but at the expense of speed and economy. In this textbook, we will focus strictly on the *electronic, digital, general-purpose computer.*

## 1.2
## IMPACT OF THE COMPUTER

Since the first sale of an electronic computer by Remington Rand in 1951, the computer industry has grown to the point that by the mid-1970s it had generated over $75 billion in sales and provided at least 700,000 jobs. The computer has revolutionized the operations of many governmental agencies, private enterprises, and public institutions, and many experts agree that the computer industry is a "young child" if not still an "infant." In this section we present a brief historical sketch of the development of the computer, provide you with a sample of computer applications, and end with an assessment of the computer's impact.

### Historical Sketch

Many conceptions and inventions dating back to the early nineteenth century were necessary precedents to the development of the computer. The first digital, general-purpose computer was completed in 1944 when Howard Aiken at Harvard University designed the **Mark I** to generate mathematical tables. Unlike electronic computers, the Mark I was a mechanical computer that operated by a system of telephone relays, mechanized wheels, and tabulating equipment. By current standards, it was *very* large, *very* unreliable, *very* slow, and *very* limited in its scope of applications. In 1946 the team of J. W. Mauchly and J. P. Eckert, Jr., from the University of Pennsylvania, completed the first *electronic* computer. This computer was named **ENIAC,** for the intimidating title Electronic Numerical Integrator and Calculator. Essentially, ENIAC was an electronic version of Mark I, in which vacuum tubes replaced the function of telephone relays; this replacement resulted in an increase of computing speed by a factor of nearly 200. Commissioned by the U.S. Army, it did an incomparable job (for the times) of generating artillery trajectory tables.

**UNIVAC I** (UNIVersal Automatic Computer), developed by Remington (now Sperry) Rand in 1951, was the first commercial computer. Unlike its predecessors, it computed using binary arithmetic and allowed the storage of instructions in internal computer memory. During this **first-generation** period, computers were developed by RCA, Philco, GE, Burroughs, Honeywell, NCR, and IBM. The first computer to achieve dominance in the industry was the IBM 650, which became the commercial leader during the period 1954–1959. These first generation machines used vacuum tubes, required air conditioning, had relatively small amounts of internal memory, and were slow by today's standards.

Subsequent generations of computers resulted in dramatic reductions in *size* and relative *cost* and increases in *speed, reliability,* and the capacity for *storage.* **Second-generation** computers during the period 1959–1965 replaced the vacuum tubes of the first generation computers with transistors. The most widely used second-generation computers were the IBM 1620, IBM 1401, and IBM 709 series.

The **third-generation** computers (1965–1970) that followed made use of the emerging field of microelectronics (miniaturized circuits) which increased the packing densities of transistorized circuits by a factor of 100. The third-generation computers were more reliable, faster, and more sophisticated than earlier computers. They also had the ability to handle several programs concurrently (multiprogramming), resulting in a more efficient use of the computer. The most prominent family of computers in this generation was the IBM System/360.

During the 1970s, a series of refinements and improvements to third-generation machines were marketed. These computers utilized large-scale integrated circuitry (LSI) and other microminiaturization features, resulting in further reductions in size and power requirements compared to earlier computers.

Another significant development in the 1970s was the use of small (in physical size and memory capacity), inexpensive, yet powerful computers referred to as **minicomputers** and **microcomputers.** The use of minicomputers is common in small to medium companies, colleges, hospitals, governmental agencies, and other organizations. Microcomputers, which are smaller than minicomputers, currently are marketed by consumer retail outlets such as Radio Shack. Today's desk-top microcomputers have more computing power than the massive first-generation machines that filled up an entire room. Moreover, the cost of a microcomputer is less than that of a first-generation computer by a factor of 10,000, or about $500 versus $5 million. Their use in small organizations and homes is expected to increase dramatically in the next decade.

## *Applications*

The computer represents a revolutionary technological tool for extending our applied capabilities. The diversity of the sample applications listed in Table 1.1 should give you an idea of the increasing influence of computers. Users of the computer include all facets of our society: individuals, private organizations such as industrial companies and banks, and public institutions such as hospitals, universities, and governmental agencies.

Basic information processing was a common early use of the computer, such as updating customer accounts, preparing payrolls, and generating status reports on personnel, sales, production, and inventories. Although these automated approaches were more effective than hours of "hand-crunching" effort by an "army" of clerks, they failed to adequately integrate the sources and uses of information in complex organizations. Today, users are calling for the design and implementation of *management information systems* (*MIS*) that can integrate and aggregate timely information for use by management in their decision-making activities.

Engineers, scientists, and mathematicians have used computers since their introduction for extensive mathematical calculations. In recent years, managers and social scientists have increasingly emphasized mathematical modeling in their decision-making activities. For example, disciplines such as *operations research* and *management science* develop and apply quantitative techniques (mathematics, probability, statistics) to help solve problems faced by managers of public and private organizations.

---

*TABLE 1.1    Sample Applications of the Computer*

---

**Information Processing**
Preparation of payroll and billings
Maintenance of inventory information
Maintenance of customer accounts
Technical processing of reference information by media and public libraries
Calculation of income taxes by the IRS
Maintenance of student records by universities
Maintenance of flight and reservation information by airlines
Cataloging of blood supplies by regional blood banks
Maintenance of checking accounts by banks
Editing and reproduction of typed manuscripts
Maintenance of criminal records by the FBI
Maintenance of property tax records by a municipality
Budgeting by organizations and individuals
Recording of monetary distributions by state and federal welfare agencies

**Mathematical Modeling**
Statistical analyses of census data, biological data, engineering data, etc.
Production scheduling and inventory control
Medical diagnosis
Orbital analysis for satellites
Management of financial portfolios
Location of fire stations in an urban area
Simulation of economic decay in a city
Dietary meal planning in institutions
Statistical forecasting
Educational planning and school bus scheduling
Design of airway and highway traffic systems
Chemical analysis
Design of solar energy systems
Planning, scheduling, and controlling complex projects (such as construction of a submarine, office building, or sports stadium)

---

The second part of Table 1.1 gives you an idea of the types of problems that lend themselves to mathematical modeling. In many cases the data required for these quantitative approaches to decision making are best provided by a MIS, which effectively integrates our two broad classes of applications.

Inevitably, the following question is asked: Can computers think? The computer cannot think in the usual sense, for it can accomplish only what people instruct it to accomplish through written programs of instruction. It is best at solving problems that are well structured, that is, problems whose solutions can be determined on a step-by-step basis which is quite explicit. Problems that require ill-defined or spontaneous actions to cope with complex or entirely new situations do not lend themselves as well to computer solution. For example, an executive can reorganize a company better than a computer; a composer writes music better than a computer; a chess master plays better chess than a computer; and an inventor is more capable of inventing than a computer.

As scientists come to better understand thinking processes behind creativity, adaptation, and judgment, programs of instruction for solving ill-structured problems will improve. This area of research, called *artificial intelligence,* has made some progress as computers have been programmed to compose music, play chess, prove theorems, and solve puzzles. Success, however, has been limited, and future progress in this area is uncertain.

## *Assessment*

Any task that can be performed by a general-purpose, digital computer can also be performed by a human being (given enough time). Of course, when it comes to the amount of data that can be stored and the speed with which these data can be manipulated, the computer is in a class by itself. In effect, therefore, the computer magnifies our own capacities. This results in both advantages and disadvantages, which we now summarize.

### *ADVANTAGES*

1.  *Power of analysis and technological advancement.* The computer can accomplish massive amounts of scientific calculation in a short span of time and can control complex processes such as steel making, automatic guidance of spacecraft, and air-ground traffic control.
2.  *Career opportunities.* The computer upgrades the skill requirements of jobs and creates new career opportunities both for labor and management; the current (and projected) supply of skilled people in this area is far short of demand.
3.  *Information needs.* As the society becomes more complex (and the individuals become more numerous), the computer provides a means to satisfy society's information needs.
4.  *Level of service.* The computer provides faster and better quality of service to members of society; examples include airline reservation systems, health care delivery systems, bank accounts, and preregistration of classes for university students. To illustrate the scale of service that the computer makes possible, consider the following:

> [The U.S. Department of Health, Education, and Welfare (HEW) provides] round-the-clock services that go directly to 115 million Americans and indirectly touch just about everybody in the nation. It is an empire, moreover, of 1,125,000 bureaucrats augmented by computers. Without its electronic marvels, HEW's accomplishments would be unthinkable. While most of the departments programs are administered from its huge Washington headquarters, Social Security data are processed in a building outside Baltimore by the most extensive computer system in the world. Every day an average of 20,000 claims are filed; every night the complete Social Security wage file, contained on 220,000 reels of tape, is run through the computers to provide information on the claimants. Next day, off go the forms that bring life-sustaining checks to the nation's aged and disabled.[1]

---

[1] "The Beneficent Monster," *Time Magazine,* June 12, 1978, p. 24.

5. *Cost savings to society.* The computer results in a more efficient delivery of services when used in applications where it is more productive than alternative approaches.

*DISADVANTAGES*

1. *Mistakes.* A survey of the public showed that 34 percent of those surveyed had a problem because of the computer.[2] Billing problems account for the majority of reported mistakes insofar as the public is concerned; in recent years, however, channels of communication for correcting errors have been improved. *The source of such mistakes is typically traced to computer personnel, rather than to the computer equipment.*
2. *Legalities.* Invasion of privacy and safeguards to programs of instruction and data have become major issues of national concern; the increasing centralization of files which contain information on individuals requires the legal protection of accuracy and confidentiality; computer crime has been one of the fastest rising categories of crime; examples of such crimes include the $2 billion Equity Funding Corporation swindle of the early 1970s, bank embezzlements which average $500,000 per swindle, and the theft of computer data tapes for ransoms.[3]
3. *Regulatory problems.* Federal and state agencies have an increasing problem in regulatory issues relating to computer product pricing policies, protection of copyrights and patents, and quality of data transmission over phone lines.
4. *Job displacement.* The creation of new jobs by the computer has resulted in the displacement of old jobs, a result which is typical of all new technologies (automobiles, airplanes, electricity, and so on); inevitably this causes psychological trauma, social displacement, and economic deprivation for the affected segment of the population.
5. *Dependence.* Our increasing dependence on the computer raises philosophical and practical issues regarding security; for example, backup systems are needed in airport traffic control should the main computer become disabled, and duplicate copies of critical data files should be maintained in case the original files are destroyed.

On balance the positive aspects of the computer far outweigh its negative aspects. As with all new technologies, however, those in positions of responsibility must strive toward correcting existing problems and, more importantly, preventing potential problems.

## 1.3
## ORGANIZATION OF A COMPUTER

Figure 1.1 should give you a "feel" for the makeup of a digital, general-purpose computer. As you can see, six components have been identified by the nature of their functions. Before describing each of these components, however, we define two terms which we use often.

[2] "A National Survey of the Public's Attitude Toward Computers," available from *Time Magazine,* Rockefeller Center, New York.
[3] See, for example, Don Parker, *Crime by Computer,* New York: Scribner's, 1976.

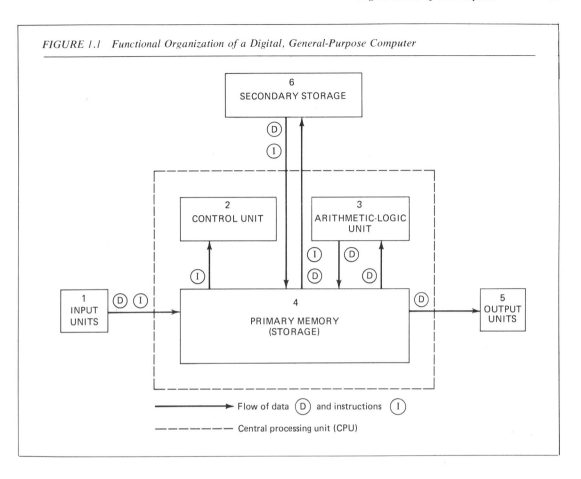

FIGURE 1.1   *Functional Organization of a Digital, General-Purpose Computer*

An **instruction** represents a specific task for the computer to accomplish. For example, the following represents three instructions:

1.  Read and store the name of a student and the grades received for the school term.
2.  Calculate and store the grade point average.
3.  Print the student's name and grade point average.

**Data** represent facts or observations which the computer is to input, manipulate, and/or output. In the above example, the student's name, grades, and grade point average all represent data.

As you read through the remainder of this section, you might find it useful to frequently look at Figures 1.1 and 1.2. The first figure relates components functionally, whereas the second figure shows photographs of specific components.

## Input Units

The input function of the computer brings data and instructions from the "outside world" to the computer's memory. To accomplish this transfer process, the data and

*FIGURE 1.2A    Functional Components of a Computer System (IBM 370). Courtesy of IBM.*

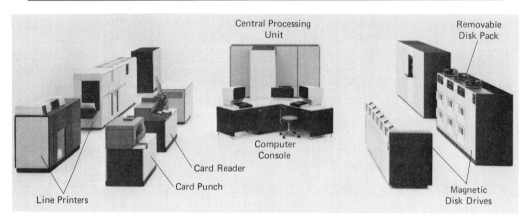

*FIGURE 1.2B    IBM 059 Keypunch Machine. Courtesy of IBM.*

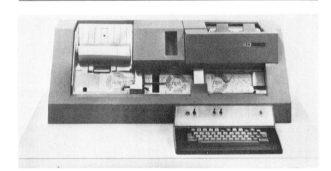

*FIGURE 1.2C    NCR 798-401 Video (CRT) Terminal. Courtesy of NCR.*

*FIGURE 1.2D    Xerox 1760 Typewriter Terminal. Courtesy of Xerox Corporation.*

*FIGURE 1.2E   IBM 3505 Card Reader Unit. Courtesy of IBM.*

*FIGURE 1.2F   IBM 3420 Magnetic Tape Drive. Courtesy of IBM.*

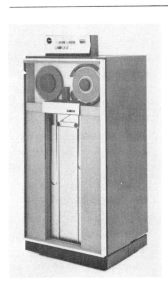

*FIGURE 1.2G   IBM 3211 Line Printer. Courtesy of IBM.*

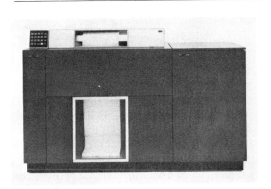

*FIGURE 1.2H   An integrated circuit. Courtesy of IBM.*

*FIGURE 1.2I   Radio Shack TRS-80 Microcomputer System. Courtesy of Tandy Corporation.*

*FIGURE 1.2J   HP 300 (left) and HP 3000 Series 33 Minicomputer Systems. Courtesy of Hewlett-Packard Corporation.*

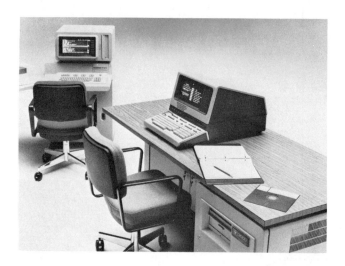

instructions must be converted into a "machine-readable" input medium. The more commonly used **input media** are punched cards, magnetic tapes, magnetic disks, punched paper tape, optical characters, and magnetic ink characters.

These media require **data preparation devices** to convert data from source documents (bills, invoices) to the desired medium. For example, the *keypunch machine* (Figure 1.2B) is a data preparation device for converting data on source documents to punched cards; a *key-to-tape machine* transfers data from source documents to magnetic tapes.

Data, once in machine-readable form, are transferred to the computer through an **input unit.** This device "reads" the coded data on the input medium and converts it into electrical impulses which are transferred to the memory unit of the computer. For example, the holes in a punched card are sensed by a *punched card reader* (Figure 1.2E) and converted to appropriate electrical signals which are submitted to the computer's memory for storage.

Table 1.2 lists some input units which are used with specific input media. By the way, MICR units are used by banks to process checks, and OCR units are widely used by universities for processing student records and grading exams.

Data and instructions also may be entered into a computer through **online terminals** (Figure 1.2C and D). The terminals are connected directly to the computer (the meaning of *online*) by either cable or telephone lines. Terminals have a keyboard for entering data and instructions, and either a visual display (video) screen or teleprinter for output.

In general, a computer system will have more than one input unit. The mix of input units in any one computer system, however, will depend on factors such as cost, the amount of data to be processed, and the method by which data originate.

## Central Processing Unit (CPU)

Input and output units are part of the computer system, but they are not generally considered the "computer"; rather they are *peripheral* to the computer. The **central processing unit**—consisting of primary memory, control unit, and arithmetic-logic unit—is what most professionals think of as *the* computer, as illustrated in Figure 1.2A.

The **primary (internal) memory** unit of the computer stores instructions and data. Sometimes this unit is called *core storage,* because in some computers primary memory is made up of thousands of "doughnut" shaped magnetic cores strung like beads on wire. More recent computer models use *semiconductor memory* where the basic memory component is the *electronic (silicon) chip,* two of which are illustrated in Figure 1.2H. These units are cheaper, faster, and more compact than core memory.

Regardless of the technology which is used to construct memory units, primary memory consists of storage locations which have numerical designations called *addresses*. Figure 1.3 represents a means of visualizing the storage locations of primary

TABLE 1.2   *Input Units and Input Media*

| MEDIUM | CORRESPONDING INPUT UNIT |
| --- | --- |
| Punched Card | Punched Card Reader (Figures 1.2A and E) |
| Punched Paper Tape | Paper Tape Reader |
| Optical Characters | Optical Character Reader (OCR) |
| Magnetic Ink Characters | Magnetic Ink Character Reader (MICR) |
| Magnetic Tape | Tape Drive (Figure 1.2F) |
| Magnetic Disk | Disk Drive (Figure 1.2A) |

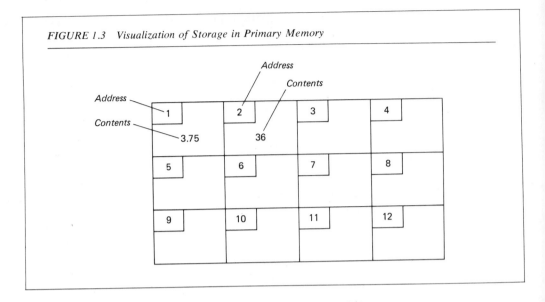

*FIGURE 1.3    Visualization of Storage in Primary Memory*

memory. Each storage location is assigned a number (**address**) that is used to reference the location whenever the item of data stored within that location (**contents**) is to be accessed. For example, in Figure 1.3, an employee's rate of pay, $3.75, is stored in location 1 and the number of hours worked by that employee, 36, is stored in location 2.

The storage capacity of computer memory may be expressed in terms of the number of characters (bytes) that can be stored. By a **character** or **byte** we mean a letter, numerical digit, comma, plus sign, and so on. Because of the way memory units are constructed, storage capacity is usually expressed as some multiple of 1024, where the number 1024 is represented by the letter K. For example, recent electronic chips smaller than the tip of your finger have quoted memory capacities of 64K, which means that each chip can store 65,536 (that is, 64 × 1024) characters of data. Primary memory units usually range in storage capacity from 4K to 8000K.

Data stored in primary storage are transferred to the **arithmetic-logic unit** whenever processing of data is required. Basic arithmetic operations such as addition, subtraction, multiplication, and division are performed within the arithmetic-logic unit. In addition, logical operations such as comparison of values can be made. This capability permits the testing of various conditions, for example, if an employee is entitled to receive overtime pay.

The **control unit** of a computer directs the operation of all other units associated with the computer, including peripheral devices (input/output units). The control unit obtains instructions from primary memory, interprets these instructions, and then transmits directions to the appropriate computer components. For example, suppose the instruction "read and store student's name and grades" is obtained from memory and interpreted by the control unit; the input unit would be directed to read these data into memory. The next instruction might be "calculate and store the grade point average"; the control unit would direct the memory unit to provide the arithmetic-logic unit with the data; then the arithmetic-logic unit would be directed to perform the calculations and to transmit the result to primary memory.

Interestingly, current technology can place an entire CPU on a single electronic chip that is less than one quarter of an inch square. These so-called **microprocessors** are as effective as small second-generation computers in terms of calculating and storage capabilities. In effect, a microprocessor that you can balance on the tip of your finger is equivalent to an early 1960s computer with a CPU as large as an office desk.

## Output Units

The function of an **output unit** is exactly opposite that of an input unit; that is, an output unit receives data from the computer in the form of electronic signals and converts these data into a form which can be used by either humans or computers. The list below summarizes output units; of these, most likely you will use online terminals.

*Line Printers.* If output of data is meant for human "consumption," then the line printer may be used. The line printer illustrated in Figure 1.2G is capable of printing 2000 lines per minute, each line having up to 132 characters. Picture yourself standing in front of such a printer. At 65 lines per page, you would see approximately 31 pages of printed output whiz by you in the time span of one minute.

*Online Terminals.* If you are using either a video or teleprinter terminal as an input unit, then most likely you are using the terminal as an output unit. This is convenient, but compared to a line printer, the speed of output is slow. Many computer systems, however, allow input through terminals and output on line printers, a feature which is advantageous if a particular job requires a high volume of output.

*Other Output Units.* Other output units include *magnetic tape drives,* which have both read (input) and write (output) capabilities using the magnetic tape medium; *paper tape units,* some of which can be attached to remote, online terminals for the purpose of both input from and output to punched paper tape; *magnetic disk drives,* which allow both input from and output to magnetized disks which resemble a stack of LP phonograph records; *card punch units,* which allow output onto punched cards; and *voice response units,* which process verbal output. Voice response units, by the way, have been used by telephone companies for many years. Without realizing it, you might have listened to the computer give you someone's new telephone number.

## Secondary Storage

**Secondary storage (auxiliary** or **external storage)** is memory that is housed outside the central processing unit. Instructions and data not currently in use are kept on secondary storage and read into primary storage when needed. Magnetic tapes, disks, drums, and data cells are used for secondary storage. Compared to primary storage, secondary storage has greater capacity at less cost, but the amount of time it takes to access data is greater.

## 1.4
## COMMUNICATING WITH THE COMPUTER

If we wish to solve a problem using a computer, we must communicate our instructions to the computer through a language. A *language* can be defined as patterns that have meaning. To a computer, these patterns are electronic; to a human being, they are symbolic (letter, numbers, punctuation). Unfortunately, no computer can understand any of the some 4000 languages practiced by peoples earthwide. It was necessary, therefore, to invent **computer languages** for the express purpose of person-machine communication. These can be classified into the three categories shown below. The designation **high-level** refers to a computer language which is far removed from the patterns ''understood'' directly by the computer. A **low-level** language, therefore, deals with patterns which are more nearly compatible with the electronic patterns of the machine.

| | |
|---|---|
| 1. Procedure- and problem-oriented languages | High-level languages |
| 2. Assembly languages | ⇑ |
| 3. Machine languages | Low-level languages |

## Procedure- and Problem-Oriented Languages

Any language can be distinguished from any other language by its *syntax,* that is, by the rules for arranging a specified set of symbols into recognizable patterns. You will be communicating your instructions to the computer using a language called **BASIC.**[4] This is one of many **procedure-oriented languages.** In general, these computer languages are easily understood by us humans (after some education, of course) and are relatively *machine-independent,* which means that they can be used across a wide variety of computers. BASIC is one of the most popular of high-level languages used for solving algebraic or scientific-type problems. By this we mean that BASIC is an excellent language for solving the types of problems which we described earlier as ''mathematical modeling.'' Moreover, BASIC can be used for ''information processing'' applications as well, although *COBOL* (*CO*mmon *B*usiness *O*riented *L*anguage) is a more widely used language for such applications.

**Problem-oriented languages** usually refer to a set of high-level languages which have been developed for solving certain special-purpose problems, such as the simulation of traffic flows in a city or the computer editing of newspaper articles.

A **computer program** is *a complete set of instructions written in a computer language for solving a specific problem.* Table 1.3 illustrates and describes a BASIC program having exactly six statements. **Statement** is another term for instruction. In the next two chapters, we will examine this program in detail (so don't be concerned about it, yet).

## Assembly and Machine Languages

Each type of computer has associated with it an assembly language and a machine language. An **assembly language** is specifically designed for a particular type of computer; hence, it can accomplish more detailed tasks for that computer than could a high-level language. Such a language, however, requires more specialized training for

---

[4] This stands for *B*eginners *A*ll-purpose *S*ymbolic *I*nstruction *C*ode. It was developed at Dartmouth College in the mid-1960s to simplify the learning of computer programming using online terminals.

TABLE 1.3   BASIC Program for Calculating and Printing Revenue for a State College Based on Tuition and Fees

| BASIC PROGRAM | HOW THE COMPUTER EXECUTES EACH INSTRUCTION (AND WHAT IT MEANS IN ENGLISH) |
|---|---|
| 10 LET C = 80 | Store a value of 80 as the contents of a storage location addressed or identified as C. (The cost per credit, C, is $80.) |
| 20 LET S = 6000 | Store 6000 in S. (The number of students, S, at this school is 6000.) |
| 30 LET B = 15*C + 250 | Multiply the contents of the storage location known as C by 15, add 250, and store this result in the location called B. (The average student bill, B, is the average number of credits (15) times the cost per credit (C, or $80) plus a fee of $250, which gives $1450.) |
| 40 LET R = B*S | Multiply the contents of B by the contents of S and store the result in R. (Total revenue due the college, R, is the average student bill, B, times the number of students, S, which gives $8,700,000.) |
| 50 PRINT "REVENUE = $";R | The computer prints the contents of R as follows:<br>  REVENUE = $ 8700000 |
| 60 END | Stop processing this program since the physical end has been reached. |

persons who would use it. In other words, it is more difficult for us to learn an assembly language than to learn a high-level language. Another disadvantage of assembly languages is that they vary from one computer type to another. Thus, if we were restricted to programming only in assembly languages, we would need to learn a new assembly language for each computer type we might use—and worse yet, every computer program which was written for one computer would have to be rewritten for use on another computer.

After all this, you might be surprised to learn that computers do not directly "understand" either high-level or assembly languages! Computers understand only machine language. An instruction in **machine language** is written in binary form as a series of 0s and 1s, as this scheme conforms to the needs of the electronic circuitry in binary computers. Needless to say, programming in machine language is tedious, which is one reason why high-level languages were developed.

## Interpreters and Compilers

How is it possible for the computer to understand the BASIC program which you write? Well, each computer manufacturer provides the means for that computer to translate your BASIC-language instruction into an equivalent instruction in machine language. This translation of a high-level language into its equivalent machine language is accomplished by a computer program called an **interpreter.** In other words, the interpreter acts as the language translator between you and the computer, much as a foreign language interpreter would translate from English into, say, Spanish.

The interpreter resides as a separate program in primary memory during the entire process of "running" your program. The interpreter first translates a single instruction into its machine language equivalent and then immediately *executes,* or carries out, this instruction. Then it processes the next instruction in the sequence in the same manner: first translation, then execution. If a particular instruction violates syntax, then the interpreter does not understand the instruction and prints an error message to that effect.

A **compiler** is similar to an interpreter, with the exception that all instructions are first translated line by line prior to execution. Providing there are no syntax errors, the result is a separate program in machine language called the **object program.** The object program is then executed by the computer. In this case, the program written in the high-level language is called the **source program.**

## 1.5
## COMPUTER SYSTEMS

Your interactions with the computer involve much more than a simple communication between you and the CPU. In fact, you will be dealing with a comprehensive computer system.

### Hardware and Software

The **computer system** is a collection of related hardware and software. As the name implies, **hardware** refers to the physical equipment: input/output (I/O) units, CPU, secondary storage, and other specialized machinery. The term **software** refers to computer programs, procedures, and specialized aids that contribute to the operation of a computer system. In general, software is classified as either systems software or applications software.

**Systems software** is a term for programs which are designed to facilitate the use of hardware. The **operating system** of a computer (supplied by the computer manufacturer) is the most important piece of systems software. This software, which is often called the *manager, monitor,* or *supervisor,* consists of a number of specialized programs for operating the computer efficiently. Among others, the following important functions are performed by the operating system.

1. Scheduling the sequence of jobs within the computer[5]
2. Supplying the appropriate compiler or interpreter
3. Allocating storage for programs and data
4. Controlling input and output operations
5. Performing "housekeeping" chores, such as accounting for the amount of CPU time used by each user

**Applications software** denotes programs which are written in either high-level or assembly language to solve specific types of problems. These programs are normally

---

[5] Each computer program which is to be run (executed) is called a *job.*

developed "in-house" (by the organization's systems analysts and programmers) to process applications such as payroll, inventories, billing, and accounts receivable.

Many computer manufacturers and independent software companies prepare generalized applications packages ("canned" software) for widely used applications. The cost of these packages range from a few hundred dollars to amounts in excess of $100,000. For example, the materials requirement planning (MRP) package provided by IBM is designed to assist a manufacturing company in managing its labor force, machines, materials, and money; Information Associates, Inc. has developed a package called *Students Records System* for generating class rosters, grade reports, and student transcripts; and SAS (*S*tatistical *A*nalysis *S*ystem), SPSS (*S*tatistical *P*ackage for the *S*ocial *S*ciences), and BMD (*BioMeDical*) are three statistical packages widely used by researchers. By the way, the types of programs that you will be writing in your computer class are examples of applications programs.

## Batch versus Time-Shared Processing

The specific configuration of hardware and software in a computer system is determined by the needs of that organization. For example, many small-to-medium-sized organizations use minicomputers for all of their data processing needs. Microcomputers in particular are becoming commonplace in small businesses and in homes. Two of the more common processing environments in academic institutions are batch processing and time-shared processing.

*Batch Processing.* Those of you who will be punching programs on cards most likely will be submitting jobs by the "batch" method. After you have punched your program onto cards, you will submit your job to the computing center personnel in order to have your program compiled and executed. In this mode of operation, programs are grouped and executed at the computing center according to job priorities established by computing center personnel. In some batch environments, each program is run serially, that is, one program at a time. In more sophisticated systems, with *multiprogramming* capabilities, several programs may be executed "simultaneously" under the control of the operating system. In either case, it may take from a few minutes to several hours before the results of your program are available to you. When you pick up your job at the computing center, errors may exist. These errors must be identified, corrected, and the job must be resubmitted. This cycle continues until you are satisfied with the results.

*Time-Shared Processing.* Most of you will be introduced to computers within a "time-sharing" environment. In a time-sharing environment many users working at online terminals have "simultaneous" utilization of the computer system. In this mode of processing jobs, you will send data and instructions to the computer via terminals, and the computer responds within seconds. This "dialogue" between you and the computer continues until you complete the task on which you are working. Thus, you code, execute, and correct programs at a terminal that is connected directly to the computer. While sitting at a terminal you may believe you have the computer to yourself. Actually, you and others who use terminals are sharing the computer's CPU in rotation under the control of the operating system (thus, the term *time sharing*).

Many of today's computer systems include two or more processing environments. For example, the computer systems in many colleges and universities include both batch and time-shared processing. Many of these same systems also feature *remote batch,* whereby *you* can submit your own jobs to the card reader and receive your results at a line printer in a location which is removed from the computer center; and *batch interface,* whereby you can bypass the use of cards altogether by entering your program at a terminal into the batch "stream" and receiving your output on either the line printer at the computer center or the online terminal.

Which system is best for you depends on many factors, some of which are listed here.

1. *Turnaround time* is usually less for time sharing than for batch processing. By turnaround time we mean the time between submission and completion of a job.

2. The *process of correcting programs* is more convenient by time sharing than by batch processing, for two reasons. First, in time sharing, it can all be done in one place. In other words, you submit your job, get results, and make corrections all at the terminal in one sitting. Second, time-sharing systems have powerful *editing* capabilities for making changes in programs. For example, if you have to change the same letter in each of 20 different lines in a program, then you must repunch each of 20 cards in the batch approach. In time-sharing, a single command may automatically make the 20 changes in your internally stored program.

3. *Direct interaction* between person and machine is facilitated by time sharing. This is useful for many types of analyses and decision processes which require the user to make a sequence of decisions based on feedback from the computer. For example, a computer program which simulates factors such as levels of world population, pollution, energy consumption, depletion of natural resources, and per capita income can be used interactively by government officials to answer "What if . . . ?" types of questions. (Such programs do exist!)

4. Jobs which require *many computations* are best handled by batch processing. This is because time-shared jobs must wait their turn for CPU time. For example, a job which requires, say, 60 minutes of CPU time would reside at least 60 minutes within the computer in a batch environment, but the same job may take several hours to complete in a relatively busy time-sharing environment. By the way, your jobs will probably use less than one second of CPU time.

5. Jobs which require *large amounts of input or output* also are best run in a batch environment. For example, a job which prints 30 pages of output may take 1 minute on a line printer and 120 minutes on a teleprinter terminal which prints 30 characters per second.

## 1.6
## BEFORE YOU LEAP

Before you "leap" into your course in BASIC, we offer some objectives for you to ponder and some advice which we believe is sound.

### Objectives

By now we should have convinced you that increasingly the computer is used as an indispensable tool for clerical purposes, to satisfy information needs, and to make decisions. Moreover, according to a survey which is already outdated, 49 percent of the public have had a job requiring either direct or indirect contact with a computer, 15 percent feel that their current job requires some knowledge of the computer, and 7 percent state that their job requires working directly with computers.[6] Given current trends these percentages will increase dramatically in coming years. In fact, the job market in computer-related fields looks quite promising for years to come.[7]

What does all of this mean to you? Well, we feel that if you do not accomplish the two objectives stated below, then you are shortchanging what will prove to be a very relevant part of your education.

*Objective 1.* Achieve a modest level of programming and problem-solving skills.
*Objective 2.* Acquire a basic knowledge of computer concepts, uses, and limitations.

The first objective is intended to develop your ability to access, utilize, and exploit the computer for the purpose of more effectively analyzing problems and making decisions, both in subsequent academic courses which you take and in your career. The second objective should serve to dispel the mystique and misconceptions surrounding computers—and to aid you in feeling "comfortable" and operating effectively in a computerized environment.

## Advice

Some of you have a great aptitude for the material which follows. Hopefully, you will get "turned on" to do fine things in this field. Others of you are less inclined to readily absorb this type of material. If you feel that you are in the latter category, then you should take the following advice seriously.

1. Pay close attention to *written detail*. The computer is not very permissive. For example, if you spell REID instead of READ, the computer will not understand.
2. Pay close attention to *logical detail*. The computer is a machine. Therefore, you must tell it what to do in rather precise detail which is broken down into logical steps.
3. Develop *good habits*. Work consistently (not constantly!). Try to rely on others as little as possible, in order to sharpen your own inherent problem-solving skills. Try to solve the "Follow-up Exercises"—before looking up answers in the back of the book.
4. Be *patient*. Don't get frustrated by your mistakes. Don't get angry at the computer if it breaks down (after all, it also works hard). Finally, give yourself time. Our years of teaching this course shows that many students take about six to eight weeks before the material crystallizes.

---

[6] "A National Survey of the Public's Attitude Toward Computers," *op. cit.*
[7] Estimates by the Bureau of Labor Statistics show over 50,000 annual new openings for programmers and systems analysts.

## Exercises

1. Can you define the following terms?

   computer
   analog computer
   digital computer
   special-purpose computer
   general-purpose computer
   minicomputer
   microcomputer
   instruction
   data
   input media
   data preparation devices
   input unit
   online terminal
   CPU
   primary or internal memory
   address
   contents
   byte
   character
   arithmetic-logic unit
   control unit
   microprocessor
   output unit

   secondary storage
   computer language
   high-level language
   low-level language
   procedure-oriented language
   problem-oriented language
   BASIC
   computer program
   statement
   assembly language
   machine language
   interpreter
   compiler
   object program
   source program
   computer system
   hardware
   software
   systems software
   applications software
   operating system
   batch processing
   time-shared processing

2. Identify and briefly discuss the three outstanding characteristics of electronic computers.
3. Identify two broad areas of computer applications. Give a sample application in each area.
4. Cite some advantages and disadvantages of the widespread use of computers. (Don't necessarily restrict yourself to what has been discussed here.)
5. Sketch the organization of a digital, general-purpose computer. Briefly describe the functions of each component.
6. Briefly describe the functions of the operating system.
7. Briefly describe the functions of the compiler. How does an interpreter differ from a compiler?
8. Compare batch and time-shared processing with respect to various criteria.
9. How are you doing?

# *Writing and Running BASIC Programs*

The process of programming is a creative, yet formalized, activity that ranges from conceptualization of the problem to implementation and maintenance of the computer program. This chapter illustrates the process of programming (1) by presenting a formal four-step procedure for writing computer programs and (2) by running a complete computer program.

## 2.1
## *STEPS IN WRITING COMPUTER PROGRAMS*

As you might recall from Chapter 1, a **computer program** is a complete set of instructions written in a computer language; its purpose is to solve a problem which has been defined by the programmer. This problem is solved when the computer program is executed in a logical sequence by the computer. Writing a computer program involves the following **four-step procedure:**

1.  Analyzing the problem
2.  Preparing the flowchart

3.  Coding the problem
4.  Debugging the computer program

### Analyzing the Problem

You must first determine what information you need to solve your problem. Our approach is to specify

1.  A general statement (in prose) which describes the nature of the problem that is to be solved
2.  The data you will provide to the computer
3.  The output you want to receive as the solution to your problem
4.  A description of the **algorithm,** the computations and logical processes the computer must perform to convert the provided data to the output data

### Preparing the Flowchart

A **flowchart** is a drawing portraying (1) the means of providing data to the computer, (2) the required output data, and (3) the logical and arithmetic steps required to solve the problem. It has two primary uses: to help you write the computer program by serving as a "blueprint" and to document the logic of the computer program for future review.

Flowcharts use specific symbols to represent different activities and written messages within each symbol to explain each activity. Table 2.1 shows the flowcharting

*TABLE 2.1    Flowcharting Symbols*

| SYMBOL | NAME | MEANING |
| --- | --- | --- |
| Terminal | Terminal | Indicates the start or end of the program. |
| Input/Output | Input/Output | Indicates when an input, read, or output operation is to be performed. |
| Process | Process | Indicates calculations or data manipulation. |
| Flowline | Flowline | Represents the flow of logic. |
| Decision | Decision | Represents a decision point or question that requires a choice of which logical path to follow. |
| Connection | Connection | Connects parts of the flowchart. |
| Preparation | Preparation | Indicates a preparation step, as in describing a FOR/NEXT loop (Chapter 5). |
| Predefined process | Predefined process | Indicates a predefined process or step where the details are not shown in this flowchart, as in calling a subprogram (Chapter 9). |

symbols we use in this textbook, and Figure 2.1 (page 29) illustrates a sample flow-chart. At this point don't worry about flowcharting technique. The art and style of constructing flowcharts will be demonstrated often by example in the chapters to come.

## Coding the Problem

**Coding** is the translation of your problem-solving logic from the flowchart into a computer program. In other words, you use the flowchart as a guide for writing your instructions to the computer.

The computer language which is to be used must be decided upon by this step in the procedure. (Quite often the same flowchart can be used regardless of the computer language.) Some languages are more suitable than others, depending on the application.

In this book we use **minimal BASIC,** a subset of the BASIC language that is compatible with the standard proposed by the American National Standards Institute (**ANSI**). This particular subset of the language will have the advantage of standardization, which means (theoretically) that the same BASIC program will run on any computer which uses BASIC compilers or interpreters that adhere to the ANSI standard.

In Part III of this book we present certain enhancements to BASIC that add considerable power to the language. Unfortunately, **enhanced BASIC** is not part of the ANSI standard. So, variations in specifics, but not generalities, exist from manufacturer to manufacturer.

BASIC is an attractive language for the following reasons:

1. It is easy to learn. The structure of the language is simple and there are only 20 instructions in minimal BASIC.
2. It has excellent mathematical capability. In addition to an algebraic orientation and built-in functions (trigonometric, logarithmic, and others), the enhanced language has matrix manipulation commands that are not available with most other popular languages.
3. It simplifies the treatment of alphabetic data. This feature is important in information-processing applications.
4. It facilitates interactive person-machine dialogue. As you will see, the language is expressly designed to facilitate ''conversation'' between computers and us.
5. It requires small interpreters. BASIC interpreters take up little storage in memory, which makes the language attractive on minicomputers and microcomputers.
6. It is becoming increasingly popular. This is so for the above reasons coupled with the rapidly expanding use by managers of time-sharing systems, minicomputers, and microcomputers.

When you are ready to code a program, you should start out by writing your code on a regular sheet of paper. After you are reasonably sure your program is correct, place the code on the appropriate input medium for your system. You will most likely use a computer terminal. Details on this procedure are presented in Section 2.2.

## Debugging the Computer Program

You will often write programs that fail to run or run improperly. (It happens to all of us.) **Debugging** is the process of locating and correcting errors, or ''getting out the bugs.'' Types of bugs and methods for correcting them are illustrated in Module A at the end of the text, which you should read after Chapter 3.

## EXAMPLE 2.1   Tuition Revenue Problem

Let's follow this four-step procedure using a specific example. Suppose that the Board of Regents who overlook the State College System wish to have an interactive program for assessing the effects of various policies on the tuition revenue collected by State College. For example, how much is revenue affected if the cost per credit is increased? What effect does a change in enrollment have on revenue? The effect of increasing student fees? Of a drop in the average number of credits taken by students?

### Step I   Analyzing the Problem

1.  Problem statement
    To develop an interactive program for assessing the revenues generated by State College. The program calculates and prints revenue given data on cost of tuition per credit, average number of credits, fees, and total number of students.
2.  Provided data
    a.  Cost of tuition per credit ($80)
    b.  Number of students at State College (6000)
    c.  Cost of fees ($250)
    d.  Average number of credits taken by students (15)
3.  Data output
    Revenue from tuition and fees
4.  Computations and Logical Processes (Algorithm)
    a.  To determine the average student bill multiply the cost per credit by the average number of credits and add the fees.
    b.  To determine revenue multiply the average student bill by the number of students.

### Step II   Preparing the Flowchart

Figure 2.1 is a flowchart that organizes the parts outlined in the preceding step (Step I). The flowchart breaks down the problem into several related components.

1.  Store the cost per credit in a memory location.
2.  Store the number of students in a memory location.
3.  Calculate the average student bill.
4.  Calculate the revenue due the college.
5.  Print the revenue.

Note that this flowchart uses only the first four symbols in Table 2.1. The other symbols are introduced in later chapters, as your programming becomes more sophisticated.

In general, a flowchart must indicate a "Start" and must have a "Stop." The flow of activities generally runs from top to bottom and from left to right. As an option, you can use arrowheads to indicate the direction of flow, which is our preference.

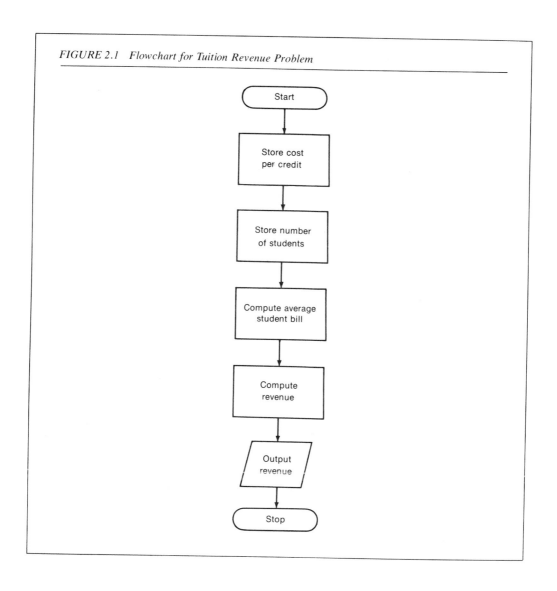

FIGURE 2.1    *Flowchart for Tuition Revenue Problem*

Although this flowchart is rather simple, and you may be tempted not to use it for such a simple problem, *we strongly suggest that you get in the habit of using flowcharts now.* As programs become more complex, you will find flowcharts increasingly helpful for coding the problem.

### Step III   Coding the Problem

| PROGRAM | COMMENTS |
| --- | --- |
| 10 LET C = 80 | Store 80 (cost per credit) in C. |
| 20 LET S = 6000 | Store 6000 (number of students) in S. |
| 30 LET B = 15∗C + 250 | Calculate average student bill (B). The symbol ∗ means multiplication. |
| 40 LET R = B∗S | Calculate revenue (R). |
| 50 PRINT "REVENUE = $";R | Print contents of R together with an identifying label. |
| 60 END | Physical end of program; stop processing. |

Note the correspondence between the program and the flowchart in Figure 2.1. For simple programs, this correspondence is *almost* one-for-one; that is, each symbol in the flowchart (except for "Start") will have a corresponding instruction in the program. As problems grow in length and complexity, however, the number of symbols in the flowchart will be less than the number of instructions in the program, for two reasons.

1.  Symbols can be used to summarize related groups of instructions in a program. For example, "Compute average student bill" and "Compute revenue" in Figure 2.1 can be combined into a single rectangle which reads "Compute average student bill and revenue."
2.  Not all instructions need be represented in a flowchart. Flowcharts need only represent what we call *executable* instructions. We take up this topic in the next chapter.

At this point, you need not worry about the exact meaning of each instruction in the program, for we provide a detailed discussion in the next chapter; however, the overall program should make some sense to you.

### Step IV   Debugging the Computer Program

The next step is to run, or execute, the program on the computer. By **run,** or **execute,** we mean that the instructions which make up the program code are processed (carried out) by the computer. Our purpose in this case is to detect and correct errors. As illustrated in the next section, this program contains no errors. In Module A, however, we purposely introduce errors to illustrate their nature, detection, diagnosis, and correction.

*2.2*
## PROCESS OF RUNNING BASIC PROGRAMS

Figure 2.2 illustrates the process of running BASIC programs. This process assumes that you are using a time-sharing system.[1]

In time sharing you communicate with the computer by entering your program at a terminal, through which information is transmitted over either a phone line or a cable to the computer.

The sign-on procedure includes turning on the terminal, establishing contact with the computer, and providing valid identification. Each of you will have a unique identification code which usually includes two parts: a *code number* (which may include letters) and a *password*. The code number is used by the computer center for accounting purposes and the password is your means of maintaining security and privacy. *The exact sign-on procedure for your system will be detailed by your instructor.*

The components and logic of the process in Figure 2.2 are mostly self-explanatory. Study the figure before reading on. In the remainder of this section this process is further explained and illustrated.

### System Commands

To communicate with the operating system when you are at the terminal requires a set of commands called **system commands.** Among other things, system commands allow you to run (execute) the program, obtain a listing of the program code, and save the program in secondary storage for future recall. Therefore, when you run programs in an interactive environment, you will have a set of system commands to learn in addition to the BASIC instructions.

Unfortunately, system commands are not universal, which means that they differ from one system to another. *Your instructor, therefore, must provide you with the system commands that are specific to your system.*

### Work Area versus Secondary Storage Area

After you sign on, the operating system assigns you a portion of primary memory which we call the **work area.** In fact, each user currently utilizing the time-sharing system is assigned a separate work area. The purpose of the work area is to store both the BASIC instructions of your program and the data the program is to work with.

Once you "sign off" a time-sharing system, the program in your work area is "erased." For this reason, each user of a time-sharing system also has an assigned **secondary storage area** (usually magnetic disk), which is often called a **library.** The secondary storage area allows you to save programs that you prepare in your work area for recall at a later date. In other words your library saves you the trouble of having to retype programs that you previously entered into your work area.

---

[1] If you are processing in a batch environment, then your instructor will provide you with instructions on running BASIC programs. If you are online to a minicomputer or microcomputer, then the process in Figure 2.2 is appropriate.

*FIGURE 2.2 Process of Running BASIC Programs*

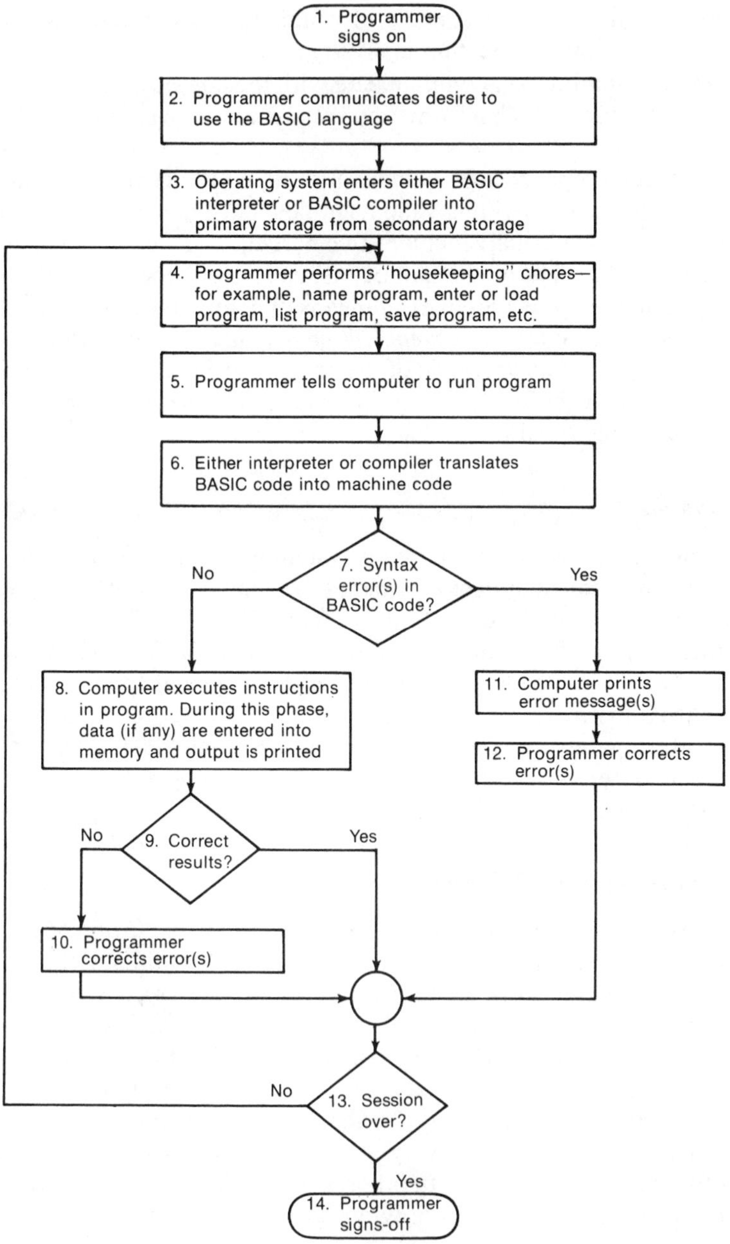

In addition to storing programs, libraries also store data that can be used as input to programs. A set of data stored in this manner is called a **data file.** We discuss this topic in Chapter 11.

## *Illustration*

In this section we illustrate a time-sharing run of the program in Example 2.1 on IBM's CALL-OS system. *If you use a different system, then your system will not operate exactly as shown in the illustration.* In this case, just pay attention to the principles, since these are universal. *Your instructor will discuss the appropriate modifications for your system.*

In what follows, boxed segments indicate the computer run and marginal notes describe the corresponding boxed segment. The numbers to the left of the boxed segments correspond to the numbers within symbols in Figure 2.2. As you read the illustration relate each boxed segment to the appropriate symbol in Figure 2.2.

To clearly point out the interactions between the user and the computer, all information typed by the computer is shaded; information typed by the user is not shaded.

1.

```
ON AT  8:44    WED  21 MAR 79
USER NUMBER,PASSWORD--
GAL101,MBBBBxbm
READY
```

Entry of identification code for signing on. *Each time you finish typing a line, you must depress the carriage return key on the terminal.* GAL101 is the code number, but the password that was entered has been printed over by the computer as a security measure.

2.

```
ENTER BASIC
READY
```

System command for using BASIC compiler. Note that the entry of a valid system command is always followed by the computer response "READY." This means that the computer is waiting for you to do something next.

4a.

```
10 LET C = 80
20 LET S = 6000
30 LET B = 15 *C + 250
40 LET R = B*S
50 PRINT "REVENUE = $";R
60 END
```

Entry of program into work area. *These are BASIC statements.* Note that the system does not respond "READY" here, since *these are not system commands.*

4b.

```
NAME REV
READY
```

System command for naming program as REV. Computer responds "READY."

5a.

```
RUN
```

System command which first compiles and then executes program. Statements in the BASIC program are processed sequentially beginning with line 10 and ending with line 60.

8a.

```
REV      8:53   WED   21 MAR 79

REVENUE = $ 8700000

TIME 0.00 SECS.
```

The computer first prints the name of the program, time, and date, then prints program output based on the PRINT statement in the program (line 50), and finally prints the amount of CPU time utilized for compilation and execution.

4c.

```
SAVE
READY
```

System command for creating in the library a duplicate copy of the program in the work area. The program now has been saved for recall at a later date.

4d.

```
CLEAR
READY
```

System command for erasing the program from the work area. (The program is still in the library.)

5b.

```
RUN
NO PROGRAM PRESENT
```

Confirmation that the program is no longer in the work area.

4e.

```
LOAD REV
READY
```

System command for creating in the work area a duplicate copy of the program in the library. This system command thus retrieves a copy of the program from the library and places it in the work area. (A copy of the program still remains in the library.)

4f.

```
LIST
```

System command to list the program in the work area. The purpose of this command is to view the program code that resides in the work area.

4g.

```
REV   8:54   WED   21 MAR 79


10 LET C = 80
20 LET S = 6000
30 LET B = 15 *C + 250
40 LET R = B*S
50 PRINT "REVENUE = $";R
60 END
```

Listing of the program in the work area. Programs need not be listed to be run.

5c.

```
RUN
```

Rerun of the program in the work area.

8b.

```
REV      8:54    WED   21 MAR 79

REVENUE  =  $ 8700000

TIME 0.01 SECS.
```

Same output as before.

14a.

```
OFF
```

System command for signing off.

14b.

```
OFF AT  8:54
PROC. TIME...     0 SEC.
TERM. TIME...    10 MIN.
```

The computer prints the time of day, the total CPU time for the entire session (to the nearest second), and the total time the terminal was "connected" to the computer system.

As you study the illustration, *keep in mind the very important distinction between a BASIC statement (instruction) and a system command.* This distinction seems to give beginning students much grief. System commands are used strictly to communicate with the operating system; they are never part of a program. BASIC statements are used only in programs.

Also, remember that *this illustration is for an IBM system. If you use a different system, then your system commands will differ.* (See Exercise 4.) As you study the illustration, *write in the appropriate system commands for your system,* and relate the illustration to Figure 2.2. Note that numbered boxes in the illustration correspond to numbered boxes in the flowchart of Figure 2.2. Errors that occur in this process are discussed in detail in Module A.

*Other System Commands.* The system commands which we have illustrated represent a small subset of the many commands available for a typical system. For example, powerful commands exist for making either editorial or debugging changes which are far superior to the process of making changes in a batch environment.

*Translation versus Execution.* As you know from Chapter 1, a high-level language such as BASIC must first be translated into the machine language of the computer. If syntax rules of the language have not been violated, then the operating system instructs the control unit of the computer to execute, or run, the program in the sequence dictated by the line numbers. Thus, in our illustration, line 10 is executed first, then line 20, line 30, and so on through line 60. As you sit at the terminal, the only evidence of execution you see visually is the execution of the PRINT statement in line 50 (the second line in boxes 8a and 8b of the illustration).

## Exercises

1. Define or explain the following terms:

   computer program                     debugging
   four-step procedure                  run
   algorithm                            execute
   flowchart                            system commands
   coding                               work area
   minimal BASIC                        secondary storage area
   enhanced BASIC                       library
   ANSI                                 data file

2. Revise Figure 2.1 so that only five flowchart symbols are used.

3. Based on the output from our tuition revenue program in the illustration, how much revenue can the college expect to collect?

4. Modify the tuition revenue illustration by writing in your system's sign-on procedure and systems commands. Now, find a terminal and try the following:

   a. Duplicate our illustrative run on your system. If you make a mistake typing a line, simply retype the line. The newly typed line will replace the old, incorrect line in your work area.

   b. Experiment. Try different things. Be bold. For example, it's OK to type lines out of numeric sequence, since the operating system rearranges lines numerically in your work area. In other words, we could have typed the lines in the sequence 20, 10, 60, 50, 30, 40, but they would be stored in the correct numeric sequence. Try it and then list the program.

5. At the beginning of Example 2.1, the Regents posed certain questions. Modify and run the tuition revenue program to answer each of the questions below. Note that each question first requires a change in the program and a new run. For example, assuming the program is already in your work area (from Exercise 4), typing

   ```
   10 LET C = 90
   RUN
   ```

   first replaces old line 10 in your work area with new line 10 and then executes the revised program. This procedure answers the first question below in part a. Note that you must change lines 10 and 20 back to the original before answering part c. Do you see why?

   a. What revenue would be generated if the cost per credit is increased to $90?

   b. What revenue would be generated if the cost per credit is increased to $90 and enrollment drops to 5500?

   c. What revenue would be generated if fees were doubled to $500? Assume all other data remain as in the original problem.

   d. What revenue would be generated if the cost per credit is raised to $100, fees are doubled to $500, enrollment drops to 5000, and the average number of credits drops to 13.5?

   e. Validate each of your computer results by hand calculation. Validation is an important part of debugging, as you will see in the next chapter.

# *PART II*

# *Minimal BASIC*

# CHAPTER 3

# *Fundamentals of BASIC*

This chapter introduces certain elements of minimal BASIC. By its conclusion, you will be writing and running complete, although simple, programs of the type presented in Example 2.1. For easy reference, the tuition revenue program of Example 2.1 is repeated here:

```
10 LET  C = 80
20 LET  S = 6000
30 LET  B = 15*C + 250
```

```
40  LET R = B*S
50  PRINT "REVENUE = $";R
60  END
```

## 3.1
## ELEMENTS OF BASIC

Nine elements describe the structure of the BASIC language. These are briefly described here for the purpose of perspective and are elaborated upon in the remainder of this chapter and other chapters.

*1.   Character Set.*   The proposed ANSI standard defines the following 60 characters:

a.   The 26 **alphabetic characters** given by the letters of the alphabet
b.   The 10 **numeric characters** or digits given by 0 1 2 3 4 5 6 7 8 9
c.   The 24 **special characters** as described below

| SPECIAL CHARACTER | DESCRIPTION |
|---|---|
|  | Space or blank |
| ! | Exclamation point |
| " | Quote |
| # | Number sign |
| $ | Dollar |
| % | Percent |
| & | Ampersand |
| ' | Apostrophe |
| ( | Open parenthesis |
| ) | Close parenthesis |
| * | Asterisk |
| + | Plus |
| − | Minus |
| / | Slant |
| . | Period |
| , | Comma |
| : | Colon |
| ; | Semicolon |
| < | Less than |
| = | Equals |
| > | Greater than |
| ? | Question mark |
| ∩ | Circumflex |
| ― | Underline |

This **character set** represents the most fundamental elements of the language, since it is used to construct the other eight elements.

2. *Strings.* A **string** is a sequence of characters. For example, the string "REVE-NUE = $" is called a *quoted string* consisting of 11 characters (the 11 characters REVENUE = $ including the two blanks around the equal sign).

3. *Numbers.* A numeric value, or **number,** in BASIC can be an **integer,** a number with no decimal point, such as 80 or −705; **real,** a number with a decimal point, such as 70. or 6.14; **exponential,** a representation used for very large or very small numbers (called *scientific notation,* or *E-notation*). These are discussed in the next section.

4. *Constants and Variables.* **Constants** and **variables** are used to represent numeric and nonnumeric data within programs. For example, the numeric variables C, S, B, and R and the numeric constants 80, 6000, 15, and 250 are used in the tuition revenue program. These we discuss fully in the next section.

5. *Key Words.* Certain words called **key words** are used either to describe an operation that is to be performed by the computer or to communicate certain information to the computer. For example, LET, PRINT, and END are key words used in the tuition revenue program. Other key words are introduced throughout the remainder of this book.

6. *Functions.* Certain operations can be performed by using **functions.** For example, we can use SQR to take square roots and LOG to find natural logarithms. These and other functions are discussed in Chapter 9.

7. *Expressions.* An **expression** is a combination of one or more variables, constants, functions, and special characters. They are used to express arithmetic calculations, logical comparisons, or string manipulations. For example, $15*C + 250$ in an arithmetic expression in the tuition revenue program. Expressions are discussed in Section 3.4.

8. *Statements.* A **statement,** or instruction, either directs the computer to perform a specific task or declares certain information which the computer needs. BASIC statements are combinations of characters, strings, numbers, variables, constants, key words, functions, and expressions. Thus, they utilize the first seven elements of BASIC. The tuition revenue program contains six statements.

9. *Line numbers.* A **line number** is a unique one- to four-digit number that must precede each statement in your program.[1] For example, the tuition revenue program uses the line numbers 10, 20, 30, 40, 50, and 60. Leading zeros are ignored, and spaces before or within the line number are not permitted. *Line numbers both order the statements in a program and attach unique labels to each statement.* The order or sequence established by the line numbers dictates the sequence of execution in the program. For example, statements in the tuition revenue program are executed in the sequence 10, 20, 30, 40, 50, 60. Moreover, these line numbers serve as labels to alter the sequence of execution, as discussed in Chapter 5.

---

[1] Some systems allow more than four digits.

It is good programming practice to number the statements in your program in increments (steps) of 5 or 10. For example, in the tuition revenue program we used an increment of 10. *This practice allows you to insert new statements between old statements should you need to correct, expand, or otherwise modify your program.*

## 3.2
## VARIABLES AND CONSTANTS

Programmers can use symbolic names rather than numbers to reference addresses or memory locations in a way that communicates the nature of the contents. For example, R in the tuition revenue program is a symbolic name which indicates that revenue is stored in this location, as opposed to, say, address location 0003, which would suggest nothing about what is stored at this address.

In BASIC a symbolic name is called a **variable.** A variable, therefore, identifies a location in memory where a particular *value* (item of data) is stored (found). Variables store either *numeric* or *string values.*

### Types of Variables

*Numeric Variables.*    A variable that stores numeric values is called a **numeric variable.** For example, the numeric value 32.7 stored under the numeric variable T can be depicted as follows:

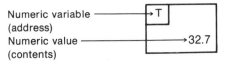

Numeric variable (address)

Numeric value (contents)

Numeric variables are classified as *simple* or *subscripted.* **Simple numeric variables** store a single numeric value whereas **subscripted numeric variables** store multiple numeric values. The use of subscripted variables requires more programming skill than you now have; so we delay this topic until Chapter 7.

Simple numeric variables consist of either a letter or a letter followed by a digit. *BASIC does not permit special characters such as % or / to be used in forming variable names.* In the tuition revenue program, C, S, B, and R are all names for simple numeric variables.

Digits in a variable name are often used to distinguish among related variables. For example, if three different types of costs are to be represented by simple numeric variables in a program, then it makes sense to label these C1, C2, and C3. This practice of selecting a variable name that has meaning simply helps you to remember the attribute that is represented by this variable.

*A good programming practice is to select variable names that have meaning to you in the context of the problem.* For example, in the tuition revenue program,

C stands for average number of Credits
S stands for number of Students
B stands for average student Bill
R stands for Revenue

*String Variables.*   The string value CLARK S. KENT stored under the string variable N$ can be illustrated as follows:

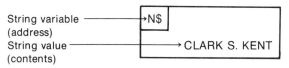

**String variables** store strings, and are named by using a letter followed by a dollar sign. For example, A$, K$, and T$ all represent string variables. These variables are primarily used to store names, addresses, text, and other nonnumeric data. In our illustration above, the string variable N$ stores 13 characters of data (including the blank after CLARK and the blank before KENT).[2]

As is true of numeric variables, string variables can be classified as **simple string variables,** those that store a single string, and **subscripted string variables,** those that store multiple strings. The variable N$ above is a simple string variable. Subscripted string variables are discussed in Chapter 7.

## Types of Constants

Not all data in a computer program need to be stored in memory locations which are referenced by variable names. In some situations you will need to use a constant (unchanging) value, such as the constant $\pi$ in the computation $\pi r^2$. In this case, you would write the number 3.14159, instead of $\pi$, directly into a BASIC program.

In the tuition revenue program the statement

30 LET B = 15*C + 250

contains two simple numeric variables, B and C, and the constants 15 and 250. The value stored in the variable may change whenever the computer executes an instruction, but the values 15 and 250 are not subject to change.

A **constant,** therefore, represents a fixed (unvarying) value that does not change during the execution of a program. As with variables, BASIC makes a distinction between numeric and string constants.

*Numeric Constants.*   A **numeric constant** is a decimal representation of a number; its value is the number represented by that constant. For example,

15    15.    250    .145    0.145    −4.6    6000    +6000

are all valid numeric constants. Note that the minus character is used to represent a negative numeric constant, as −4.6 illustrates. Positive numeric constants need not be preceded by a plus character. Also note that the above list of constants has four *integer* constants and four *real* constants.

Very small or very large numeric constants can be represented by using scientific notation, or **E-notation,** as follows:

---

[2] Many versions of BASIC allow a string variable to be written as a letter, followed by a digit, followed by a dollar sign. We might also note that all systems have a limit on the number of characters that can be stored under a string variable. Systems that limit this number to one character essentially require the use of subscripted variables, as discussed in Chapter 7.

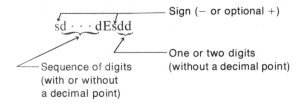

Table 3.1 shows several examples of conventional scientific notation and the equivalent E-notation used in the BASIC language. Thus, E represents "times ten to the power given by the digits following." In other words, E6 in the constant $-.845E6$ says to multiply $-0.845$ by 10 raised to the power 6, or multiply $-0.845$ by $10^6$, giving $-0.845 \times 1000000$, or $-845000$. In "plain English," E6 simply denotes move the decimal point six places to the *right* and E-8 says move the decimal point eight places to the *left*.

You will most likely first see E-notation when reading computer output, since systems store and print large numeric values using this convention. Thus, an understanding of E-notation facilitates the reading of computer output.

You should be aware of the following issues when using numeric constants:

1.  Commas and other special characters are not permissible within a numeric constant. For example, both the constants 6,000 and $54.50 would provoke errors from a BASIC interpreter.
2.  The maximum number of digits stored in a numeric constant differs from system to system. Most systems store six to eight digits. In most versions of BASIC, an integer value which contains eight or less digits is stored as is. However, if the number of digits in your constant exceeds eight digits, the number is rounded to six significant digits and stored as a decimal number with an exponent. For example, the integer value 12345678 would be stored as is, but the integer value 987654321

---

TABLE 3.1   *E-Notation Examples*

| E-NOTATION | SCIENTIFIC NOTATION | STANDARD NOTATION | COMMENT |
|---|---|---|---|
| 7.2E+12<br>7.2E12<br>+7.2E12 | $7.2 \times 10^{12}$ | 7200000000000 | Move decimal point 12 places to the right (multiply by $10^{12}$) |
| −.845E06<br>−.845E6<br>−.845E+06<br>−.845E+6 | $-0.845 \times 10^6$ | −845000 | Move decimal point six places to the right (multiply by $10^6$) |
| 5E−8<br>5.E−8 | $5 \times 10^{-8}$ | 0.00000005 | Move decimal point eight places to the left (divide by $10^8$). |
| .5E−7 | $0.5 \times 10^{-7}$ | 0.00000005 | This constant is identical to the preceding. |

would be stored as 9.87654E08. On most systems, a real value with a fractional part is stored as is, unless the value has more than six digits, in which case the number is rounded to six digits. For example, the real value 500.618 is stored as is, the real value 50027.689 is stored as 50027.7 (note the rounding), and the real value 9876543.21 is stored as 9.87654E06.

3. The maximum value allowed for a number in E-notation differs from system to system. According to the proposed ANSI standard, all systems accommodate a range of at least 1E-38 to 1E38 ($10^{-38}$ to $10^{38}$). Thus, a value such as 2.5E82 may be too large for most systems. Values that exceed the maximum limit are said to cause **overflow;** values smaller than the lower limit are said to cause **underflow.** The computer prints an error message whenever overflow or underflow occurs during execution, as we illustrate in Module A.

*String Constants.*     A **string constant** consists of a string enclosed in quotations; its value is the string of characters between the quotations. For example,

"REVENUE = $"

identifies a string constant in line 50 of the tuition revenue program. Note that the length of this string constant is 11 characters, including the single space on each side of the equal sign. Also note that the string constant itself (its value) does not include the quotes.

Other terms for a string constant include *quoted string, literal constant, literal string,* and *character string.* In Section 3.5 we show how string constants are used to print labels, report headings, messages, and other text. Additional uses for string constants are illustrated in subsequent chapters.

You should be aware of the following facts when using string constants:

1. Spaces are not ignored within string constants; that is, don't forget that a space counts as a valid character in a quoted string.
2. The maximum number of characters (length) that can be included in a string varies from one version of BASIC to another. In some versions a string cannot exceed 15 characters, while in others as many as 4095 characters can be represented. Check with your instructor for limits on your system.

**Follow-up Exercises**

1. Identify what is wrong, if anything, with each of the following simple numeric variables.

   a.  1T                          b.  T 1
   c.  T1                          d.  7
   e.  A7                          f.  B+
   g.  PROFIT                      h.  $P
   i.  P$                          j.  P
   k.  %K

2. Identify what is wrong, if anything, with each of the following constants.
   a. 1,000,000
   b. 1000000
   c. 1E6
   d. +7.3
   e. 7.3
   f. 614.25−
   g. −614.25
   h. 7 05
   i. 7*5
   j. 2.5E175
   k. 2.5E1.5
   l. "COST
   m. "CO ST"
   n. $500
   o. 65789024517
   p. 154.612876
3. Express the following constants using E-notation.
   a. $-6.142 \times 10^{15}$
   b. $-6142 \times 10^{12}$
   c. 0.00007
   d. $7 \times 10^{-5}$
4. Express the following constants using standard notation.
   a. 123E9
   b. .123E12
   c. 456E-4
   d. 4.56E-2

## 3.3
## END STATEMENT

Statements are classified as those which are executable and those which are nonexecutable. An **executable statement** is one that causes activity within the CPU *during execution of the program*. The LET, PRINT, and END statements in the tuition revenue program are all examples of executable statements.

As illustrated in the tuition revenue program, each program *must* end with the statement:

> *line no.* **END**

This statement not only defines the physical end of a BASIC program but also causes execution of the program to terminate. Since the END statement is the last statement in your program, it follows that you must assign it the highest line number.

A **nonexecutable statement** is used to provide or declare certain information to the CPU during compilation or interpretation of the program. *Nonexecutable statements are ignored during execution of the program.* We introduce the first nonexecutable statement in Section 3.6.

## 3.4
## LET STATEMENT

A **LET statement** is used (1) to perform and store calculations, (2) to assign a constant to a storage location, or (3) to copy the contents of one storage location into another. In the tuition revenue program, the statement

    10 LET C = 80

is an example of a LET statement. This statement stores the numeric value 80 in the storage location named C.

## *Structure*

In more general terms, the LET statement is structured as follows:

line no. **LET** variable = expression

On the left side of the equal sign, a single variable following the key word LET identifies a storage location in internal computer memory.[3] The right side of the equal sign is either a string expression or an arithmetic expression.

*String Expressions.*   A **string expression** is either a string variable or a string constant.[4] For example, execution of

  10 LET L$ = "I LOVE BASIC"

would store the following in memory:

L$

I LOVE BASIC

In this case the string expression is the 12-character string constant I LOVE BASIC (including the two blank characters). The LET statement thus tells the computer to "replace the contents of L$ by the expression to the right of the equal sign."
  If the computer next executes

  20 LET P$ = L$

then memory for these two string variables would appear as follows:

L$

I LOVE BASIC

P$

I LOVE BASIC

The string expression to the right of the equal sign is the single string variable L$. Note that the LET statement simply copies the contents of L$ into P$, leaving the contents of L$ unaffected. If the computer next executes

  30 LET L$ = "I'M NOT SO SURE"

then memory would appear as follows:

L$

I'M NOT SO SURE

P$

I LOVE BASIC

---

[3] The key word LET can be omitted on some systems.
[4] A string expression also may include string functions, which we do not discuss in this book.

Thus, *the equal sign in a LET statement dictates that the storage content of the variable to the left of the equal sign is to be replaced by the value of the expression to the right of the equal sign.*

*Arithmetic Expressions.*    An **arithmetic expression** may consist of a single numeric constant, a single numeric variable, or a combination of numeric constants and numeric variables separated by parentheses and arithmetic operation symbols.[5] An **arithmetic operation symbol** indicates the type of computation that is desired. Five symbols are used in the BASIC language to indicate the type of arithmetic operation, as described in Table 3.2.

Table 3.3 illustrates three possible arithmetic uses of LET statements. In the first illustration, the constant 5000 is placed in the storage location identified by V. In the second case, the contents of the storage location called M are copied by the storage location called C. Note, however, that this transfer is electronic; that is, whatever is in M remains there, but whatever was in C gets replaced by whatever is in M. Finally, the third illustration places the computational result of $7*V - C$ in the storage location called P. This means that the contents of C will be subtracted from seven times the contents of V, and the result will be stored in P. Note that $*$ *must* be used for multiplication; implied multiplication such as 7V would give a syntax error.

Again *you should carefully note the meaning of the equal sign (=) in BASIC*. It means "place the value indicated by the expression on the right in the storage location indicated by the variable on the left." Because of this meaning, a LET statement such as

200 LET I = I + 1

makes sense in BASIC but not in algebra. Note that each time this statement is executed by the computer, the content (value) of I gets increased by 1. In other words, this statement instructs the computer to "add 1 to the contents of I and place this result in

---

TABLE 3.2   *Arithmetic Operation Symbols*

| OPERATION SYMBOL | ARITHMETIC OPERATION |
|:---:|:---|
| + | Addition |
| − | Subtraction |
| / | Division |
| * | Multiplication |
| ** | Exponentiation (raise to a power)† |

† The proposed ANSI standard recommends the circumflex ∩ as the symbol for exponentiation; some terminals may use the upward arrow ↑ for exponentiation; some systems may not allow ** for exponentiation. Ask your instructor.

---

[5] In Chapter 9 we include functions in this definition.

TABLE 3.3   *Three Arithmetic uses of LET Statements*

**LET** *arithmetic variable = arithmetic expression*

| TYPE | ILLUSTRATION |
|---|---|
| LET variable = constant | 30 LET V = 5000 |
| LET variable = variable | 35 LET C = M |
| LET variable = combination of constants and variables separated by operation symbols | 40 LET P = 7∗V – C |

I.'' This type of statement is used quite often in BASIC programs for the purpose of ''counting,'' as you will see in the chapters which follow.

Try to avoid the following two language violations: *two operation symbols must never appear adjacent to one another,* as this would cause a syntax error;[6] *avoid raising a negative value to a nonintegral power,* as this would cause an error during execution. Negative values may be raised only to whole-number powers. (See Follow-up Exercise 5.)

Finally, we should mention that the *precision* with which arithmetic expressions are evaluated varies from system to system. Most systems, however, maintain at least six digits of precision.

---

**EXAMPLE 3.1**

In the tuition revenue program, four LET statements were used.

    10 LET C = 80
    20 LET S = 6000
    30 LET B = 15∗C + 250
    40 LET R = B∗S

In the first two LET statements, the expression is a single constant; hence the values 80 and 6000 are simply stored in the respective memory locations named C and S, as indicated below.

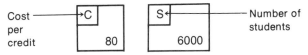

The third statement instructs the computer to multiply the constant 15 (average number of credits) by the contents of the memory location named C, add the

---

[6] Note that ∗∗ is treated as a single operation symbol for exponentiation.

constant 250 (fees), and store the result in the memory location B. After this calculation, the memory locations appear as follows:

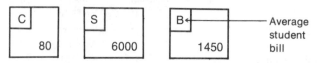

The fourth statement tells the computer to multiply the contents of B by the
contents in S and to store the result in the memory location R. After this calculation,
the memory locations appear as follows:

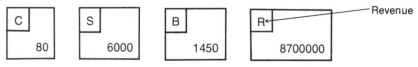

Note that these statements are executed sequentially: first line 10, then 20, 30, and
40.

**Follow-up Exercises**

5. Identify what is wrong, if anything, with each of the following LET statements.

   a.  05 LET B + C = A          b.  10 LET D = 4.*−X
   c.  15 LET 5 = A              d.  20 LET X = Y = 5.3
   e.  25 LET K = J**3.2, where J stores    f.  30 LET K = J**3, where J stores a
       a negative value.              negative value.
   g.  35 L = 8**K + 4

6. Consider the following sequence of instructions

       05 LET A = 37/C
       10 LET B = A + 1.6
       15 LET D = B**2

   and the current contents of the specified storage locations given below.

   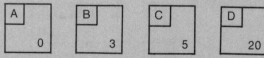

   Indicate the new contents following the execution of the above statements.

7. Given the instructions

       100 LET K = K + 1
       110 LET S = S + X

and the current contents

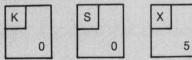

determine the new contents if these instructions are executed three times in sequence.

**8.** For the sequence of instructions in Table 3.3, indicate the contents of V, C, and P if M contains 25000.

## Arithmetic Hierarchy

Computers do arithmetic on only two numbers at a time (pairwise arithmetic). Therefore, an arithmetic expression involving several computations must be computed in a certain sequence.

In BASIC the sequence for performing arithmetic operations is

First: All exponentiation is performed.
Second: All multiplication and division is completed.
Third: All addition and subtraction is performed.

We illustrate this so-called arithmetic hierarchy through examples.

### EXAMPLE 3.2

The calculation of average student bill in the tuition revenue program is performed by the statement:

    30 LET B = 15*C + 250

When C has a value of 80, then 1450 is stored in B. This value is arrived at through the following steps:

First: C is multiplied by 15 because multiplication is completed before addition. The result is 1200.
Second: 250 is added to 1200. The result is 1450.

### EXAMPLE 3.3    Costing Problem

An analyst for Prangles Potato Chips, a competitor of Pringles, wishes to determine the area of the top which would be required of a super-economy-size cylindrical container of radius 5 inches. As you might recall, the area of a circle is computed by using the formula Area $= \pi r^2$, where $r$ is the radius. This can be written in BASIC as

    50 LET A = 3.14159*R**2

If the variable R has the value 5, then 78.5398 is stored in A. This result is achieved as follows:

First: R is raised to the second power because exponentiation is performed before multiplication. The result is 25.

Second: The number 3.14159 is multiplied by 25. The result is 78.5398.

## Left-to-Right Rule

The exact order of computation when two or more operations are at the same level of arithmetic hierarchy will differ depending on the complexity of the arithmetic expression and the particular computer system. However, *the computational result will be consistent with a left-to-right scan of the arithmetic expression,* as the following examples illustrate.

### EXAMPLE 3.4   Percentages

The percentage of business students relative to the university enrollment is calculated using the following statement:

750 LET P = B/U*100

If 1000 is stored in B and 5000 is stored in U, then 20 is stored in P. The value of 20 is determined by the following sequence:

First: B is divided by U because division and multiplication are at the same level, so that operations are from left to right. The result is 0.2.

Second: The number 0.2 is multiplied by 100. The result is 20.

Note that the left-to-right rule prevents the wrong sequence of first multiplying U by 100 (giving 500000) and then dividing this result into B (giving 0.002 for P).

### EXAMPLE 3.5   Microeconomics Problem

The daily cost in dollars of operating a small manufacturing firm is described by the equation

$$\text{Cost} = \text{Units}^3 - 6 \cdot \text{Units}^2 + 250$$

where Units represents the number of units produced by the firm per day. The equivalent LET statement in BASIC is

75 LET  C = U**3 − 6*U**2 + 250

If U has the value 20, then 5850 will be stored in C. The value 5850 is determined as follows:

First: U is raised to the third power because exponentiation is the first operation performed, and U∗∗3 appears to the *left* of U∗∗2. The result is 8000.

Second: U is raised to the second power. The result is 400.

Third: The number 6 is multiplied by 400 because multiplication is performed before addition and subtraction. The result is 2400.

Fourth: The number 2400 is subtracted from 8000 because the subtraction operation is found to the left of the addition operation. The result is 5600.

Fifth: The number 250 is added to 5600, giving 5850.

## *Use of Parentheses*

The insertion of parentheses within arithmetic expressions changes the order of computation according to the following rules:

The operations enclosed within parentheses are computed before operations not included in parentheses. Parentheses may be embedded inside other parentheses in complicated expressions. The innermost set of parentheses contains the computations done first.

We might note that within parentheses, themselves, the hierarchy and left-to-right rules apply.

### EXAMPLE 3.6   Temperature Conversion

Conversion of temperatures from Fahrenheit to Celsius is a procedure you should become accustomed to as the United States converts to metric measurements. The appropriate formula is

$$\text{Celsius} = 5/9 \cdot (\text{Fahrenheit} - 32)$$

In BASIC the formula is written

20 LET C = 5/9∗(F − 32)

If 212 is stored in F, then 100.000 will be stored in C according to the following steps:

First: The number 32 is subtracted from F because this operation is enclosed in parentheses. The result is 180.

Second: The number 5 is divided by 9 because the division operation is found to the left of the multiplication operation. The result is 0.555556.

Third: The number 0.555556 is multiplied by 180. The result is 100.000.

Note that division of 5 by 9 actually gives the irrational number 0.555555555 · · · , that is, the 5s never end. We expressed the result to six significant digits, assuming a computer that works with six-digit precision. When this six-digit number is multiplied by 180, the precise result is 100.00008, which we have expressed to six digits as 100.000.

### Follow-up Exercises

It is very important that you pay close attention to hierarchy, left-to-right, and parentheses rules when you are writing BASIC expressions. *Inattention to these rules is a leading cause of logic errors.* The following exercises emphasize this point.

9. In Example 3.6, what would be stored under C if the LET statement were as follows:

   20 LET C = 5/9*F - 32

10. Indicate what would be stored in A for each of the following, given that 3 is in B and 2 is in C.
    a.  80 LET A = (4 + B**3 - C)*C**2
    b.  82 LET A = (4 + B**(3 - C))*C**2
    c.  84 LET A = (4 + B**(3 - C))*(C**2)
    d.  86 LET A = 9/B*C + 5/C
    e.  88 LET A = 9/(B*C) + 5/C
    f.  90 LET A = 9/B/C + 5/C
    g.  92 LET A = 9/B*(C + 5)/C

11. Write BASIC arithmetic expressions for each of the following algebraic expressions.
    a. $x^{i+1}$
    b. $x^i + 1$
    c. $\dfrac{s^2}{p - 1}$
    d. $\dfrac{(x - a)^2}{p - 1}$
    e. $(y - 3^{x-1} + 2)^5$
    f. $(7 - x)^{1/2}$
    g. $\sqrt{\dfrac{(x - a)^2}{p - 1}}$

12. Modify the tuition revenue program on page 49 by eliminating B as a variable and incorporating the average student bill calculation directly into the revenue calculation.

## 3.5
## PRINT STATEMENT

The **PRINT statement** is used to output

1. Numeric constants
2. Value of numeric expressions
3. Value of variables (the contents of memory locations)
4. String constants (labels, report headings, and so on)

The usual output device for those programming in BASIC is the terminal, whereby the execution of a PRINT statement causes printed output on either paper or a video screen.

A general form of the PRINT statement is given by

> *line no.* **PRINT** *list*

where *list* refers to

1.  A constant (numeric or string)
2.  A variable (numeric or string)
3.  An arithmetic expression
4.  Any combination of constants, variables, and expressions separated by commas or semicolons

## Printing Numeric Constants, Variables, and Expressions

To illustrate various versions of the PRINT statement, we turn to a familiar example.

---

### EXAMPLE 3.7   Revised Tuition Revenue

Consider the following revision of our earlier version:

| PROGRAM | COMMENTS |
|---|---|
| 10 LET C = 80 | |
| 20 LET S = 6000 | |
| 30 LET B = 15*C + 250 | |
| 40 LET R = B*S | |
| 50 PRINT 250 | Print numeric constant |
| 60 PRINT 15*C | Print arithmetic expression. |
| 70 PRINT B | Print numeric variable B. |
| 80 PRINT R,S | Print list of two variables, R and S. (Note use |
| 90 END | of comma to separate S from R.) |

When this program is run (executed), the following four lines are printed:

Print Column

```
        11111111112
1234567890123456789 0 . . .
```

Print line 1     250 ◄——————— Execution of line 50. The constant 250 is printed beginning in column 2 of print line 1. The printing element (carriage) on terminal then goes to beginning of next print line.

Print line 2     1200 ◄——————— Execution of line 60. The value of expression is printed beginning in column 2 of print line 2. The printing element then goes to beginning of print line 3.

Print line 3     1450 ◄——————— Execution of line 70. The value stored in B is printed.

Print line 4     8700000     6000

Output of R beginning in column 2 of print line 4.          Output of S beginning in column 17 of print line 4.

---

Study the above output and carefully note the following:

1.  When execution of a PRINT statement is completed, the printing element or carriage on the terminal automatically goes to the beginning (column 1) of the next **print line.**

2.  The output of positive numeric values is preceded by a blank space to account for the plus sign (the plus sign is not printed for positive numbers). Thus, the first four numbers printed begin in **print column** 2. If any of these numbers had been negative, then the negative sign would have been printed in column 1 (the negative sign is always printed for negative numbers). Also, all printed numeric values are always followed by a single blank space.

3.  Output on a print line is divided into **print zones.** A typical system divides a 75-column print line into five print zones of 15 columns each.[7] For example, the execution of line 80 requires the use of two print zones since two variables are in the list. Thus, the value of R is printed within the first print zone and the value of S is printed within the second print zone. Virtually all systems print **left justified** within a print zone. In other words, the value of R is printed in the leftmost portion of the first print zone (print column 1 when we account for the imaginary plus sign) and the value of S is printed in the first column associated with the second print zone (column 16 in this case has a blank because of the suppressed + sign).

4.  The width of print zones varies slightly from system to system, so ask your instructor about yours or solve Exercise 13. If you're using a terminal that has more than, say, 75 print columns, then your system may accommodate more than the usual number (four or five) of print zones. Check out your system.

5.  If the number of numeric values to be printed on a print line exceeds the number of print zones on your system, and you use commas to separate the elements in the list of the PRINT statement, then printing continues on the next print line once the current print line is filled. For example, if lines 50 through 80 are replaced by

    ```
    75 PRINT 250,15,15*C,B,R,S
    ```

    then on a five-zone print line we would get the following output:

    ```
    250    15    1200    1450    8700000
    6000
    ```

    The sixth element in the list of the PRINT statement gets printed in the first zone of the next line.

6.  If the number of digits in a numeric value exceeds the maximum for the system (usually six for real values and eight for integer values), then the printed value will be expressed in E-notation. For example, if we replace old lines 10 and 20 by

    ```
    10 LET C = 160
    20 LET S = 40000
    ```

---

[7] Some systems vary from this norm. For example, IBMs CALL system uses four print zones of 18 characters each for print lines of 72 characters.

then the output for an eight-digit integer system would appear as follows:

```
250
2400
2650
1.06E8     40000
```

Revenue equals $106,000,000; since this
nine-digit number exceeds the system's maximum,
the system switches to E-notation.

## *Printing String Constants*

As you know by now, the print list can include string constants for the purpose of printing labels, report titles, columns headings, and other textual matter.

---

### EXAMPLE 3.8   String Constants by Themselves

When the following program is executed,

```
 5 PRINT "BASIC PROGRAMMING"
10 PRINT "IS MY FAVORITE"
15 PRINT "SUBJECT!"
20 END
```

we get the output shown below.

```
┌─Print column 1
↓
BASIC PROGRAMMING
IS MY FAVORITE
SUBJECT!
```

Thus, execution of each PRINT statement causes the computer to literally print the string of characters within the quotes. Note that the string constant for each PRINT statement is printed left-justified (beginning in column 1) of the first print zone.

### EXAMPLE 3.9   String Constants as Labels for Numeric Output

String constants are often included in a print list as labels for numeric output, as the following illustrates.

```
 5 LET  P1 = 40.05
10 LET  C  = 45.20
15 LET  P2 = P1 − C
20 PRINT "PRICE IS   $",P1
25 PRINT "COST IS    $",C
30 PRINT "PROFIT IS  $",P2
35 END
```

Output would be printed as follows:

```
|◄──── Print Zone 1────►|◄──── Print Zone 2 ──►|
                   1 1 1 1 1 1 1 1 1 1 2 2 2 2 2 2 2 2 2 2 3
1 2 3 4 5 6 7 8 9 0 1 2 3 4 5 6 7 8 9 0 1 2 3 4 5 6 7 8 9 0 . . .
```

```
PRICE  IS   $      40. 05
COST   IS   $      45. 20
PROFIT IS   $     − 5 . 15
```

Note that each print list has two elements, a string constant and a numeric variable. Thus, the value of the string constant is printed left-justified in the first print zone of a print line, and the value of the numeric variable is printed left-justified in the second print zone of the same print line. Did you notice how we spaced the dollar signs within the quotes in the print lists so that they would align in the printed output? Little efforts (and ideas) of this type can make a big difference in the visual appeal of printed output.

### EXAMPLE 3.10    Length of String Constant Greater than Width of Print Zone

If the length of a string constant exceeds the width of a print zone, then the printed string utilizes the next available print zone, as the following illustrates.

```
10 PRINT "NAME:  W. W.", "AGE:  2001"
20 PRINT "NAME:  WONDER WOMAN", "AGE:  2001"
30 END
```

Output for a 75-character line with five zones of width 15 characters each would appear as follows:

```
|◄────Zone 1 ────►|◄──── Zone 2────►|◄──── Zone 3────►|
             1 1 1 1 1 1 1 1 1 1 2 2 2 2 2 2 2 2 2 2 3 3 3 3 3 3 3 3 3 4 4 4 4 4 4
1 2 3 4 5 6 7 8 9 0 1 2 3 4 5 6 7 8 9 0 1 2 3 4 5 6 7 8 9 0 1 2 3 4 5 6 7 8 9 0 1 2 3 4 5 . .
```

```
NAME :  W .W .      AGE :   2001
NAME :  WONDER WOMAN         AGE :   2001
```

The string constants in line 10 have lengths of 12 and 10 characters, respectively. Thus, each fits within print zones 1 and 2, respectively. The 19-character length of the first string constant in line 20, however, exceeds the width of the first zone; hence, its output "overlaps" into zone 2 as shown. Therefore, the second string constant in line 20 is printed beginning in zone 3.

## Output Spacing

Certain variations in the use of the PRINT statement allow you to better control horizontal and vertical spacing of printed output. Here are some points that will allow you to spread spacing, compact spacing, suppress printing on the next line, and achieve blank lines.

1. When a *comma* is used to separate items in a print list, it has the effect of moving the print element on the terminal to the next zone; that is, it *prints blank spaces for the remainder of the current zone.*

2. Use of a *semicolon* to separate items in a print list "packs" the zones. **Packed zones** allow you to fit more output data on a print line. The semicolon causes the terminal to generate zero blank spaces, so that printing continues at the next print column on the line.

3. A comma or semicolon at the end of the list in a PRINT statement, called a **trailing comma** or **trailing semicolon,** instructs the terminal to suppress the carriage return and line feed operations, and causes the terminal to print the next output on the same print line. Thus, a trailing comma causes the printing element to "stay on the current line and proceed to the beginning of the next print zone." On the other hand, the trailing semicolon causes the carriage to "stay in its current location."[8]

4. Commas can appear consecutively in the list of a PRINT statement. Each extra comma positions the print element on output at the beginning of the next zone, thus allowing you to print a **blank zone.** In this way you can achieve horizontal spacing.[9]

5. If you omit the list of items in a PRINT statement, then a **blank line** is "printed." In effect, this allows you to control vertical spacing by moving the carriage down the page or video screen.

We now illustrate these points by example. Assume that 42 is stored in A, 4 is stored in D, 5.75 is stored in W, and 15-column print zones. Study the variations shown in Table 3.4.

The descriptions below should help you with the finer points of using the PRINT statements illustrated in Table 3.4. (Note that ƀ signifies the space character in these descriptions.)

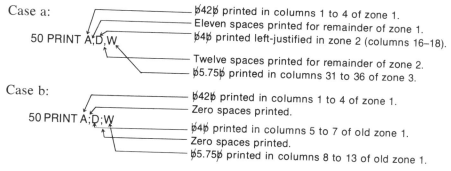

Case a:

50 PRINT A,D,W

- ƀ42ƀ printed in columns 1 to 4 of zone 1.
- Eleven spaces printed for remainder of zone 1.
- ƀ4ƀ printed left-justified in zone 2 (columns 16–18).
- Twelve spaces printed for remainder of zone 2.
- ƀ5.75ƀ printed in columns 31 to 36 of zone 3.

Case b:

50 PRINT A;D;W

- ƀ42ƀ printed in columns 1 to 4 of zone 1.
- Zero spaces printed.
- ƀ4ƀ printed in columns 5 to 7 of old zone 1.
- Zero spaces printed.
- ƀ5.75ƀ printed in columns 8 to 13 of old zone 1.

Note that *printed numeric values are automatically followed by a single blank space as part of that numeric output.* As before, positive numeric values are preceded by a single blank space to account for the suppressed + sign. Unfortunately, not all systems treat the semicolon as described above when it follows a numeric variable. As noted in

---

[8] Not all systems treat the semicolon as described above when it follows a numeric variable. Some systems insert additional spaces in the packed field following numeric output.

[9] The proposed ANSI standard recommends commas for generating blank zones. For systems that do not allow commas for this purpose, the string constant " " can be used to generate a blank zone.

TABLE 3.4  Output Spacing Examples

| CASE | STATEMENTS | PRINT COLUMNS (output) | COMMENTS |
|---|---|---|---|
| a. | 50 PRINT A,D,W | `42` (cols 1–2), `4` (col 15), `5.75` (cols 31–34) | Normal zones. |
| b. | 50 PRINT A;D;W | `42` `4` `5.75` (packed) | Packed zones. |
| c. | 50 PRINT A, <br> 55 PRINT D, <br> 60 PRINT W | `42` `4` `5.75` (same as case a) | Trailing commas. Results identical to case a. |
| d. | 50 PRINT A; <br> 55 PRINT D; <br> 60 PRINT W | `42` `4` `5.75` (packed, same as case b) | Trailing semicolons. Results identical to case b. |
| e. | 50 PRINT A <br> 55 PRINT ,D <br> 60 PRINT ,,W | `42` (line 50), `4` in zone 2 (line 55), `5.75` in zone 3 (line 60) | Line 55 prints one blank zone and line 60 prints two blank zones. |
| f. | 50 PRINT "AGE =",A <br> 55 PRINT "DEPENDENTS =",D <br> 60 PRINT "WAGE RATE =",W | `AGE =` `42` <br> `DEPENDENTS =` `4` <br> `WAGE RATE =` `5.75` | Normal zones |
| g. | 50 PRINT "AGE =";A <br> 55 PRINT <br> 60 PRINT "DEPENDENTS =";D <br> 65 PRINT <br> 70 PRINT "WAGE RATE =";W | `AGE =42` <br> (blank) <br> `DEPENDENTS =4` <br> (blank) <br> `WAGE RATE =5.75` | Packed zones and blank print lines. |

**h.**
```
50 PRINT "AGE";"DEPENDENTS"
60 PRINT A;D
```
Packing strings runs them together in print line.

AGEDEPENDENTS
42 4

**i.**
```
50 PRINT "AGE","DEPENDENTS"
60 PRINT A,D
```
Better appearance than case h.

AGE                DEPENDENTS
42                 4

**j.**
```
50 PRINT "AGE";"ḃḃḃDEPENDENTS"
60 PRINT A;"ḃḃḃḃḃ";D
```
Better appearance than case h and more closely spaced than case i.

AGE   DEPENDENTS
42        4

**k.**
```
50 PRINT "AGE = ";A,"DEPENDENTS = ";D
```
Mixed strings, variables, commas, and semicolons.

AGE = 42           DEPENDENTS = 4

**l.**
```
50 PRINT "AGE = ";A,"DEPENDENTS = ";D
```
Same as case k except all zones are packed.

AGE = 42 DEPENDENTS = 4

footnote 8, *some systems insert additional spaces in the packed field following numeric output, while other systems use different output formats from the above.*

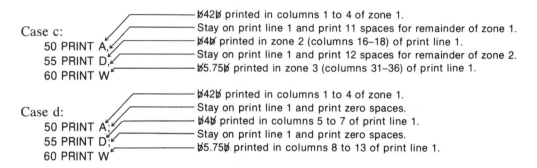

Case c:
    50 PRINT A,
    55 PRINT D,
    60 PRINT W

— Ø42Ø printed in columns 1 to 4 of zone 1.
— Stay on print line 1 and print 11 spaces for remainder of zone 1.
— Ø4Ø printed in zone 2 (columns 16–18) of print line 1.
— Stay on print line 1 and print 12 spaces for remainder of zone 2.
— Ø5.75Ø printed in zone 3 (columns 31–36) of print line 1.

Case d:
    50 PRINT A;
    55 PRINT D;
    60 PRINT W

— Ø42Ø printed in columns 1 to 4 of zone 1.
— Stay on print line 1 and print zero spaces.
— Ø4Ø printed in columns 5 to 7 of print line 1.
— Stay on print line 1 and print zero spaces.
— Ø5.75Ø printed in columns 8 to 13 of print line 1.

In case e note that an extra comma in a print list has the effect of filling in an entire zone with blanks. If $n$ commas appear at the beginning or end of a list, then $n$ zones are blanked out; if $n$ commas appear between two items in a print list, then $n - 1$ blank zones are printed between the two printed items.

Cases f through l illustrate various combinations of string constants, numeric variables, commas, and semicolons within print lists. Note that case g illustrates a method for vertical spacing: the statements

    55 PRINT
    65 PRINT

simply "print" two blank lines by causing the carriage to skip a line for each PRINT statement.

### Follow-up Exercises

**13.** Run the following program on your system:

    10 PRINT "000000000111111111122222222223333333333334"
    15 PRINT "123456789012345678901234567890123456789012345678901234567890"
    20 LET A = −5.4
    30 PRINT A,A,A,A,A,A,A
    40 END

How long is each zone on your system? How many zones fit on a print line? Ask your instructor if it is possible to increase the length of the print line on your system.

**14.** In Exercise 13, change line 30 as follows:
   a.    30 PRINT ,,,A
   b.    30 PRINT A,,,A
   c.    30 PRINT A,,,
         35 PRINT A

Describe the print line for each case. *Note:* If these cause errors on your system, then see footnote 9 on page 59.

**15.** Describe printed output for your system by running the following program:

```
10 LET A = 7.500
20 LET B = 0.55
30 LET C = 1234.
40 LET D = 123456789
50 LET E = 1234.56789
60 PRINT A,B,C,D,E
70 PRINT A;B;C;D;E
80 END
```

**16.** First describe the print lines for each case below. Then run these on your system. Assume −5 is stored in X, 10 is stored in Y, and 15 is stored in Z.

| CASE | STATEMENTS |
|------|------------|
| a. | 15 PRINT X,Y;Z |
| b. | 15 PRINT X;Y,Z |
| c. | 15 PRINT X;Y,<br>20 PRINT Z |
| d. | 15 PRINT X;Y;<br>20 PRINT Z |
| e. | 15 PRINT X,Y,,,Z |
| f. | 15 PRINT "X=";X<br>20 PRINT<br>25 PRINT "Y=",Y<br>30 PRINT<br>35 PRINT<br>40 PRINT "Z EQUALS";Z;"%"<br>45 LET L\$ = "Z EQUALS"<br>50 PRINT L\$;Z;"%" |
| g. | 15 PRINT "X","Y"<br>20 PRINT X,Y |
| h. | 15 PRINT "ƀXƀ";"ƀƀY"<br>20 PRINT "------"<br>25 PRINT X;Y |

**17.** The following PRINT statements contain some common errors for beginning programmers. Make necessary corrections.

a. PRINT A = A
b. PRINT "B ="B
c. PRINT QUANTITY PRICE REVENUE
d. PRINT A B C
e. PRINT "MY NAME IS

> **\*18.**  Modify the program in Example 3.7 on page 55 to print the following output:
>
> | | |
> |---|---|
> | FEES: | 250 |
> | TUITION: | <u>1200</u> |
> | BILL: | 1450 |
>
> REVENUES OF $ 8700000 ARE EXPECTED
> FOR A STUDENT BODY OF 6000

## 3.6
## REM STATEMENT

The statement

line no. **REM** *unquoted string*

is used to document programs, as the following example illustrates.

---

**EXAMPLE 3.11   Tuition Revenue with Documentation**

```
010 REM      TUITION REVENUE PROGRAM
020 REM      ------------------------
030 REM      VARIABLE KEY
040 REM       INPUT:
050 REM        NONE
060 REM       OUTPUT:
070 REM        R = REVENUE
080 REM       OTHER:
090 REM        B = AVERAGE STUDENT BILL
100 REM        C = COST PER CREDIT
110 REM        S = NUMBER OF STUDENTS
120 REM      ------------------------
210 LET C = 80
220 LET S = 6000
230 LET B = 15*C + 250
240 LET R = B*S
250 PRINT "REVENUE = $";R
260 END
```

---

Thus, REM statements are used in programs to identify (line 10) or describe the program, to define the variables (lines 20 to 120), and to describe segments of complicated programs. *Good programming style dictates that programs be well documented,* since such programs are easier to change, modify, or otherwise update at a later time.

---

\* Answers to single-starred exercises are not given in this book. Ask your instructor.

Note that the REM statement is a *nonexecutable* statement. When this program is run, the first statement executed is the LET in line 210. Thus, REM statements are ignored during execution. They simply serve to document programs for users whenever we view listings of the programs.

## 3.7
## AUTOMOBILE FINANCING PROBLEM

Many consumer automobile loans require the borrower to pay the same amount of money to the lending institution each month throughout the life of the loan. The monthly payment is based on the amount borrowed (purchase price – trade in of used

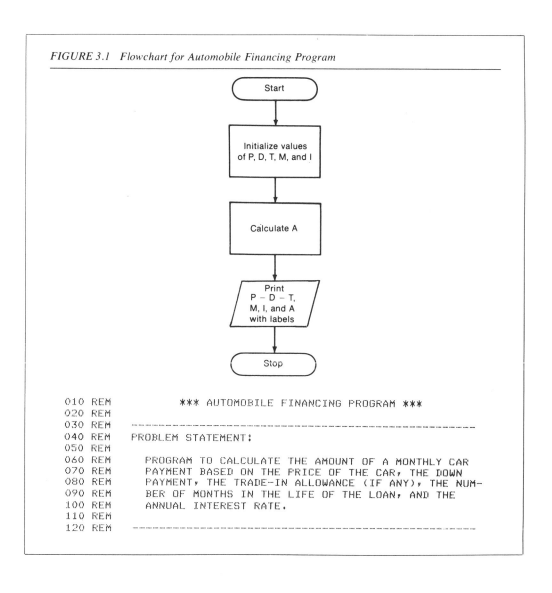

FIGURE 3.1   *Flowchart for Automobile Financing Program*

```
010 REM           *** AUTOMOBILE FINANCING PROGRAM ***
020 REM
030 REM    -----------------------------------------------------------------
040 REM    PROBLEM STATEMENT:
050 REM
060 REM       PROGRAM TO CALCULATE THE AMOUNT OF A MONTHLY CAR
070 REM       PAYMENT BASED ON THE PRICE OF THE CAR, THE DOWN
080 REM       PAYMENT, THE TRADE-IN ALLOWANCE (IF ANY), THE NUM-
090 REM       BER OF MONTHS IN THE LIFE OF THE LOAN, AND THE
100 REM       ANNUAL INTEREST RATE.
110 REM
120 REM    -----------------------------------------------------------------
```

```
130 REM    PROVIDED DATA:
140 REM
150 REM      P=PRICE OF CAR
160 REM      D=DOWN PAYMENT
170 REM      T=TRADE-IN-ALLOWANCE
180 REM      M=NUMBER OF MONTHS IN LIFE OF LOAN
190 REM      I=ANNUAL INTEREST RATE
200 REM
210 REM    -------------------------------------------------------
220 REM    DATA OUTPUT:
230 REM
240 REM      P-D-T, AMOUNT BORROWED ($)
250 REM      M
260 REM      I
270 REM      A, MONTHLY CAR PAYMENT ($)
280 REM
290 REM    -------------------------------------------------------
300 REM    COMPUTATIONS AND LOGICAL PROCESSES:
310 REM
320 REM      A=I/12*(P-D-T)*((1+I/12)**M/((1+I/12)**M-1))
330 REM
340 REM    -------------------------------------------------------
350 REM    THE FLOWCHART:
360 REM
370 REM      SEE FIGURE 3.1
380 REM
390 REM    -------------------------------------------------------
400 REM    PROBLEM CODE:
410 REM
420 LET P=6200
430 LET D=1000
440 LET T=1300
450 LET M=48
460 LET I=.1
470 LET A=I/12*(P-D-T)*((1+I/12)**M/((1+I/12)**M-1))
480 PRINT "******************************"
490 PRINT
500 PRINT "AMOUNT BORROWED: $";P-D-T
510 PRINT "NUMBER OF MONTHS: ";M
520 PRINT "INTEREST RATE:     ";100*I;"% PER YEAR"
530 PRINT
540 PRINT "MONTHLY PAYMENT: $";A
550 PRINT
560 PRINT "******************************"
570 END



******************************

AMOUNT BORROWED: $ 3900
NUMBER OF MONTHS:  48
INTEREST RATE:     10.  % PER YEAR

MONTHLY PAYMENT: $ 98.921

******************************

TIME 0.03 SECS.
```

car − down payment), the time required for repayment, and the interest rate. A lending institution uses the following formula to determine the car buyer's monthly payment:

$$a = i \cdot (p - d - t) \cdot \left( \frac{(1 + i)^m}{(1 + i)^m - 1} \right)$$

where

$a$ = monthly payments
$p$ = purchase price of car
$d$ = down payment
$t$ = trade-in allowance
$i$ = monthly interest rate
$m$ = total number of monthly payments

If the interest rate is expressed on an annual basis, then $i$ in the above formula is replaced by $i/12$.

In this section we illustrate a program that includes the four-step procedure in its documentation. The last step on debugging is illustrated by a run of the program. Segments of the program itself are not documented, since the logic is simple. First, study Figure 3.1, the documentation, the program logic, and the output, and then answer the follow-up exercises.

### Follow-up Exercises

**19.** With respect to the calculation of A:
   a. State its algebraic formula based on the arithmetic expression in line 470.
   b. Confirm the output for A by using a calculator.
**\*20.** Modify and run the program to calculate and output the following:
   a. Total payments over the life of the loan: A · M
   b. Total interest over the life of the loan: A · M − (P − D − T)
   c. Proportion interest: [A · M − (P − D − T)] ÷ A · M
**\*21.** Modify and run the program to answer the following: What are the effects on monthly payment, total payments, total interest, and proportion interest over the life of the loan if we
   a. Increase the downpayment to $2000?
   b. Change the life of the loan to 36 months? (D remains at the original $1000.)
   c. Get a reduction of 0.5 percent (0.005) in the interest rate? (D remains at $1000 and M at 48.)
**\*22.** Try making the following modifications to the program:
   a. Change a LET statement in the program that eliminates the need to compute I/12 three times in line 470. What argument can you give for justifying this modification?
   b. Shorten the program by eliminating all LET statements except for A, modifying the LET statement for A, and modifying the first three PRINT statements. Can you think of advantages and disadvantages of this approach over the original approach?

## Additional Exercises

We strongly recommend studying Module A (see page A–1) before attempting any of the programming exercises.

**23.** Define or explain the following:

| | |
|---|---|
| character set | E-notation |
| alphabetic characters | overflow |
| numeric characters | underflow |
| special characters | string constant |
| string | executable statement |
| number | nonexecutable statement |
| integer | LET statement |
| real | string expression |
| exponential | arithmetic expression |
| constant | arithmetic operation symbol |
| variable | arithmetic hierarchy |
| key word | PRINT statement |
| function | print line |
| expression | print column |
| statement | print zone |
| line number | left-justified |
| numeric variable | packed zones |
| simple numeric variable | trailing comma |
| subscripted numeric variable | trailing semicolon |
| string variable | blank zones |
| simple string variable | blank line |
| subscripted string variable | REM statement |
| numeric constant | |

**24.** Identify and briefly discuss the nine elements of BASIC.

**25.** Distinguish between
- a. A variable and a value
- b. A variable and a constant
- c. A numeric variable and a string variable
- d. A simple numeric variable and a subscripted numeric variable

**26.** Why is it a bad idea to number lines in your program as follows: 1, 2, 3, 4, . . . ?

**27.** **Temperature Conversion.** Write a program that explicitly assigns values to degrees Fahrenheit and outputs degrees Fahrenheit and its equivalent degrees Celsius. (See Example 3.6.) Don't forget to specify the first three steps in the four-step procedure and to document your program. Run the program to determine degree Celsius equivalents of $-10$, 0, 32, 80, and 100 degrees Fahrenheit. Do a nice job of labeling your output. Note that a change in a LET statement followed by a separate run is required for each degree equivalent.

**28.** **Costing Problem.** Consider the scenario in Example 3.3. Suppose that each top costs $C$ dollars per square inch of surface and $X$ containers are needed. Write a computer program which determines the total cost of $X$ containers. Treat $R$, $C$, and $X$ as variables that are explicitly assigned values through LET statements. Don't forget to specify the first three steps in the four-step procedure and to document your program. What is the total cost of 500,000 container tops, where each top has a radius of 5 inches and costs 2 cents per square inch? What if the cost is $\frac{1}{2}$ cent per square inch, all other things the same? Do a nice job of labeling the output of $R$, $C$, $X$, and total cost. Note that a change in a LET statement followed by a separate run is needed to answer the second question.

29. **Microeconomics Problem.** Consider the scenario in Example 3.5. Suppose that all units produced can be sold at a constant price of $100 per unit. Noting that daily revenue is price times the number of units produced and sold in one day and that daily profit is daily revenue less daily cost, write a program which calculates daily profit. Treat U as a variable that is initialized through a LET statement, and print with labels the daily revenue, daily cost, and daily profit. Don't forget to specify the first three steps in the four-step procedure and to document your program. How many units should be produced to maximize profit? *Hint:* Try values of 1, 2, 3, . . . , 10 for U. Note that a change in a LET statement followed by a separate run is required to assess each new value of U.

30. **Blood-Bank Inventory Problem.** Decision making relating to the management of physical inventories is an established area in the management sciences which in recent years has been applied increasingly in semiprivate and public organizations.

Suppose that whenever a hospital replenishes its supply of a certain type of blood, it orders from a regional blood bank the amount indicated by the following formula:

$$Q = \sqrt{\frac{2 \cdot C \cdot D}{H}}$$

where

$Q$ = number of pints of blood to order
$C$ = administrative and shipping cost (in dollars) of placing the order
$D$ = average weekly demand (usage) for this type of blood
$H$ = cost (dollars per pint per week) of refrigerating the blood

Also, it can be shown that the cost per week of this inventory policy is given by the formula

$$W = \sqrt{2 \cdot C \cdot H \cdot D}$$

where

$W$ = expected cost (dollars) per week.

Write a computer program that assigns values to $C$, $H$, and $D$ and determines how much blood to order and the cost of such a policy. Don't forget to specify the first three steps in the four-step procedure and to document your program. Output the values of $C$, $D$, $H$, $Q$, and $W$ with labels.

How many units of blood should be ordered if it costs $50 to place an order, weekly demand averages 3000 pints, and it costs 20 cents per week per pint of blood to refrigerate? How much should be ordered if the refrigeration cost increases to 30 cents? What is the expected cost per week for each of the above? Comment on the logic of changes in the output values of Q and W based on changes in the value of H. Note that a change in a LET statement followed by a separate run is needed to answer the second question. *Hint:* See the answers to Exercise 11g to evaluate the expressions for Q and W.

31. **Forecasting Population Growth.** In recent years, the prediction of world population levels into the next century has been a concern of many political, environmental, and agricultural planners. The following equation can be used to predict future levels of world population:

$$p = c \cdot [1 + (b - d)]^n$$

where

$p$ = predicted level of future population
$b$ = birth rate
$c$ = current level of population
$d$ = death rate
$n$ = number of years into the future

Write a program that can be used to predict future population level given the current level, the birth rate, the death rate, and the number of years into the future. Assign values to $c$, $b$, $d$, and $n$ using LET statements. Don't forget to specify the first three steps in the four-step procedure and to document your program. Output the values of $c$, $b$, $d$, $n$, and $p$ with labels. Predict the earth's population in the year 2000. The population in 1976 was approximately 4 billion.

    a.   Assume a birth rate of 0.025 (2.5 percent) per year and a death rate of 0.009 (0.9 percent), both of which are expected to remain constant until the year 2000.

    b.   How would your prediction change if the birth rate fell to 0.02?

    c.   How many years before the earth's population doubles? Use the birth and death rates given in part a. *Hint:* Try different values for $n$ and observe the output values for $p$.

  **d.   Go to your library and look up comparable $c$, $b$, and $d$ figures for the United States or your state. Make some predictions.

Note that a change in a LET statement followed by a separate run is needed to answer each additional question.

32. **Depreciation Problem.** The concept of *depreciation* plays a prominent role in the financial accounting of organizations which report profits and pay taxes. Write a program to calculate the amount of depreciation *in the first year* for a capital asset (building, automobile, machine, and so on) using

    a.   *The straight-line method.* This method uses the following formula to determine depreciation in any given year.

$$\text{Depreciation} = \left( \begin{matrix} \text{Cost of} \\ \text{asset} \end{matrix} - \begin{matrix} \text{Salvage value} \\ \text{of asset} \end{matrix} \right) \cdot \left( \frac{1}{\text{Life of asset}} \right)$$

---

** Exercises that have a double asterisk either require more than the usual effort or are of above average difficulty.

b. *The double-declining balance method* (a method used to increase the amount of depreciation in early years). This method uses the formulas:

$$\begin{matrix} \text{Book value} \\ \text{of asset} \end{matrix} = \begin{pmatrix} \text{Cost of} \\ \text{asset} \end{pmatrix} - \begin{pmatrix} \text{Accumulated depreciation} \\ \text{from all prior years} \end{pmatrix}$$

$$\text{Depreciation} = \begin{pmatrix} \text{Book value} \\ \text{of asset} \end{pmatrix} \cdot (2) \cdot \begin{pmatrix} \dfrac{1}{\text{Life of asset}} \end{pmatrix}$$

Data assigned through LET statements should include cost, salvage value, and life of the asset. Output should include the depreciation in the first year by each method. Note that accumulated depreciation should be initialized to zero for this calculation. Don't forget to specify the first three steps of the four-step procedure and to document your program.

A small business firm has just purchased a car costing $4200. The owners intend to "run the car into the ground" in four years, at which time they will be happy to get $200 salvage for the car. How much depreciation is allowed in the first year under the straight-line method? The double-declining balance method? What happens to the amount of depreciation if the life of the asset were two years? eight years? Note that a change in a LET statement followed by a separate run is needed to answer each additional question.

# Additional Input and Output

In the last chapter you learned two ways of providing data to a program:

1.  By using constants in an arithmetic expression
2.  By assigning values to variables using the LET statement.

In this chapter you will learn two additional approaches that provide data:

1.  INPUT statement
2.  READ and DATA statements.

You will also learn a new means of controlling your output: the TAB function.
In addition, we show you how to process string variables.

## 4.1
## INPUT STATEMENT

The INPUT statement allows you to supply data to the program while the program is running. In other words, when the computer executes the INPUT statement, it prints a question mark (?) at your terminal and waits for you to enter the data for this program.

### General Form

The general form of the INPUT statement is

> *line no.* **INPUT** *list of variables*

where the "list of variables" contains variable names (separated by commas) in the exact sequence that data items are to be entered.

---

**EXAMPLE 4.1  Tuition Revenue Problem with Data Input**

We can rewrite the tuition revenue program of Example 2.1 using the INPUT statement to provide data:

```
10 INPUT C, S
20 LET R = (15*C + 250)*S
30 PRINT "REVENUE = $"; R
40 END
```

Figure 4.1 shows an appropriate flowchart for this program. Note the use of the parallelogram symbol for the INPUT statement.
Data input is as follows while the program is running:

System
command————→RUN                    *Note:* Shaded segments
                                   are printed by the
Data                               computer.
entry ————————→ ? 80,6000

Computer
output ————————→ REVENUE = $ 8700000

The execution of line 10, the INPUT statement, directs the computer to print a question mark. Next, the computer pauses as it waits for you to enter two values separated by a comma. Once you enter the values, you must hit the carriage return key on your terminal to transmit these values to the computer. Following this procedure the two memory locations for C and S appear as follows:

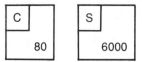

Having completed the execution of the INPUT statement, the computer then executes the next executable statement in the program (in this case the LET in line 20).

FIGURE 4.1    *Flowchart Showing Input Process*

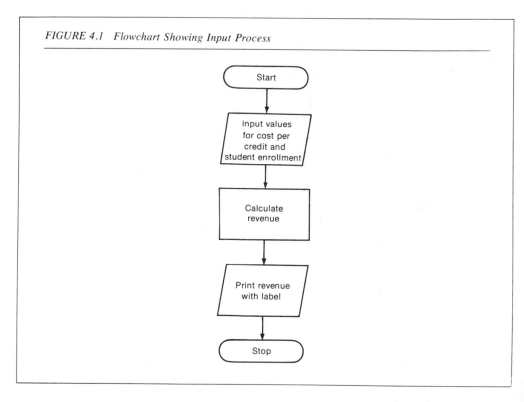

## Conversational Programming

A good programming practice is to print a "prompting" message reminding the program user of what data are to be entered next. This is accomplished by placing a PRINT statement containing a description of the input data *immediately before* the corresponding INPUT statement. For example, the program of Example 4.1 could be revised as in the next example.

---

**EXAMPLE 4.2   Tuition Revenue Problem with Conversation**

```
05 PRINT "PLEASE ENTER COST PER CREDIT AND ENROLLMENT"
07 PRINT "SEPARATED BY A COMMA"
10 INPUT C,S
20 LET R = (15*C + 250)*S
30 PRINT "REVENUE = $";R
40 END
```

The input and output now appear as follows:

```
PLEASE ENTER COST PER CREDIT AND ENROLLMENT
SEPARATED BY A COMMA
?80,6000
 REVENUE = $ 8700000
```

Many programmers prefer to see the question mark on the same line as the message. In this case, the PRINT statement that immediately precedes the INPUT statement should end with a trailing semicolon.[1] For example, the statements

```
05 PRINT "PLEASE ENTER COST PER CREDIT AND ENROLLMENT"
07 PRINT "SEPARATED BY A COMMA";
10 INPUT C,S
```

Trailing
semicolon

cause the following

```
PLEASE ENTER COST PER CREDIT AND ENROLLMENT
SEPARATED BY A COMMA? 80,6000
```

Semicolon causes
print of question
mark here.

---

As you can see, the INPUT statement facilitates **interactive** or **conversational programming,** whereby the computer and the user carry out a "dialogue." In this type of program design, each PRINT statement that precedes an INPUT statement prints "conversation" in the form of a computer request. The INPUT statement then accepts the user's response.

### *Matching Input Data to List*

Whenever an INPUT statement is executed and a question mark is printed, you should enter a corresponding value for each variable in the list of the INPUT statement. If

---

[1] A trailing comma could be used, but then the question mark is not "packed" next to the message.

there is more than one variable in the list, then the usual procedure is to enter all requested values on the same line, each value separated from the other by a comma. For example, if we wish to store the following

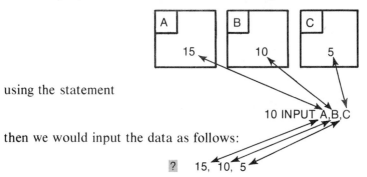

using the statement

then we would input the data as follows:

Otherwise, one of two procedures will apply:

1. If too many values are entered, then either the excess data on that line are ignored, or held for future use, or a nonfatal execution error occurs. For example, if we had entered the following for A, B, and C,

    ? 15,10,5,2

    then some systems will ignore the 2, other systems will "hold" the 2 for the next time an INPUT statement is executed, and still other systems will print an error message requesting correct input.

2. If too few values are entered, compared with the variable list of the INPUT statement, then most systems print another question mark to indicate "at least one more data item is needed." Consider the following sequence in the input of A, B, and C:

    ? 15◄─────We type 15 for A and then press the return key on the terminal.
    ? 10,5 ◄───Computer prints another question mark and we type 10 for B and 5 for C.

If we had only typed the 10 following the second question mark, then the computer would have typed a third question mark for the entry of C. Some systems precede these additional question marks by error messages.

## Advantages

Prior to the INPUT statement you had only two means of providing data: constants in arithmetic expressions and initialization using LET statements. For example, the Chapter 3 version of the tuition revenue program provided data as follows:

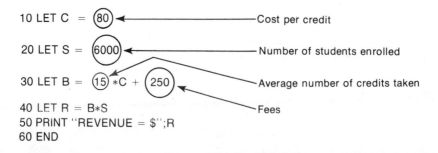

In our latest version, we replaced lines 10 and 20 with the statement

```
10 INPUT C, S
```

The INPUT statement is an alternative approach to storing data in memory locations, and *is preferred to the LET statement whenever variables have a high likelihood of changing values each time the program is executed.* For example, if we need to assess the effects of 10 different values for C, then it is much easier to type RUN and to enter the appropriate value for C following the question mark than to change a LET statement for C 10 different times. Moreover, *conversational programs are essential when used by those who are not themselves programmers.* For example, most nonscientific commercial time-sharing programs are conversational since they are mostly used by managers who have no programming experience.

### Follow-up Exercises

1. Construct PRINT and INPUT statements for the following:

    a. ENTER SOCIAL SECURITY NUMBER AND AGE
       ? ←————————————————————— Values for S and A

    b. ENTER PRINCIPAL? ←———————— Value for P

       ENTER NUMBER OF YEARS? ←———— Value for N

       ENTER INTEREST RATE? ←———— Value for I

2. Run the following program and deliberately enter too few and then too many data items, in order to familiarize yourself with this type of execution error on your system.

    ```
    10 INPUT A,B,C
    20 PRINT A;B;C
    30 END
    ```

3. Suppose you were to enter your data in Example 4.1 as

    ```
    ? 6000, 80
    ```

    What result would you get?

4. Modify Example 4.2 so cost per credit and enrollment are entered as follows:

    ```
    COST PER CREDIT? 80
    ENROLLMENT? 6000
    ```

5. Modify Example 4.2 for input as follows:

    PLEASE ENTER COST PER CREDIT, ENROLLMENT,
    FEES, AND AVERAGE CREDITS? ←———————— Values for C, S, F, A

    Don't forget to modify line 20. Run this program to answer the questions posed in Exercise 5 of Chapter 2 on page 36. Why is the interactive version of the program preferred?

*6. **Automobile Financing Problem.** Modify the program of Section 3.7 on page 66 by treating P, D, T, M, and I as input variables. Include appropriate conversation and answer Exercise 21 on page 67 by running your new version. Why is this interactive version preferred?

## 4.2
## READ AND DATA STATEMENTS

The use of READ and DATA statements is a fourth approach to providing data. In this case, unlike the INPUT statement, data are supplied within the program prior to execution.

### General Form

The READ statement stores values in computer memory that are initially typed onto a DATA statement. The general form of the READ statement is

> *line no.* **READ** *list of variables*

where the "list of variables" contains variable names (separated by commas) in the same sequence as the items of data that are to be entered into memory.

The READ instruction must be used with a nonexecutable instruction called the *DATA statement*. The DATA statement contains the data items (values) that correspond to the list of variables in the READ statement. The general form of the DATA statement is

> *line no.* **DATA** *list of data items*

where each data item is either a numeric constant or a string constant, separated by a comma from the preceding data item.

The READ statement, when executed, retrieves as many values from one or more DATA statements as variables in the list of the READ statement. For example, if the list of a READ statement contains five numeric variables, then execution of this READ statement processes five numeric values from one or more DATA statements. The variables in the READ statement and the values in the DATA statement are matched in an ordered fashion; that is, the first variable with the first data value, the second variable with the second value, and so on.

---

**EXAMPLE 4.3   Tuition Revenue Program with READ/DATA**

We can rewrite and run the tuition revenue program using the READ and DATA statements as follows:

```
10 READ C,S
20 LET R = (15*C + 250)*S
30 PRINT "REVENUE = $";R
40 DATA 80,6000
50 END

RUN

REVENUE = $ 8700000
```

The flowchart for this program is the same as the flowchart in Figure 4.1, except the word *INPUT* is replaced by the word *READ*.

The execution of the READ statement causes the transfer of the two values from the DATA statement to the memory locations C and S. After the READ instruction is executed the memory locations appear as follows:

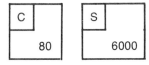

## Data Blocks

The data values from *all* DATA statements in your program are combined by the BASIC compiler into a single sequence of data sometimes referred to as a **data block.** The data values are placed into the block in the order of their appearance in the program; that is, data values on lower line numbers are placed ahead of values on higher line numbers, and data values to the left are placed ahead of data values to the right.

**EXAMPLE 4.4   Exam Averaging Program**

A program to average a student's three exam scores can be written as follows:

```
010 READ E1
020 READ E2
030 READ E3
040 LET S = E1 + E2 + E3
050 LET A = S/3
060 PRINT "AVERAGE IS"; A
070 DATA 83
080 DATA 91
090 DATA 87
100 END
```

The data in the three DATA statements are combined into a data block that can be visualized as

| 83 |
|----|
| 91 |
| 87 |

Even if the data were typed

```
70 DATA 83,91
80 DATA 87
90 END
```

or

    70 DATA 83,91,87
    80 END

the computer still combines the data into the data block

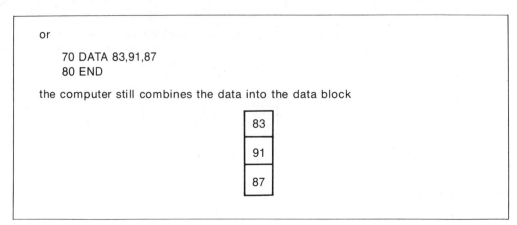

When your program is run, the computer maintains a conceptual pointer to the next item of data to be read into a memory location. When the program begins execution this pointer points to the first item in the block of data values. Each time a READ statement is executed values from the data block are assigned to the variables in the READ statement based on the location of the pointer. When the execution of a READ statement is completed the pointer is advanced to the data value immediately following the last data value read in.

To illustrate how this works, consider the following description of data activities during the execution of the exam averaging program.

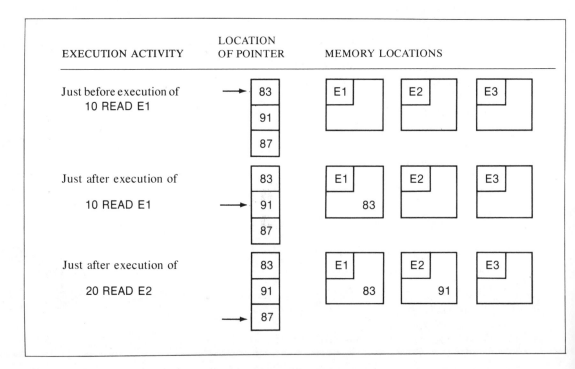

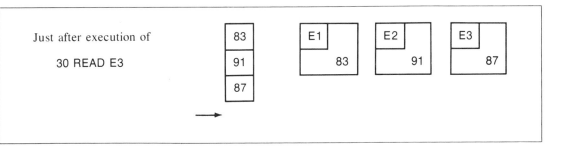

## Other Considerations

You should realize that the READ statement is executable, but not the DATA statement. In other words, when execution reaches a line containing a DATA statement, that line is ignored and execution proceeds to the next line. Since DATA statements only serve the purpose of creating a data block, and the data block is formed prior to execution, it follows that DATA statements can be placed anywhere in the program prior to the END statement. Many programmers prefer to place all DATA statements in a group just before the END statement, since this "gets them out of the way," thereby allowing users to more easily follow programming logic.

As was true of the INPUT statement, the READ/DATA statements give us more flexibility in providing data than do LET statements and the use of constants in arithmetic expressions. Technically, however, programs strictly using READ/DATA statements are not interactive. So, if the program is to be used by nonprogrammers and data are likely to change from run to run, then careful instructions must be given in the use and placement of DATA statements.

If large amounts of data need to be provided and stored for future use, then the READ/DATA alternative is preferred to the use of INPUT statements. For example, if we had to type in test scores for 200 students, then READ/DATA statements have the following advantages over the INPUT statement:

1. Errors in the data list can be corrected easily.
2. The same data can be processed more than once without having to retype it.

For either small amounts of data or the need to process interactively, the INPUT statement is preferred over the READ/DATA statements. In some cases, program design might call for the use of both INPUT and READ/DATA statements in the same program. It simply depends on the needs that the program is to fulfill.

### Follow-up Exercises

7. Modify the program in Example 4.4 such that one READ statement reads in values for E1, E2, and E3. Do the DATA statements need changing?
8. What do you think would happen during execution if line 90 were omitted in the program of Example 4.4?

9. Solve Exercise 5 on page 77 using READ/DATA statements in place of the INPUT statement. Which approach do you prefer?

*10. **Automobile Financing Problem.** Solve Exercise 6 on page 77 using READ/DATA statements in place of the INPUT statement. Which approach do you prefer?

11. Specify which of the indicated sets of DATA statements yield the block:

| 10 |
|----|
| 20 |
| 30 |
| 40 |
| 50 |

a. 100 DATA 10
   102 DATA 20
   104 DATA 30
   106 DATA 40
   108 DATA 50

b. 100 DATA 10,20,30,40,50

c. 100 DATA 50,40,30,20,10

d. 100 DATA 10, 20
   102 DATA 30,40,50

e. 10 DATA 10, 20
   20 ⎫
   30 ⎬ Executable statements
   40 ⎪
   50 ⎭
   60 DATA 30,40,50

12. Consider the following READ statements:

   20 READ A, B, C
   30 READ D, E

For the data block in the preceding exercise, indicate the location of the pointer and contents in memory for the following:
a. Just before line 20 is executed.
b. Just after line 20 is executed.
c. Just after line 30 is executed.

## 4.3
## RESTORE STATEMENT

In certain instances it is necessary to reread the same data within the same program. This can be accomplished by using the RESTORE statement.

A general form of this statement is

```
line no. RESTORE
```

The RESTORE statement resets the pointer back to the beginning of the data block, so that the next READ statement executed will read data from the beginning again. For example, consider the following:

```
10 READ A, B
20 PRINT "A ="; A, "B ="; B
30 RESTORE
40 READ C, D
50 PRINT "C = "; C, "D = "; D
60 DATA 100, 150
70 END
```

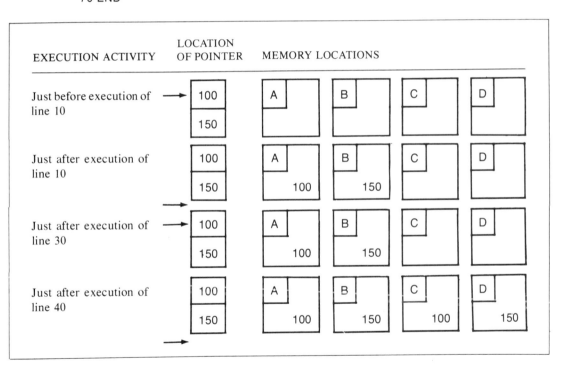

Output from the program would appear as follows:

```
A = 100     B = 150
C = 100     D = 150
```

## Follow-up Exercise

**13.** What output would you expect if line 30 is removed from the program?

## 4.4
## PROCESSING STRING VARIABLES

For simplicity we have emphasized programs where the input, read, and output data were numeric. This is unrealistic for many problems. Data about particular entities such as students, customers, and inventories often contain alphabetic, special, and numeric characters. For example, a "student file" may contain name, address, city, state, zip code, phone number, and grade point average. BASIC processes this type of **character** (or **nonnumeric** or **alphanumeric** or **alphameric**) **data** in the form of *strings*. As you know from Chapter 3, a *string* is a sequence of characters (letters, numbers, special characters) treated as a unit.

Up to now you have used *string constants* in PRINT statements to print messages and label output. For example, in the statement

30 PRINT "REVENUE = $"; R

REVENUE = $ is an 11-character string constant enclosed in quote marks.

Just as numbers can be stored, retrieved, and manipulated by using a numeric variable so can character data be stored, retrieved, and manipulated by using a *string variable*. As you might recall from the last chapter, string variables are named by specifying a letter followed by a dollar sign.

The number of characters that can be stored within memory identified by a string variable varies from system to system. A typical range is anywhere from 15 to 256 characters per memory location.[2]

### Processing with READ/DATA Statements

The READ/DATA statements can be used to store character data within a string variable. For example, the execution of

050 READ N$,H,R
100 DATA "WALTER MITTY",40,3.25

yields the following storage:

 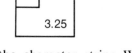

Notice that quote marks were used to enclose the character string WALTER MITTY. This type of string is termed a **quoted string**. The **unquoted string** in the DATA statement

100 DATA WALTER MITTY,40,3.25

also could have been used on some but not all systems. Unfortunately, unquoted strings promote potential errors, since most systems do not permit leading and trailing zeros,

---

[2] Some systems store only one character per memory location, which forces the processing of character data through subscripted variables, as illustrated in Chapter 7. Ask your instructor how many characters can be stored under a string variable on your system.

embedded commas, apostrophes, and other special characters in unquoted strings (these characters generally serve other purposes in data lists). For example, the statements

  10 READ D$
  90 DATA "JULY 21, 1984"

store the following in memory

but the statements

  10 READ D$
  90 DATA JULY 21, 1984

would store

since the comma is commonly used to separate items in a data list. Our advice: *Use quoted strings in the list of DATA statements if spaces, commas, and other special characters are in the strings.*

Also notice that the *list of data items in the DATA statement must match the list of variables in the READ statement by type.* That is, string variables must be paired with string constants and numeric variables must be paired with numeric constants.

### Processing with INPUT Statement

The INPUT statement also can be used to enter character data into string variables. For example, suppose the execution of

      .
      .
      .
  50 PRINT "DO YOU WANT TO ENTER MORE DATA";
  60 INPUT R$
      .
      .
      .

yields the following:

  DO YOU WANT TO ENTER MORE DATA? "YES"

In this case, the response "YES" stores the following:

For such simple responses, the use of an unquoted string presents no problems. For example, we could have processed as follows:

DO YOU WANT TO ENTER MORE DATA? YES

However, the same cautions in using unquoted strings apply here as in DATA statements.

## Processing with PRINT Statement

The following program illustrates the output of string variables.

---

**EXAMPLE 4.5   Psychological Self-Analysis (PSA) Program**

Study the following program and its input/output. In particular, pay close attention to the execution of lines 130 to 210.

```
010 PRINT "*** PSA PROGRAM ***"
020 PRINT
030 PRINT "THIS PROGRAM WILL HELP YOU FEEL BETTER!"
040 PRINT
050 PRINT
060 PRINT "PLEASE ENTER YOUR NAME, STREET, CITY, STATE"
070 PRINT "AND ZIP AS FIVE SEPARATE ENTRIES SEPARATED"
080 PRINT "BY COMMAS AND ENCLOSED IN QUOTES."
090 PRINT
100 INPUT A$,B$,C$,D$,E$
110 PRINT
120 PRINT "PSA FOR:"
130 PRINT A$
140 PRINT B$
150 PRINT C$;", ";D$;"    ";E$
160 PRINT
170 PRINT "WHAT IS TROUBLING YOU, ";A$;
180 INPUT F$
190 PRINT "YOU REALLY SHOULDN'T WORRY ABOUT SUCH THINGS AS"
200 PRINT F$;"."
210 PRINT "JUST STAY COOL AND LEARN TO MEDITATE."
220 END
RUN

*** PSA PROGRAM ***

THIS PROGRAM WILL HELP YOU FEEL BETTER!


PLEASE ENTER YOUR NAME, STREET, CITY, STATE
AND ZIP AS FIVE SEPARATE ENTRIES SEPARATED
BY COMMAS AND ENCLOSED IN QUOTES.

?"M. E. GROVER", "2001 SESAME ST.","NEW YORK,","NY","10013"
```

```
PSA FOR:
M. E. GROVER
2001 SESAME ST.
NEW YORK, NY 10013

WHAT IS TROUBLING YOU, M. E. GROVER?"I FAILED MY BASIC EXAM"
YOU REALLY SHOULDN'T WORRY ABOUT SUCH THINGS AS
I FAILED MY BASIC EXAM.
JUST STAY COOL AND LEARN TO MEDITATE.
```

## Follow-up Exercises

14. Construct READ/DATA statements that will assign values in the following situations:
    a. The month (M$) is July, the day (D) is 4, and the year (Y) is 1976.
    b. Faculty name (F$) is Newman, the rank (R$) is Instructor-1, and salary (S) is 14000 dollars.

15. Specify INPUT statements for the data in the preceding exercise and indicate how these values are to be input.

16. Suppose that the statements

        050 READ N$,H,R
        100 DATA "WALTER MITTY", 40,3.25

    are used in a program and we wish the following output:

            NAME:  WALTER MITTY
           HOURS:  40
        PAY RATE:  $ 3.25

    Specify the appropriate PRINT statements.

17. Indicate what would happen for each of the following errors:

    a. 20 READ A, B$
       30 READ C
       40 DATA 4.5,10,"FALSE"

    b. 10 INPUT A$
       ?COSMIC,J.B.

    c. Confirm exactly what happens on your system for the errors in parts a and b by processing the following program:

            10 INPUT A$
            15 PRINT A$
            20 READ A,B$
            25 PRINT A,B$
            30 READ C
            35 PRINT C
            40 DATA 4.5,10,"FALSE"
            50 END .

    Make necessary corrections after your initial run.

**18.** The input response "I FAILED MY BASIC EXAM" in Example 4.5 is a string of 22 characters. Not all systems store a string of this length under one variable. If the maximum length on your system is less than 50 characters, then the following program can be used to determine this maximum:

```
10 READ M$
20 DATA 12345678901234567890123456789012345678901234567890
30 PRINT M$
40 END
```

Run this program on your system. Result?

**19. Tuition Revenue Program.** Modify Example 4.2 on page 75 as follows:

  a.  On the same line, input college name (N$), cost per credit, and enrollment.

  b.  Output should read

REVENUE FOR . . . IS PROJECTED AT $ 8700000

Whatever college
name you input

**\*20. Automobile Financing Problem.** Modify

  a.  The program of Exercise 6 on page 77

  b.  The program of Exercise 10 on page 82 to enter and print the name (N$), address (A$,C$,S$,Z$), and phone number (P$) of the customer. The output report should be headed as follows:

AUTOMOBILE FINANCING INFORMATION FOR:

··· ◄─────────── Your name

··· ◄─────────── Your street

···, ··· ··· ◄─────────── Your city, state and ZIP code

PHONE -- ··· ◄─────────── Your phone

## 4.5
## PRINT STATEMENT AND THE TAB
## FUNCTION[3]

The use of the comma (,) and the semicolon (;) to space output may not be adequate in creating attractive output in some cases. The TAB function is a formatting feature which allows more exact spacing in your output. This function can be used only with the PRINT statement. Its general form is

**TAB** *(argument)*

where the "argument" represents a numeric constant, numeric variable, or arithmetic expression which is evaluated and rounded to the nearest integer value. The value of the

---

[3] Some systems lack this feature of BASIC. We might also note that many programmers prefer to precisely control output by using the enhancement (PRINT USING statement) discussed in Chapter 10.

argument determines the print column where the next character is to be printed. For instance, compare the following illustrations:

```
10  LET  B = 15                    10  LET  B = 15
20  PRINT  "COST =";B              20  PRINT TAB (10); "COST =";B
30  END                            30  END
        Print Column                       Print Column
1 2 3 4 5 6 7 8 9 10 11 12 13 14 15 16 17 18 19 20 . . .    1 2 3 4 5 6 7 8 9 10 11 12 13 14 15 16 17 18 19 20 . . .
```

```
COST  =  1 5                                    COST  =  1 5
```

Note in the first case that the string COST = is printed beginning at the first print column, whereas in the second case the string begins in the 10th column as specified by the TAB (10) function. Also, note that *the semicolon separator is used following the TAB function;* otherwise, output may revert back to the standard zone prints.

Additional considerations when using the TAB function include the following:

1.  The TAB function can be used several times within a single PRINT statement. For example,

    ```
    10 LET A = 5
    20 LET B = −10
    30 PRINT  TAB (10);A;TAB(25);B
    40 END
    ```

    results in

    ```
            Print Column
    1 2 3 4 5 6 7 8 9 10 11 12 13 14 15 16 17 18 19 20 21 22 23 24 25 26 27 28 29 30 . . .
    ```

    ```
              5                        − 1 0
    ```

    Notice that the numeric value 5 is printed in column 11 because its suppressed + sign takes up column 10. As expected, the negative sign for the value of B is printed in column 25.

2.  The TAB function causes the printing element (carriage) to skip to the next line when the current print column position of the printing element is beyond the column position specified in the TAB function.[4] Printing begins on the next line at the print column specified by the value in the TAB function. For example,

    ```
    10 LET A = 5
    20 LET B = −10
    30 PRINT  A,TAB(12);B
    40 END
    ```

    results in

    ```
            Print Column
    1 2 3 4 5 6 7 8 9 10 11 12 13 14 15 . . .
    ```

    ```
      5
              − 1 0
    ```

[4] On some systems the TAB function is ignored and printing continues on the same line.

In this case the comma following A in the print list causes the printing element to space over to the beginning of the second zone (column 16 on our hypothetical system) on the same print line as the 5. The current print column (16), therefore, is beyond the column position specified by the TAB function (12); hence, the value of B is printed on the next print line beginning in column 12. This error can be corrected by using the semicolon separator following A in the PRINT statement. In general, we advise that you *use the semicolon separator exclusively in the list of a PRINT statement that uses TAB functions.*

---

### EXAMPLE 4.6   Tuition Revenue Program with Report Headings

In this program we use the TAB function to conveniently space headings and output for a report. Study the correspondence between the program and the output.

```
10 PRINT TAB(10);"COLLEGE";TAB(22);"COST PER"
20 PRINT TAB(10);"NAME";TAB(22);"STUDENT";TAB(35);"REVENUE"
30 READ A$,C,S
40 LET B = 15*C + 250
50 LET R = B*S
60 PRINT
70 PRINT TAB(10);A$;TAB(22);B;TAB(34);R
80 DATA "SACRAMENTO",30,12000
90 END

RUN
```

Print
Line    Print Column
1 2 3 4 5 6 7 8 9 10 11 12 13 14 15 16 17 18 19 20 21 22 23 24 25 26 27 28 29 30 31 32 33 34 35 36 37 38 39 40 41 42 43 44 45 . . .

| Line | | |
|---|---|---|
| 1 | COLLEGE | COST PER |
| 2 | NAME | STUDENT     REVENUE |
| 3 | | |
| 4 | SACRAMENTO | 7 0 0     8 4 0 0 0 0 0 |

---

### Follow-up Exercises

**21.** Modify the program in Example 4.6 so that
  a. The label ($) is printed in columns 24 to 26 and columns 37 to 39 of print line 3. The output of A$, B, and R now appears in print line 5.
  b. The heading CODE is printed beginning in column 1 of print line 2; the string variable C$ is the fourth variable in the list of the READ statement; and the code SC105 is the fourth data item in the DATA statement. Modify the output accordingly.
**22.** Describe output given the following storage in memory:

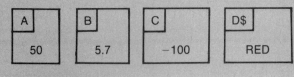

| A | B | C | D$ |
|---|---|---|---|
| 50 | 5.7 | -100 | RED |

a. 75 PRINT A,TAB(25);C      b. 75 PRINT A;TAB(25),C
c. 75 PRINT A;TAB(25);C      d. 75 PRINT TAB(15);B
e. 75 PRINT TAB(15);C      f. 75 PRINT TAB(15);D$
g. 75 PRINT TAB(B);D$      h. 75 PRINT TAB(2*B);D$
i. 75 PRINT TAB(C);D$

**\*23.** Supply PRINT statements that incorporate the TAB function for the following output:

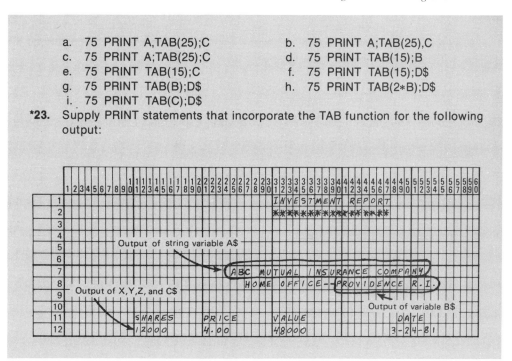

## 4.6
## BANK SAVINGS ACCOUNT PROGRAM

To complete your introduction to read/input and output statements, we present another problem scenario for which we write a complete BASIC program.

Suppose that we have $1000 to invest in a savings account which yields interest of 0.015 ($1\frac{1}{2}$ percent) per quarter (every three months). If we deposit the $1000 now, then one quarter from now we have our original $1000 plus $15 interest ($1000 \times 0.015$), or a total of $1015. This calculation can be written as follows:

$$1015 = 1000 + 1000 \times 0.015$$
$$= 1000 \times (1 + 0.015)$$

Now, consider how much we would have two quarters from now: the $1015 at the end of the first quarter plus the new interest of $15.22 on this amount ($1015 \times 0.015$), or a total of $1030.22. In other words,

$$1030.22 = 1015 + 1015 \times 0.015$$
$$= 1015 \times (1 + 0.015)$$

But we already know that

$$1015 = 1000 \times (1 + 0.015)$$

Thus,

$$1030.22 = 1015 \times (1 + 0.015)$$
$$= 1000 \times (1 + 0.015) \times (1 + 0.015)$$
$$= 1000 \times (1 + 0.015)^2$$

Do you see an emerging pattern? In general, if $A$ represents our accumulated funds, $N$ represents the number of quarters into the future, $P$ represents the principal we start off with, and $R$ represents the quarterly interest rate, then

$$A = P \cdot (1 + R)^N$$

Today's banks have computerized virtually all computational aspects dealing with savings and checking accounts, mortgages, loans, and investments. Suppose that you have been hired (after you graduate, of course) by a large bank with many branches. As your first assignment, you are asked to develop an interactive program for answering queries regarding accumulated funds in a savings account. It seems that tellers at many branch banks are getting harassed by customers who come in with their savings book asking that their entries be updated to reflect earned interest since the last entry.

To illustrate, suppose a customer's savings book shows $4025 as of the end of the third quarter in 1978. Let's say that currently we are in the second quarter of 1981. This means that 10 complete quarters have passed since the book was updated: the fourth in 1978, the four quarters in 1979, the four quarters in 1980, and the first quarter in 1981. If the account earns 1.5 percent interest per quarter, then we have $P = 4025, R = 0.015$, and $N = 10$, so that

$$A = 4025 \cdot (1 + 0.015)^{10} = \$4671.12$$

This means that $646.12 was earned in interest since the last entry, or

$$I = A - P$$
$$= 4671.12 - 4025 = \$646.12$$

So, what we need is a conversational program that performs these calculations for tellers at a branch bank. Each branch bank, of course, has a terminal that is connected to the bank's central computer at the home office.

### Step I. Analysis

1. *Statement*
   To develop an interactive program for determining accumulated funds and earned interest given the principal, quarterly interest rate, and number of quarters.
2. *Data Input*
   a. Customer name (N$)
   b. Account number (A$)
   c. Principal (P)
   d. Quarterly interest rate (R)
   e. Number of quarters (N)
3. *Data Output*
   a. Customer name
   b. Account number
   c. Accumulated funds since last entry (A)
   d. Earned interest since last entry (I)
4. *Algorithm*

   $A = P \cdot (1 + R)^N$
   $I = A - P$

***Step II. Flowchart.***   See Figure 4.2.

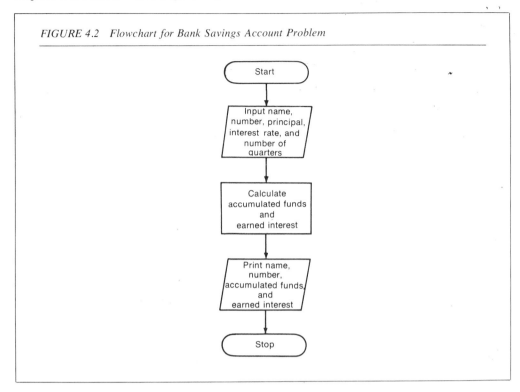

*FIGURE 4.2   Flowchart for Bank Savings Account Problem*

***Step III. Code***

```
100 REM     BANK SAVINGS ACCOUNT PROGRAM
110 REM
120 REM     VARIABLE KEY:
130 REM       N$ = CUSTOMER NAME
140 REM       A$ = ACCOUNT NUMBER
150 REM        P = PRINCIPAL
160 REM        R = QUARTERLY INTEREST RATE
170 REM        N = NUMBER OF QUARTERS
180 REM        A = ACCUMULATED FUNDS SINCE LAST ENTRY
190 REM        I = EARNED INTEREST SINCE LAST ENTRY
200 REM
210 PRINT "ENTER NAME AND NUMBER";
220 INPUT N$,A$
230 PRINT "ENTER PRINCIPAL";
240 INPUT P
250 PRINT "ENTER RATE";
260 INPUT R
270 PRINT "ENTER QUARTERS";
280 INPUT N
290 REM
300 LET A=P*(1+R)**N
310 LET I=A-P
320 REM
330 PRINT "*************************************************"
```

```
340 PRINT
350 PRINT TAB(29);"NAME:";TAB(39);N$
360 PRINT TAB(27);"NUMBER:";TAB(39);A$
370 PRINT
380 PRINT TAB(25);"INTEREST:";TAB(38);I
390 PRINT TAB(22);"NEW BALANCE:";TAB(38);A
400 PRINT
410 PRINT "*******************************************************"
420 END
```

## Step IV. Debugging

```
RUN

ENTER NAME AND NUMBER? "S. HOLMES","SY101"
ENTER PRINCIPAL? 4025
ENTER RATE? .015
ENTER QUARTERS? 10
*******************************************************

                         NAME:      S. HOLMES
                       NUMBER:      SY101

                     INTEREST:      646.12
                  NEW BALANCE:      4671.12


*******************************************************

TIME 0.02 SECS.

RUN

ENTER NAME AND NUMBER? "DR. WATSON","SY102"
ENTER PRINCIPAL? 50000
ENTER RATE? .02
ENTER QUARTERS? 20
*******************************************************

                         NAME:      DR. WATSON
                       NUMBER:      SY102

                     INTEREST:      24296.12
                  NEW BALANCE:      74296.12


*******************************************************

TIME 0.02 SECS.
```

### Follow-up Exercises

24. Why is it best to use INPUT statements rather than LET or READ/DATA statements to store values of N$, A$, P, R, and N?

25. Suppose all accounts earn 1.5 percent interest per quarter. Modify the program to eliminate the input of R; discuss three means of incorporating the value of 0.015. Which do you prefer and why?

*26. Usually interest rates are expressed on an annual basis. For example, 6 percent per year is equivalent to 1.5 percent per quarter. Also, some accounts may earn interest monthly (12 periods per year) and others may earn interest daily (assume 365 periods per year). Modify the program by defining R as an annual rate, N as number of periods since the last entry, and M as a new input variable that represents the number of times in a year the account earns interest (4 for quarterly, 12 for monthly, and 365 for daily). Run the following data through the program:

a.   P = 4025, R = 0.06, N = 10, M = 4
b.   P = 4025, R = 0.06, N = 30, M = 12
c.   P = 4025, R = 0.06, N = 130, M = 52
d.   P = 4025, R = 0.06, N = 912.5, M = 365

Compare the input data for N and M, study the output, and draw some conclusions.

## 4.7
## COMMON ERRORS

Errors in entering data are quite common. If you study the following common errors, you might save yourself some grief.

### Input Errors

*1.   Too Few Values Entered.*   For example, suppose we wish to input the values 10, 20, and 30 during the execution of

50 INPUT A, B, C

and we proceed as follows:

? 10,20          Carriage return key is hit following entry of 20.
? 10,20,30       Most systems print a second question mark to request the remaining data items, but we enter all three values from the beginning. System ignores the 20 and 30 and stores 10 in C instead of the desired 30. We should have typed only 30 following the second question mark.

*2.   Variables and Values Mismatched by Type.*   The list of variables in the INPUT statement must match the list of values in the input list following the printed question mark; that is, match numeric variable with numeric value and string variable with string constant. Suppose we wish to store the numeric constant 3 in R and the string constant FALSE in A$ using

75 INPUT A$,R

If we proceed as follows

? 3,"FALSE"

then the system stores 3 in A$ ("thinking" the 3 is an unquoted string) but prints an execution error when it tries to store the string constant FALSE in the numeric variable R. We should have typed:

? "FALSE", 3

We might note that many programmers prefer to use separate INPUT statements for string and numeric data to avoid problems associated with mixing strings and numeric data on the same line.

*3. Quotes Omitted around String Constant.* For example, if we wish to store the name MARNER, SILAS in the string variable N$ during the execution of

    100 INPUT N$

and we proceed as follows

    ?MARNER, SILAS

then the system stores MARNER in N$ because the comma signals the end of a data item. When an embedded comma is part of a string constant, you must enclose the entire string in quotes:

    ?"MARNER, SILAS"

Try to avoid the use of unquoted strings for all but simple input.

### Read Errors

*4. Too Few Values in Data Block.* For example, suppose we run the following program:

    10 READ A,B
    20 PRINT A,B
    30 DATA 50
    40 END

When line 10 is executed, most systems will print an "out of data" execution error message, and processing will terminate. If *n* variables are to be read in a program, then the data block must have at least *n* values.

*5. Variables and Values Mismatched by Type.* If the program

    10 READ A$,R
    20 PRINT A$,R
    30 DATA 3,"FALSE"
    40 END

was processed, a fatal execution error would occur. If your data block has both numeric and nonnumeric values, make sure that their sequence corresponds with the sequence of variable types in the lists of READ statements.

*6. Quotes Omitted around String Constant.* If we pair

    10 READ N$

with

    90 DATA MARNER, SILAS

then N$ stores MARNER instead of the intended MARNER, SILAS. Try to avoid the use of unquoted strings except when they are simple.

7. *Trailing Comma Inserted in DATA Statement.* Don't place a comma at the end of a data line. For example,

```
100 DATA 50, 75,
```

may cause a syntax error.

8. *Wrong Sequence of Statements.* Sometimes output is attempted before the appropriate value has been stored in a memory location. For example,

```
10 PRINT A
20 READ A
30 DATA 50
40 END
```

either yields a *logic error* when a system initializes all variables to zero (the output will be 0 instead of 50) or yields an *execution error* because the value in A is undefined when line 10 is executed.

## *Mirror or Echo Printing*

To check your data storage for logic errors, place a PRINT statement immediately after each READ or INPUT statement. The paired READ/PRINT or INPUT/PRINT statements must have identical variable lists. Once you have confirmed that the stored data are correct, remove these PRINT statements.

9. *String Overflow.* All systems limit the number of characters that can be stored under a string variable. For example, consider the program segment

```
10 INPUT A$
20 PRINT A$
   .        .
   .
   .
```

and assume a system that stores only 18 characters per string variable. The following input/output would occur based on lines 10 and 20:

```
?"12345678901234567890"
123456789012345678
```

Thus, the system only stores the first 18 characters and ignores the remaining 2, which is clearly confirmed by the echo PRINT in line 20.

## *Unaligned Output*

Output which is other than trivial involves careful planning. For instance, if you have to output aligned headings and values for several variables, then *before writing your PRINT statements you can save yourself some grief by outlining your output on a sheet of plain paper, graph paper, or* **print chart.** To illustrate, consider the following layout on a print chart:

**150/10/6 PRINT CHART**     PROG. ID _____     PAGE _____

(SPACING: 150 POSITION SPAN, AT 10 CHARACTERS PER INCH, 6 LINES PER VERTICAL INCH)     DATE _____

PROGRAM TITLE _____

PROGRAMMER OR DOCUMENTALIST: _____

CHART TITLE _____

| | | Row | Content |
|---|---|---|---|
| | | 1 | ************************************************ |
| | | 2 | |
| | | 3 | NAME:   XXXXXXXXXXXXXX |
| | | 4 | NUMBER:   XXXXX |
| | | 5 | |
| | | 6 | INTEREST:   XXXXX |
| | | 7 | NEW BALANCE:   XXXXXXXX |
| | | 8 | |
| | | 9 | ************************************************ |
| | | 10 | |
| | | 11 | |
| | | 12 | |

This layout was done *before* the PRINT statements in lines 330 through 410 on page 94 were written. You should confirm that the PRINT lines and actual output exactly correspond to the output plan on the print chart.

## Additional Exercises

**27.** Define or explain the following:

| | |
|---|---|
| INPUT statement | alphanumeric data |
| interactive programming | alphameric data |
| conversational programming | quoted string |
| READ statement | unquoted string |
| DATA statement | TAB function |
| data block | mirror print |
| RESTORE statement | echo print |
| character data | print chart |
| nonnumeric data | |

**28.** Under what circumstances are INPUT statements preferred to READ/DATA statements in program design? When is it advantageous to use READ/DATA statements over INPUT statements?

**29. Temperature Conversion.** Rework Exercise 27 of Chapter 3 on page 68 by replacing selected LET statements with READ and INPUT statements. Design and run two programs as follows:

    a. Use READ and DATA statements exclusively where appropriate.

    b. Use INPUT statements exclusively when appropriate, accompanied by conversation.

Include the read/input/output of your name through a string variable. Output for both programs should appear as follows:

Row 1: `PERSONALIZED TEMPERATURE CONVERSION FOR XXXXXXXXXXXXXXXXXX`
Row 3: `XXX    DEGREES FAHRENHEIT IS THE SAME AS`    your name
Row 4: `XXXXXXX DEGREES CELSIUS`

Include a flowchart for each program.

**30. Costing Problem.** Rework Exercise 28 of Chapter 3 on page 68 by replacing selected LET statements with READ and INPUT statements. Design and run two programs, as follows:

    a. Use READ and DATA statements exclusively where appropriate.

    b. Use INPUT statements exclusively where appropriate, accompanied by conversation.

Include the read/input/output of product name through a string variable. Output for both programs should appear as follows:

product name

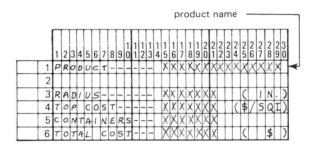

Row 1: `PRODUCT------ XXXXXXXXXXXXXXX`
Row 3: `RADIUS-------- XXXXXX    ( IN.)`
Row 4: `TOP COST------ XXXXXX  ($/SQI)`
Row 5: `CONTAINERS--- XXXXXXX`
Row 6: `TOTAL COST---- XXXXXX    ( $ )`

Include a flowchart for each program.

**31. Microeconomics Problem.** Rework Exercise 29 of Chapter 3 on page 69 as follows:

    a. Use READ and DATA statements exclusively where appropriate.

    b. Use INPUT statements exclusively where appropriate, accompanied by conversation.

Include the read/input/output of product name through a string variable. Output for both programs should appear as follows:

Row 1: `PRODUCT NAME = XXXXXXXXXXXXXX`
Row 3: `UNITS = XXXXXXX`
Row 4: `DAILY REVENUE = $ XXXXXXX`
Row 5: `DAILY COST = $ XXXXXXX`
Row 6: `DAILY PROFIT = $ XXXXXXX`

Include a flowchart for each program.

**32. Blood-Bank Inventory Problem.** Rework Exercise 30 of Chapter 3 on page 69 as follows:

a. Use READ and DATA statements exclusively where appropriate.

b. Use INPUT statements exclusively where appropriate, accompanied by conversation.

Include the read/input/output of hospital name (make one up) through a string variable. Output for both programs should appear as follows:

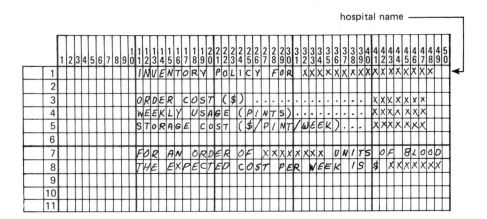

Include a flowchart for each program.

**33. Forecasting Population Growth.** Rework Exercise 31 of Chapter 3 on page 70 as follows:

a. Use READ and DATA statements exclusively where appropriate.

b. Use INPUT statements exclusively where appropriate, accompanied by conversation.

Include the read/input/output of the object of the forecast (Earth, United States, etc.) through a string variable. Output for both programs should appear as follows:

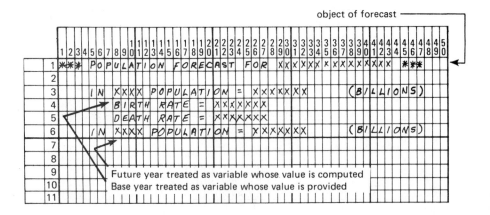

Include a flowchart for each program.

34. **Depreciation Problem.** Rework Exercise 32 of Chapter 3 on page 70 as follows:
   a. Use READ and DATA statements exclusively where appropriate.
   b. Use INPUT statements exclusively where appropriate, accompanied by conversation.

   Include the read/input/output of the name of the capital asset through a string variable. Output for both programs should appear as follows:

```
CAPITAL ASSET = XXXXXXXXXXXXXXXXX    <-- name
COST           = $ XXXXXXX
SALVAGE VALUE  = $ XXXXXXX
LIFE           = XX YEARS

FIRST YEAR DEPRECIATION BY STRAIGHT-LINE METHOD    = $ XXXXXXX
FIRST YEAR DEPRECIATION BY DOUBLE-DECLINING METHOD = $ XXXXXXX
```

   Include a flowchart for each program.

35. **Revised Tuition Revenue Problem.** Suppose that the cost per credit charged by the college directly affects student enrollment according to the following *demand curve:*

$$S = D1 - D2 \cdot C$$

   where

   $S$ = number of students enrolled
   $C$ = cost ($) per credit
   $D1$ = first parameter in demand curve
   $D2$ = second parameter in demand curve

   For example, if the tuition charge is $80 per credit, $D1$ is 14,000 and $D2$ is 100, then the number of students that will enroll is estimated by

$$S = 14000 - 100 \cdot 80 = 6000$$

   If the cost per credit is increased to $90, then the estimated enrollment drops to

$$S = 14000 - 100 \cdot 90 = 5000$$

   Design your program to read in the following using READ and DATA statements: fee ($250), average number of credits (15), name of college (make one up), $D1$ (14000), and $D2$ (100). Input $C$ using an INPUT statement accompanied by appropriate conversation. Your output should appear as follows:

```
                        AVERAGE      COST PER   AVERAGE   EXPECTED    EXPECTED
        COLLEGE    FEE  CREDITS      CREDIT     BILL      ENROLLMENT  REVENUE

XXXXXXXXXXXXXXXXX  XXX  XX           X X X      XXXX      XXXXX       XXXXXXXX
```

Don't forget to include a flowchart for your program. Answer the following questions based on repeated runs of your program: What tuition charge (cost per credit) do you recommend in order to maximize revenue for the college? How would your recommendation change if $D2$ were 25 instead of 100?

**36.   Retirement Contribution.** The personnel department of a large corporation is offering a new pension plan to its employees that works as follows. The employee contributes an amount $C$ that is deducted from each biweekly paycheck. The company then matches this amount (also contributes $C$) and invests the money at an annual interest rate $R$. At the end of $Y$ years, when it is time for the employee to retire, the employee can withdraw sum $S$. The necessary biweekly employee contribution to achieve $S$ after $Y$ years when the fund is compounded biweekly at rate $R$ per year is given by

$$C = \frac{S}{2} \cdot \frac{R/26}{(1 + R/26)^{26Y} - 1}$$

Thus, if the interest rate is 0.07 per year, 30 years remain toward retirement, and the employee desires \$40,000 at retirement, then the employee must contribute

$$C = \frac{40000}{2} \cdot \frac{0.07/26}{(1 + 0.07/26)^{26 \cdot 30} - 1} = \$7.54$$

every two weeks. Design a program that inputs $R$ using appropriate conversation; reads employee name, $Y$, and $S$ using a READ statement; and prints the following output:

Don't forget to include a flowchart.

Run the program repeatedly to determine contributions for the following employees:

| NAME | Y | S |
|---|---|---|
| Tahiti Joe | 30 | \$ 40,000 |
| Jet-Set Sal | 40 | 200,000 |
| Too-Late Leroy | 5 | 10,000 |

What would be the effect of an increase in the interest rate to 8 percent per year?

**37.   Bank Drive-In Queuing System.** A queue is a waiting line of customers requiring service from one or more servers. Queuing systems have been the object of intense study by analysts in management, engineering, and computer science because of their widespread applicability. For example, mathematical

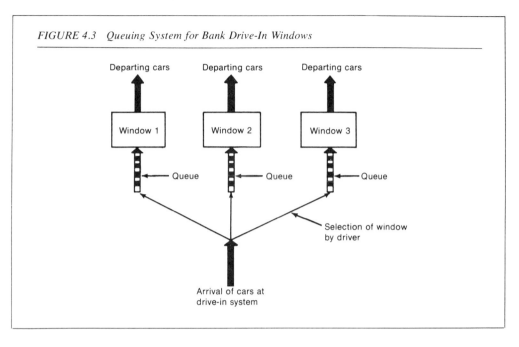

*FIGURE 4.3    Queuing System for Bank Drive-In Windows*

queuing formulas have been developed to study the arrival and servicing of patients in hospitals, the arrival and departure of airplanes at airports, the flow of customers in restaurants and of traffic in cities, and (yes!) the processing of computer programs by operating systems. Suppose a large commercial bank with many branches is in the process of studying proposed designs for drive-in window queuing systems. Figure 4.3 illustrates one such design together with relevant data. If certain assumptions are made about this queuing process[5], then the following formulas predict what are called *operating characteristics of the system:*

$$I = \left(1 - \frac{A/C}{S}\right)^C$$

$$W = \left(\frac{A/C}{S}\right)^C$$

$$N = \frac{A}{S - A/C}$$

$$Q = \frac{A^2}{C^2 \cdot S \cdot (S - A/C)}$$

$$T1 = \frac{1}{S - A/C}$$

$$T2 = \frac{A}{C \cdot S \cdot (S - A/C)}$$

[5] For an explanation of these assumptions, see F. Budnick, R. Mojena, and T. Vollman, *Principles of Operations Research for Management,* Homewood, Illinois: Irwin, 1977, pp. 440–445.

where

$I$ = proportion of time (probability) the system is idle (no cars are in the queuing system)

$W$ = probability an arriving car has to wait for service (all servers are busy)

$N$ = average number of cars in system

$Q$ = average length of the queue in front of each window (not including the car being served)

$T1$ = Average amount of time (minutes) a car is in the system (wait plus service)

$T2$ = average amount of time (minutes) a car waits in the queue

$A$ = arrival rate, or average number of cars that arrive at the bank per minute

$S$ = service rate, or average number of cars per minute that get serviced by one teller

$C$ = number of tellers (three tellers or windows in the illustration)

For example, if we have three windows, cars arrive at the rate of 0.9 per minute, and 0.4 cars get serviced per minute by one teller (that is, it takes 1/0.4, or 2.5 minutes to service a car on the average), then $C = 3$, $A = 0.9$, and $S = 0.4$, so that

$$I = \left(1 - \frac{0.9/3}{0.4}\right)^3 = 0.015625$$

$$W = \left(\frac{0.9/3}{0.4}\right)^3 = 0.421875$$

$$N = \frac{0.9}{0.4 - 0.9/3} = 9$$

$$Q = \frac{(0.9)^2}{(3)^2 \cdot (0.4) \cdot (0.4 - 0.9/3)} = 2.25$$

$$T1 = \frac{1}{0.4 - 0.9/3} = 10$$

$$T2 = \frac{0.9}{(3) \cdot (0.4) \cdot (0.4 - 0.9/3)} = 7.5$$

Thus, about 1.5 percent of the time (0.015625) all three tellers are idle; about 42 percent of the time (0.421875) all three tellers are busy; on the average, 9 cars are in the entire drive-in system and 2.25 cars are in front of each window waiting to be serviced; and it takes on the average 10 minutes for a car to enter and leave the system and 7.5 minutes of waiting to be serviced.

Design a flowchart and program that reads $A$, $S$, and the name of the branch (make one up) from one data line, inputs $C$ interactively, and outputs values for $I$, $W$, $N$, $Q$, $T1$, and $T2$. Label your output as follows:

```
        BRANCH:      XXXXXXXXXXXXXX
        ARRIVAL  RATE:  XXX
        SERVICE  RATE:  XXX

NO. OF      IDLE          WAIT       CARS IN   QUEUE     TIME IN   TIME IN
WINDOWS   PROBABILITY   PROBABILITY  SYSTEM    LENGTH    SYSTEM    QUEUE

  X       XXXXXXX       XXXXXX       XXXXXXX   XXXXXXX   XXXXXXX   XXXXXXX
```

Use the given values for *A* and *S* and run the program repeatedly in order to calculate operating characteristics for three, four, . . ., nine windows. How many windows are needed to ensure simultaneously an idle probability below 6 percent and time in the system below 5 minutes? Answer the same question if the arrival rate were to increase to 1.1.

**CHAPTER 5**

# *Introduction to Control Statements*

5.1   GO TO STATEMENT

5.2   IF/THEN STATEMENT

5.3   FOR/NEXT LOOPS
Loop Mechanics
The Fine Points

5.4   ACCUMULATING A SUM

5.5   COMMON ERRORS

ADDITIONAL EXERCISES

The computer programs up to now have been simple in the sense that the computer executed the instructions sequentially from the first instruction to the last, and then stopped. The statements in this chapter will allow you to control the flow of execution within the program. These so-called **control statements** not only permit ''multiple passes'' for processing new data but also greatly improve your ability for solving intricate problems.

## 5.1
## GO TO STATEMENT

The GO TO statement causes the computer to interrupt the normal sequential execution of a program and branch (jump or transfer control) to some other executable instruction in the program that is not the next instruction in the normal sequence. This process of breaking the sequential flow of a program is referred to as **branching** or **transfer of control.**

The basic form of the GO TO statement is

line no. **GO TO** line number

For example, when the statement

   30 GO TO 80

is executed, transfer of control goes to the statement labeled with line number 80; that is, the next statement executed is found on line 80.

## 5.2
## IF/THEN STATEMENT

The IF/THEN statement is a BASIC instruction that requires the computer to test a condition and then, based on one of two possible results, to take a proper transfer of control action. The general form of this instruction is

> line no. **IF** *relational expression* **THEN** *line number*

The *relational expression* is used to construct the condition that you want tested. The result of this test is either "true" or "false." If the result is true, then control is transferred to the line number specified after the relational expression. If the result is false, however, then the statement following the IF/THEN is executed.

---

### EXAMPLE 5.1   Sales Commissions

A salesperson earns a base salary of \$150 plus a 2 percent commission on sales if weekly sales are above \$5000; otherwise, no commission is added to the base salary. The following program determines the appropriate pay.

```
010 REM     SALES COMMISSION PROGRAM
020 REM
030 REM     READ VARIABLES:
040 REM      N$ = SALESPERSON'S NAME
050 REM      S$ = SALESPERSON'S SOCIAL SECURITY NUMBER
060 REM      S  = WEEKLY SALES
080 REM     OUTPUT VARIABLES:
090 REM       N$, S$
100 REM       T = TOTAL PAY
110 REM     OTHER VARIABLES:
120 REM       B = BASE PAY
130 REM       C = COMMISSION
200 LET B = 150
220 LET C = 0
240 READ S$,N$,S
260 IF S < = 5000 THEN 300
280 LET C = .02*S
300 LET T = B + C
320 PRINT "EMPLOYEE NAME","SS NUMBER","TOTAL PAY"
340 PRINT N$,S$,T
901 DATA "266-62-8431","B. FLINTSTONE",4150
999 END
```

The salesperson's base salary of $150 is stored in a variable named B and the IF/THEN statement determines whether or not the salesperson receives the 2 percent commission.

The relational expression S $<=$ 5000 represents the condition "sales less than or equal to $5000," where $<$ stands for "less than" and $=$ stands for "equal to". When executed, the IF/THEN statement tests this condition, giving one of two results: true or false. If, in fact, the value of S is less than or equal to 5000, then the result of the test is true, and the transfer of control to the right of the relational expression is executed. In other words, the computer next executes line 300:

300 LET T = B + C

However, if the result of the test is false, the THEN portion to the right of the relational expression is skipped and control immediately goes to the first statement below the IF/THEN, in this case line 280.

Since 4150 is stored in S according to the READ/DATA statements, it follows that control branches to line 300 based on the IF/THEN test; the execution sequence goes as follows: 200, 220, 240, 260, 300, 320, 340, and 999. Printed output would appear as follows:[1]

```
EMPLOYEE NAME   SS NUMBER     TOTAL PAY
B . FLINTSTONE  266-62-8431     150
```

Every **relational expression** takes the form of an expression (arithmetic or string), then a relational operator, and then another arithmetic or string expression. A **relational operator** indicates a mathematical comparison such as less than, equal to, or greater than. BASIC uses six relational operators, as indicated in Table 5.1. To test a condition, you will use one of these relational operators "wedged" between the two arithmetic or string expressions. As in Chapter 3, *arithmetic expressions* may consist of a single numeric variable, a single numeric constant, or a combination of numeric variables and numeric constants separated by parentheses and arithmetic operators. A *string expression* is either a string variable or a string constant.[2]

The flowchart symbol ◇ is used whenever a decision or test is made. The test is described within the diamond and arrows show the alternate paths that your program may take from that decision point. The symbol ○ indicates transfer of control points in the program.

---

[1] Some systems allow an executable statement to the right of THEN in the IF/THEN statement. For example, we could eliminate line 280 and use

260 IF S $>$ 5000 THEN LET C = .02*S

[2] Functions also may be used in arithmetic expressions (Chapter 9) and string expressions (not discussed in this text).

TABLE 5.1   *Relational Operators in BASIC*

| MATHEMATICAL COMPARISON | RELATIONAL OPERATOR | MEANING |
|---|---|---|
| $=$ | $=$ | Equal to |
| $\neq$ | $<>$ | Not equal to† |
| $<$ | $<$ | Less than |
| $\leq$ | $<=$ | Less than or equal to |
| $>$ | $>$ | Greater than |
| $\geq$ | $>=$ | Greater than or equal to |

† Some systems use # in place of $<>$.

The following examples further illustrate the use of the IF/THEN statement for testing conditions within your program.

**EXAMPLE 5.2**

| FLOWCHART | BASIC STATEMENT | EXPLANATION |
|---|---|---|

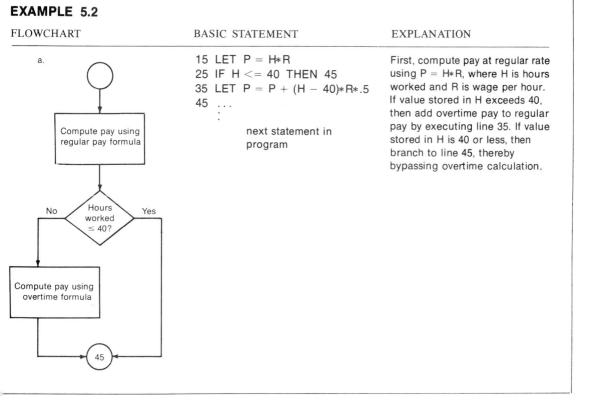

a.

Compute pay using regular pay formula

Hours worked ≤ 40?   No / Yes

Compute pay using overtime formula

45

15 LET P = H∗R
25 IF H <= 40 THEN 45
35 LET P = P + (H − 40)∗R∗.5
45 ...

next statement in program

First, compute pay at regular rate using P = H∗R, where H is hours worked and R is wage per hour. If value stored in H exceeds 40, then add overtime pay to regular pay by executing line 35. If value stored in H is 40 or less, then branch to line 45, thereby bypassing overtime calculation.

## EXAMPLE 5.2 (Continued)

| FLOWCHART | BASIC STATEMENT | EXPLANATION |
|---|---|---|
| b. 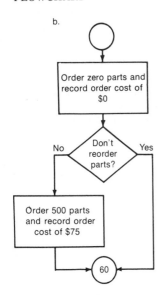 | 10 LET Q = 0<br>20 LET C = 0<br>30 IF I+A > R THEN 60<br>40 LET Q = 500<br>50 LET C = 75<br>60 ... | Set size of order (Q) and order cost (C) to zero in lines 10 and 20. If inventory level (I) plus amount on order (A) is greater than reorder point (R), then bypass placement of order by going to line 60; otherwise, execute lines 40 and 50. |
| c. 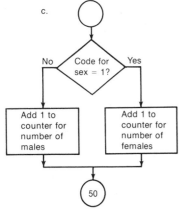 | 10 IF S = 1 THEN 40<br>20 LET C2 = C2 + 1<br>30 GO TO 50<br>40 LET C1 = C1 + 1<br>50 ... | A **code** is the representation of words or groups of words by numbers, letters, or symbols. Codes are used by organizations to provide meaningful identification for descriptions that otherwise would be awkward to store and manipulate. For example, the code for employee sex is 1 or 2—1 for female and 2 for male. If the value stored in S is 1, then branch to line 40 and add 1 to count of females; otherwise, branch to line 20 and add 1 to count of males. Note that the GO TO 50 bypasses the female counter whenever the male counter is updated. |

## EXAMPLE 5.2 (Continued)

| FLOWCHART | BASIC STATEMENT | EXPLANATION |
|---|---|---|

d.

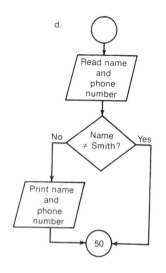

```
10  READ  N$,P
20  IF N$ <> "SMITH" THEN 50
30  PRINT "NAME: ";N$
40  PRINT "PHONE NUMBER: ";P
50  ...
      :
```

This example illustrates how character data in the form of string variables and/or string constants can be compared. In the program segment, if the name is SMITH, then the person's name and phone number are printed. Otherwise, the program branches to line 50 without any output.

e.

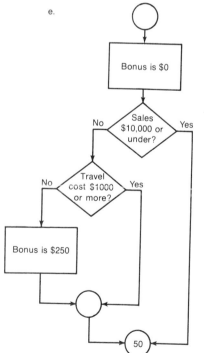

```
10  LET B = 0
20  IF S <= 10000 THEN 50
30  IF T >= 1000 THEN 50
40  LET B = 250
50  ...
      :
```

This example illustrates the use of two IF/THEN statements to make the required test. First, the bonus (B) is set to zero. Next, if the value stored in S is 10,000 or under then control is transferred to line 50. However, if the value stored in S is greater than 10,000, a second test is made which determines if the value stored in T is greater than or equal to 1000; if true, then control is transferred to line 50; otherwise, control is transferred to line 40.

It is important to note that *good program design requires simplicity in branching*. For example, the following illustrates poor design for the logic in part a of Example 5.2:

```
15 IF H > 40 THEN 45
25 LET P = H*R
35 GO TO 55
45 LET P = 40*R + (H − 40)*R*1.5
55 ...
   :
   :
```

As you can see, the transfer of control logic is more complicated than the original version because of the need to branch over line 45 whenever line 25 is executed, thereby requiring a GO TO statement.

A corollary to good program design is *minimize the use of GO TO statements*. A program with excessive GO TO statements is difficult to follow, inefficient with respect to CPU time, and unreliable in the sense that the greater the number of transfers the greater the likelihood of an incorrect transfer.

You might ask, "Both versions accomplish the same end, so why worry about good design?" In recent years the cost of software has surpassed the cost of hardware. Thus, organizations can lower costs by promoting good program design, since well-designed programs require less time to debug and change than poorly designed programs.[3]

## Follow-up Exercises

1. Indicate whether a true or false condition exists for each relational expression.

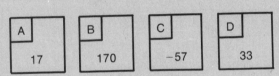

| A | B | C | D |
|---|---|---|---|
| 17 | 170 | −57 | 33 |

   a. A < B
   b. B <= D
   c. C > −58
   d. D = 33
   e. A + D >= B − C
   f. B/A <> C + D

2. Flowchart the program in Example 5.1.
3. Modify the program of Example 5.1 to incorporate the fact that base pay varies from salesperson to salesperson.
4. Write IF/THEN statements for the following tests:
   a. At line 10, if credits taken (C) are 12 or more, than transfer control to line 500.
   b. At line 20, if part-name (P$) is "WRENCH," then transfer to line 750.
   c. At line 25, if fixed cost (F) plus variable costs (V) are less than profit (P), then transfer control to line 100.
   d. At line 30, if student's major (M$) equals first preference (A$) or second

---

[3] Module B discusses this topic in detail.

preference (B$) of employer, then transfer to line 50; otherwise, transfer to line 80.

   e.  At line 40, if Age (A) is between 25 and 35 branch to line 50; otherwise, transfer to line 75.

**5.**  Code each flowchart into a segment of a BASIC program.

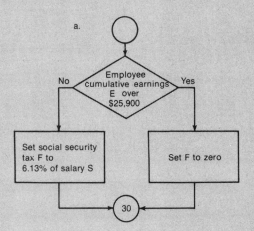

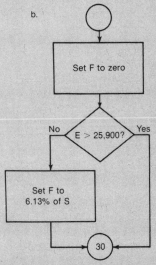

Why is this version preferable to the version in part a?

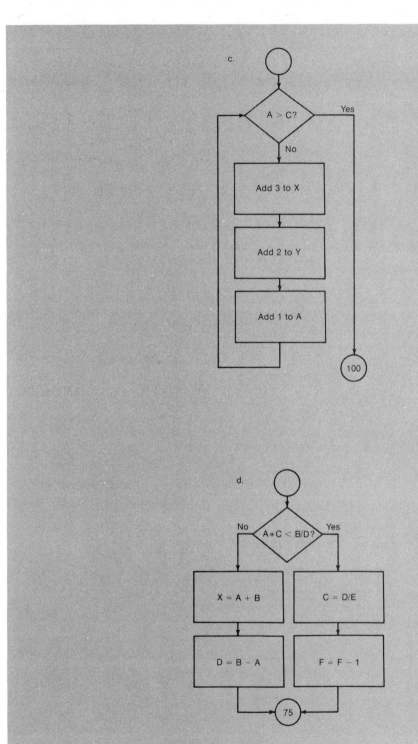

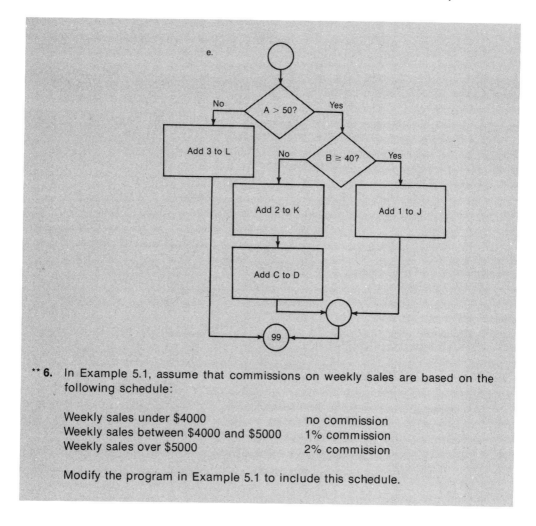

**\*\* 6.** In Example 5.1, assume that commissions on weekly sales are based on the following schedule:

Weekly sales under $4000      no commission
Weekly sales between $4000 and $5000      1% commission
Weekly sales over $5000      2% commission

Modify the program in Example 5.1 to include this schedule.

## 5.3
## FOR/NEXT LOOPS

Each program up to now has processed a single set of data, since we have not introduced the ability to "loop back" or "return" to statements previously executed. As you know, this "single pass" through the program forces you to run the program separately each time you have new data.

The computer can repeat a group of instructions over and over again within a program, without running the program each time you have new data. This ability of repeating a series of instructions is called **looping.**

In this section we present a common type of loop called the FOR/NEXT loop. Looping by this method is used when we know beforehand the number of loop

---

\*\* Exercises marked with double asterisks (\*\*) either are more difficult or require more effort than the typical exercise. Answers to these are not given in the back of the text.

iterations—the number of times the loop is to be repeated. In this case, the FOR and NEXT statements are used to handle automatically all details of looping.

## Loop Mechanics

The FOR statement indicates the beginning of the loop, whereas the NEXT statement represents the end of the loop. All executable instructions in between these two are the instructions to be repeated. Those statements between the FOR and NEXT are called the **body** of the loop.

The general form of the FOR statement is

| line no. **FOR** | control (index) variable | = | initial value of control variable | **TO** | terminal value of control variable | **STEP** | incremental value of control variable |
|---|---|---|---|---|---|---|---|

For example,

    40 FOR I = 1 TO 3 STEP 1

represents a specific case of the FOR statement.

In the FOR statement you must

1. Specify the simple *numeric* variable called the **control variable** or **index.** The variable I is the control variable in the above example.
2. Specify the initial value of the control variable. In this example I is first set to 1.
3. Set the terminal value that the control variable must exceed before your loop is terminated. (I must exceed 3 before the loop is terminated.)
4. Establish the increment for the control variable. (I is incremented or changed by 1 each time the loop is processed.)

The NEXT statement defines the end of the loop. The general form of this statement is

| line no. **NEXT** | control variable |
|---|---|

For example,

    40 FOR I = 1 TO 3 STEP 1
        .
        .  } body of loop
        .
    120 NEXT I

illustrates a FOR/NEXT loop, whereby the FOR statement defines the beginning of the loop and the NEXT statement defines the end of the loop. In this case the body of the loop is processed three times as I changes from 1 to 2 to 3. *Note that matched FOR/ NEXT statements must have the same control variable (I in the above example).*

### EXAMPLE 5.3  Sales Commission Program with FOR/NEXT Loop

In Example 5.1 we processed data for one salesperson. That program is now rewritten to automatically process three salespersons using the FOR/NEXT loop.

```
200 LET B = 150
205 PRINT "EMPLOYEE NAME","SS NUMBER","TOTAL PAY"
210 PRINT "_____"
215 FOR I = 1 TO 3 STEP 1
220    LET C = 0
240    READ S$,N$,S
260    IF S <= 5000 THEN 300
280    LET C = .02*S
300    LET T = B + C
320    PRINT N$,S$,T
330 NEXT I
901 DATA "266-62-8431","B. FLINTSTONE",4150
902 DATA "375-41-6215","P. RABBIT",6000
903 DATA "154-25-1298","B. B. BABBLE",2020
999 END
```

Notice that the body of the FOR/NEXT loop is within the boundaries of the FOR and NEXT statements. Thus, these two statements act as "visual brackets" for your loop and improve the readability of your program. We also indent the body of the loop to make it stand out. *We will follow the convention of indenting loops to better identify them visually.* Although it's not necessary to do this, it is yet another programming practice that promotes good program design.

When the FOR statement is executed the first time, the control variable is set equal to its initial value (I set equal to 1). The control variable is then tested to determine if it is less than or equal to the terminal value defined in the FOR statement. If the value stored in I is less than or equal to the terminal value (3 in this example), then the computer executes the statements following the FOR statement (body of the loop).

At the end of the loop, when the NEXT statement is executed, the value of the control variable is changed by the incremental value, and control returns to the test built into the FOR statement. When the control variable (I) reaches a value greater than the terminal value (I is 4), the statement following the NEXT statement is executed (in this case END). The flowchart in Figure 5.1 illustrates the logic of the FOR/NEXT loop.[1]

Table 5.2 illustrates the successive values stored in memory for the variables as the loop goes through three iterations. In this case, the "snapshot" of memory is taken just before the execution of the NEXT statement.

[1] On some systems, the test for the control variable is between the body and incrementation. We might note that the structure of the FOR/NEXT loop is a special case of the DO WHILE structure discussed in Module B.

**FIGURE 5.1**   *Logic of FOR/NEXT LOOP*

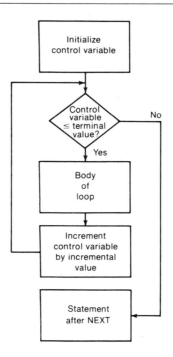

**TABLE 5.2**   *Successive Values in Memory*

| I | B | S$ | N$ | S | C | T |
|---|---|---|---|---|---|---|
| 1 | 150 | 266-62-8431 | B. FLINTSTONE | 4150 | 0 | 150 |
| 2 | 150 | 375-41-6215 | P. RABBIT | 6000 | 120 | 270 |
| 3 | 150 | 154-25-1298 | B. B. BABBLE | 2020 | 0 | 150 |

The output from this program is given by

```
EMPLOYEE NAME    SS NUMBER              TOTAL PAY
---------------------------------------------------
B.  FLINTSTONE   266 - 62 - 8431           150
P.  RABBIT       375 - 41 - 6215           270
B.  B.  BABBLE   154 - 25 - 1298           150
```

Note that the output within the loop due to the PRINT statement in line 320 gives the appearance of a "table," and that column headings for this table must be printed before the loop, as done in lines 205 and 210.

For a loop whose index starts at 1 and increases by 1 at each iteration, *the terminal value represents the total number of iterations.* Thus, in Example 5.3, the terminal value 3 turns out to be the number of times the loop is processed. For such loops, a good programming practice is to *define the terminal value as a variable.* This makes for more flexible programs, since the number of times we wish to loop can be provided through an INPUT or READ statement. The next example illustrates this approach.

---

**EXAMPLE 5.4    FOR/NEXT Loop with Terminal Value Stored in Variable**

```
200 LET B = 150
205 PRINT "EMPLOYEE NAME","SS NUMBER","TOTAL PAY"
210 PRINT "_____"

212 READ N

215 FOR I = 1 TO  N  STEP 1
220     LET C = 0
240     READ S$,N$,S
260     IF S <= 5000 THEN 300
280     LET C = .02*S
300     LET T = B + C
320     PRINT N$,S$,T
330 NEXT I

900 DATA 3

901 DATA "266-62-8431","B. FLINTSTONE",4150
902 DATA "375-41-6215","P. RABBIT",6000
903 DATA "154-25-1298","B. B. BABBLE",2020
999 END
```

The portions enclosed in boxes show the only differences between this program and that in Example 5.3. In this case line 212 reads the terminal value (3) from the DATA statement in line 900 into memory location N. The use of N in the FOR statement (line 215) thus generalizes the number of loop iterations. In other words, if the number of employees to be processed differs from run to run, then we need only make changes in the DATA statements and not in the logic of the program itself. *This type of design thus reduces subsequent software maintenance (future changes in the program), thereby reducing computer costs.*

---

**Follow-up Exercises**

7. Consider the following modifications to the sales commission program:
   a. Suppose we have to process data on 325 salespeople. How would you modify Example 5.3? Example 5.4?

b. Replace line 210 with a FOR/NEXT loop having a PRINT statement with a single dash in its list. Do you prefer this approach?

8. What values get printed for each of the following loops? How many times does each loop iterate?

a. 50 FOR K = 1 TO 10 STEP 1
   60    PRINT K
   70 NEXT K

b. Same as part a except STEP 2

c. 75 FOR L = 2 TO 5 STEP 1
   80    PRINT L
   85 NEXT L

d. Same as part c except L = 5 TO 5

e. Same as part c except L = 6 TO 5

*9. **Counter Method of Looping.** Code the equivalent of the FOR/NEXT loop in Example 5.4 by using only an IF/THEN statement and a GO TO statement to construct the loop. *Hint:* Use Figure 5.1 as your guide. Specify a control variable or *counter* (I) by using LET statements and slightly revise the test in Figure 5.1. Why is the FOR/NEXT approach preferable to this approach?

## The Fine Points

Try to keep in mind the following points when using the FOR and NEXT statements:

1. Each FOR statement must have a corresponding NEXT statement with the same control variable. For each FOR statement there can be only one NEXT statement.

2. If the incremental value is not specified, then it is assumed to be equal to 1. For example,

    215 FOR I = 1 TO N

   is treated the same as

    215 FOR I = 1 TO N STEP 1

3. The initial, terminal and incremental values of the FOR statement can be either a numeric constant, numeric variable, or arithmetic expression. For example,

    20 READ M,N
    25 FOR I = M TO M*N STEP N − 1
        .
        .
        .
    90 NEXT I

   is permitted.
   In addition, these values can be either positive or negative and either integer or decimal. For example,

```
10 FOR R = .05 TO .25 STEP .01
        .
        .
        .
50 NEXT R
```

and

```
60 FOR K = 10 TO 1 STEP −1
        .
        .
        .
90 NEXT K
```

are allowed.

Whenever a step (incremental value) is negative, the initial value should be greater than the terminal value, and looping continues until the value of the control variable is less than the terminal value.

4. The control variable can be utilized within the body of the loop. For example,

```
10 LET X = 1980
20 FOR I = 1 TO 10
30    LET Y = X + I
40    PRINT "YEAR IS";Y
50 NEXT I
        .
        .
        .
```

is legitimate. However, *care should be taken not to redefine the value of the control variable, or to change its initial, terminal, or incremental value within the FOR/NEXT loop.*

5. Branching within the loop is allowed, as illustrated in Example 5.4 when control is transferred to line 300, thereby bypassing line 280 whenever S is less than or equal to 5000. *Transfers within the loop directly to the FOR statement, however, either are not allowed or result in an infinite loop (depending on the compiler).* An **infinite loop** is one that "never" ends; that is, the computer continues to process the loop until a fatal execution error is encountered (such as an out-of-data error message) or until the user aborts the run. For example, consider a program segment that prints the names of students who have a grade point average above 3.25:

```
100 FOR I = 1 TO N
110    READ N$,G
120    IF G<= 3.25 THEN 100
130    PRINT N$;" IS ON DEAN'S LIST"
140 NEXT I
```

The transfer from line 120 to line 100 may result in an infinite loop. (The value of the index is always reset to 1.) Instead, the transfer of control to process the next student should be based as follows:

```
120    IF G<= 3.25 THEN 140
```

Thus, we go on to the next iteration of the loop by a transfer to the NEXT statement.

6. Transferring control out of an "active" FOR/NEXT loop is permissible. This "forced" or "unnatural" exit from the FOR/NEXT loop (before the control variable achieves its terminal value) preserves the current value of the control variable. For example, the segment

```
10 FOR I = 1 TO 500
20    READ A
30    IF A < 18 THEN 80
        .
        .
        .
60 NEXT I
        .
        .
        .
80 PRINT "EMPLOYEE";I,"IS UNDER AGE"
        .
        .
        .
```

prints a value of 75 for I if the 75th employee in the data list is under 18 years of age. We might point out, however, that *good program design generally discourages a transfer out of an active FOR/NEXT loop.*[5]

7. After a normal exit from the FOR/NEXT loop the value of the control variable may or may not be retained depending on the system. For example, the segment

```
50 FOR J = 1 TO 50
        .
        .
        .
80 NEXT J
85 PRINT J
```

might print 50, or 51, or an undefined value for J.

8. Branching into the body of a FOR/NEXT loop from outside the loop either is not permitted by the system or is not advisable. For example,

---

[5] Multiple transfers out of a loop impede readability. Moreover, this practice may create dependencies between the loop and other parts of the program, which violates basic principles in styles of programming called *structured programming* and *modular programming*. (See Module B.)

```
      ⋮
100 IF K <> 0 THEN 210

      ⋮
                    •
200 FOR I = 1 TO N
          READ X

      ⋮
      ⋮
300 NEXT I

      ⋮
      ⋮
```

may provoke a syntax or execution error. If you need to activate the loop at line 100, then transfer control to line 200:

```
100 IF K <> 0 THEN 200
```

9. There is no standard notation for specifying a FOR/NEXT loop in a flowchart. One common approach is to use the hexagon-shaped symbol to define the start of the loop (FOR statement) and the circle symbol to indicate the end of the loop (NEXT statement). Figure 5.2 illustrates this approach for Example 5.4. Note that the loop returns to the first executable statement following the FOR statement, not to the FOR statement itself. Another flowcharting alternative for the FOR/NEXT loop is illustrated in Figure 5.1 on page 118. In this case the behavior of the control variable and the loop test are explicitly shown.

Carefully study Example 5.5, as it illustrates many of the topics covered in Sections 5.3 and 5.4.

---

### EXAMPLE 5.5   Finding the Minimum Value

The Department of Health, Education, and Welfare (HEW) has a data file that includes the per capita income (that is, total income divided by total number of people) for each standard metropolitan statistical area (SMSA) in the country. An administrator wishes to determine the SMSA code that has the smallest per capita income. The program below illustrates the determination of this minimum and its associated SMSA.

```
010 REM    HEW PROGRAM
020 REM --------------------------------------------------------------
030 REM    KEY:
040 REM      C  = CODE FOR SMSA
050 REM      I  = PER CAPITA INCOME OF SMSA
060 REM      C1 = CODE OF SMSA WITH MINIMUM I
070 REM      I1 = MINIMUM I
080 REM      N  = TOTAL NUMBER OF SMSA'S
090 REM --------------------------------------------------------------
```

FIGURE 5.2     *Flowchart Illustrating FOR-NEXT Loop of Example 5.4*

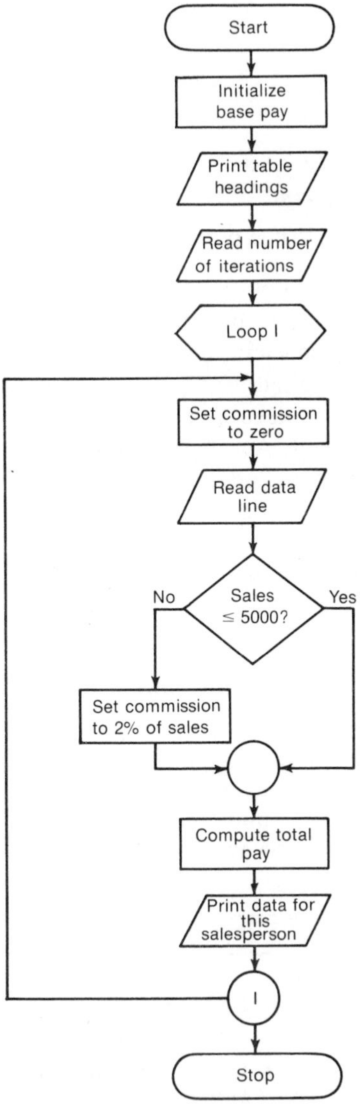

```
100  LET I1 = 1E30
110  READ N
120  FOR J = 1 TO N
130     READ C,I
140     IF I>= I1 THEN 170
150     LET I1 = I
160     LET C1 = C
170  NEXT J
180  PRINT "SMSA NUMBER";C1
190  PRINT "HAS THE MINIMUM PER CAPITA INCOME OF";I1
900  DATA 5
901  DATA 147,5165
902  DATA  56,7860
903  DATA  75,6350
904  DATA  41,4293
905  DATA 105,5415
999  END
```

Note that the variable which stores the minimum value (I1) is initially set equal to a very large number (1E30). This assures that one of the data items will be the minimum value.

**Follow-up Exercises**

10. Draw a flowchart for the program of Example 5.5. Check the logic of the flowchart and program by roleplaying (with you as computer) through the provided test data. Indicate below the values stored successively, where the "snapshot" of memory is taken at each iteration just before the execution of the NEXT statement.

| J | C | I | I1 | C1 | N |
|---|---|---|----|----|---|
|   |   |   |    |    |   |

Show exactly how the output would look.

11. Indicate why each of the following would be wrong in the program of Example 5.5:
   a.  150 LET J = I
   b.  140 IF I >= I1 THEN 120
   c.  195 RESTORE
       197 GO TO 130

**12. Modify the program of Example 5.5 to find and output the largest per capita income (I2) and its associated SMSA (C2), in addition to I1 and C1. Draw the flowchart.

**13.** What values get printed for each of the following loops? How many times does each loop iterate?

a.  ```
    10 FOR J = 10 TO 0 STEP −1
    20    PRINT J
    30 NEXT J
    ```

b.  Same as part a except STEP −3

c.  ```
    40 FOR R = .05 TO .25 STEP .01
    50    PRINT R
    60 NEXT R
    ```

d.  Same as part c except STEP .05

e.  ```
    10 FOR K = 1 TO 5 STEP .5
    20    PRINT K
    30 NEXT K
    ```

f.  Same as part e except place a second PRINT after NEXT:

    ```
    40 PRINT K
    ```

g.  Same as part f except add:

    ```
    25 IF K > 2.5 THEN 40
    ```

h.  ```
    40 FOR I = 1 TO 50
    50    LET X = I**2 + 5
    60    IF X > 15 THEN 80
    70 NEXT I
    80 PRINT I,X
    ```

i.  ```
    10 READ M,N
    15 FOR I = M TO M*N STEP N − 1
    20    PRINT I
    25 NEXT I
         .
         .
         .
    90 DATA 4,3
    ```

**14.** Which of the following are valid FOR/NEXT loops? If invalid, state reason(s).

a.  ```
    30 FOR K = 1 TO 5
    35    PRINT K
    40 NEXT K
    45 FOR K = 1 TO 5
    50    PRINT K
    55 NEXT K
    ```

b.  ```
    60 FOR K = 1 TO 5 STEP −1
    65    PRINT  K
    70 NEXT K
    ```
    ```

```
c.  20 GO TO 60
      .
      .
      .
    40 FOR L = 1 TO 50
    50    LET K = L**.5
    60    LET L = K/2
    70    PRINT L,K
    80    GO TO 40
    90 NEXT K
```

# 5.4
# ACCUMULATING A SUM

Accumulating and printing sums for one or more variables is a common computation in programming. For example, a payroll program computes gross pay, deductions, and net pay for each employee and also computes the total gross pay, total deductions, and total net pay for all employees of a firm. To illustrate how the computer can accumulate a sum, we return to our sales commission problem.

---

**EXAMPLE 5.6   Sales Commission Program With Sum**

The sales manager of the company needs to know the total amount of money the company pays to all its salespeople. Conceptually, we set aside a memory location (that is, assign a variable) which represents the sum. The sum is initialized to zero, and then each time the computer computes the total pay of a salesperson, the sum is increased by this amount. In effect the sum can be thought of as a running total whose final value is not known until all the data are read in and processed. For our test data, the total pay for each salesperson is $150, $270, and $150. As the program is computing, the sum will be

```
    After the first salesperson:    0 + 150 = 150
   After the second salesperson: 150 + 270 = 420
    After the third salesperson: 420 + 150 = 570
```

Thus a running total accumulates.

The flowchart in Figure 5.3 illustrates the steps needed to accumulate a sum. In the program below, A is the variable that stores the accumulated amount paid to all salespeople. Note that this program is identical to the program in Example 5.4, except for the segments shown within boxes.

---

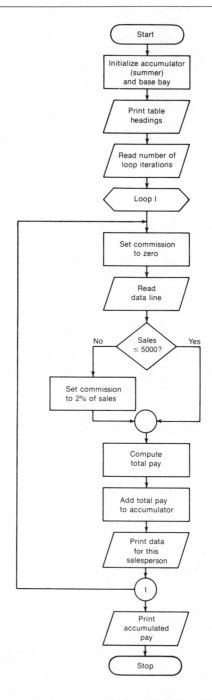

FIGURE 5.3   *Accumulating Total Commissions*

```
195 LET A = 0
200 LET B = 150
205 PRINT "EMPLOYEE NAME","SS NUMBER","TOTAL PAY"
210 PRINT "_____"
212 READ N
215 FOR I = 1 TO N
220     LET C = 0
240     READ S$,N$,S
260     IF S <= 5000 THEN 300
280     LET C = .02*S
300     LET T = B + C
310     LET A = A + T
320     PRINT N$,S$,T
330 NEXT I
340 PRINT
350 PRINT "TOTAL PAYROLL:" ,,A
900 DATA 3
901 DATA "266-62-8431","B. FLINTSTONE",4150
902 DATA "375-41-6215","P. RABBIT",6000
903 DATA "154-25-1298","B. B. BABBLE",2020
999 END
```

First we explicitly initialize A to zero for the reasons outlined on page A-3 of Module A. Even though our system initializes all variables to zero, it is good programming practice to explicitly initialize the variables that need initializing. This makes the program more "portable," since it would also work on a system that does not initialize variables to zero. By placing the instruction

310 LET A = A + T

within the loop the value stored in T is added to the value stored in A, and the result of the addition is stored in A, replacing the value previously stored in A.

As the program is executed, the contents of memory locations A and T change as follows.

After initialization:

After the first person is processed:

After the second person is processed:

After the third person is processed:

Now the output would appear as follows:

```
EMPLOYEE NAME    SS NUMBER              TOTAL PAY
- - - - - - - - - - - - - - - - - - - - - - - - - - - -

B.  FLINTSTONE   266 - 62 - 8431         150
P.  RABBIT       375 - 41 - 6215         270
B.  B.  BABBLE   154 - 25 - 1298         150

TOTAL  PAYROLL:                          570
```

Notice that when the FOR/NEXT loop is completed, the computer branches to line 340 and prints the total amount paid to all salespersons, $570.

were placed before

LET T = C + B

c. Describe the output if

PRINT "TOTAL PAYROLL:",,A

were placed just before the NEXT I instruction?

d. Describe the output if

PRINT "EMPLOYEE NAME","SS NUMBER","TOTAL PAY"

were placed right after

READ S$,N$,S

e. Why is it a good idea to explicitly initialize A to zero in line 195?

**16.** Modify the program of Example 5.6 by calculating and printing the mean or average pay per employee (M).

**\*17.** Modify the program in Example 5.6 to accumulate and print three sums: cumulative base pay, cumulative commissions, and cumulative total pay. *Hint:* You need a separate variable to accumulate each total. Can you think of simplifications in the program which make use of the fact that once you have two of these sums you automatically have the third?

# 5.5
# COMMON ERRORS

Beginning programmers are likely to make at least one of the errors below when applying the material in this chapter. Will you?

*1. Nonexistent line numbers.* A common syntax error that's fatal is to transfer control to a nonexistent line number, as when we have

50 GO TO 110

and line 110 is missing. This is an easy error to make in long programs with many transfers, particularly if you've been renumbering lines a lot while setting the code down on paper. For this type of error you might get an error message such as UNDEFINED LINE NUMBER.

*2. Transfer to wrong line number.* This logic error is common when we set down a long code on paper and subsequently make a series of line changes, insertions, and deletions. Make it a habit to give your program a final "once over" to make sure your transfers are to the intended statements. By the way, this is another reason to keep GO TO statements to a minimum.

3.  *Transfer to DATA statement.*   Do you see anything wrong with the following?

```
    .
    .
    .
150 READ A
    .
    .
    .
250 GO TO 610
    .
    .
    .
610 DATA 5.4
    .
    .
```

If you wish to read the next item of data, then transfer control to the READ statement, not to the DATA statement itself. Do you see why? The DATA statement is *nonexecutable*. Transferring control to a nonexecutable statement is a logic error, since the statement that will be executed is the first executable statement following the nonexecutable statement to which "control" was transferred. To correct the above error, type

```
250 GO TO 150
```

4.  *Order of relational operators.*   The order of relational operators is important. For example, the statement

```
75 IF Q =< 80
```

might provoke a fatal syntax error. The statement should read

```
75 IF Q <= 80
```

as illustrated in Table 5.1.

5.  *Don't use unquoted strings in relational expressions.*   For example,

```
120 IF B$ = YES THEN 50
```

would give a syntax error. The string YES must be written "YES."

6.  *Redundant IF/THENs.*   Study the following:

```
    .
    .
    .
240 IF S < 10 THEN 290
245 IF S >= 10 THEN 250
250 IF S < 20 THEN 310
    .
    .
```

Technically, we don't have an error here, but line 245 is unnecessary since control always goes to line 250 when the test in line 240 is false. This is a common programming inefficiency.

7.  *Improper FOR parameters.*   These errors are subtle:

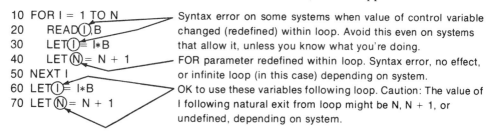

20 FOR I = 1 TO 5 STEP ⊖ ◄——— Control variable cannot reach 5 since step is negative and initial value is below terminal value. Result:
infinite loop.

40 FOR K = 1 TO Ⓝ ◄——————— Execution error or bypass of entire loop if N not
explicitly assigned a value and system stores zero
in N.

60 FOR J = J1 TO J2 STEP Ⓙ③ ◄— When J1 < J2 then infinite loop if J3 not explicitly
assigned a value and system stores zero for J3.

80 FOR L = 50 TO 1          Loop bypassed since 50 > 1. STEP – 1 needs to be
inserted.

8.  *Redefining control variable.*   It doesn't make sense, but it happens.

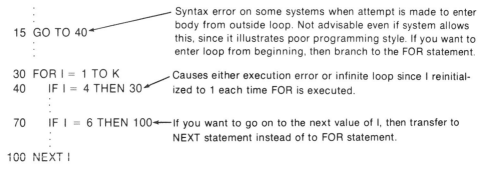

10 FOR I = 1 TO N ———————— Syntax error on some systems when value of control variable
20    READ Ⓘ,B               changed (redefined) within loop. Avoid this even on systems
30    LET Ⓘ = I∗B            that allow it, unless you know what you're doing.
40    LET Ⓝ = N + 1 ———————— FOR parameter redefined within loop. Syntax error, no effect,
50 NEXT I                    or infinite loop (in this case) depending on system.
60 LET Ⓘ = I∗B ———————————— OK to use these variables following loop. Caution: The value of
70 LET Ⓝ = N + 1            I following natural exit from loop might be N, N + 1, or
undefined, depending on system.

9.  *Improper transfers.*   Several incorrect transfers are possible:

:
:
15  GO TO 40 ◄—————— Syntax error on some systems when attempt is made to enter
body from outside loop. Not advisable even if system allows
this, since it illustrates poor programming style. If you want to
enter loop from beginning, then branch to the FOR statement.

30  FOR I = 1 TO K ———— Causes either execution error or infinite loop since I reinitial-
40    IF I = 4 THEN 30 ◄— ized to 1 each time FOR is executed.
:
:
70    IF I = 6 THEN 100 ◄—— If you want to go on to the next value of I, then transfer to
NEXT statement instead of to FOR statement.
:
100 NEXT I

10. *Too many NEXT statements.*   Here's one we've seen often when the student
wishes to transfer to the end of the loop from within the body:

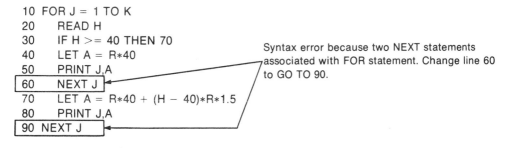

10 FOR J = 1 TO K
20    READ H
30    IF H >= 40 THEN 70
40    LET A = R∗40              Syntax error because two NEXT statements
50    PRINT J,A                 associated with FOR statement. Change line 60
60    NEXT J ◄                  to GO TO 90.
70    LET A = R∗40 + (H – 40)∗R∗1.5
80    PRINT J,A
90 NEXT J ◄

11. *Incomplete FOR/NEXT pair.* Always make sure you pair a unique NEXT statement with a FOR statement.

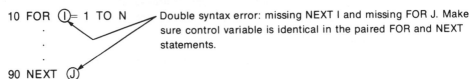

10 FOR Ⓘ= 1 TO N      Double syntax error: missing NEXT I and missing FOR J. Make sure control variable is identical in the paired FOR and NEXT statements.

90 NEXT Ⓙ

### Additional Exercises

**18.**   Define or explain the following:

| | |
|---|---|
| control statements | looping |
| GO TO statement | FOR/NEXT loop |
| branching | iterations |
| transfer of control | FOR statement |
| IF/THEN statement | NEXT statement |
| relational expression | body of FOR/NEXT loop |
| relational operator | control variable |
| code | index |
| | infinite loop |

**19. Temperature Conversion.** Modify the program and flowchart of part a *or* b in Exercise 29 in Chapter 4 (page 98) as follows:

a. Convert degrees Fahrenheit to degrees Celsius by using a FOR/NEXT loop that varies degrees Fahrenheit (F) from its initial value (F1) to its terminal value (F2) in increments of F3. Run the program for the following sets of values:

| F1 | F2 | F3 |
|---|---|---|
| 20 | 40 | 1 |
| −30 | 120 | 5 |

For example, your output for the first run should look like this:

| DEGREES FAHRENHEIT | DEGREES CELSIUS |
|---|---|
| 20 | −6.67 |
| 21 | −6.11 |
| 22 | −5.56 |
| . | . |
| . | . |
| . | . |
| 40 | 4.44 |

21 rows

**b. Include an "outer" loop which processes as many sets of data as desired (two sets for the above data). Note that the loop of part a is completely within this outer loop.

**20. Costing Problem.** Modify the program and flowchart of part a *or* b in Exercise 30 in Chapter 4 (page 99) as follows:

a. Calculate and output total cost based on different values of cost per square inch (C). Use a FOR/NEXT loop that varies C from its initial value (C1) to its terminal value (C2) in increments of C3. Run the program for the following three sets of values:

| C1 | C2 | C3 | R | X |
|----|----|----|----|----|
| 0.005 | 0.100 | 0.005 | 5.0 | 500000 |
| 0.005 | 0.100 | 0.005 | 5.2 | 500000 |
| 0.010 | 0.150 | 0.010 | 5.2 | 650000 |

For example, your output for the first run should look like this:

| | COST PER SQUARE INCH | TOTAL COST |
|----|----|----|
| | 0.005 | 196349 |
| | 0.010 | 392699 |
| | 0.015 | 589048 |
| 20 rows | · | · |
| | · | · |
| | · | · |
| | 0.100 | 3926991 |

**b. Include an "outer" loop which processes as many sets of data as desired (three sets for the above data). Note that the loop of part a is completely within this outer loop.

**21. Microeconomics Problem.** Modify the program and flowchart of part a *or* b in Exercise 31 of Chapter 4 (page 99) as follows:

a. Calculate and print daily revenue, daily cost, and daily profit based on different values of U. Use a FOR/NEXT loop that varies U from 1 to a maximum (M) in increments of 1. Input or read M for the following four sets of data:

| M | Price |
|----|----|
| 15 | 80 |
| 15 | 100 |
| 15 | 120 |
| 15 | 140 |

For example, your output for the first run should look like this:

| UNITS PRODUCED | DAILY REVENUE | DAILY COST | DAILY PROFIT |
|---|---|---|---|
| 1 | 80 | 245 | −165 |
| 2 | 160 | 234 | −74 |
| 3 | 240 | 223 | 17 |
| . | . | . | . |
| . | . | . | . |
| . | . | . | . |
| 15 | 1200 | 2275 | −1075 |

**b.  Include an "outer" loop which uses price as the index. In other words, the loop in part a is completely within this outer loop. Define initial (P1), terminal (P2), and incremental (P3) prices as input or read variables, along with M. The above input/read data now appear as follows:

| P1 | P2 | P3 | M |
|---|---|---|---|
| 80 | 140 | 20 | 15 |

The computer now prints all four tables in one run. Note that the computer run terminates after the price index reaches P2. Just before each table, print the price that corresponds to that table.

22. **Blood-Bank Inventory Problem.** Modify the program and flowchart of part a *or* b in Exercise 32 of Chapter 4 (page 100) as follows:

a.  Calculate and print the number of pints to order (Q) and the expected cost per week (W) based on different values of cost of refrigeration (H). Use a FOR/NEXT loop to vary H from its initial value (H1) to its terminal value (H2) in increments of H3. Input or read H1, H2, H3, administrative and shipping cost (C), and average weekly demand (D) for the following three sets of values:

| H1 | H2 | H3 | C | D |
|---|---|---|---|---|
| 0.20 | 0.30 | 0.01 | 50 | 2500 |
| 0.20 | 0.30 | 0.01 | 50 | 3000 |
| 0.20 | 0.30 | 0.01 | 50 | 3500 |

For example, your output for the first run should look like this:

| | COST OF REFRIGERATION | ORDER QUANTITY | COST PER WEEK |
|---|---|---|---|
| 11 rows | 0.20 | 1118 | 223.61 |
| | 0.21 | 1091 | 229.13 |
| | . | . | . |
| | . | . | . |
| | . | . | . |
| | 0.30 | 913 | 273.86 |

Draw conclusions with respect to the behavior of Q and W as H and D change.

**b. Include an "outer" loop which uses D as the index. In other words, the loop in part a is completely within this outer loop. Define initial (D1), terminal (D2), and incremental (D3) demands as input or read variables, along with H1, H2, H3, and C. The above input/read data now appear as follows:

| H1 | H2 | H3 | C | D1 | D2 | D3 |
|---|---|---|---|---|---|---|
| 0.20 | 0.30 | 0.01 | 50 | 2500 | 3500 | 500 |

The computer now prints all three tables in one run. Note that the computer run terminates after the demand index reaches D2. Just before each table, print the demand that corresponds to that table.

23. **Property Tax Assessment.** The property tax rate in a town is set at an increasing rate according to the following table.

**Annual Property Tax Schedule**

| Value of Property | Tax Rate (%) |
|---|---|
| Less than $10,000 | 3 |
| $10,000 and above | 4 |

a. Prepare a flowchart and write a program to read in the value of the property, then determine and print the tax charge. Use a FOR/NEXT loop to process the following test data:

| Lot Number | Owner's Name | Property Value |
|------------|--------------|----------------|
| 613 | A. Smith | $8,900 |
| 975 | A. B. Smith | 25,000 |
| 152 | B. C. Smith | 42,000 |
| 1642 | C. B. Smith | 37,000 |
| 1785 | Deaf Smith | 75,000 |

*Sample Output*

| LOT NUMBER | OWNER | PROPERTY VALUE | TAX CHARGE |
|------------|-------|----------------|------------|
| 613 | A. SMITH | 8900 | 267 |
| 975 | A. B. SMITH | 25000 | 1000 |
| 152 | B. C. SMITH | 42000 | 2100 |
| 1642 | C. B. SMITH | 37000 | 1850 |
| 1785 | DEAF SMITH | 75000 | 3750 |

b. Modify the program in part a such that it prints the sum of property values, the total tax charge, the average property value, and the average tax charge.

**c. Instead of the Tax Schedule in part a use the following:

| Value of Property | Tax Rate (%) |
|-------------------|--------------|
| Less than $10,000 | 3 |
| $10,000 but under $30,000 | 4 |
| $30,000 but under $60,000 | 5 |
| $60,000 and over | 6 |

24. **Factorials.** The factorial of a number $N$ (written $N!$) is a useful calculation in many problems in mathematics and statistics. By definition $N!$ is given by the product

$$N \cdot (N - 1) \cdot (N - 2) \ldots 2 \cdot 1$$

For example, if the value of $N$ is 5, then

$$5! = 5 \cdot 4 \cdot 3 \cdot 2 \cdot 1 = 120$$

a. Design an interactive program that inputs $N$ and calculates and prints $N!$ What is the factorial of 1, 5, 10, 25, 50, and 100?

b. Did you get overflow in part a? By trial and error determine the maximum value of $N$ whose factorial your computer can process. Then design your program to check each input of $N$ to make sure it is within the allowable range of zero to the maximum value. If it is not, print a message to the user to this effect and then request another input value.

    c.  The factorial of zero is defined as having a value of one. Ensure that your program is capable of printing out the correct value of 0! should a user input zero for *N*.

\*\* d.  Design an "outer" loop in your program for the purpose of processing *K* different values of *N*. For example, the data in part a would require six iterations of this loop.

\*\* e.  Instead of the "outer" loop in part d, design an outer loop that processes values of *N* from some initial value (N1) to some terminal value (N2) in increments of N3. Print a table of *N* values and their factorials. Try two test runs: the first processes *N* from 1 to 10 in increments of 1; the second processes *N* from 10 to 50 in increments of 5.

**25. Quadratic Roots.** A quadratic equation is defined by

$$y = ax^2 + bx + c$$

where *a*, *b*, and *c* are constants called *parameters.* Many mathematical applications require the "roots" of this equation. By definition, a root is a value of *x* that when substituted into the equation yields a value of zero for *y*. The following familiar *quadratic formula* determines the appropriate roots:

$$x = \frac{-b \pm (b^2 - 4ac)^{\frac{1}{2}}}{2a}$$

Prepare a flowchart and write a program to calculate and print quadratic roots for the following read/input values of *a*, *b*, and *c*:

| a | b | c |
|---|---|---|
| 5 | 6 | 1.35 |
| 1 | 10 | −1 |
| 1 | 2 | 1 |
| 7 | 4 | 2 |

Use a FOR/NEXT loop to process these values. Your program should have three separate branches within the loop depending on the value of the expression $b^2 - 4ac$. If this expression is negative, then have the computer print "IMAGINARY ROOTS"; if the expression equals zero exactly, then evaluate the single root using $x = -b/(2a)$; if the expression is positive, then use the above quadratic formula to calculate the two roots. *Note:* Instead of raising the expression $b^2 - 4ac$ to the 0.5 power, you might want to use the SQR function illustrated on page 258.

**26. Personnel Benefits Budget.** A budget officer for the State Agency of Education is in the process of preparing the personnel budget for the next fiscal year. One phase of this process is to prepare a budget of personnel expenditures paid by the state in addition to salaries. The additional expenditures include the following:

    1.  Social security. The state contributes 6.13 percent of an employee's salary up to $22,900. No deduction is made for earnings above that amount.

2. Retirement. The state contributes 9.6 percent of total salary if the employee belongs to the state retirement plan; 9 percent is contributed by the state if the employee elects a private plan; and nothing is contributed by the state if the employee is not eligible for a retirement plan (for example, employees under 30 years of age are not eligible for a retirement plan).
3. Group life insurance. The state contributes $1.30 for every $1000 of salary paid to the employee. For example, a yearly salary of $11,200 results in a $14.56 contribution (11.200 × 1.30).

The data line for each employee consists of

1. Name
2. SS number
3. Annual salary
4. Code for retirement: 1 = not eligible; 2 = state plan; 3 = private plan

Prepare a flowchart and write a program which outputs each employee's name, SS number, salary, social security contribution, retirement contribution, group life contribution, and total contribution. After all employees have been processed, print the totals of each budget category (the four contribution columns) for all employees. Use the test data below to debug your program.

| Name | SS Number | Salary | Retirement Code |
|------|-----------|--------|-----------------|
| TEST 1 | 111-11-1111 | 17,000 | 2 |
| TEST 2 | 222-22-2222 | 19,500 | 3 |
| TEST 3 | 333-33-3333 | 21,300 | 2 |
| TEST 4 | 444-44-4444 | 23,800 | 1 |
| TEST 5 | 555-55-5555 | 22,900 | 2 |
| TEST 6 | 666-66-6666 | 10,750 | 1 |
| TEST 7 | 777-77-7777 | 24,375 | 2 |
| TEST 8 | 888-88-8888 | 15,600 | 3 |

27. **Affirmative Action Search.** A personnel file in a large firm consists of the following items:

| | |
|------|------|
| Employee name | (up to 15 characters) |
| Employee number | (four-digit number) |
| Age | (nearest whole number) |
| Sex | (1 = male, 2 = female) |
| Marital status | (1 = single, 2 = married, 3 = divorced) |
| Education | (1 = high school, 2 = some college, 3 = college degree, 4 = masters degree) |
| Annual salary | (five-digit number) |

The affirmative action officer wants to determine if there is any difference in salaries paid to males and females of comparable age and education levels.

a. For purposes of this assignment, prepare a flowchart, write a program, and use the test data below to determine the average salary for males under 35 years of age with a masters degree; find the average salary for a similar group of females. Conclusion?

**Test File**

| Name | Number | Age | Sex | Marital Status | Education | Annual Salary |
|------|--------|-----|-----|----------------|-----------|---------------|
| Test 1 | 1111 | 50 | 1 | 2 | 3 | 27,000 |
| Test 2 | 2222 | 25 | 2 | 2 | 4 | 18,000 |
| Test 3 | 3333 | 29 | 2 | 1 | 2 | 12,000 |
| Test 4 | 4444 | 27 | 1 | 3 | 4 | 22,000 |
| Test 5 | 5555 | 40 | 1 | 2 | 4 | 31,000 |
| Test 6 | 6666 | 35 | 1 | 1 | 2 | 15,000 |
| Test 7 | 7777 | 41 | 2 | 2 | 4 | 25,000 |
| Test 8 | 8888 | 32 | 1 | 3 | 4 | 21,000 |
| Test 9 | 9999 | 38 | 1 | 2 | 3 | 24,000 |
| Test 10 | 1000 | 30 | 2 | 2 | 4 | 20,000 |
| Test 11 | 1100 | 28 | 1 | 1 | 4 | 26,000 |
| Test 12 | 1200 | 21 | 2 | 1 | 4 | 19,000 |

** b. Generalize your program such that the affirmative action officer can compare average salaries of males versus females by age category, on the one hand, and by education, on the other. For example, the required input to answer the question in part a would be 35 (for age cutoff) and 4 (for education level). Use this program to answer other interesting questions which might occur to you.

28. **Computerized Matching—A File Search.** The placement office on a college campus is designing an interactive program for the computerized matching of employers and graduating seniors looking for a job. Each student that registers with the placement office provides the following information:

1. Name
2. Student ID
3. Address
4. Major (codes 1 to 10)
5. Grade point average
6. Willing to relocate?  (1 = no, 2 = yes)
7. Willing to travel?  (1 = no, 2 = yes)

a. A firm is looking for a business major (code=6) with a GPA of 3.25 or better who is willing to relocate and travel. Search the Placement Office file and print the name and address of each student that meets the criteria for this job. Include a flowchart with your program. Hint: Store the file in your program by using DATA statements; then read this file one line at a time within a loop.

**b.   Generalize your program such that the placement office can output the name and address of each student who satisfies criteria which the firm specifies as part of the input. In other words, define input variables in your program for: (1) desired major, (2) desired minimum grade point average, (3) relocation requirement, and (4) travel requirement. Thus, for the criteria in part (a), the input for these variables would be 6, 3.25, 2, and 2, respectively. Assume that those students who are willing to relocate or travel would also be willing to accept a job that does not require relocation or travel. Test your program by running the following data for inquiries on the above four variables:

| (1) | (2) | (3) | (4) |
|-----|-----|-----|-----|
| 6 | 3.25 | 2 | 2 |
| 3 | 3.00 | 1 | 1 |
| 8 | 3.70 | 2 | 1 |

*Placement Office File*

| Name | ID | Address | Major | GPA | Relocate | Travel |
|------|-----|---------|-------|-----|----------|--------|
| Iris Abbot | 2119 | 11 Estell Drive | 6 | 3.45 | 1 | 2 |
| Calvin Budnick | 3112 | Burnside Dorm | 8 | 2.75 | 2 | 2 |
| Susan Dent | 4112 | 12 Upper College Rd. | 3 | 2.50 | 2 | 2 |
| Ken Driden | 4819 | RR3 | 4 | 2.85 | 1 | 1 |
| Flo Further | 5811 | 107 Ocean Rd. | 1 | 3.00 | 1 | 2 |
| Ben Lewis | 6237 | Heath Dorm | 3 | 3.25 | 1 | 1 |
| Bella Senate | 6331 | 71 Boston Neck Rd. | 6 | 3.75 | 1 | 2 |
| Wally Tenure | 6581 | 15 South Rd. | 8 | 3.25 | 2 | 1 |
| Alice Tillitson | 8211 | 97 North Rd. | 6 | 3.30 | 2 | 2 |
| Martin Wiener | 9112 | 10 Ballentine | 6 | 3.70 | 2 | 1 |

**29.  Credit Billing.** Design a flowchart and write a program that prints monthly bills (statements) for Muster Charge, an internationally reknown credit card company. Use the following data for three customers.

| Name | Address | Credit Limit | Previous Balance | Payments | New Purchases |
|------|---------|--------------|------------------|----------|---------------|
| Napoleon B. | 19 Waterloo St. Paris France | $ 800 | $ 300.00 | $ 100.00 | $700.00 |
| Duke Welly | 1 Thames Ave. London GB | 1500 | 1350.70 | 1320.70 | 645.52 |
| Betsy Ross | 1776 Flag St. Boston MA USA | 2000 | 36.49 | 36.49 | 19.15 |

Output for these three customers would appear as follows:

```
NAPOLEON B.
19 WATERLOO ST   PREVIOUS                    FINANCE    NEW           NEW
PARIS FRANCE     BALANCE  - PAYMENTS + CHARGE  + PURCHASES = BALANCE
                 300.00   - 100.00    + 3.00    + 700.00    = 903.00
                                      MINIMUM PAYMENT DUE = 183.00
**WARNING**
YOU HAVE EXCEEDED YOUR CREDIT LIMIT
CONTROL YOURSELF, OR ELSE. . . .
```

---

```
DUKE WELLY
1 THAMES AVE     PREVIOUS                    FINANCE    NEW           NEW
LONDON GB        BALANCE  - PAYMENTS + CHARGE  + PURCHASES = BALANCE
                 1350.70  - 1320.70   + .45     + 645.52    = 675.97
                                      MINIMUM PAYMENT DUE = 67.60
```

---

```
BETSY ROSS
1776 FLAG ST     PREVIOUS                    FINANCE    NEW           NEW
BOSTON MA USA    BALANCE  - PAYMENTS + CHARGE  + PURCHASES = BALANCE
                 36.49    - 36.49     + 0.      + 19.15     = 19.15
                                      MINIMUM PAYMENT DUE = 19.15
```

---

Certain conditions must be reflected by the program:
1.  The finance charge is 1.5 percent of the difference between the previous month's balance and the payments made since the previous month.
2.  The minimum payment due is determined according to one of three results.
    a.  If the new balance exceeds the credit limit, then the minimum payment is the difference between the new balance and the credit limit plus 10 percent of the credit limit. Thus, for the first statement, $(903.00 - 800.00) + 10\% (800)$ gives $183.00.
    b.  If the new balance is $100 or more and does not exceed the credit limit, then the minimum payment is 10 percent of the new balance. Thus, for the second statement, $10\% (675.97)$ gives $67.60.
    c.  If the new balance is less than $100, then the minimum payment is set to the new balance (see the third statement).
3.  A warning is printed if the credit limit is exceeded by the new balance (Muster Charge doesn't fool around).
4.  Printout for each person should take up exactly 12 lines in order to conform to the size of the billing statement. In other words, the printout should appear exactly as illustrated.

**30. Student Fee Bill.** The bursar's office at State University would like you to design a flowchart and write a program that prepares student fee bills for *N* students each term.

The fee structure is outlined by the following chart:

|  | Undergraduate | | Graduate | |
|---|---|---|---|---|
|  | In-state | Out-of-state | In-state | Out-of-state |
| Full Time | | | | |
| Tuition | $715 | 1715 | 770 | 1500 |
| Fees | 250 | 250 | 200 | 200 |
| Part Time † | | | | |
| Tuition | $ 66/credit | 160/credit | 90/credit | 150/credit |
| Fees | 10 | 10 | 25 | 25 |

† Less than 12 credits for an undergraduate student; less than 9 credits for a graduate student.

In addition, students living on campus pay room rent of $375 and/or board of $400 per term.

a.  The following data are stored in the student file:
1.  Student ID number
2.  Last name
3.  First name
4.  Class code (1 = undergraduate; 2 = graduate)
5.  Residence (1 = in-state; 2 = out-of-state)
6.  Campus housing (1 = yes; 2 = no)
7.  Board contract (1 = yes; 2 = no)
8.  Credits

Sample Output

```
FEE BILL--STATE UNIVERSITY
NAME--
TUITION   xxxx
FEES      xxxx
ROOM      xxxx
BOARD     xxxx

TOTAL     xxxxx
```

Sample Data

| (1) | (2) | (3) | (4) | (5) | (6) | (7) | (8) |
|-----|-----|-----|-----|-----|-----|-----|-----|
| 6391 | BOLLES | FRAN | 1 | 1 | 1 | 1 | 14.0 |
| 8242 | CARSON | JIMMY | 1 | 2 | 2 | 2 | 8.0 |
| 8577 | DALE | ROBERT | 2 | 1 | 1 | 2 | 10.0 |
| 8699 | HEALY | HEATHER | 2 | 2 | 2 | 1 | 9.0 |
| 8811 | LUCKY | SONIA | 1 | 2 | 2 | 1 | 12.0 |
| . . . make these up . . . | | | 2 | 2 | 2 | 2 | 12.0 |
| . . . make these up . . . | | | 1 | 2 | 1 | 1 | 15.5 |
| . . . make these up . . . | | | 2 | 2 | 1 | 1 | 11.0 |

    b. After all fee bills have been printed, print summary totals for tuition, fees, room, board, and overall total.

    c. Print a summary which categorizes total amount billed by

       1. Full time vs. part time
       2. Undergraduate vs. graduate
       3. In-state vs. out-of-state

\*\* d. Include error detection to ensure that all codes are either 1 or 2 and the number of credits is 3 or greater and less than 22. If an error is encountered, then print an appropriate error message that includes the student's name and ID, bypass the calculations and printout for this student, and go on to the next student. Add new data to test each of the possible data errors.

**31. Police Car Replacement.** A police administrator would like to estimate the mileage at which a police cruiser should be replaced. Data analyses show that the *cost of operation* (gasoline, maintenance, and so on) is approximated by

$$c = f + vm + sm^2$$

where *f, v,* and *s* are called *parameters,* and *m* is the mileage reading (in thousands) on the odometer. For example, a cruiser which is driven for 30,000 miles and is characterized by $f = 1000, v = 200,$ and $s = 2$ incurs an operating cost of approximately

$$c = 1000 + (200)(30) + (2)(30)^2 = \$8800.$$

    The police department has an arrangement with the automaker for trade-ins of used police cruisers. The automaker has agreed to reduce the price of a new cruiser by the following amount:

$$r = pd^m$$

where *r* is the tradein (salvage) value of a used cruiser, *p* is the original (new) car price, *d* is some depreciation factor, and *m* is defined as before. For example, if $p = \$10,000, d = 0.95,$ and $m = 30,$ then

$$r = (10000)(0.95)^{30} = \$2146.$$

This means that the police department pays $10,000 for a new cruiser, drives it for 30,000 miles, and gets $2146 on a tradein. The *depreciation cost* in this case is $7,854, or the difference between the new car price and the salvage price.

Thus, a cruiser which is driven for 30 (thousand) miles costs $8800 to operate and $7854 in depreciation cost, for a total cost of $16,654. If this type of cruiser is replaced by a new cruiser of the same type at 30,000-mile intervals, then the total cost per 1000 miles is approximately $555 (that is, $16,654 \div 30$)

a. Prepare a flowchart and write a program which determines the mileage (to the nearest thousand) at which cruisers should be replaced. Input/read should include *f, v, s, p,* and *d*. Output should appear as follows:

| m | c | c ÷ m | Depreciation Cost | Depreciation Cost ÷ m | Total Cost per 1000 miles |
|---|---|---|---|---|---|
| (1) | (2) | (3) = (2)/(1) | (4) | (5) = (4)/(1) | (6) = (3) + (5) |
| 1 | | | | | |
| 2 | | | | | |
| 3 | | | | | |
| . | | | | | |
| . | | | | | |
| . | | | | | |
| 100 | | | | | |

Thus, the best mileage at which to replace a cruiser is that which gives the smallest value in column (6). Note that 100,000 miles is the maximum replacement mileage that the police administrator is willing to consider.

The police administrator is evaluating several types of cruisers, one of which must be selected. Their characteristics follow.

| Cruiser Type | f | v | s | p | d |
|---|---|---|---|---|---|
| 1 | 1000 | 200 | 2·0 | 10000 | 0.95 |
| 2 | 800 | 300 | 2·5 | 8000 | 0.93 |
| 3 | 1200 | 225 | 1·6 | 13000 | 0.98 |

At what mileage should each type be replaced and what is the total cost per 1000 miles? Which cruiser is the cheapest on a total cost per 1000 mile basis?

**b. Add an "outer" loop for processing all three cruisers in one computer run.

**c. Design your program such that the program itself determines and outputs the best cruiser type and its associated total cost per 1000 miles.

**d. As you go down column (6) in this type of table, costs typically begin high, decrease to a minimum, and begin increasing again. Design your program to exit from the table loop once total cost begins to increase. What is the advantage of this approach? Any disadvantages?

# CHAPTER 6

# *Additional Control Concepts and Statements*

This chapter treats several extensions and variations to looping, and introduces two new statements: ON/GO TO and STOP.

## 6.1
## NESTED FOR/NEXT LOOPS

FOR/NEXT loops are said to be **nested** when one FOR/NEXT loop lies entirely within another FOR/NEXT loop, as illustrated below.

```
              ┌ 10 FOR I = 1 TO 2
Outer Loop──► 20  ┌ FOR J = 1 TO 3
Inner Loop╲   30  │    PRINT I;J
          │   40  └ NEXT J
          └ 50 NEXT I
              60 END
```

For each value of the index I in the outer loop, the inner loop gets "exhausted" (J changes from 1 to 2 to 3 to 4) before I is incremented to its next value. Thus, the inner loop is said to "vary the fastest." Each time the inner loop is exhausted, its index is reset to its initial value (J gets reset to 1 since line 20 gets executed for each new value of I). For example, the output from the above program would appear as follows:

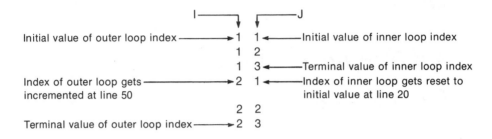

The sequence of execution is as follows:

1.   Line 10—I initialized to 1
2.   Line 20—J initialized to 1
3.   Line 30—1    1    gets printed
4.   Line 40—J incremented to 2
5.   Line 30—1    2    gets printed
6.   Line 40—J incremented to 3
7.   Line 30—1    3    gets printed
8.   Line 40—J incremented to 4 (inner loop exhausted)
9.   Line 50—I incremented to 2 (index of outer loop incremented)
10.  Line 20—J initialized to 1 (index of inner loop reset)
11.  Line 30—2    1    gets printed
12.  Line 40—J incremented to 2
13.  Line 30—2    2    gets printed
14.  Line 40—J incremented to 3
15.  Line 30—2    3    gets printed
16.  Line 40—J incremented to 4 (inner loop exhausted)
17.  Line 50—I incremented to 3 (outer loop exhausted)
18.  Line 60—Execution ends

The above illustration shows nesting to a "depth" of two, which is quite common. Nesting to a depth of three is less common:

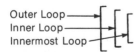

Nesting to greater depths is also conceptually possible, the maximum depth depending on the system.

When constructing nested FOR/NEXT loops, *be careful that your loops do not overlap*, as shown below.

```
┌─10 FOR I = 1 TO 2
├─20    FOR J = 1 TO 3
│  30       PRINT I; J
│└─40    NEXT I
└──50 NEXT J
   60 END
```

In this case you would get a syntax error, since the translator matches the first NEXT with the last FOR, thereby realizing a mismatch between the index I in the NEXT and the index J in the FOR.

---

**EXAMPLE 6.1   Sales Commission Program with Nested FOR/NEXT Loops**

Example 5.4 on page 119 is now modified by assuming that the company has two sales regions—an eastern region and a western region. Separate sales commission reports are prepared for each region. In this revision, an outer loop is set up to process M regions; the inner loop processes each commission calculation. Moreover, assume that the base pay (B) now varies from salesperson to salesperson as specified in the data lines. Figure 6.1 shows the revised flowchart for the new program.

```
160 PRINT "***SALES COMMISSION REPORT***"
165 READ M
170 FOR J = 1 TO M
175    READ R$,N
180    PRINT
185    PRINT
190    PRINT R$;" REGION"
195    PRINT
205    PRINT "EMPLOYEE NAME","SS NUMBER","TOTAL PAY"
210    PRINT "_____"
215    FOR I = 1 TO N
220       LET C = 0
240       READ S$,N$,B,S
260       IF S <= 5000 THEN 300
280       LET C = .02*S
300       LET T = B + C
320       PRINT N$,S$,T
330    NEXT I
335 NEXT J
899 DATA 2
900 DATA "EAST",3
901 DATA "266-62-8431","B. FLINTSTONE",150,4150
902 DATA "375-41-6215","P. RABBIT",200,6000
903 DATA "154-25-1298","B. B. BABBLE",175,2020
910 DATA "WEST",2
911 DATA "275-14-9876","MURPH SURF",125,3000
912 DATA "185-45-1721","B. REDFORD",250,10500
999 END
```

*FIGURE 6.1   Flowchart Illustrating Nested FOR/NEXT Loops*

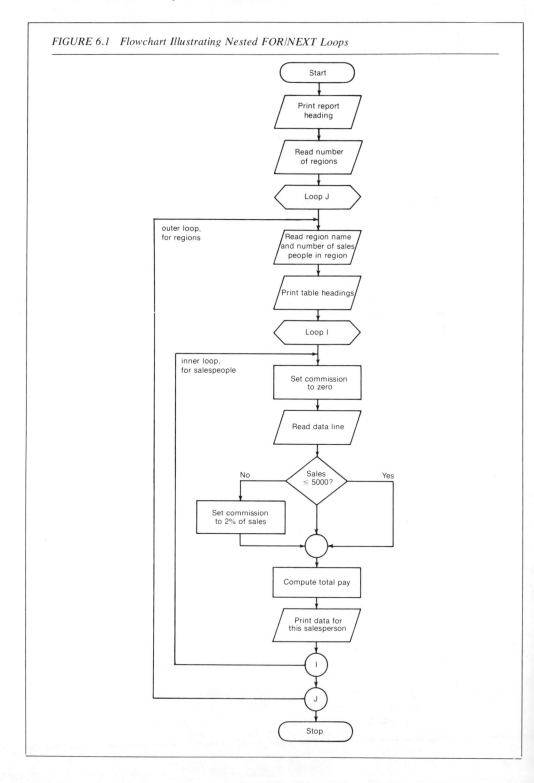

Output from the program would appear as follows:

\*\*\*SALES COMMISSION REPORT\*\*\*

EAST REGION

| EMPLOYEE NAME | SS NUMBER | TOTAL PAY |
| --- | --- | --- |
| B. FLINTSTONE | 266-62-8431 | 150 |
| P. RABBIT | 375-41-6215 | 320 |
| B. B. BABBLE | 154-25-1298 | 175 |

WEST REGION

| EMPLOYEE NAME | SS NUMBER | TOTAL PAY |
| --- | --- | --- |
| MURPH SURF | 275-14-9876 | 125 |
| B. REDFORD | 185-45-1721 | 460 |

## Follow-up Exercises

1. In Example 6.1,
   a. Define the variable R$.
   b. Explain the data items in lines 899, 900, and 910.
   c. What changes would have to be made in the program if the company segments the country into six regions?
   d. Roleplay computer by "executing" this program. Indicate below the values stored successively, where the "snapshot" of memory is taken at each iteration just before the execution of the NEXT I statement.

| J | R$ | N | I | B | S | C | T |
| --- | --- | --- | --- | --- | --- | --- | --- |

\*2. Modify Figure 6.1 and the program of Example 6.1 such that three totals are printed as follows:

```
                                    150
                                    320
                                    175
                                    ----------
                                              645

                                    125
                                    460
                                    ----------
                                              585
                                    ----------
                                             1230
```

3. Specify the printed output and number of iterations for each of the following nested loops:
   a. 10 FOR J = 1 TO 4
      15    FOR K = 1 TO 2
      20       PRINT J,K
      25    NEXT K
      30 NEXT J
   b. Same as part a except K = 1 TO 2 STEP .2
   c. 10 FOR I = 1 TO 2
      15    PRINT I
      20    FOR J = 1 TO 3
      25       PRINT ,J
      30       FOR K = 1 TO 4
      35          PRINT ,,K
      40       NEXT K
      45    NEXT J
      50 NEXT I

4. What is wrong, if anything, in each segment?
   a. 10 FOR X = 1 TO P
      15    FOR Y = R TO S
      20       PRINT "I LOVE NESTED LOOPS"
      25    NEXT X
      30 NEXT Y

   b. 35 FOR I = 1 TO 3
      40 FOR J = 1 TO 4
      45 FOR I = 1 TO 5
      50 PRINT "NOT ME"
      55 NEXT I
      60 NEXT J
      65 NEXT I

# 6.2
# DO UNTIL LOOPS

The FOR/NEXT loop is a popular type of loop, but it is not appropriate for all types of looping. Some problems require the type of looping illustrated in Figure 6.2. The **DO UNTIL loop** first processes a set of statements called the **body of the loop,** after which a condition (relational expression) is tested. If the result of the test is false, then control goes back to the beginning of the loop and the body is processed once more; if the result is true, then control is transferred out of the loop. Thus, we are telling the computer to "DO" the loop "UNTIL" the condition tests true.

### EXAMPLE 6.2  The Inflation Curse

High rates of inflation in a "free" market economy can have devastating effects. For individuals, particularly those on fixed incomes such as retirees, purchasing power (the ability to buy goods and services) can erode dramatically over time. For the economy as a whole, it can lead to recession and unemployment due to factors such as uncertainty and high interest rates.

To illustrate, suppose an item currently costs $100 and increases at a 10 percent rate of inflation per year. The future cost of this item 1 year from now would be $110, determined as follows:

$$100 + (100)(0.1) \quad \text{or} \quad 100(1 + 0.1)$$

Two years from now it would cost $110 plus an additional 10 percent for the price increase in the second year, or

$$110(1 + 0.1)$$

which is $121. Thus, if we define

$C$ = current cost of item
$R$ = rate of inflation
$F$ = future cost of item 1 year from now

then we have

$$F = C(1 + R)$$

for the cost at the end of 1 year and

$$F = (\text{previous year's } F)(1 + R)$$

for future costs in subsequent years.

Figure 6.3 and the program below illustrate an algorithm that prints successive future costs by years until the future cost equals or exceeds double the current cost. Variable J in the program is called a **counter,** since it keeps track of the number of times the loop is repeated (1,2,3,4 . . .). Note that J is *initialized* to 0 before the loop (line 10) and *incremented* by 1 within the loop (line 60).

FIGURE 6.2   DO UNTIL *Loop*

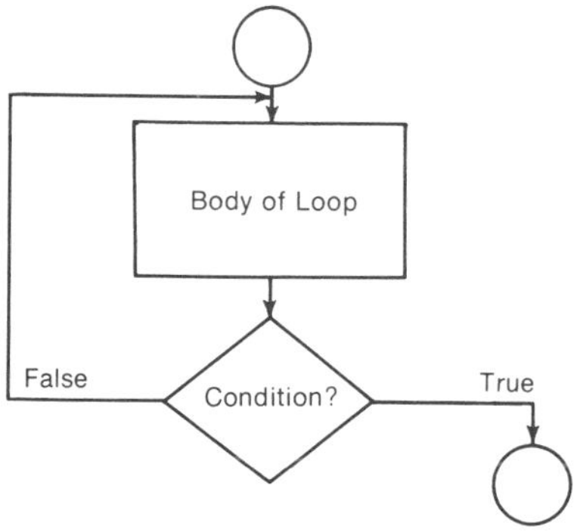

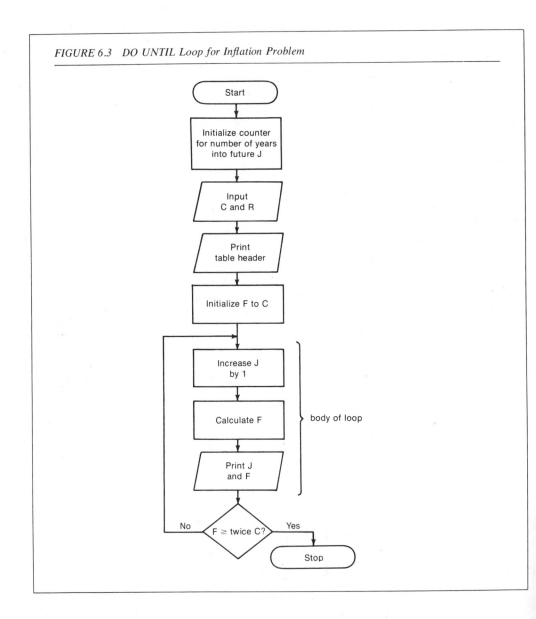

FIGURE 6.3   DO UNTIL Loop for Inflation Problem

```
010 LET J = 0
020 PRINT "ENTER C & R";
030 INPUT C,R
040 PRINT "YEARS INTO FUTURE,bbbbFUTURE COST"
050 LET F = C
060 LET J = J + 1
070    LET F = F*(1 + R)
080    PRINT TAB (7);J;TAB (23);F
090    IF F >= 2*C THEN 999
100 GO TO 60
999 END
```

As in FOR/NEXT loops, we indent all but the first and last statements in the DO UNTIL loop to improve its readability.

To illustrate the program, suppose we wish to calculate and print the future cost of a house that increases year by year at a constant rate of inflation. Assume a current cost of $60,000 and a 10 percent rate of inflation.

RUN

```
ENTER C & R? 60000, .1
YEARS INTO FUTURE       FUTURE COST
       1                66000
       2                72600
       3                79860
       4                87846
       5                96630.6
       6                106294
       7                116923
       8                128615
```

Thus, just to keep up with inflation, the house must sell at the indicated future costs. In the eighth year, the future cost exceeds double the initial cost, so execution terminates based on the test in line 90.

## Follow-up Exercises

5. Confirm the output by roleplaying the computer. As you do this, fill in the contents of the indicated storage locations below as if a snapshot of memory were taken at line 90.

|     J     |     C     |     R     |     F     |
| --- | --- | --- | --- |

In particular, pay attention to lines 50 to 70 and the test performed in line 90.

What would happen if
a. The statement in line 50 were omitted?
b. Line 70 read as follows?

   70 LET F = C*(1 + R)

c. J were initialized to 1 in line 10? What change would you have to make within the loop to compensate for an initial value of J = 1?

**6.** Why would it be unwise to use the following test?

   90 IF F = 2*C THEN 999

**7.** Modify line 90 to eliminate the need for a GO TO statement. Technically, do we now have a DO UNTIL loop? Explain.

**8.** Modify the program such that the user specifies an input value for the multiplicative factor (M). In the example, M has a value of 2 (that is, the loop terminates when the cost exceeds double the current cost).

**\*9. Nested Loops.** Incorporate a FOR/NEXT loop into the program that allows you to process N sets of data. Note that the DO UNTIL loop is entirely contained within the FOR/NEXT loop. Run the program for the following sets of values:

| C | R |
|---|---|
| $60,000 | 0.100 |
| 60,000 | 0.050 |
| 60,000 | 0.025 |
| 90,000 | 0.100 |
| 120,000 | 0.100 |

First, flowchart your program. What's the advantage of this approach? Draw some interesting conclusions from your output about the nature of this type of growth in cost.

## 6.3
## LAST-RECORD-CHECK (LRC) LOOPS

FOR/NEXT loops are convenient when we know beforehand the number of desired loop iterations, and DO UNTIL loops are useful when exit from the loop is based in a computational result within the loop. If we do not wish to specify in advance (or know) the exact number of times the loop is to be repeated, then the **last-record-check (LRC)** loop may be appropriate.

The construction of an LRC loop requires a special data item that signals the end of the data. This special data item, sometimes called a **trailer number,** has a "unique" number (or string constant) assigned to one of the input/read variables. By a *unique* number, we mean one that would never be part of regular provided data. For example, in the sales commission program, weekly sales (S) of −99 might serve as a trailer number since normally sales are positive. After each salesperson's line of data is read into the computer a test is made to determine whether the data just read in contains the trailer number. If the computer determines that a particular value of S is the trailer

*FIGURE 6.4    Sales Commission Problem With LRC Loop*

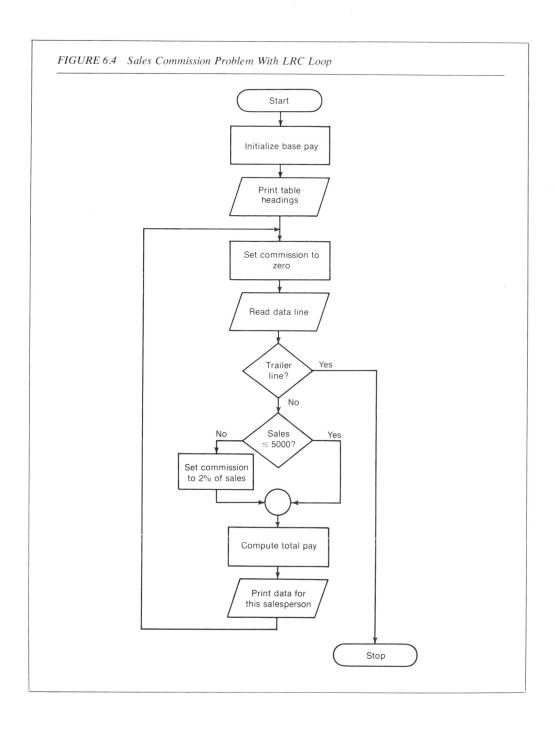

number, then the computer branches out of the loop; otherwise, the computer continues looping. Figure 6.4 illustrates this method for the sales commission example, and Example 6.3 illustrates the corresponding program.

---

### EXAMPLE 6.3   Sales Commission Program With LRC Loop

```
200 LET B = 150
205 PRINT "EMPLOYEE NAME","SS NUMBER","TOTAL PAY"
210 PRINT "------------------------------------------------"
220 LET C = 0
240     READ S$,N$,S
250     IF S = -99 THEN 999
260     IF S <= 5000 THEN 300
280     LET C = .02*S
300     LET T = B + C
320     PRINT N$,S$,T
325 GO TO 220
901 DATA "266-62-8431","B. FLINTSTONE",4150
902 DATA "375-41-6215","P. RABBIT",6000
903 DATA "154-25-1298","B. B. BABBLE",2020
904 DATA " "," ",-99
999 END
```

The *trailer line* (line 904) has the trailer number $-99$ assigned to the salesperson's weekly sales. This line number does not represent another salesperson; it is placed at the end of the data to indicate no more data. When the computer reads this line, it has already processed data for all salespersons. The instruction

250 IF S = -99 THEN 999

needs further explanation. Immediately after reading in the SS number, name, and sales for a given salesperson, the computer checks for the trailer number by testing the value of S against $-99$. After the data for the first salesperson are read in, the location S contains the value 4150, which is not equal to $-99$. Thus, the relational expression "S = $-99$" is tested as false. As a result, control drops to line 260, which is to say that the computer next computes and prints the total pay, and returns to line 220 to reinitialize commission and read in more data. For the second and third salespeople the same process is repeated; that is, the program again bypasses the instruction "THEN 999" and executes the next instruction (line 260). Finally, when the trailer line is processed, the contents of S test true against the value $-99$. As a result, control is transferred to the END statement (line 999) and processing terminates.

Output from a run of the program is as follows:

| EMPLOYEE NAME | SS NUMBER | TOTAL PAY |
|---|---|---|
| B. FLINTSTONE | 266-62-8431 | 150 |
| P. RABBIT | 375-41-6215 | 270 |
| B. B. BABBLE | 154-25-1298 | 150 |

As usual statements within the loop, except the first (line 220) and last (line 325), are indented to improve identification of the loop.

**Follow-up Exercises**

10. If we were to use zero as the trailer number, how would you change the program in Example 6.3? Is there a danger in using zero?
11. Do you see any problem with placing the test for the trailer number immediately after the PRINT instruction (line 320)? Why or why not?
12. Do you need data entries for SS number and name on the trailer line? Do these have to be blank? Explain.
13. Change the program such that SS number is used to test the last line of data. Use the string constant "NO MORE DATA" as the trailer "number." What would happen if we were to use the following as our last line of data?

        904 DATA "NO MORE DATA"

14. How would the output change if we were to place the first PRINT statement (line 205) at a point within the loop just before the PRINT statement in line 320?
15. Explain the execution logic of this program.

        05 LET S = 0
        10 PRINT "ENTER A VALUE";
        20     INPUT V
        30     LET S = S + V
        40     PRINT "DO YOU WANT TO CONTINUE";
        50     INPUT R$
        60 IF R$ = "YES" THEN 10
        70 PRINT S
        80 END

    In your explanation, indicate all input/output as if you were to run this program. Process the following values of V: 10, 20, and 30.

*16. **Bank Savings Account Program.** Change the bank savings program of Section 4.6 on page 91 by inserting an LRC loop to process customers. Use an appropriate trailer number for the input of customer name. Include a flowchart.

# 6.4
# ON/GO TO STATEMENT

The ON/GO TO statement is a multiple transfer of control statement whereby control is passed to one of a group of instructions based on the integer value of an expression. expression.

The general form of this statement is[1]

> *line no.* **ON** $^{arithmetic}_{expression}$ **GO TO** $^{line}_{number,}$ $^{line}_{number,}$ . . . , $^{line}_{number}$

To illustrate this statement, consider the two equivalent program segments below.

| Version A | Version B |
|---|---|
| 10 IF L = 2 THEN 50 | 10 ON L GO TO 20,50 |
| 20 LET K1 = K1 + 1 | 20 LET K1 = K1 + 1 |
| . | . |
| . | . |
| . | . |
| 40 GO TO 100 | 40 GO TO 100 |
| 50 LET K2 = K2 + 1 | 50 LET K2 = K2 + 1 |
| . | . |
| . | . |
| . | . |

In either version, control is transferred to line number 50 when the value stored in L is 2 and to line 20 when 1 is stored in L.

The arithmetic expression (the variable L in this example) must store an *integer* value (if the value is a decimal number the fractional part of the number is ignored) that falls within the range of 1 and the total number of line numbers in the ON/GO TO statement. In our example, L must be a 1 or 2 because there are only two line numbers in the instruction. The program branches to the first line number specified after GO TO if the value of the expression is 1, control passes to the second line number if the value is 2, the third line number if the value is 3, and so on. In our example, if L stores a value of 1, then the program branches to the line number in the first position, or line 20; if L stores a 2, then the program branches to the line number in the second position, or line 50.

If the integer value of the expression is *out of range* (less than 1 or greater than the total number of line numbers indicated in the instruction), then an error occurs and execution of the program stops.[2] For example,

```
05 LET L = 3
10 ON L GO TO 20,50
       .
       .
       .
```

would cause a fatal execution error.

---

[1] Some systems have variations of this statement. For example, the form of the statement on IBM's CALL system is

> *line no.* **GO TO** $^{line}_{number,}$ $^{line}_{number,}$ . . . , $^{line}_{number}$ **ON** $^{arithmetic}_{expression}$

[2] Some systems ignore this out-of-range condition by transferring control to the next executable statement following the ON/GO TO statement.

In our simple example, only two branches were illustrated, so the segment in version B is no more efficient than the segment in version A. *As the number of branches increases, however, you should appreciate that the use of the ON/GO TO statement over multiple IF/THEN statements increases clarity and realizes efficiencies regarding length of program and CPU time.*

The ON/GO TO statement is often used when a data item has been coded by category (for example, 1 = freshman, 2 = sophomore, 3 = junior, 4 = senior) and each category requires a different set of calculations, as we illustrate next.

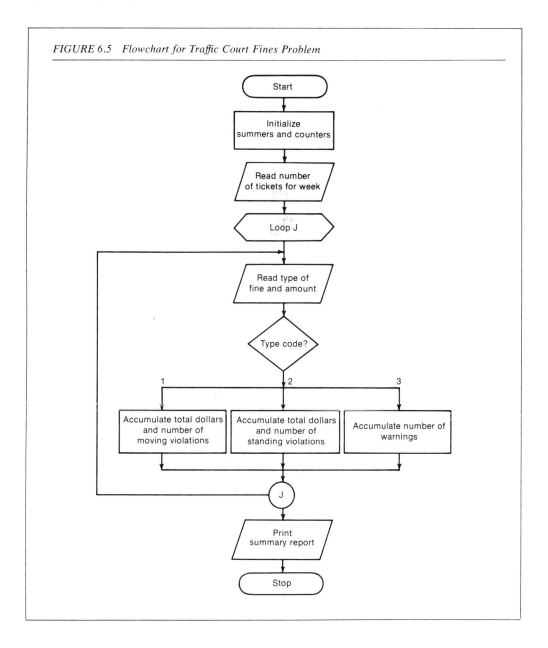

FIGURE 6.5   *Flowchart for Traffic Court Fines Problem*

## EXAMPLE 6.4  Traffic Court Fines

Each week the clerk in traffic court summarizes the fines collected for traffic violations by major categories: moving violation, standing violation, and warning. The data on each violation include traffic violation type (1 = moving; 2 = standing; 3 = warning) and amount of fine.

Figure 6.5 is a flowchart which presents the steps necessary to summarize the traffic violations data. In the program below M1 accumulates the dollar amount (total fines) collected for moving violations and M2 counts the number of moving violations; S1 and S2, respectively, accumulate the total fines collected and number of fines for standing violations; W2 counts the number of warnings (warnings do not involve a fine). When T = 1, the violation is a moving violation; when T = 2, the violation is a standing violation; when T = 3, the violation is a warning. N is the number of tickets issued for the week, and F is the amount of fine for the ticket.

|  Program | Comments |
|---|---|

```
05 REM TRAFFIC COURT FINES
10 REM----------------------------------------------------------------------------------------
15 REM READ VARIABLES
20 REM    N = NUMBER OF TICKETS
25 REM    T = TYPE OF VIOLATION
30 REM    F = FINE
35 REM----------------------------------------------------------------
40 REM OUTPUT VARIABLES
45 REM    M1 = ACCUMULATED DOLLAR AMOUNT OF MOVING VIOLATIONS
50 REM    M2 = ACCUMULATED NUMBER OF MOVING VIOLATIONS
55 REM    S1 = ACCUMULATED DOLLAR AMOUNT OF STANDING VIOLATIONS
60 REM    S2 = ACCUMULATED NUMBER OF STANDING VIOLATIONS
65 REM    W2 = ACCUMULATED NUMBER OF WARNINGS
70 REM----------------------------------------------------------------
100 LET M1 = 0
110 LET M2 = 0
120 LET S1 = 0
130 LET S2 = 0
140 LET W2 = 0
150 READ N
160 FOR J = 1 TO N
170    READ T,F
180    ON T GO TO 200, 300, 400
200       LET M1 = M1 + F
210       LET M2 = M2 + 1
220    GO TO 500
300       LET S1 = S1 + F
310       LET S2 = S2 + 1
320    GO TO 500
400       LET W2 = W2 + 1
500 NEXT J
510 PRINT "TYPE","NUMBER","AMOUNT"
520 PRINT
530 PRINT "MOVING",M2,M1
540 PRINT "STANDING",S2,S1
550 PRINT "WARNING",W2
900 DATA 7
901 DATA 1,50
902 DATA 2,15
903 DATA 2,20
904 DATA 1,75
905 DATA 3,0
906 DATA 2,10
907 DATA 2,15
999 END
```

Comments:

Initialize summers and counters (Lines 100–140)

Moving violations branch (Lines 200–220)

Standing violations branch (Lines 300–320)

Warnings branch (Line 400)

Note how indentation within branches (lines 200, 210, 300, 310, 400) improves their identification.

## Follow-up Exercises

17. Roleplay computer by "executing" this program. Indicate below the values stored successively, where the snapshot of memory is taken at each iteration just before the execution of the NEXT statement.

| J | T | F | M1 | M2 | S1 | S2 | W2 |
|---|---|---|----|----|----|----|----|
|   |   |   |    |    |    |    |    |

Show the exact output that gets printed.
Did you notice the purposeful numbering of lines in the program? Why did we number lines this way?

18. Construct an ON/GO TO statement for each situation below:
   a. If faculty code (F) is 1 through 4, then transfer control to lines 100, 150, 200, 250, respectively.
   b. If code (C) is 1 or 2, transfer to line 100; if code is 3, transfer to 200; and if code is 4, 5, or 6, transfer to 300.
   c. If the code in part a is to reflect 20 possible values (1, 2, . . . , 20), then how many IF/THEN statements would be required to achieve the same effect as one ON/GO TO statement?

19. Based on the results of the ON/GO TO statement, what line number would be executed next?
   a. 10 READ A,B
      20 DATA 5,2
      30 ON A-B GO TO 40, 50, 10
      40 . . .
         :
         :
      50 . . .
         :
         :
   b. Change line 20 to DATA 5,3
   c. Change line 20 to DATA 5,4
   d. Change line 20 to DATA 5,5
   e. Change line 20 to DATA 5,1

## 6.5
## STOP STATEMENT

The STOP statement terminates the logical processing of a program at any point in the program. The general form is

```
line no.   STOP
```

Any number of STOP statements can be used in a program, and they can appear anywhere before the END statement.

One major use of the STOP statement is in conjunction with **error routines.** Most commercial programs include logic which tests for errors in the read/input data. If an error is detected, then the program branches to an error routine that specifies appropriate action. For instance, in the traffic court program, the only valid values for type of ticket are 1, 2, or 3. If any other number is typed, then an error exists in the data. In this case, an error routine might first print an error message that identifies the incorrect item of data and then stop execution.

---

### EXAMPLE 6.5   Traffic Court Fines With Error Routine

We now revise the program of Example 6.4 to include a routine that checks for errors in the read in of the violation code T. New statements associated with error detection and the error routine are enclosed in boxes.

```
100 LET M1 = 0
110 LET M2 = 0
120 LET S1 = 0
130 LET S2 = 0
140 LET W2 = 0
150 READ N
160 FOR J = 1 TO N
170     READ T,F
174     IF T < 1 THEN 450
176     IF T > 3 THEN 450
180     ON T GO TO 200,300,400
200         LET M1 = M1 + F
210         LET M2 = M2 + 1
220     GO TO 500
300         LET S1 = S1 + F
310         LET S2 = S2 + 1
320     GO TO 500
400         LET W2 = W2 + 1
410     GO TO 500
450         LET L = 900 + J
460         PRINT "DATA ERROR IN LINE";L;"T=";T
470         STOP
500 NEXT J
510 PRINT "TYPE","NUMBER","AMOUNT"
520 PRINT
530 PRINT "MOVING",M2,M1
540 PRINT "STANDING",S2,S1
550 PRINT "WARNING",W2
```

```
900 DATA 7
901 DATA 1,50
902 DATA 4,15
903 DATA 2,20
904 DATA 1,75
905 DATA 3,0
906 DATA 2,10
907 DATA 2,15
999 END
```

### Follow-up Exercises

**20.** Explain how this error routine works. Specifically,
   a. How does control get transferred to the program sequence beginning with line 450?
   b. What does L represent?
   c. What gets printed when this program detects an error? Do you see an error in the data?
   d. What happens after the error message is printed?
   e. Why must the data be arranged as shown, rather than by placing all of the data on one data line?

**21.** Modify the flowchart in Figure 6.5 to incorporate the error routine in Example 6.5.

**\*\* 22.** Design the error routine such that after an error message is printed, execution continues to the next read in of data rather than terminating. When the loop is exhausted, the report is printed as usual. Also, modify the code-check logic such that if the code T is out of range, then it gets set to a value of 4. Now the error routine is entered through a fourth branch in the ON/GO TO statement. What is the advantage of this approach? Draw the revised flowchart before setting down code.

**\*\* 23.** In the preceding exercise, normal output would be printed even if the data contained errors. In some situations it would be undesirable to do so, as when large volumes of incomplete results get printed. Modify the program in Exercise 22 so that the output report is not printed if any errors have been detected. *Hint:* Set up a variable, called a *flag,* which is initially assigned a value of 1, meaning "It's OK to print the report." If an error is detected, then set the flag to 2, meaning "Do not print the report." Draw the revised flowchart before setting down code.

## 6.6
## INTERACTIVE PRICE QUOTATION PROGRAM

The vice-president of marketing for Mopups, a fast-selling motorized bike which gets 155 miles per gallon, has determined a new rate schedule for shipments to dealers.

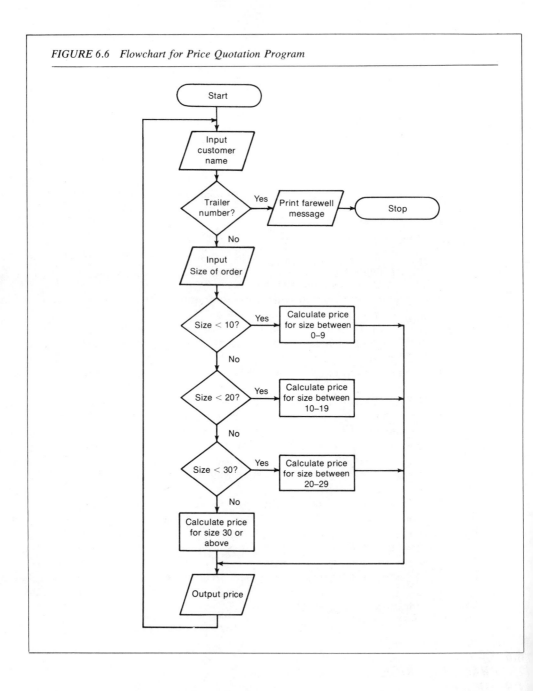

*FIGURE 6.6   Flowchart for Price Quotation Program*

To illustrate, an order for 15 Mopups would cost a total of $3690, or $2250 for the first nine Mopups at $250 each plus $1440 for the remaining six Mopups at $240 each.

| SIZE OF ORDER | MARGINAL PRICE PER BIKE |
|---|---|
| 9 or less | $250 |
| 10–19 | 240 |
| 20–29 | 225 |
| 30 or more | 205 |

The VP heard recently through the company "grapevine" that a recent college graduate is a "hotshot" programmer. With little effort, VP found Hotshot under a deck of spilled cards and wasted no time in assigning Hotshot the task of developing an interactive program that quotes the price to charge a dealer for a shipment of Mopups. Within an hour, Hotshot returned with the results shown below.

### Step I. Analysis
1. *Problem statement*

   Develop an interactive price quotation system that determines the total price to charge a dealer for a shipment of Mopups based on the size of the order.
2. *Data input*

   a.  Name of customer (N$)

   b.  Size of order (S)
3. *Data output*

   Total price (T) to charge for each order.
4. *Algorithm*

   Based on rate schedule.

### Step II. Flowchart
See Figure 6.6.

### Step III. Code

```
100 REM     INTERACTIVE PRICE QUOTATION SYSTEM    250    IF S<20 THEN 310
110 REM                                           260    IF S<30 THEN 330
120 REM     KEY:                                  270    LET T = 205*(S-29) + 6900
130 REM        N$ = CUSTOMER NAME                 280    GO TO 340
140 REM        S = SIZE OF ORDER                  290    LET T = 250*S
150 REM        T = TOTAL PRICE OF ORDER           300    GO TO 340
160 REM                                           310    LET T = 240*(S-9) + 2250
170 PRINT "---------------------------------- "   320    GO TO 340
180    PRINT                                       330    LET T = 225*(S-19) + 4650
190    PRINT "CUSTOMER NAME";                      340    PRINT
200    INPUT N$                                    350    PRINT "PRICE:   $";T
210    IF N$="EOD" THEN 900                        360    PRINT
220    PRINT "SIZE OF ORDER";                      370 GO TO 170
230    INPUT S                                     900 PRINT
240    IF S<10 THEN 290                            910 PRINT "ANOTHER DAY, ANOTHER DOLLAR"
                                                   999 END
```

### Step IV.  Debugging

```
----------------------------------------------

        CUSTOMER NAME?RENT-A-BIKE
        SIZE OF ORDER?25

        PRICE:   $ 6000

---------------------------------------------

        CUSTOMER NAME?BIKE-A-GO-GO
        SIZE OF ORDER?12

        PRICE:   $ 2970

---------------------------------------------

        CUSTOMER NAME?FEET LAST
        SIZE OF ORDER?29

        PRICE:   $ 6900

---------------------------------------------

        CUSTOMER NAME?IBM
        SIZE OF ORDER?55

        PRICE:   $ 12230

---------------------------------------------

        CUSTOMER NAME?MOM & POP
        SIZE OF ORDER?6

        PRICE:   $ 1500

---------------------------------------------

        CUSTOMER NAME?EOD

        ANOTHER DAY, ANOTHER DOLLAR

        TIME 0.03 SECS.
```

*Note 1:* Did you notice that the test for a last record check is done by entering the string constant EOD (end of data) as the customer name? The customer name (N$) is immediately compared with the string constant EOD. When EOD is stored in the variable N$, the program branches to a farewell message and terminates the run; otherwise, customer processing continues.

*Note 2:* You should carefully relate the logic in the flowchart to the logic in the program. In particular, pay close attention to the method of branching which guarantees one and only one price calculation for each dealer. Also, notice how we branch to the PRINT statement following each T calculation.

*Note 3:* To make sure you understand the calculation of T for each category, you should "handcrank" the test data through the program: that is, you should roleplay the computer by "processing" the program using the test input data. In doing so, make sure you confirm the constants (2250, 4650, 6900) used in the LET statements. (See Exercise 24.)

## Follow-up Exercises

**24.** Illustrate how we determined the constants 2250, 4650, and 6900 in lines 310, 330, and 270. Validate the program by roleplaying the computer for our input data in the illustration.

**25.** A common error associated with this type of logic is the omission of the statement GO TO 340 in lines 280, 300, and 320. What output would such an error produce?

**26.** Place a counter in the loop to assign a number to each quotation (or each time we loop). Number quotations consecutively as 1, 2, 3, . . . . . For example, the illustrated run has a total of five quotations, numbered 1, 2, 3, 4, 5. Print the quotation number in column 32 on the same line as the price.

**\*27.** Modify the program so that the overall total (T1) and average price per order (A) are calculated and printed for *all* dealers; that is find the sum and average of T. Determine their values for the test data. For the illustrated run, ending output should appear as follows:

```
CUSTOMER NAME? EOD
ANOTHER DAY, ANOTHER DOLLAR
TOTAL VALUE OF ALL QUOTATIONS:   $ 29600
AVERAGE VALUE PER QUOTATION:     $ 5920
```

**\*\*28.** Modify the program as follows:

a. Use READ/DATA statements to read in the rate schedule. Use the variables L1, L2, and L3 to store the class limits 9, 19, and 29; use M1, M2, M3, and M4 to store the marginal prices 250, 240, 225, and 205.

b. Based strictly on L1, L2, L3, M1, M2, and M3, calculate the values 2250, 4650, and 6900 and store these in C1, C2, and C3, respectively.

c. Modify lines 240, 250, 260, 270, 290, 310, and 330 such that all numeric constants are eliminated in favor of the variables, L1, L2, L3, M1, M2, M3, M4, C1, C2, and C3.

Explain why this version of the program would be desirable in a setting where the rate schedule is likely to change often.

## 6.7
## COMMON ERRORS

The variety of topics in this chapter promotes fertile ground for errors. If you look out for the following common errors, you will be a happier programmer.

*1.   Improper nesting.*   Watch out for this type of crossover:

```
10  FOR I = 1 TO M
20  FOR J = 1 TO N
        .
        .
80  NEXT I
90  NEXT J
```

Lines 80 and 90 must be switched to avoid syntax error. Proper indentation of the inner loop would tend to avoid this error.

*2.   Improper nesting.*   Avoid use of the same index within nested loops; otherwise, you get a syntax error.

```
10  FOR X = A TO B
20     FOR (X) = B TO C
            .
            .
80     NEXT (X)
90  NEXT X
```

Either change this index or change the other.

*3.   Unnecessary Processing.*   When designing an LRC loop, beginning programmers often place the IF/THEN test at the end of the loop rather than immediately after the READ or INPUT statement at the beginning of the loop. Thus, the loop is processed unnecessarily one additional time. Although this does not provoke a syntax or execution error, it does promote programming inefficiency.

*4.   Infinite Loop.*   In designing the IF/THEN test for a DO UNTIL loop, take care that the condition tests true sometime during the processing of the loop. If the condition were to always test false, then you have committed a logic error called an *infinite loop*. In this case, the body of the loop continues to be processed until you stop execution by hitting the "break" key on the terminal. *A common cause of infinite loops is the use of the relational operator = in the IF/THEN test.* If the test is based on a computational result, then the resulting value may never *exactly* equal the test value. To illustrate what we mean, answer Exercise 6 on page 156.

*5.   Code value outside ON/GO TO range.*   Make sure the value of your code variable is always within the range given by 1, 2, . . . , number of line numbers in ON/GO TO statement.

```
180  ON (T) GO TO 200,300,400
200  ...
       .
```

If T is less than 1 or greater than 3, then we get either execution error or default to line 200, depending on system.

To be safe, a range test should precede an ON/GO TO statement, as in Example 6.5.

6.  *Missing GO TO statement within logical branch.*   An ON/GO TO statement transfers control to one of several logical branches. The GO TO statement usually needs to
be inserted between each branch in order to avoid the inadvertent execution of statements in other branches. For example, a common error in the program of Example 6.4
on page 162 would be the following:

```
180    ON T GO TO 200,300,400
200    LET M1 = M1 + F
210    LET M2 = M2 + 1
300    LET S1 = S1 + F            ──────> Missing GO TO 500
310    LET S2 = S2 + 1
400    LET W2 = W2 + 1
500 NEXT J
```

7.  *Algorithmic logic errors.*   Now that you are designing more complicated algorithms,
you need to validate your programs carefully and systematically during the debugging
phase. *The key to this procedure is the deliberate selection of test data.* Always select test
read/input data that validates each logical segment or branch in your program. For
example, the data in the price quotation run on page 168 were selected to test each
branch in the flowchart on page 166. The output from the program was then checked
against a set of hand-calculated results.

Where appropriate, "extreme" data values should be selected to test potential
problems. For example, select a data item that might cause division by 0 and check the
computer's reaction. If the result is unwanted, then you must program an error routine.
This was the reasoning behind the error routine in Example 6.5 on page 164. A common
cause of this type of error is incorrect input/read data, as when mistakes are made
keying in data.

The test data we give in exercises at the end of chapters are generally designed to
aid you in debugging. You should always check the data for thoroughness, however, and
add your own when warranted. To complete the validation, confirm the correctness of
computer output by parallel hand calculations.

In general, you should program "defensively" by testing all parts of your program
and by training yourself to anticipate potential errors which can be overcome by good
program design.

### Additional Exercises

**29.**   Define or explain the following:

| | |
|---|---|
| nested loops | LRC loop |
| DO UNTIL loop | trailer number |
| body of loop | ON/GO TO statement |
| counter | STOP statement |
| last-record-check loop | error routine |

**30. Revised Tuition Revenue Problem.** Change the program and flowchart of Exercise 35 in Chapter 4 (page 101) as follows:

a.  Design a FOR/NEXT loop that varies cost per credit (C) from C1 to C2 in steps of C3. This loop outputs a table of four columns: cost per credit, average bill, expected enrollment, and expected revenue. Just prior to this table, print the name of the college, the fee, and average number of credits. As before, fee, average number of credits, name of college, D1, and D2 are read in from one data line prior to this loop. C1, C2, and C3, however, are to be input interactively.

   Run this program by varying C from $50 to $80 in steps of $2. As before, use $250 for fee, 15 for average number of credits, 14000 for D1, and 100 for D2.

b.  Immediately after the table gets printed, print the maximum revenue and its corresponding cost per credit.

c.  After the table gets printed ask the user, "Do you wish to print another table for the same college using different costs per credit?" If the user responds "yes," then loop back to the input of C1, C2, and C3 and print a new table. Thus, this part adds a second loop that is outer to the first loop. Its function is to better "zero-in" on the cost per credit that maximizes revenue.

d.  Add a third loop that is outer to the other two so as to process N colleges. Run the following test data through your program.

| Name | Fee | Average No. of Credits | D1 | D2 |
|---|---|---|---|---|
| Test 1 | 250 | 15 | 14000 | 100 |
| Test 2 | 250 | 15 | 14000 | 25 |
| Test 3 | 500 | 13.5 | 30000 | 25 |

What tuition (cost per credit) should be charged at each college in order to maximize revenue? Would you say there's a flaw in the algorithmic logic if students freely change colleges within the system based on tuition?

**31. Retirement Contribution.** Change the program and flowchart of Exercise 36 in Chapter 4 (page 102) as follows:

a.  Design a FOR/NEXT loop that varies S from S1 to S2 in steps of S3. This loop outputs a table of two columns: retirement sum and biweekly contribution. Just prior to this table, print the name of the employee and years to retirement. As before, the value of R (0.07) is to be input interactively. Data lines should include name of the employee, Y, S1, S2, and S3. Run this program by varying S from $20,000 to $60,000 in steps of $5000. Assume this run is for Tahiti Joe, who has 30 years left to retirement.

b.  Add an outer FOR/NEXT loop that processes N employees. Run the following test data through the program:

| Name | Y | S1 | S2 | S3 |
|------|---|-----|-----|-----|
| Tahiti Joe | 30 | $ 20,000 | $ 60,000 | $ 5,000 |
| Jet-Set Sal | 40 | 100,000 | 300,000 | 50,000 |
| Too-Late Leroy | 5 | 5,000 | 15,000 | 1,000 |

Comment on the effects of Y and S on C.

c. Add a third FOR/NEXT loop outer to the other two. This loop processes different values of R, from R1 to R2 in steps of R3. Input the values 0.06, 0.08, and 0.01 for R1, R2, and R3, respectively. Comment on the effects of R.

**32. Bank Drive-In Queuing.** Change the program and flowchart of Exercise 37 in Chapter 4 (page 102) as follows:

a. Design a FOR/NEXT loop that varies C from C1 to C2 in steps of C3. This loop outputs the table that is illustrated in the original exercise. Now, the data line for a branch bank contains the name of the bank, A, S, C1, C2, and C3. Run this program using 0.9 for A, 0.4 for S, 3 for C1, 9 for C2, and 1 for C3.

b. Add a second FOR/NEXT loop that processes M branch banks. Run the following test data through your program:

| Name of Branch | A | S | C1 | C2 | C3 |
|----------------|-----|-----|-----|-----|-----|
| Test 1 | 0.9 | 0.4 | 3 | 9 | 1 |
| Test 2 | 1.1 | 0.4 | 3 | 9 | 1 |
| Test 3 | 1.1 | 0.3 | 4 | 12 | 1 |

Comment on the effects of A, S, and C on operating characteristics.

**c. In the queuing system described previously, each drive-in window had its own queue. An alternative design is to have a *single* queue feed into all tellers. In this case, the following formulas apply (don't panic):

$$ I = \cfrac{1}{1 + \left( \sum_{J=1}^{C-1} \cfrac{(A/S)^J}{J!} \right) + \cfrac{(A/S)^C}{C! \left( 1 - \cfrac{A}{C \cdot S} \right)}} $$

$$ W = \frac{(A/S)^C \cdot S \cdot C \cdot I}{C!(S \cdot C - A)} $$

$$ N = \frac{I \cdot (A/S)^{C+1}}{(C - 1)!(C - A/S)^2} + \frac{A}{S} $$

$$ Q = N - \frac{A}{S} $$

$$ T1 = \frac{Q}{A} + \frac{1}{S} $$

$$ T2 = \frac{Q}{A} $$

*Note 1:* The summation $\sum_{J=1}^{C-1}$ implies a FOR/NEXT loop whose index $J$ runs from 1 to $C - 1$ in steps of 1. The quantity being summed for each value of $J$ is $(A/S)^J/J!$.

*Note 2:* The term $J!$ is called $J$ *factorial.* This is short form mathematical notation for the product $1 \cdot 2 \cdot 3 \cdots J$. For example, 4! is $1 \cdot 2 \cdot 3 \cdot 4$, or 24. A loop is required to calculate a factorial.

Try to confirm the following by hand calculation and then by computer: If $C = 3$, $A = 0.9$, and $S = 0.4$, then $I = 0.0748$, $W = 0.57$, $N = 3.95$, $Q = 1.70$, $T1 = 4.39$, and $T2 = 1.89$. Design your program such that two tables are now printed for each branch bank: The first table gives operating characteristics for the original $C$-queue system and the second table gives operating characteristics for the 1-queue system with $C$ windows. Based on your output, which design appears more desirable?

33. **Forecasting Population Growth.** Modify the program and flowchart of part a *or* b in Exercise 33 of Chapter 4 (page 100) as follows:

a. Use an LRC loop to output predicted population based on the different sets of data. Select an appropriate trailer number to terminate the loop.

b. Let N be a counter in an "inner" DO UNTIL loop that lies entirely within the "outer" loop in part a. This inner loop increments N by 1, calculates P, and prints N, corresponding year (Y), and P. Initialize N by defining an input or read variable called N1. Exit from the loop when the ratio of predicted population (P) to current population (C) exceeds a desired ratio (R). Run the program for the following three sets of values:

| C | Base Year | B | D | N1 | R |
|---|---|---|---|---|---|
| 4 | 1976 | 0.025 | 0.009 | 10 | 2 |
| 4 | 1976 | 0.025 | 0.009 | 25 | 3 |
| 4 | 1976 | 0.020 | 0.009 | 30 | 3 |

For example, your output for the first run should look like this:

| | YEARS INTO FUTURE | CORRESPONDING YEAR | PREDICTED POPULATION |
|---|---|---|---|
| | 10 | 1986 | 4.688 |
| | 11 | 1987 | 4.763 |
| 35 rows | ⋮ | ⋮ | ⋮ |
| | 43 | 2019 | 7.915 |
| | 44 | 2020 | 8.042 |

Note that the counter is initialized by N1 and that this loop terminates when the predicted population *exceeds* (not equals) double (R has a value of 2) the current population. Comment on the number of years it takes the current world population to double and triple relative to changes in the birth rate.

**34. Mailing List.** A professional group of computer specialists is planning a regional meeting in New Orleans. A subgroup of information system specialists within this professional group is having a well-known computer scientist as a guest speaker. The chairperson of this subgroup plans to send meeting notices to members in two regions—southeast (code 3) and southwest (code 5)—who have an interest in information systems (code 15) or computer science (code 18).

a. Design a flowchart and write a program that prepares mailing labels for members of the organization that satisfy the location and area of interest criteria.

The organization maintains the following data on each member:
1. Last name
2. First name
3. Address
4. City
5. State
6. Zip
7. Region code (one digit; there are nine regions overall)
8. Interest code (two digits; there are 20 interest areas overall)

*Sample Data File*

| 1 | 2 | 3 | 4 | 5 | 6 | 7 | 8 |
|---|---|---|---|---|---|---|---|
| Fastcode | Frank | 11 Flower | Dallas | TX | 75215 | 5 | 15 |
| Burden | Kathy | 193 West St | Warwick | RI | 02886 | 1 | 18 |
| Peripheral | Leslie | 18 Grande | Slidell | LA | 70808 | 5 | 20 |
| Crowley | M.I.S | 1 Hope Rd | Atlanta | GA | 30901 | 3 | 15 |
| Deff | Doris | 111 High St | Hartford | CT | 06518 | 7 | 12 |
| Aides | Clyde | 963 Main St | Orlando | FL | 32407 | 3 | 18 |
| Frick | Ford | 2 Rose Way | Boston | MA | 01906 | 9 | 18 |

*Sample Output (The First Mailing Label)*

FRANK FASTCODE
11 FLOWER
DALLAS, TX 75215

b. Include error detection for region and interest codes. If an error is found, then print an appropriate error message and go on to the next member. Add new data with incorrect codes to debug your error logic.

c. Generalize your program so mailing labels can be prepared for any region and/or area of interest criteria. Specifically, design your program to provide the following options:

| Option Code | Criteria |
|---|---|
| 1 | Specific region only |
| 2 | Specific interest area only |
| 3 | Specific region or interest area |
| 4 | Specific region and interest area |

This version is more general than part a, but requires more computer runs to print labels for multiple regions and interest areas. For example, the run in part a requires four separate runs for option 4: region 3 and interest area 15; region 3 and interest area 18; region 5 and interest area 15; region 5 and interest area 18.

35. **Telephone Company Billing.** "Flat rate service" charges for telephone service is a method of billing which includes some fixed amount for the main station (main telephone, switchboard, and so on) plus a variable amount per extension phone in service. Distinctions also are made between residential and business customers according to the table below.

| Customer Type | Code | Type of Service | Monthly Flat Rates ($) | |
|---|---|---|---|---|
| | | | Main Station | Each Extension |
| Residential | 1 | Main phone/extensions | 13 | 3 |
| Business | 2 | Main phone/extensions | 50 | 10 |
| Business | 3 | PBX/extensions | 150 | 5 |
| Business | 4 | Centrex/extensions | 500 | 3 |

Public branch exchange (PBX) service uses a switchboard for the main station, off of which extensions can be wired. Centrex service is for large-scale business firms and governmental agencies which require such a large number of extensions that the telephone switching equipment is located on the customer's premises.

In actual practice, PBX and Centrex include many special features. For example, options include fully automatic equipment versus partly manual equipment, facilities for data transmission, private lines which ring at specific locations when the receiver is picked up (PLs), facilities for foreign exchange (FX), and many others.

To illustrate a calculation, consider a business customer with PBX equipment and 50 extensions. In this case, the monthly flat rate is $400 (or $150 + 50 × 5) which, of course, excludes long distance charges, taxes, and charges due to special features.

a. Prepare a flowchart and write a program that calculates flat rate service charges and outputs customer name, phone number, and charge. Test your program with the following data:

| Customer<br>Name | Customer Phone<br>Number | Code | Number of<br>Extensions |
|---|---|---|---|
| Test 1 | 783-5123 | 2 | 5 |
| Test 2 | 792-7541 | 4 | 400 |
| Test 3 | 445-8162 | 4 | 550 |
| Test 4 | 612-6148 | 3 | 75 |
| Test 5 | 783-1235 | 1 | 0 |
| Test 6 | 445-2164 | 1 | 3 |
| Test 7 | 789-5849 | 2 | 7 |
| Test 8 | 789-7812 | 4 | 730 |
| Test 9 | 792-2674 | 1 | 1 |
| Test 10 | 615-6513 | 3 | 50 |

Terminate customer read in when ∗∗∗ is encountered for customer name.
b.  Modify the program in part a to include the calculation and output of the following:
1.  Total number of customers by code category
2.  Percent number of customers by code category
3.  Total charges by code category
4.  Overall total charges
Try to design your output for easy readability.
c.  Include error detection for code. If an error is found, then print an appropriate error message and go on to the next customer. Do not include that customer's data in the output of parts a or b. Add new data with incorrect codes to debug your error logic.

36. **Aging Customer Accounts.** Aging of customer accounts requires that the date of the sale be compared with the current date; the difference between these dates is the age of the account. For example, assume the current date is July 1 (182nd day) and a sale was made on February 16 (47th day); then the transaction is 136 days old (183 − 47). Note that 1 must be added to the current date (or 1 must be subtracted from the sale date) in order to compute the correct age.

In the terminology of accounting, this is called *aging accounts receivables.* Reports of this type serve a useful purpose in assessing the collection practices and assets of a company.

Output for the report should conform to the following:

AGED CUSTOMER ACCOUNTS

| | DOLLAR<br>AMOUNTS | NUMBER OF<br>CUSTOMERS |
|---|---|---|
| O V E R  6 0  DAYS OLD | xxxxx.xx | xxx |
| B E T W E E N  30 − 60 DAYS OLD | xxxxx.xx | xxx |
| U N D E R  3 0 DAYS OLD | xxxxx.xx | xxx |
| TOTALS | xxxxxx.xx | xxxx |

The data for your program include
1.  Current date (entered as a three-digit number)
2.  Customer file consisting of date of sale (entered as a three-digit number—for example, February 16 would be entered as 47, while December 26 would be 360) and amount of sale.
a.  Prepare a flowchart and write a program that produces the report described above. Process the data given below. Check the output from your program after aging the accounts by hand. Current date: July 1. End your loop by using an appropriate trailer number.

| Sale Date | Amount of Sale ($) |
|---|---|
| January 10 | 310.52 |
| February 20 | 168.40 |
| March 24 | 278.29 |
| April 21 | 125.10 |
| May 5 | 25.13 |
| May 17 | 64.79 |
| June 3 | 37.05 |
| June 13 | 105.15 |
| June 27 | 75.98 |
| June 30 | 44.15 |
| (Assume 28 days in February) | |

b.  Add a new column to the report next to "Number of Customers" which reads "Average Dollar Amounts." This column is computed as "Dollar Amounts" divided by corresponding "Number of Customers" in each category.
c.  As part of your data line, include the name and address of the customer. Make up your own names and addresses. Prior to the output of the report on aging accounts receivables, print the name, address, and amount of sale for each customer. (Assume one transaction per customer.)
**d.  Enter your data for current and sale dates as two two-digit numbers, where the first two digits represent the month and the last two digits, the day. For example, April 21 would be entered as 4 (fourth month) and 21 (21st day). Then, design the logic of your program such that the elapsed time is computed (111 for April 21).

37. **Sales Forecasts.** Design a flowchart and write a program that calculates and prints sales forecasts by quarters for future years based on current sales and projected annual growth rate. For example, if currently we are at the end of the second quarter in the year 1980 and sales this quarter were $1.2 million with a projected growth rate of 2 percent per quarter, then forecasts through 1982 should appear as follows:

```
**SALES FORECAST FOR OUIJA BOARD**

CURRENT YEAR QUARTER SALES
      1980      2    $1.2 M

YEAR   QUARTER    SALES
------ ---------- ------

1980      3       1.224
1980      4       1.248
1981      1       1.273
1981      2       1.299
1981      3       1.325
1981      4       1.351
1982      1       1.378
1982      2       1.406
1982      3       1.434
1982      4       1.463
```

Note that the next forecast is always the last forecast increased by the growth rate.
a.   Run your program for the following two sets of data:

| Product Name | Current Year | Current Quarter | Current Sales | Growth Rate | Years into Future |
|---|---|---|---|---|---|
| OUIJA BOARD | 1980 | 2 | 1.20 | 0.02 | 2 |
| STAR TREK CHARM | 1981 | 4 | 0.85 | 0.05 | 4 |

Note that the sample output is based on the first set of data.
b.   Design your program so that you have an outer FOR/NEXT loop for processing $N$ product forecasts. In other words, the data given in part a represent two iterations of this loop.
**c.   **Graphical Output.** To the right of each sales forecast, print the asterisk character in a graph format. Do this as follows: Reserve columns 30 through 70 for graphical output. In this case, column 30 really represents 0 on a graph and column 70 represents 40 (that is, there are 40 print columns between 30 and 70). This means that all sales forecasts must be scaled to a range between 0 and 40:

$$\text{Scaled forecast} = \left( \frac{\text{forecast}}{\text{maximum forecast}} \right) \cdot 40$$

For example, the scaled forecast for the fourth quarter in 1981 is (1.351/1.463) · 40, or 36.9. This means that we wish an asterisk printed in column 66 (or 30 + 36) of the print line where 1.351 is printed for sales. Use the TAB function to help you, where the argument in the function is given by the expression (30 + scaled forecast).

38. **Installment Loan.** When a consumer purchases a capital good such as an automobile, stereo, or refrigerator, more often than not credit is arranged in the form of an installment loan. This means that the consumer makes a down payment ($D$) on the purchase price ($P$) and finances (borrows) the rest, with a signed agreement to pay installments (or fixed amounts of money) each month until the loan and interest are paid off. The amount of money which must be paid each month ($A$) is determined from

$$A = \frac{P - D}{F}$$

Note that the amount borrowed is given by $P - D$. The interest factor ($F$) is calculated from

$$F = \frac{1}{(1 + R/12)} + \frac{1}{(1 + R/12)^2} + \frac{1}{(1 + R/12)^3} + \cdots + \frac{1}{(1 + R/12)^N}$$

where $R$ is the annual interest rate and $N$ is the number of months it takes to pay off the loan.[3]

These same formulas, by the way, also are used by banks to determine monthly mortgage payments for homes.

a. Prepare a flowchart and write a program which reads $P$, $D$, $R$, and $N$; calculates $A$; and outputs ($P - D$), $R$, $N$, $A$, and name of item, all with appropriate labels. Process the following data:

| Item | Purchase Price ($) | Down Payment ($) | Annual Interest Rate | Number of Months |
|------|------|------|------|------|
| 1. Debug | 50 | 20 | 12.* | 4 ($A = 32$) |
| 2. Stereo | 3,000 | 300 | 0.18 | 24 ($A = 134.80$) |
| 3. Car | 6,500 | 1,000 | 0.14 | 48 |
| 4. Car | 6,500 | 3,000 | 0.14 | 48 |
| 5. Car | 6,500 | 1,000 | 0.15 | 60 |
| 6. Home | 60,000 | 12,000 | 0.10 | 300 |
| 7. Home | 60,000 | 18,000 | 0.10 | 300 |
| 8. Home | 60,000 | 12,000 | 0.09 | 300 |

*This figure is 1200 percent, not 12 percent. It's unrealistic in actual practice, but serves nicely to debug the program. You should confirm $A = 32$ by hand to make sure you understand the calculations.

[3] Alternatively, the formula used in Section 3.7 on page 67 can be used, after suitable modifications for variable definitions.

Design your program such that the first data item is the number of times you wish to calculate *A* (eight for the above data). Draw conclusions for each of the following comparisons:

Item 3 versus item 4
Item 3 versus item 5
Item 6 versus item 7
Item 6 versus item 8

b. Modify your program to include the calculation and output of the total interest paid over the life of the loan.

**c. Incorporate the option of printing a table as follows, where the sample calculations are based on item 1 in part a.

AMORTIZATION TABLE

| MONTH | BEGINNING BALANCE | INTEREST | PRINCIPAL REPAYMENT | ENDING BALANCE |
|---|---|---|---|---|
| 1 | 30 | 30 | 2 | 28 |
| 2 | 28 | 28 | 4 | 24 |
| 3 | 24 | 24 | 8 | 16 |
| 4 | 16 | 16 | 16 | 0 |

TOTAL INTEREST: 98
RATIO OF TOTAL INTEREST TO LOAN = 3.27

1. The first beginning balance is $P - D$. Subsequent beginning balances are simply the preceding month's ending balance.
2. Interest for any month is calculated as the monthly interest rate times the beginning balance for that month. In the example, the annual interest rate is 12 (1200 percent), which must be divided by 12 to convert to a monthly interest rate. The interest in month 1, therefore, is $(1.) \cdot (30.00)$, or $30.00; in month 2, it is $(1.) \cdot (28.00)$, or $28.00.
3. Principal repayment for any month is the monthly installment less the interest for that month. Thus, the principal repayment in month 3 is $32.00 - 24.00$, or $8.
4. The ending balance is the beginning balance less the principal repayment. For month 3, it is $24.00 - 8.00$, or $16.00.

Note that the ending balance should be exactly 0, except perhaps for rounding error. Also note that this table is an option in the program; that is, *it should not be printed automatically for each item*. In your computer run, print this table for items 1, 2 and 4.

**39. Checking Account Report.** Prepare a flowchart and write a program which produces a monthly checking account report for each customer. Checking charges are calculated on the basis of the following information:

1. If the ending balance is less than $200, then the following service charges are assessed: a monthly fee of 80 cents plus a charge of 10 cents per honored check (withdrawal). No charges are assessed for deposits.

2. If the ending balance is $200 or more, then no service charges are assessed.
3. If a check "bounces" (that is, if the balance were to become negative when the bank attempts to honor a check), then a charge of $5.00 is assessed, and the current balance is reduced by this amount. This charge is made for each check that bounces. Checks that bounce are not honored. In other words, a withdrawal is not made from the account, since the person to whom the check was made out does not get paid. Also the $200 limit does not apply to this bounce charge; that is, if a check bounces, then the $5.00 charge is assessed regardless of the ending balance.

For each bank customer

1. The first line of data contains four items:
   Item 1. The bank account number[4]
   Item 2. Name
   Item 3. Number of transactions ($N$), or total number of withdrawals and deposits
   Item 4. Beginning balance
2. $N$ lines follow the first line, each line representing a single transaction. If the value is negative, the transaction is a withdrawal; if the value is positive, the transaction is a deposit.

*Sample Input*

```
614275,"WENDY BRANDON",3,741.62
50.75
-125
-260.50
216422,"RICHARD R. WEEKS",4,250.15
-115
-80.75
100
-236.80
-99," ",0,0
```

*Sample Output*

BANK STATEMENT

| | | |
|---|---|---|
| WENDY BRANDON | 614275 | |
| BEGINNING BALANCE | 741.62 | |
| TOTAL DEPOSITS | 50.75 | 11 lines |
| TOTAL WITHDRAWALS | 385.50 | |
| CHARGES | 0 | |
| ENDING BALANCE | 406.87 | |

----

[4] If the bank account number is −99, there are no more customer transactions to be processed.

⎫
⎬  6 blank lines and
⎭  the next bank statement

                    BANK  STATEMENT       ⎫
                                          |
    RICHARD  R.  WEEKS          216422    |
                                          |
    BEGINNING  BALANCE         250.15     |
                                          |
    TOTAL  DEPOSITS            100.00     |
    TOTAL  WITHDRAWALS         195.75     ⎬  15 lines
    CHARGES                    6          |
                                          |
    ENDING  BALANCE            148.40     |
                                          |
    **TOTAL  NOT  HONORED**               |
                                          |
              236.80                      ⎭

⎫
⎬  2 blank lines and
⎭  the next bank statement

Debug your program using the above data and the following additional data:

| Account Number | Name | N | Beginning Balance | Trans-actions |
|---|---|---|---|---|
| make these up . . . |  | 4 | 240.00 | −50.00 |
|  |  |  |  | −35.00 |
|  |  |  |  | −175.00 |
|  |  |  |  | +200.00 |
| make these up . . . |  | 7 | 450.00 | −300.00 |
|  |  |  |  | −125.00 |
|  |  |  |  | +200.00 |
|  |  |  |  | −75.00 |
|  |  |  |  | −35.00 |
|  |  |  |  | +150.00 |
|  |  |  |  | −66.00 |

Before designing your program, make sure you understand the logic by solving these problems by hand. Note that each bank statement takes up exactly 17 lines of output in order to conform to a standardized form. By the way, this is a good program to use diagnostic PRINT statements (traces) for current balance and charges during the debugging phase.

**40. Crew Selection—A Combination Problem.** An oceanographic food firm is planning extensive underwater experiments in aquaculture (sea farming). These experiments require people to live together in an isolated underwater environment for extended periods of time. To avoid problems associated with incompatibility, the firm has decided to run isolation tests for the purpose of judging compatibility. These tests require individuals to live together for two weeks under monitored conditions in an above-ground capsule which is cut off from the outside world.

As an example, suppose that four people are available for the experiments, but only two are required to live together underwater. How many subgroups of two persons are possible from among four? If we let *P1* represent the first person, *P2* the second person, and so on, then we have the following six distinct subgroups of two persons each: (*P1, P2*), (*P1, P3*), (*P1, P4*), (*P2, P3*), (*P2, P4*), (*P3, P4*). Right? This means that six separate isolation tests would have to be conducted in the capsule so as to select the most compatible two persons.

This approach of listing groups works fine when we are dealing with small numbers, but becomes impractical when the numbers get large. For instance, if 10 people are available and we need four for the experiments, then we have 210 distinct groups of four each. If you have had a course in statistics, then most likely you realized that this is a so-called combination problem.

Given that *n* people are available and *k* are needed, then the number of combinations of *n* taken *k* at a time is given by the formula

$$C = \frac{(n)\cdot(n-1)\cdot(n-2)\cdots(2)\cdot(1)}{[(n-k)\cdot(n-k-1)\cdots(2)\cdot(1)]\cdot[(k)\cdot(k-1)\cdots(2)\cdot(1)]}$$

For the first example above, $n = 4$ and $k = 2$, so that

$$C = \frac{4\cdot3\cdot2\cdot1}{(2\cdot1)\cdot(2\cdot1)} = 6$$

For the second example, $n = 10$ and $k = 4$, so that

$$C = \frac{10\cdot9\cdot8\cdot7\cdot6\cdot5\cdot4\cdot3\cdot2\cdot1}{(6\cdot5\cdot4\cdot3\cdot2\cdot1)\cdot(4\cdot3\cdot2\cdot1)} = 210$$

a.  Prepare a flowchart and write an interactive program which calculates *C* given *n* and *k*. Output should include *C* and the total number of days required for all isolation experiments given that each experiment takes 14 days. Run the following data through your program:

| n | k |
|---|---|
| 6 | 2 |
| 10 | 4 |
| 10 | 6 |
| 10 | 10 |
| 20 | 4 |
| 40 | 4 |
| 40 | 6 |
| 60 | 6 |

Design your program such that the above data are processed by either an LRC loop or a FOR/NEXT loop.

**b. Did you have numeric overflow when $n = 60$ and $k = 6$? Certain efficiencies can be realized in the calculation of $C$ by dividing terms in the numerator by terms in the denominator. For example, for $n = 60$ and $k = 6$, we can write

$$C = \frac{60 \cdot 59 \cdot 58 \cdot 57 \cdot 56 \cdot 55}{6 \cdot 5 \cdot 4 \cdot 3 \cdot 2 \cdot 1}.$$

Design your program to take advantage of this efficiency.

**41. Bracket Search Algorithm.** Read once more Section 4.6 on page 91. Suppose that we are given $A$, $P$, and $N$ in

$$A = P \cdot (1 + R)^N$$

and we wish to solve for the interest rate $R$. One way to go about this is to divide both sides by $P$, take the $N$th root, and solve for $R$. This algebraic approach gives

$$R = \left(\frac{A}{P}\right)^{1/N} - 1$$

Another approach is to solve for $R$ by trial and error. That is, select a test value for $R$ and calculate a trial value for $A$. If the trial value for $A$ is less than the actual value for $A$, then the trial value for $R$ must be increased by some increment. If trial $A$ is greater than actual $A$, however, then trial $R$ must be reduced by the increment. Each time we "bracket" the actual value of $A$, then the increment can be made smaller, and the procedure can be repeated until the desired degree of accuracy is achieved. The following set of calculations illustrates this bracket search algorithm for $A = 1500$, $P = 1000$, and $N = 4$:

| Trial R | Trial A | Increment in R | Comment |
|---------|---------|----------------|---------|
| 0.2 | 2074 | 0.1 | Reduce trial $R$, since $2074 > 1500$. |
| 0.1 | 1464 | 0.01 | Actual $A$ has been bracketed, since $1464 < 1500$. Increment changed by factor of 10, and trial $R$ is increased. We now know that actual $R$ is between 0.1 and 0.2. |
| 0.11 | 1518 | 0.001 | Again actual $A$ bracketed. Actual $R$ between 0.10 and 0.11. |
| 0.109 | 1513 | 0.001 | Reduce trial $R$. |
| 0.108 | 1507 | 0.001 | Reduce trial $R$. |
| 0.107 | 1502 | 0.001 | Reduce trial $R$. |
| 0.106 | 1496 | | Actual $R$ between 0.106 and 0.107. |

In this case, the algebraic approach gives 0.1066819197. Prepare a flowchart (very important!) and write a program which solves for $R$ by this trial-and-error method. To check the result, have the program output the algebraic solution as well. Process the following data:

| A | P | N |
|---|---|---|
| 1500 | 1000 | 4 |
| 3000 | 1000 | 10 |
| 3000 | 1000 | 20 |
| 100000 | 20000 | 20 |

In each case, terminate the algorithm when the increment in $R$ drops below 0.00001.

# One-Dimensional Arrays

Most programs you've written or studied up to this point had this structure:

1. Read in or input a set of data.
2. Process the data.
3. Print the results.
4. Return to step 1 if more data are available.

In some problems you may want to store all data before you begin any computations. This was not possible in many earlier programs because storing a new set of data automatically erased the values stored from the previous set, thus preventing access to the stored data of the previous set, that is, unless you reentered or restored the data.

## 7.1
## MOTIVATION

An **array** is a group of consecutive memory locations that have the same name. The use of arrays

1.   Permits access to any data item that has been stored previously.
2.   Provides simple yet powerful capabilities to name and manipulate a large number of storage locations.

To help you visualize this concept, the illustration below shows three storage locations for an array named D:

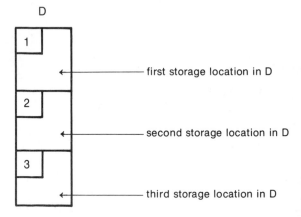

Just how we specify and manipulate arrays will become clear in the next two sections. First, however, we motivate their use through the following example.

---

### EXAMPLE 7.1   Analysis of Bank Deposits

The vice-president of marketing for a small branch bank wants to compare the percent of deposits that each branch contributes to the bank's total deposits. The number of deposits for each of the three branches is given below.

| Bank | Number of Deposits |
| --- | --- |
| 1 | 3500 |
| 2 | 5000 |
| 3 | 4000 |

Let's first try and solve this problem using the approach used in prior chapters. A program such as the following might be written.

| Program | Comments |
|---|---|
| 005 LET T = 0 | Initialize total deposits (T) to zero |
| 010 FOR I = 1 TO 3 | |
| 020   READ D | Read in a branch's deposits (D) |
| 030   LET T = T + D | Accumulate total deposits |
| 040 NEXT I | |
| 050 RESTORE | Reset pointer to beginning of data block |
| 060 FOR I = 1 TO 3 | |
| 070   READ D | |
| 080   LET P = D/T*100 | Compute percent (P) |
| 090   PRINT D,P | |
| 100 NEXT I | |
| 110 DATA 3500,5000,4000 | |
| 120 END | |

In the first loop (lines 10–40), the three data items are read in and total deposits (T) are accumulated for the bank. Next, the RESTORE statement moves the data block pointer back to the first data item so that we can reenter the data by consecutively executing the READ statement in line 70. In the second loop (lines 60–100), each of the three iterations reads in the number of deposits for a bank, calculates its percentage, and prints the number of deposits and the corresponding percentage, as follows:

```
3500     28
5000     40
4000     32
```

This approach works, but it is inefficient since the reading of data is a time-consuming machine task, and this version reads the same set of data twice.
   Now consider the following approach.

```
010 READ D1,D2,D3
020 LET T = D1 + D2 + D3
030 LET P = D1/T*100
040 PRINT D1,P
050 LET P = D2/T*100
060 PRINT D2,P
070 LET P = D3/T*100
080 PRINT D3,P
090 DATA 3500,5000,4000
100 END
```

This program gives output identical to the first program, but it is very rigid and inefficient. It works for three branches, but if you wish to add a fourth branch, the program would have to be rewritten. Worse yet, visualize this program written for the hundreds of Chase Manhattan branch banks in New York City. What a long and tedious program it would be for such a simple problem!
   A simpler solution to this problem is to use an array, as follows:

```
010  DIM D(3)
015  LET T = 0
020  FOR I = 1 TO 3
030     READ D(I)
035     LET T = T + D(I)
040  NEXT I
060  FOR I = 1 TO 3
065     LET P = D(I)/T*100
070     PRINT D(I),P
080  NEXT I
100  DATA 3500,5000,4000
110  END
```

In this program the first loop reads the number of deposits for each branch bank, storing them in an array called D and accumulates the total deposits for all branches in T. The second loop references each element in the array, divides the number of deposits for each branch by the total deposits, multiplies the fraction by 100 to give a percentage, and prints the number of deposits and the relative percent of total deposits for each branch bank. At this point, don't worry about the exact nature of the array or about the DIM statement. We discuss these topics next.

## 7.2
## SUBSCRIPTS

When programming with arrays, a number of unique memory locations "belong" to the same variable name; each memory location in the array is referred to as an **array element,** which can be referenced by its relative position in the array through the use of a subscript.

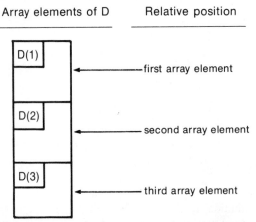

A **subscript** acts as an index or pointer to locate a specific array element. In BASIC, subscripts are written within parentheses following the array name. For example, the illustration below identifies the first array element in our sample program.[1]

---

[1] Some versions of BASIC allow a subscript of zero to identify the first array element.

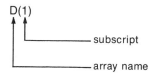

D(1)

subscript

array name

When each array element is referenced by only one subscript, the array is called a **one-dimensional array.**

The elements of an array are also called **subscripted variables,** since each element in the array is identified by a variable name followed by a subscript enclosed in parentheses. In most versions of BASIC, an array which is to store *numeric* values is named by a single alphabetic character. An *alphanumeric* or *string* array stores character strings and is named by a letter followed by a dollar sign. Each string array element commonly stores from 15 to 256 string characters, depending on the system.

The use of subscripted variables in BASIC gives the language great ease and flexibility in naming and manipulating a large number of *related* values. This feature is "borrowed" from algebra, as the following illustrates:

| Stock Number | Price of Stock ($) | Subscripted Variables in Algebra | Subscripted Variables in BASIC |
|---|---|---|---|
| 1 | 75 | $x_1$ | X(1) |
| 2 | 42 | $x_2$ | X(2) |
| 3 | 24 | $x_3$ | X(3) |
| . | . | . | . |
| . | . | . | . |
| . | . | . | . |
| 500 | 105 | $x_{500}$ | X(500) |

For example, if we are dealing with a series of 500 numbers, where each number represents the price of a stock at the end of a given day on the New York Stock Exchange, then the algebraic notation $x_3$ refers to the price of the third stock and $x_{75}$ refers to the price of the seventy-fifth stock. Similarly, in BASIC, X(3) refers to the storage location for the price of the third stock and X(75) identifies the storage location for the price of the seventy-fifth stock. Naming and manipulating this many related variables would be quite tedious and impractical without the use of subscripts. For example, you wouldn't recommend a scheme such as A, B, C, . . . , A0, B0, C0, . . . , A1, B1, C1, . . . , to name 500 variables, would you? These names are cumbersome, are difficult to manipulate, cause inefficient coding, and do not in themselves suggest contextual meaning. As you will see, the use of arrays overcomes each of these difficulties.[2]

You should keep in mind the following additional points when working with subscripted variables.

1. Subscripts must be unsigned integer constants, variables that store positive integer values, or expressions having positive integer values. For example,

---

[2] We couldn't even name 500 simple numeric variables in this manner, since the maximum in BASIC is 286. Can you figure out how we got the number 286?

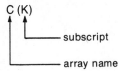

uses the variable K as a subscript. When you use a variable as a subscript you may reference any element in the array based upon the value you assign that variable. For example, the program segment

```
75  LET K = 3
80  LET S(K) = 700
```

stores 700 in the third location of the array S.

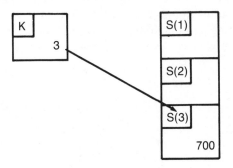

In the last program of Example 7.1 storage is accomplished as follows:

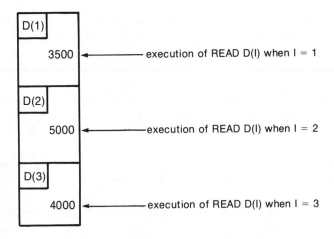

2.  You can use a single variable name as a subscript to reference corresponding elements in different arrays. For example, the program segment

```
90  LET K = 2
95  LET P(K) = S(K) – C(K)
```

subtracts the second array element in C from the second array element in S and stores the result in the second array element of P.

3. Subscripts are not part of the array name; thus T(J) and T(I) both reference the array T. In addition, if I and J are equal, then T(J) and T(I) reference the same element in T.
4. If a subscript is a decimal number, then the computer *truncates* (not rounds) the fractional part of the number and uses the integer part as the subscript. For example, if 10 is in X and 5 is in Y, then the execution of

    50  LET B(X + Y/2) = 1000

stores 1000 in B(12), the twelfth element in B.

## 7.3
## DIM STATEMENT

Because an array occupies more than one memory location, these locations must be reserved for the array through the use of a DIM statement. The general form of the DIM statement for one-dimensional arrays is

> *line no.* **DIM** $\dfrac{array}{name}$ $\left(\dfrac{integer}{constant}\right)$, $\dfrac{array}{name}$ $\left(\dfrac{integer}{constant}\right)$, . . . .

This statement declares to the compiler which variables in your program represent arrays and defines the maximum number of locations or elements in each array as specified by the value of the constant. In Example 7.1 the statement

    010  DIM D(3)

reserves three memory locations[3] for the array named D, which can be depicted in the usual way:

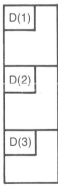

[3] The proposed ANSI standard and some versions of BASIC use a lower bound of zero instead of one for the value of the subscript. Thus, the statement DIM D(3) would actually reserve four locations: D(0), D(1), D(2), and D(3). In this case, it is best to conceptualize the integer value in the DIM statement as the *upper bound* on the value of the subscript. As a compromise on the issue of a lower bound, the standard specifies the new command

        *line no.* **OPTION BASE 0**
or
        *line no.* **OPTION BASE 1**

for explicitly declaring the lower bound of the subscript.

Note that the contents (stored values) of these locations are left blank;[4] they are filled in with the appropriate values when the READ statement is executed three times in the FOR/NEXT loop. If we had used

    10 DIM D(5)

then five memory locations would have been reserved for D:

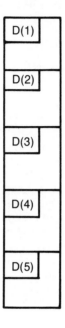

However, the program of Example 7.1 still would utilize only the first three of these locations.

More than one array can be dimensioned in a single DIM statement by using commas to separate each array specification. For example,

    5 DIM C(80),R(50),P(50)

reserves 80 locations for an array named C, another 50 locations for array R, and 50 more locations for P.

Here are some additional points to keep in mind when working with arrays.

1.  The DIM statement is a *nonexecutable* statement which normally is placed at the beginning of a program, but may appear anywhere in the program before the array is used.[5]
2.  The constant that specifies the size of the array *must* be an integer value. For example,

        DIM S(N)

---

[4] Some versions of BASIC automatically initialize all array elements to zero.
[5] Some versions of BASIC may treat the DIM statement as an executable statement.

would yield a syntax error, since a variable is *not* permitted within parentheses in the DIM statement.

3. You can reserve more locations for an array than are actually used in a particular program; however, the opposite is not true. If you reserve only five locations for an array and need seven, an error message may occur during the execution of your program when the value of your subscript exceeds five, or in some complex programs a logic error may occur.

4. On some systems, the DIM statement may be omitted; in this case, a one-dimensional array is automatically assigned an upper dimension of 10. Thus, it is not always necessary to define arrays through the use of the DIM statement. However, *we recommend you use the DIM statement even if its use is optional.* This way not only do you avoid errors by forgetting the DIM statement when needed but also your programs more clearly identify arrays.

**Follow-up Exercises**

1. Can you reason why a variable is not permitted in place of the integer constant in the DIM statement?
2. Indicate what is wrong, if anything, with each of the following program segments.

   a.  10  READ K,X(K)
       20  DIM X(K)
          ⋮

   b.  10  LET M = 5
       20  LET N = 8
       30  LET A(0) = 100
       40  LET A(15) = 500
       50  LET A(M − 2∗N) = M∗N
          ⋮

   c.  10  DIM D(10),E(10)
       20  FOR I = 1 TO 26
       30     LET D(I) = I∗∗2
       40  NEXT I
       50  FOR I = 1 TO 19
       60     LET E(I + 1) = D(I)∗D(I + 1)
       70  NEXT I
          ⋮

   What would be stored in E(3), once the program is corrected?

**∗∗3.** Indicate the storage contents of specific array elements for the following.

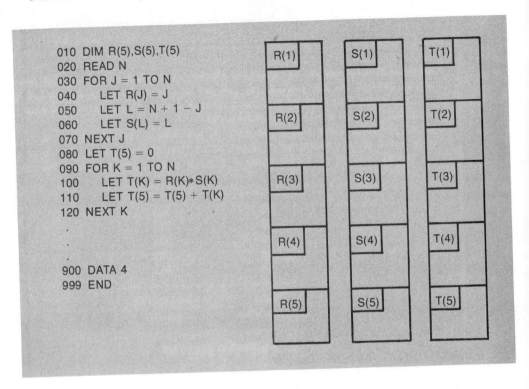

```
010  DIM R(5),S(5),T(5)
020  READ N
030  FOR J = 1 TO N
040      LET R(J) = J
050      LET L = N + 1 − J
060      LET S(L) = L
070  NEXT J
080  LET T(5) = 0
090  FOR K = 1 TO N
100      LET T(K) = R(K)*S(K)
110      LET T(5) = T(5) + T(K)
120  NEXT K
   .
   .
   .
900  DATA 4
999  END
```

## 7.4
## READ, INPUT, AND OUTPUT

In the discussions which follow, assume that we wish to read, input, or print every element in the array, beginning with the first element and moving sequentially through the array until the last element.

### Read/Input

The FOR/NEXT statements are a convenient device for the read in or input of array values. In this case the *index* or *counter* of the FOR statement may be used as a subscript which takes on values that coincide with each element in the array.

The program segment

```
010  DIM D(3)
020  FOR I = 1 TO 3
030      READ D(I)
040  NEXT I
100  DATA 3500,5000,4000
```

reads data found in the DATA statement and stores them in the array D, according to the following procedure: Initially, I is set equal to 1 (from the FOR statement), and the first data item is read into D(1).

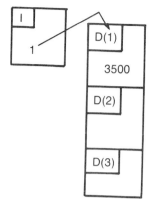

Then, I is incremented to 2, the READ statement is executed a second time, the second data item is entered, and 5000 is stored in D(2).

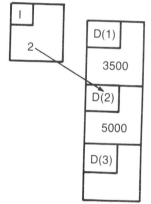

Finally, I is incremented to 3, and the third memory location for D is filled.

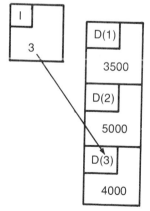

*Note that a new value is processed each time the READ statement in the FOR/NEXT loop is executed.*

In essence, the FOR/NEXT loop is equivalent to the following:

```
20 READ D(1)
30 READ D(2)
40 READ D(3)
```

In other words, identical results would be obtained if the FOR/NEXT loop were replaced with the above three statements. If we were reading in deposits for 200 banks, then you should readily appreciate the power of the FOR/NEXT approach.

## Output

This looping technique using the FOR/NEXT statement also can be used for output. For example, the statements

```
60 FOR I = 1 TO 3
70    PRINT D(I)
80 NEXT I
```

give *column output* for the contents of array D as follows:

```
3500
5000
4000
```

*Note that a new output line is written each time the PRINT statement is executed.* In effect, this FOR/NEXT loop is equivalent to the following:

```
60 PRINT D(1)
70 PRINT D(2)
80 PRINT D(3)
```

If *row output* rather than column output is desired, then a trailing comma or semicolon should be used in the PRINT statement, as follows:

```
60 FOR I = 1 TO 3        Note trailing semicolon
70    PRINT D(I);
80 NEXT I
```

This would give the output

```
3500  5000  4000
```

which is equivalent to the restrictive and cumbersome use of

```
60 PRINT D(1); D(2); D(3)
```

Note, however, that *row output using a FOR/NEXT loop requires a PRINT statement with a blank list following the NEXT statement if the program is to print subsequent output.* This ensures that subsequent output is not mixed on the same line as the row output. For example, if we have

```
60 FOR I = 1 TO 3
70    PRINT D(I);
80 NEXT I
90 PRINT "ENTER CODE"
```

then the following output is printed:

    3500  5000  4000 ENTER CODE

If the prompt ENTER CODE is to appear on the line below the row output, then we need

    85 PRINT

to fill in blank characters for the remainder of the row output line.

---

**Follow-up Exercises**

4. With respect to the third program (the one using array D) in Example 7.1 on page 190:
   a. Change the program to process 100 branch banks. How many more statements would be needed in the *second* program on page 189 to accomplish the same task? How about the length of the statement that calculates T? Do you now see why arrays give us a simple yet powerful means to name and manipulate a large number of storage locations?
   b. Generalize the program so it can handle any number of branch banks (N) up to 500.

5. Consider the following program segment for the input of 50 values into an array named M:

    ```
    100 DIM M(50)
    110 INPUT M(1)
    120 INPUT M(2)
    130 INPUT M(3)
        :
        :
    600 INPUT M(50)
    ```

   Rewrite this segment using the FOR/NEXT statement. In general, which approach is more efficient?

6. Describe output for the following:
   a.
    ```
    100 DIM A(100),B(100),C(100)
    110 READ M
    120 FOR I = 1 TO M
    130     READ A(I),B(I)
    140     LET C(I) = A(I)/B(I)*100
    150 NEXT I
    160 FOR K = 1 TO M
    170     PRINT A(K);B(K);C(K)
    180 NEXT K
    900 DATA 4
    901 DATA 10,20
    902 DATA 15,20
    903 DATA 10,40
    904 DATA 20,50
    999 END
    ```

b. Change line 170 to

170 PRINT A(K);B(K);C(K),

c. How would you change the program to get the following output?

| | | | |
|---|---|---|---|
| 10 | 15 | 10 | 20 |
| 20 | 20 | 40 | 50 |
| 50 | 75 | 25 | 40 |

*7. Given the following data:

| Cost | Sales |
|------|-------|
| 40 | 100 |
| 20 | 125 |
| 75 | 95 |

a. Write an efficient program segment to read these data into the arrays C and S. What might be the most logical way of placing data on DATA statements?
b. Write the code to output these data so they appear as presented in the above table.
c. Write the code to output these data as follows:

| | | | |
|---|---|---|---|
| COST | 40 | 20 | 75 |
| SALES | 100 | 125 | 95 |

# 7.5
# MANIPULATING ARRAYS

This section presents four examples that illustrate techniques of manipulation for one-dimensional arrays.

## EXAMPLE 7.2   Initialization

Often it is necessary to set each element in an array to some.initial value. For example, to initialize all values in a 100-element array to 50, you could write the following instructions:

```
10 FOR I = 1 TO 100
20    LET S(I) = 50
30 NEXT I
```

As the value of I changes from 1 to 100, each of the 100 locations in the array S is set to 50. After this segment of the program is executed, array S appears as follows:

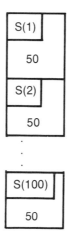

## EXAMPLE 7.3   Accumulation of a Sum

Quite often it is necessary to perform arithmetic operations on all the elements in an array. The following segment from Example 7.1 illustrates the accumulation of a sum:

```
15  LET T = 0
20  FOR I = 1 TO 3
30    READ D(I)
35    LET T = T + D(I)
40  NEXT I
```

As the value of I changes from 1 to 3, each element of the array D is added to the variable T. When I = 1, we are actually executing

$$T = T + D(1) \quad \text{or} \quad T = 0 + 3500$$

when I = 2, we are executing

$$T = T + D(2) \quad \text{or} \quad T = 3500 + 5000$$

and when I = 3, we are executing

$$T = T + D(3) \quad \text{or} \quad T = 8500 + 4000$$

Thus, 12500 gets stored in T. Note that T is explicitly initialized to 0 in line 15, as we advised in Example 5.6 on page 127.

## EXAMPLE 7.4 Correspondence Among Arrays

Sometimes we need to perform operations among corresponding elements of different arrays. For example, assume that a banking program has stored the current month's total dollar deposits in array C and the total dollar withdrawals in array W. A third array can be used to accumulate the new balance (B), as follows:

```
10 FOR I = 1 TO N
20     LET B(I) = B(I) + C(I) − W(I)
30 NEXT I
```

where N represents the number of customers to be processed. Note that the appearance of B(I) on the right side reflects the previous value of B(I), that is, last month's balance for the Ith account.

## EXAMPLE 7.5 String Arrays[6]

String arrays are particularly useful when we need to store and manipulate a set of data with related alphanumeric values, such as days of the week, months of the year, names of employees working for a specific company, and so on. Study the following program and then answer Exercise 11.

```
100 DIM D$(7)
110 FOR J = 1 TO 7
120     READ D$(J)
130 NEXT J
140 INPUT K
150     IF K < 1 THEN 999
160     IF K > 7 THEN 999
170     PRINT D$(K)
180 GO TO 140
901 DATA "MONDAY","TUESDAY","WEDNESDAY","THURSDAY"
902 DATA "FRIDAY","SATURDAY","SUNDAY"
999 END
```

### Follow-up Exercises

8. Suppose that prior to running the program segment in Example 7.4, memory appears as follows:

---

[6] Some versions of BASIC do not support string arrays.

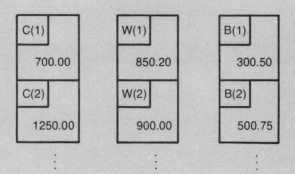

What changes would occur for the first two customer accounts following execution of the program segment in Example 7.4?

9. A student, wishing to initialize an array with 200 elements to 0, wrote the following:

```
10 DIM T(200)
20 T(K) = 0
```

On seeing this, a friend (who also takes BASIC programming) says that the above doesn't make sense because K is undefined. Perhaps, they reason, we can try the following approach:

```
10 DIM T(200)
20 T = 0
```

Explain why each approach would be incorrect. Correct this segment of the program.

10. **Mean and Standard Deviation.** The following program illustrates the calculation of the arithmetic mean (average) and standard deviation (a measure of variability of the data about the mean) for a set of data. Algebraically, the mean is defined by

$$m = \frac{x_1 + x_2 + \cdots + x_n}{n}$$

and the standard deviation by

$$s = \sqrt{\frac{(x_1 - m)^2 + (x_2 - m)^2 + \cdots + (x_n - m)^2}{n - 1}}$$

```
100 DIM X(1000)
110 LET M = 0
120 READ N
```

```
130 FOR I = 1 TO N
140    READ X(I)
150    LET M = M + X(I)
160 NEXT I
170 LET M = M/N
180 LET S = 0
190 FOR I = 1 TO N
200    LET S = S + (X(I) − M)**2
210 NEXT I
220 LET S = (S/(N − 1))**.5
230 PRINT M,S
900 DATA 3
901 DATA 5,4,3
999 END
```

a.  Roleplay the computer by filling in the following memory locations

| Snapshot | N | I | M | S | X(1) | X(2) | X(3) | X(4) |
|---|---|---|---|---|---|---|---|---|
| Just before line 160 | 3 | | | | | | | |
| | 3 | | | | | | | |
| | 3 | | | | | | | |
| Just before line 190 | 3 | | | | | | | |
| Just before line 210 | 3 | | | | | | | |
| | 3 | | | | | | | |
| | 3 | | | | | | | |
| Just before line 230 | 3 | | | | | | | |

b.  What gets printed?

c.  Does M represent the mean throughout? Explain our use of M.

d.  Does S represent the standard deviation throughout? Explain our use of S.

e.  Why do we explicitly initialize M and S?

f.  Why would you not advise dimensioning X to 3? Up to how many items of data can this program process? Why would you not advise dimensioning X to, say, 100,000?

11. With respect to Example 7.5,

a.  What gets stored in D$(1), D$(2), . . . , D$(7)?

b.  Indicate output for the successive input

```
? 2
? 6
? 4
? 0
```

c. Revise the program such that the input of

   ? 7, 4, 1776

   results in the output

   JULY 4, 1776

# 7.6
# SELECTED APPLICATIONS

This section illustrates three common applications of one-dimensional arrays.

---

### EXAMPLE 7.6  Table Look-Up

The term *table look-up* refers to procedures for accessing data that are stored in a table. These procedures satisfy a very common need across a wide variety of professional fields and occupational areas. In this example we work with one-dimensional "tables"; in the next chapter, two-dimensional tables are treated.

Suppose that a life insurance company uses the following premium schedule to bill its customers. In this case, the annual premium is based on the age of the policyholder. For example, a policyholder who is 47 years old would pay a premium of $327 per year.

**Premium Schedule**

| Upper Age Limit | Annual Premium ($) |
|:---:|:---:|
| 25 | 277 |
| 35 | 287 |
| 45 | 307 |
| 55 | 327 |
| 65 | 357 |

When looking up information in a table, three basic elements are required. First, there is the "search key," which is the item of information that helps you to locate the right place within the table. In the case of the life insurance company, each policyholder's age is the search key.

The table that is to be searched usually makes up the other two sets of elements needed for the search: (1) The set of "keys" used to access the proper location and (2) the set of "function values." In the premium schedule the set of keys is the limit on the various age classes, and the corresponding premiums are the function values.

Figure 7.1 illustrates the flowchart for the interactive program below, which answers inquiries by determining the appropriate premium for a potential policyholder.

| Program | Comments |
|---|---|

```
010 REM ---- TABLE LOOKUP ----
020 REM         VARIABLE KEY
030 REM         A=ARRAY CONTAINING UPPER AGE LIMITS
040 REM         P=ARRAY CONTAINING PREMIUMS
050 REM         N$=NAME OF POLICYHOLDER
060 REM         A1=AGE OF POLICYHOLDER
070 REM ----------------------
100 DIM A(5),P(5)
110 FOR I=1 TO 5
120    READ A(I),P(I)
130 NEXT I
300 PRINT "POLICYHOLDER'S NAME";
310    INPUT N$
320    IF N$ = "EOD" THEN 999
330    PRINT "POLICYHOLDER'S AGE";
340    INPUT A1
400    FOR I=1 TO 5
410      IF A1 <= A(I) THEN 430
420    NEXT I
430    PRINT "PREMIUM IS ";P(I)
440    PRINT
450 GO TO 300
901 DATA 25,277
902 DATA 35,287
903 DATA 45,307
904 DATA 55,327
905 DATA 65,357
999 END
```

Lines 110 to 130 read the premium schedule.

Test for end of run.

Lines 400 to 420 search age limits to determine location of appropriate premium. This represents the table look-up logic.

```
RUN

POLICYHOLDER'S NAME? CLARK S.   KENT
POLICYHOLDER'S AGE? 42
PREMIUM IS   307

POLICYHOLDER'S NAME? LOIS S. LANE
POLICYHOLDER'S AGE? 28
PREMIUM IS   287

POLICYHOLDER'S NAME?EOD

TIME 0.02 SECS.
```

The premium schedule is read into two one-dimensional arrays: A and P. Memory locations for these arrays appear as follows just before line 300 is executed:

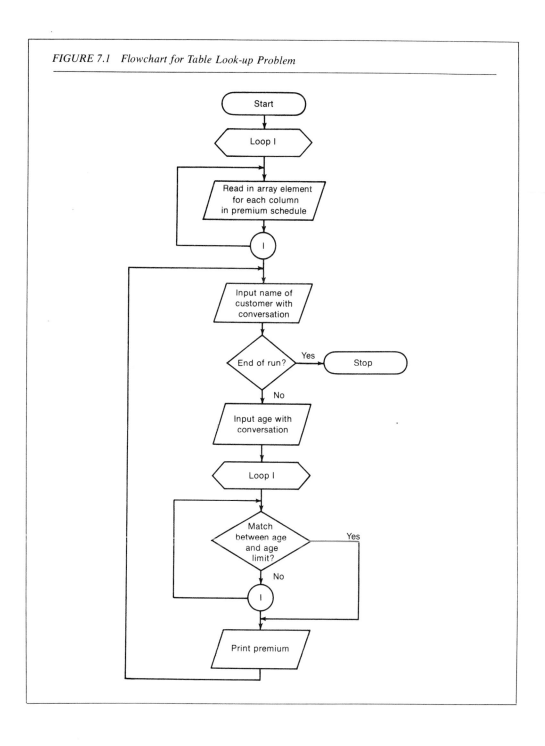

FIGURE 7.1 *Flowchart for Table Look-up Problem*

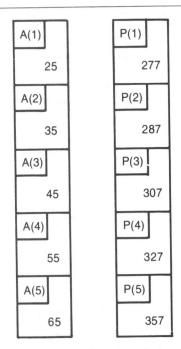

Next, the customer's name is entered and tested against the trailer number ("EOD"), after which the customer's age is entered. The table look-up logic is found in lines 400 to 420. In this case, the search key is the value stored in A1 and the set of keys is given by the array elements in A. The loop scans each element of A until the proper age class is found, that is, until the age of the policyholder (the search key) is less than or equal to an age limit value in the array A. When this condition is satisfied, the appropriate premium (function value) is identified as the array element of P which corresponds to the matching age class. For example, when 42 is stored in A1, lines 400 to 420 operate as follows:

| I | Is A1 less than or equal to A(I)? | Result |
|---|---|---|
| 1 | No; 42 is not less than or equal to 25 | Next I |
| 2 | No; 42 is not less than or equal to 35 | Next I |
| 3 | Yes; 42 is less than or equal to 45 | Go to line 430 |

Thus, when line 430 is executed, the value of 3 in I (age class) is used as the subscript of P. In this case, the contents of P(3) are printed, which gives a premium of $307 for someone aged 42.

## Follow-up Exercises

**12.** With respect to Example 7.6,
  a.  What premium value would be output if you entered

POLICYHOLDER'S NAME?  RIP VAN WINKLE
POLICYHOLDER'S AGE?    99

b.  Modify the program to print the message

OVER 65--UNINSURABLE

on the line that otherwise prints the premium.

13.  Instead of reading in the premium schedule as in lines 200 to 220, some beginning programmers will insert a READ statement between lines 400 and 410 as follows:

```
400 FOR I = 1 TO 5
405     READ A(I),P(I)
410     IF A1 <= A(I) THEN 430
420 NEXT I
```

Explain why this approach will not work.

**\*\*14.**  Recent styles of programming called *modular* and *structured programming* (which we discuss in Module B) discourage exit from a FOR/NEXT loop other than through the NEXT statement, as this procedure implies two exit points, thereby impairing readability. Write alternative code for lines 400 to 420 by designing a DO UNTIL loop that includes a counter for the subscript. Which approach is more "readable"?

---

## EXAMPLE 7.7   Direct Access to Array Element—SAT Scores

A more efficient method of utilizing arrays in some applications is to access or process values *directly* from one array location without moving sequentially through an entire array. To illustrate the direct access concept, consider the following problem.

Every year State College prints a Fact Book that includes average SAT scores of students categorized as freshmen, sophomore, junior, and senior. Figure 7.2 and the following program illustrate how an array can be used to accumulate these data.

| Program | Comments |
|---|---|

```
010 REM   *** SAT STATISTICS ***
020 REM
030 REM   VARIABLE KEY
035 REM      N  = NUMBER OF LOOPS
040 REM      K  = CLASS CODE
045 REM      S1 = SAT MATH
050 REM      S2 = SAT VERBAL
055 REM      S  = COMBINED MATH AND VERBAL
060 REM      C  = ARRAY COUNT OF STUDENTS BY CLASS
065 REM      T  = ARRAY ACCUMULATED SAT SCORES BY CLASS
070 REM
```

```
100 DIM C(4),T(4)
200 FOR K = 1 TO 4
210    LET C(K) = 0                      Initialize array elements.
220    LET T(K) = 0
230 NEXT K
300 READ N
310 PRINT "CLASS","AVERAGE","NUMBER"
400 FOR J = 1 TO N
410    READ K,S1,S2
420    LET S = S1 + S2
430    LET C(K) = C(K) + 1               Direct access logic illustrated by lines 430
440    LET T(K) = T(K) + S               and 440.
450 NEXT J
500 FOR K = 1 TO 4
510    PRINT K,T(K)/C(K),C(K)            Note calculation of average SAT score in
520 NEXT K                              PRINT statement.
600 DATA 5
610 DATA 2,580,640
620 DATA 3,720,680
630 DATA 2,610,560
640 DATA 4,415,563
650 DATA 1,560,590
999 END
```

| CLASS | AVERAGE | NUMBER |
|-------|---------|--------|
| 1 | 1150 | 1 |
| 2 | 1195 | 2 |
| 3 | 1400 | 1 |
| 4 | 978 | 1 |

```
TIME 0.03 SECS.
```

*Note 1.* N represents "number of students" and K represents "class code." The variable K stores coded values 1 through 4, which represent 1 for freshmen, 2 for sophomore, 3 for junior, and 4 for senior. The array C is used to store the accumulated count of students in each class. For example, C(1) represents number of freshmen, C(2) represents number of sophomores, and so forth. The array T stores the sum of combined SAT scores by class. For example, T(1) will contain the sum of combined (math and verbal) SAT scores for all freshmen.

*Note 2.* If a student has a class standing of 2, then the statement

$$C(K) = C(K) + 1$$

increments by 1 the second storage location in C. In other words, the equivalent statement given by

$$C(2) = C(2) + 1$$

is executed. Thus, K acts as a "pointer" (subscript) to the specific location in C that is to be manipulated. The same approach is used to manipulate or update the array T.

*Note 3.* In this particular example, the concept of *direct access* is illustrated by the fact that we need not loop through the entire array each time we wish to update (increment or sum) the contents of a specific location in C or T. The pointer K conveniently serves to locate specific elements in C and T.

*FIGURE 7.2   Flowchart for Example 7.7*

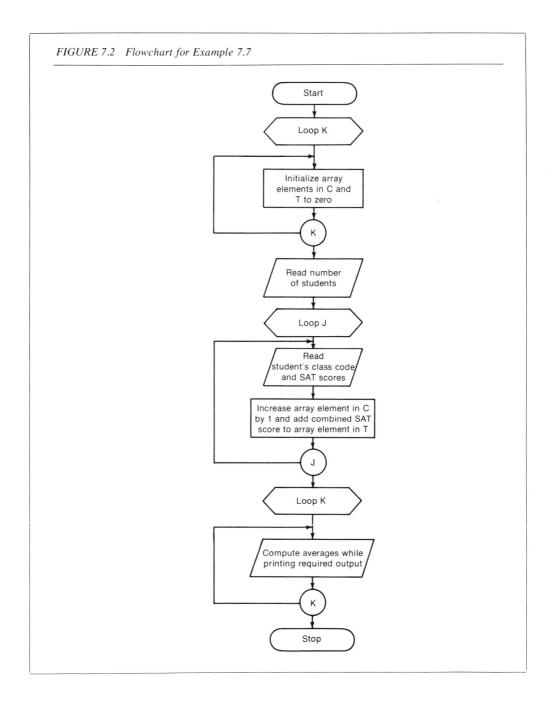

**Follow-up Exercise**

15. For the program in Example 7.7:
    a. Indicate how the specified storage locations appear just before each execution of line 450.

    | K | S1 | S2 | S | C(1) | C(2) | C(3) | C(4) | T(1) | T(2) | T(3) | T(4) |
    |---|----|----|---|------|------|------|------|------|------|------|------|
    | — | — | — | — | 0 | 0 | 0 | 0 | 0 | 0 | 0 | 0 |

    b. Where do average SAT scores get computed? Can you think of another way of computing these averages such that they get stored in array A?

## EXAMPLE 7.8   Sorting

One of the most common operations performed in data processing, called **sorting,** is arranging data either numerically or alphabetically into sequential order according to some criterion. For example, a student file contains a number of records, one for each student. Each record contains student name and identification number in addition to other data. We could sort the file either by ID number in ascending or descending order or we could arrange the file alphabetically using the student names. In either case, the item in the record which is used to sort the file is known as the *sort key.*

Let's assume we want a listing of students in *ascending* numeric order according to their ID number. For simplicity, let's further assume we have only four students. The one-dimensional array called L is used to store and sort ID numbers, as shown below.

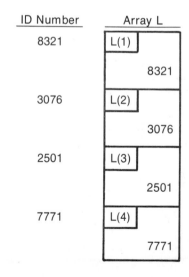

For this problem, we use the **exchange method** of sorting. On each pass through the array, the first element is compared with the second: the smaller number is stored in the first position, and the larger number is stored in the second position. Then, the second element of the array is compared to the third: the smaller number is placed in the second position, and the larger number is placed in the third position. This process of comparison and rearranging continues throughout the entire array. When this first pass through the array is complete, the array is processed again, from beginning to end. This procedure continues until no exchanges take place in a pass through the entire array. The exchange method is also called a **bubble sort,** since items which are below their correct positions in the array tend to move upward to their proper places, like bubbles in a carbonated drink.

Figure 7.3 illustrates the flowchart for the sorting program below.

| Program | Comments |
|---|---|

```
010 REM----SORT ROUTINE----
015 REM
020 REM    VARIABLE KEY
025 REM       N=NUMBER OF VALUES TO BE SORTED
030 REM       L=ARRAY OF VALUES TO BE SORTED
040 REM       S=SWITCH; 0=SORT COMPLETE, 1=SORT NOT COMPLETE
045 REM       T=TEMPORARY HOLDER
050 REM
100 DIM L(500)
200 READ N
210 FOR I=1 TO N
220   READ L(I)
230 NEXT I
300 LET S=0                          Set switch to zero.
310   FOR I=2 TO N
320     IF L(I) >= L(I-1) THEN 370
330     LET T=L(I)
340     LET L(I)=L(I-1)              Bubble sort logic.
350     LET L(I-1)=T
360     LET S=1
370   NEXT I
380 IF S=1 THEN 300                  Sort is not complete whenever
400 PRINT "SORT COMPLETED"           switch equals one.
410 PRINT
420 FOR I=1 TO N
430   PRINT L(I);
440 NEXT I
900 DATA 4
901 DATA 8321,3076,2501,7771
999 END

RUN

SORT COMPLETED

 2501     3076     7771     8321
TIME 0.02 SECS.
```

The logic in lines 310 to 370 illustrates the bubble sort. The subscripts I and I − 1 are used to compare values stored in adjacent array elements. When an exchange

FIGURE 7.3    *Flowchart for Sorting Program*

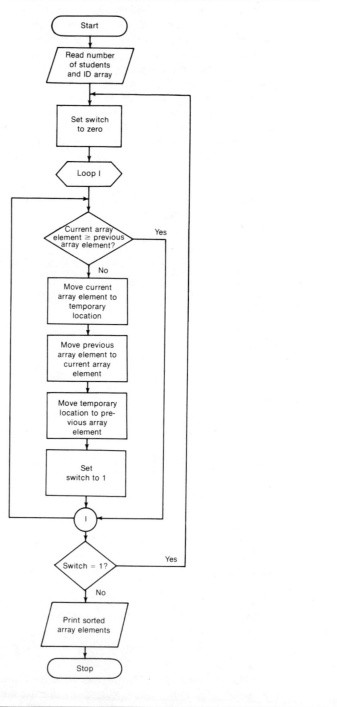

takes place between two adjacent elements, a separate memory location (T) serves as a temporary location to hold one of the values while the exchange takes place. To understand exactly what's happening, follow the diagram and steps below for the case I = 2.

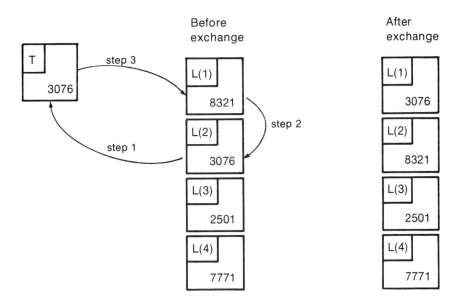

The variable S acts as a "switch" or "flag" by storing either 0 or 1. If the value in S is 1 after a complete pass through the array L, then the sort is not complete and the entire array must be scanned again for numbers out of sequence. If the value in S is 0 after a complete pass through the array L, then the sort is complete.

## Follow-up Exercises

**16.** Fill in the following table based on the data in the example, just before execution of line 370.

| I | T | L(1) | L(2) | L(3) | L(4) | S |
|---|------|------|------|------|------|---|
| 2 | 3076 | 3076 | 8321 | 2501 | 7771 | 1 |
| 3 | | | | | | |
| 4 | | | | | | |
| 2 | | | | | | |
| 3 | | | | | | |
| 4 | | | | | | |
| 2 | | | | | | |
| 3 | | | | | | |
| 4 | | | | | | |

How many passes through the entire array does it take to sort the array? How many passes does it take to terminate execution?

**\*17.** Make appropriate changes in the program for a numeric sort in descending order. Test your program by tracing through the given data.

**\*\*18.** Is it possible to sort alphabetic data using the program in Example 7.8? Make necessary modifications to the program and run it on your system to sort the following data: SMITH, JONES, DAVIS, KELLY.

## 7.7
## COMMON ERRORS

Arrays are great for giving a lot of practice in debugging. Often one "small" error will result in an "avalanche" of error messages. Pay attention to the following and you might avoid apoplexy.

*1. Declaration of array.* Don't forget to declare your array by using the DIM statement. Some systems allow you to omit the DIM statement for arrays that utilize 10 or less elements. In this case, you will get an execution error if the subscript of an array exceeds 10 during execution. On other systems, if you forget to dimension an array, then you will get a *syntax* error message for *each* line containing a subscripted variable. So, if you get an error message such as "UNDEFINED ARRAY" or "UNDEFINED FUNCTION" for each line where the subscripted variable appears, then check on whether or not you dimensioned the array.

Also, don't forget to declare arrays before their use in the program. To be safe, place your DIM statement prior to all other executable statements in the program.

Finally, you must use an integer constant to declare the size of your array. Don't try the following

    DIM X(N)

unless you like to see syntax errors. A variable number of locations is not permitted.

*2. Subscripts.* If you get an *execution* error message such as "SUBSCRIPT OUT OF BOUNDS" or "SUBSCRIPT OUT OF RANGE," then a subscript is negative, zero (in the case of systems that don't allow this lower bound), or greater than the upper bound specified in the DIM statement. Two kinds of mistakes are possible here: either you reserved too few locations for your array, or you made a logic error in assigning values to subscripts. In the latter case, you might want to diagnose the error by using a *trace* to print subscript values, as illustrated by the following simple example.

```
10 DIM X(5)
20 FOR J = 1 TO 5
30    LET K = J + 1
40    PRINT J,K
50    LET X(K) = J**3
60 NEXT J
```

Output

| | |
|---|---|
| 1 | 2 |
| 2 | 3 |
| 3 | 4 |
| 4 | 5 |
| 5 | 6 |

SUBSCRIPT OUT OF BOUNDS

The error message is the result of a 6 in the subscript K, which exceeds the upper bound of 5 in the DIM statement.

*3. Array names.* A common point of confusion among beginning programmers is just what portion of a subscripted variable represents the array name. For example, are B(J) and B(I) one and the same array? Yes. In this case, the array name is B, not B(J) or B(I). B(J) and B(I) simply reference specific elements in the array B.

A related issue is the use of the same letter to represent both a numeric array and a simple numeric variable within the same program. For example, A(I) would be treated as an array and A would be treated as a simple variable in the statement

    50 PRINT A(I),A

We don't recommend this practice, however, since it makes programs more difficult to follow.

If you name an array incorrectly, then you will get a syntax error for each line that uses this array. For example, many systems do not allow the optional digit permitted with simple variables. Thus subscripted variables such as B2(J), A1(3), and N1$(K) would cause syntax errors on these systems.

*4. Initialization.* If the elements in an array are to accumulate a sum, then don't forget to initialize the array elements to zero, as illustrated in Example 7.7 on page 209. Some compilers automatically initialize all storage locations to zero, but others don't. If yours does not, then you will get an execution error the first time your program attempts to use an uninitialized counter or summer.

*5. Data Entry and Output.* Don't forget to use a loop to enter or output an array. We often see the following approaches as attempts to output the entire contents of an array:

    50 PRINT A(I)
    60 PRINT A

Line 50 either prints one element (if a positive integer within the bounds of the array is stored for I) or results in an execution error. Line 60 either gives an execution error or prints the stored value of a simple numeric variable A.

### Additional Exercises

**19.** Define or explain each of the following:

| | |
|---|---|
| array | DIM statement |
| array element | OPTION BASE statement |
| subscript | sorting |
| one-dimensional array | exchange method |
| subscripted variables | bubble sort |

**20. Mopups Revisited.** Rewrite the program in Section 6.6 on page 165 as follows:

   a. Use one-dimensional arrays to store the rate schedule. Treat the number of rows in the rate schedule as a variable that is read in. *Hint:* Let the numbers 10, 20, and 30 represent the "set of keys." See Exercise 28a–b in Chapter 6.

   b. After all dealers have been processed, print the total number of bikes ordered, the sum of total prices, and the average price per bike. Nicely label your output.

  \*\*c. Design your program such that the program itself calculates and stores the values 2250, 4650, and 6900. *Hint:* See Exercise 28c in Chapter 6.

**21. Property Tax Assessment Revisited.** Solve Exercise 23 in Chapter 5 on page 137 as follows:

   a. Store the tax schedule, lot numbers, property values, and tax charges in one-dimensional arrays. Treat the number of rows in the rate schedule as a variable that is read in. Use a FOR/NEXT loop for your loop. Label your output. Following the output table, print the sum of property values and the total tax charge. *Hint:* Let the numbers 10,000, 30,000, and 60,000 represent the set of keys.

  \*\*b. Following the output in part a, print a second table that shows tax charges (together with corresponding lot numbers and property values) in descending order.

**22. Crime Data Summary.** The data below represent the number of arrests for felony crimes in a state over a 3 year period.

**Arrest Data by Year**

| | 1 | 2 | 3 |
|---|---|---|---|
| Homicide | 1000 | 1000 | 1000 |
| Robbery | 10000 | 9000 | 11000 |
| Burglary | 27000 | 24000 | 28000 |
| Assault | 13000 | 15000 | 16000 |
| Theft | 19000 | 20000 | 23000 |
| Forgery | 10000 | 9000 | 10000 |

   a. Write a flowchart and program to read the data into several one-dimensional arrays. Print out the data in a table format which includes a new row for total arrests in each year and a new column for average arrests for each crime over the past 3 years. No need to label rows and columns here.

b. In the output of part a, label your columns 1, 2, 3, and AVERAGE. Label your rows according to the felony names in the above table, the last row being TOTALS. Preferably, the output of felony names should be handled through the use of arrays.

c. Print a second table which gives the percent of arrests for each crime to the total number of arrests in that year.

**23. Support Facility for Oil Drilling Platforms.** Consider the coordinate system below, where the plotted points 1 through 5 represent the coordinate loca-

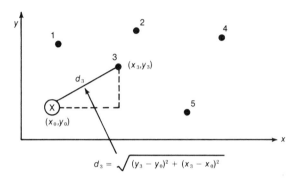

$$d_3 = \sqrt{(y_3 - y_0)^2 + (x_3 - x_0)^2}$$

tions of offshore oil drilling platforms and the plotted point labeled 0 is a possible location for a support facility. The figure also illustrates the distance $d_3$ between the support facility and platform 3. The formula for calculating $d_3$ is called the *Euclidian distance formula*. The coordinates in miles are given below:

| Platform $i$ | $x_i$ | $y_i$ |
|:---:|:---:|:---:|
| 1 | 5 | 20 |
| 2 | 15 | 22 |
| 3 | 12 | 15 |
| 4 | 25 | 21 |
| 5 | 21 | 5 |

a. Design a flowchart and write an interactive program that calculates and prints distance between each platform and the following proposed locations for the support facility:

| $x_0$ | $y_0$ |
|:---:|:---:|
| 4 | 6 |
| 20 | 14 |
| 20 | 18 |
| 23 | 20 |

Include the *total* distance $(d_1 + d_2 + \cdots + d_5)$ as part of your output.

b.  Use your program interactively to determine the coordinate (to the nearest mile) for the support facility that minimizes total distance. In other words, by trial and error input a proposed location, and based on the output make a judgment regarding your next proposed coordinate. Repeat this procedure until you're satisfied you have converged on the coordinate that minimizes total distance.

**c.  Instead of the trial-and-error search in part b, design your program to systematically vary $x_0$ and $y_0$ between chosen ranges. Include $x_0$, $y_0$, and total distance in your output. Also, have the program print the coordinate, of the ones considered, that minimizes total distance.

*Note:* Instead of using the exponent 0.5 to take square roots you might want to use the SQR function illustrated on page 258.

24.  **Revenue-Sharing.** Consider the allocation program whereby the federal government apportions certain federal funds to the states on the basis of each state's population to the total U.S. population. The table below provides population figures for all fifty states according to a recent census.

Population by State (in Thousands)

| | | | |
|-----|--------|-----|--------|
| ME | 1,059 | NC | 5,451 |
| NH | 808 | SC | 2,818 |
| VT | 468 | GA | 4,926 |
| NA | 5,199 | FL | 8,327 |
| RI | 938 | KY | 3,396 |
| CT | 3,080 | TN | 4,188 |
| NY | 18,101 | AL | 3,614 |
| NJ | 7,322 | MS | 2,364 |
| PA | 11,841 | AR | 2,068 |
| OH | 10,745 | LA | 3,762 |
| IN | 5,313 | OK | 2,681 |
| IL | 11,160 | TX | 12,017 |
| MI | 9,117 | MT | 748 |
| WI | 4,566 | ID | 820 |
| MN | 3,905 | WY | 374 |
| IA | 2,857 | CO | 2,534 |
| MO | 4,772 | NM | 1,147 |
| ND | 636 | AZ | 2,224 |
| SD | 681 | UT | 1,206 |
| NB | 1,541 | NV | 592 |
| KS | 2,266 | WA | 3,544 |
| DE | 577 | OR | 2,288 |
| MD | 4,089 | CA | 20,876 |
| VA | 4,967 | AK | 341 |
| WV | 1,803 | HI | 854 |

a.  Write a program which uses one array for the names of the states and another array for the population figures. Read these arrays, calculate how much revenue should go to each state if $380 million is available for allocation, and output a table with appropriate labels which lists each state and its allocated amount. Include a flowchart.

b. Modify the preceding program to include a loop which processes more than one allocation. For example, if three allocation programs are to be run, then the output should appear as follows:

DOLLAR AMOUNTS ALLOCATED UNDER
EACH PROGRAM

| STATE | 1 | 2 | 3 | TOTALS |
|---|---|---|---|---|
| ME | XXXXXXX | XXXXXXX | XXXXXXX | XXXXXXXX |
| NH | XXXXXXX | XXXXXXX | XXXXXXX | XXXXXXXX |

The number of allocations to be made (three in the above example) should be a variable. Note that the total amount which is to be allocated to each state is given by row sums and output under the column labeled "TOTALS." Test your program by processing the following funds available for allocation under three programs: $380 million, $800 million, $500 million.

**c. Modify your output in either part a or part b such that the states are listed in alphabetical order. *Hint:* The bubble sort can be used for alphabetic data.

25. **Alphanumeric Distribution.** The Interstate Commerce Commission (ICC) routinely receives written complaints regarding illegal, fraudulent, and other unsavory business practices. Below is a test file that stores the type of complaint (code 1, 2, or 3) and the state (abbreviation) where the complaint originated.

| Complaint Code | State |
|---|---|
| 1 | OH |
| 1 | RI |
| 3 | CA |
| 2 | FL |
| 3 | MA |
| 1 | MA |
| 2 | NY |
| 3 | CA |
| 4 | GA |
| 2 | CA |
| 1 | PA |
| 3 | NY |
| 1 | CA |
| 2 | NJ |
| 1 | NY |
| 1 | MD |
| 2 | TX |
| 1 | LA |
| 2 | MI |
| 5 | IL |
| 1 | ++ |

Note that ++ is the trailer number.

a.  Design a flowchart and write a program that reads this test file and prints the following:

```
**ERROR ON NUMBER 9  INVALID CODE = 4
**ERROR ON NUMBER 20 INVALID CODE = 5
```

**SUMMARY BY CODE**

Part a

| CODE | FREQUENCY | PERCENT |
|------|-----------|---------|
| 1 | 8 | 44 |
| 2 | 6 | 33 |
| 3 | 4 | 22 |
|   | 18 | 99 |

**SUMMARY BY STATE**

Part b

| STATE | FREQUENCY | PERCENT |
|-------|-----------|---------|
| CA | 4 | 36 |
| MA | 2 | 18 |
| NY | 3 | 27 |
| OH | 1 | 9 |
| RI | 1 | 9 |
|    | 11 | 99 |

Right after the program reads a data line, the code should be checked for validity. A valid complaint code is a 1, 2, or 3; any other number in this field is invalid. Then determine the frequency and percentage of complaints by type of complaint.

b.  In addition to the output in part a, output the frequency and percentage of complaints by state. (This version of the program prints a summary for only five states. In actual practice we would treat all 50 states.)

26.  **Exam Grading.** Consider an N-question multiple choice exam, where only one answer is correct for each question.

a.  Write a flowchart and program to grade the exam and print the student's name, the number right, the number wrong, and the final grade. The final grade is the percent number right. The data consist of

1.  One line for N
2.  One line containing N integers representing the N correct answers (answer key)
3.  One line indicating the number of students in the class who took the exam (M)
4.  M lines, one for each student, containing the student's name and N answers.

Use two one-dimensional numeric arrays to store the answer key and a student's answers. Test your program with the following test data:

20
1,3,5,4,4,1,1,2,3,5,5,1,2,3,4,4,5,3,2,1
5
"PETROCELLI",1,3,4,4,4,1,1,2,3,3,5,1,2,3,4,4,5,1,1,1
"BAKER",1,3,5,4,3,2,1,2,3,4,3,2,2,3,3,3,5,1,2,1
"VALENTINO",1,3,5,4,4,1,1,2,3,5,5,1,2,3,4,4,4,3,2,1
"SIMPSON",1,2,5,4,4,2,2,3,3,1,2,1,3,3,3,5,5,3,1,1
"CARTER",2,3,5,4,4,1,1,3,3,5,4,1,5,4,4,4,5,2,1,3

  b.  Print the name and grade of the student with the highest grade.

**c.  Modify your output in part a such that the required output is in alphabetical order according to last name. *Hint:* The bubble sort can be used for alphabetic data.

**d.  Print a frequency distribution of final grades for the exam, as follows:

| | |
|---|---|
| 90 OR ABOVE | XX |
| 80 BUT UNDER 90 | XX |
| 70 BUT UNDER 80 | XX |
| 60 BUT UNDER 70 | XX |
| 50 BUT UNDER 60 | XX |
| BELOW 50 | XX |
| ------------------------- | |
| | XX |

AVERAGE GRADE FOR EXAM = XX.X

**27.  **Polynomial Root Search.** A polynomial function of degree *n* is given by

$$y = b_0 + b_1 x + b_2 x^2 + b_3 x^3 + \cdots + b_n x^n$$

where $b_0, b_1, \ldots, b_n$ are called *parameters.* This type of mathematical function has numerous applications across a wide variety of disciplines. In many applications, particularly in calculus, it's necessary to find the root(s) of this equation. By definition, a *root* of the above polynomial is a value of *x* that yields a value of zero for *y*. For example, the graphical sketch below illustrates roots for two given polynomials.

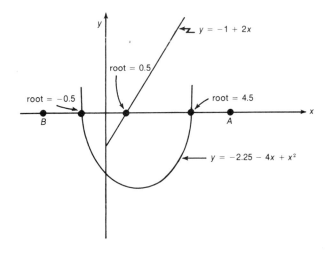

Notice that the first-degree polynomial has one real root and the second-degree polynomial has two real roots. In general, the degree of the polynomial gives the maximum number of possible real roots. Thus, an $n$-degree polynomial does not necessarily have $n$ real roots. In fact, some polynomials, depending on the values of the parameters, do not have any real roots; that is, the function does not cross the $x$ axis.

Design a flowchart and write a program that finds the root(s) of a polynomial, if any, by a trial-and-error search procedure. To illustrate consider the function $y = -1 + 2x$ given in the graph. We might proceed as follows:

| Trial $x$ | Trial $y$ | Increment in $x$ | Comment |
|---|---|---|---|
| 3 | 5 | 1 | Trial $x$ and increment selected arbitrarily. Trial $y$ calculated from function. |
| 4 | 7 | 1 | Trial $x$ increased by increment. Since 7 is further from 0 than 5, trial $x$ must be reduced by increment. |
| 3 | 5 | 1 | Change in trial $y$ is in direction toward 0; therefore, continue to reduce trial $x$ by increment. |
| 2 | 3 | 1 | |
| 1 | 1 | 1 | |
| 0 | −1 | 0.5 | Trial $y$ has crossed over 0. Thus, we know that root is between $x = 1$ and $x = 0$. Increment reduced by 50 percent and trial $x$ increased by new increment. |
| 0.5 | 0 | 0.5 | Root found at $x = 0.5$. |

In designing your program, consider the following words of wisdom:
1. First design your flowchart. When you're satisfied the algorithm is correct, then and only then write down the code.
2. Because of machine arithmetic, trial $y$ will rarely test out to 0. Check your trial $y$ against an acceptable range of error about 0, such as $\pm 0.00001$.
3. Start the search with an arbitrarily large value for the increment in $x$, for example, 100. This tends to ensure a relatively rapid crossover when a real root exists.
4. If trial $y$ fails to change in an expected direction, then you might have "overshot" the region of roots, as illustrated by a change in trial $x$ from point $A$ to point $B$ in the above graph. In this case, reduce the increment and try again.
**5. Think about how your algorithm is going to detect cases where (a) a real root does not exist and (b) more than one real root exists.

In your test runs, process the following data:

| $n$ | $b_0$ | $b_1$ | $b_2$ | $b_3$ |
|---|---|---|---|---|
| 1 | $-1$ | 2 | | |
| 2 | $-2.25$ | $-4$ | 1 | |
| 2 | 200 | 400 | 700 | |
| 3 | 100 | 900 | $-50$ | 1 |

Store the parameters in a one-dimensional array and calculate trial values of $y$ using a FOR/NEXT loop.

# CHAPTER 8

# *Two-Dimensional Arrays*

8.1 MOTIVATION

8.2 SUBSCRIPTS

8.3 DIM STATEMENT

8.4 READ, INPUT, AND OUTPUT

8.5 MANIPULATING ARRAYS

8.6 SELECTED APPLICATIONS
Financial Report
Income Tax Program

8.7 COMMON ERRORS

ADDITIONAL EXERCISES

In many situations it is convenient to store data in arrays with more than one dimension. Some computer systems allow several dimensions, but we will focus here on the more common two-dimensional arrays.

## 8.1
## MOTIVATION

Generally, it is desirable to use two-dimensional arrays whenever we wish to store and manipulate data that are characterized by two attributes. For example, the Premium Schedule of Example 7.6 on page 205 incorporates the attributes "upper age limit" and "annual premium." Other examples include the following:

Occupied beds in a hospital are tabulated by day of the week and by ward.
Deposits for a major bank are recorded for all branch banks on a quarterly or monthly basis.

Enrollments at a college are tabulated by major and by class standing.

Exam scores for a course are recorded for all students.

Ten financial ratios from the Fortune 500 list of major U.S. corporations are recorded for all 500 corporations.

## 8.2
## *SUBSCRIPTS*

You will more easily understand **two-dimensional arrays** (those with two subscripts) if you visualize a group of memory locations as a grid of boxes (table) arranged in rows and columns as shown below.

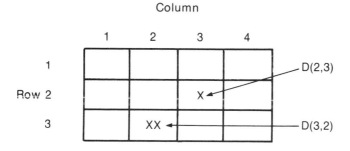

An element within a two-dimensional array is referenced by specifying two subscripts: row number and column number.

For example, in the 3-row by 4-column array below, the memory location that is marked with an X is found by looking at row 2, column 3; the memory location marked with XX is found in row 3, column 2.

As you can see, two subscripts are needed when you use two-dimensional arrays. In BASIC, the subscripts must be enclosed in parentheses and separated by a comma. For example, if the above array is named D, then the location where the X is found would be referenced as D(2,3) and the location where the XX is found would be referenced as D(3,2). Notice that, in accordance with mathematical convention, the subscripts are always given in the order

    array  ( row        column   )
    name   ( subscript,  subscript )

Other than the use of two subscripts according to the above convention, subscripts for two-dimensional arrays are treated in the same manner as for one-dimensional arrays.

Storage of two-dimensional arrays is best conceptualized as a table. For example, the 12-element array named D can be visualized as a 3-row by 4-column table in memory, as follows:

| D(1,1) | D(1,2) | D(1,3) | D(1,4) |
|--------|--------|--------|--------|
| D(2,1) | D(2,2) | D(2,3) | D(2,4) |
| D(3,1) | D(3,2) | D(3,3) | D(3,4) |

In actual practice, storage locations for two-dimensional arrays do not "look" like a table in memory, but that need not concern us since the BASIC convention treats it like a table.

In this chapter we deal exclusively with *numeric* two-dimensional arrays; *string* two-dimensional arrays are not permitted in many versions of BASIC.

## 8.3
## DIM STATEMENT

Just as with one-dimensional arrays, two-dimensional arrays must be dimensioned in order to reserve memory locations for the array. In addition to identifying one-dimensional variables, the DIM statement can indicate which variables are two-dimensional and establishes the number of rows and columns that will be reserved in memory for the array.

The general form of the DIM statement for use with two-dimensional arrays is

$$\text{line no. } \textbf{DIM} \begin{smallmatrix} array \\ name \end{smallmatrix} \left( \begin{smallmatrix} row \\ constant, \end{smallmatrix} \begin{smallmatrix} column \\ constant \end{smallmatrix} \right), \begin{smallmatrix} array \\ name \end{smallmatrix} \left( \begin{smallmatrix} row \\ constant, \end{smallmatrix} \begin{smallmatrix} column \\ constant \end{smallmatrix} \right), \ldots$$

For example, we might store the number of deposits for three branch banks in each of four quarters in a 3-row by 4-column two-dimensional array named D, where each row stores the quarterly data for one branch. The DIM statement would be specified as

    10 DIM D(3,4)

If you wanted D to store branch deposits for each month of the year, then you could set up an array with 3 rows and 12 columns. In this case, the DIM statement would be given by

    10 DIM (3,12)

In the first case, D has 12 elements in memory, whereas in the second case, 36 locations are reserved in memory.[1]

Both one and two-dimensional arrays can be dimensioned in a single DIM statement by using commas to separate each array specification. For example,

```
20 DIM S(5,10),E(8,10),T(5)
```

This results in the reservation of 50 locations for the two-dimensional array S, 80 locations for the two-dimensional array E, and 5 locations for the one-dimensional array T.[2]

## 8.4
## READ, INPUT, AND OUTPUT

The read/input/output of two-dimensional arrays is best accomplished by the use of two FOR/NEXT loops, one nested within the other. For the example that follows, assume that the two-dimensional array D stores the following data on the number of deposits by branch and by quarter.

|  |  | \multicolumn{4}{c}{Quarter} |
|  |  | 1 | 2 | 3 | 4 |
|---|---|---|---|---|---|
| | 1 | 1000 | 800 | 500 | 1200 |
| Branch | 2 | 500 | 2000 | 2000 | 500 |
| | 3 | 1500 | 300 | 700 | 1500 |

**Example 8.1    Read/Output with Nested FOR/NEXT Loops**

Consider the following program segment for reading D:

```
              005    DIM D(3,4)
  inner       010   ┌FOR R = 1 TO 3
  loop        020   │ ┌FOR C = 1 TO 4
              030   │ │   READ D(R,C)
  outer       040   │ └NEXT C
  loop        050   └NEXT R
                :
                :
              500 DATA 1000, 800, 500,1200
              510 DATA   500,2000,2000, 500
              520 DATA 1500, 300, 700,1500
              999 END
```

[1] As in one-dimensional arrays, some versions of BASIC use a zero subscript; thus DIM D(3,12) would reserve 4 rows and 13 columns, or 52 locations, including the element D(0,0).

[2] As in one-dimensional arrays, the omission of the DIM statement on some systems causes the implicit assignment of an upper bound of 10 on each subscript. As stated in the last chapter, however, the omission of the DIM statement, even when allowed, is not a good programming practice.

The flowchart in Figure 8.1 should help you visualize how the nesting of FOR/NEXT loops works. The key concept that you need to understand here is the exact manner in which the subscripts change values. (It might help you to review Section 6.1 beginning on page 147). Carefully look at the program and the flow-chart to confirm that the subscripts of D change values as follows:

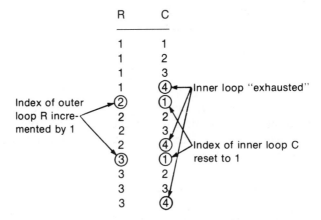

The first time through the loops, R = 1 and C = 1; so the first data item is read into D(1,1).

| D(1,1) | D(1,2) | D(1,3) | D(1,4) |
|--------|--------|--------|--------|
| 1000   |        |        |        |
| D(2,1) | D(2,2) | D(2,3) | D(2,4) |
|        |        |        |        |
| D(3,1) | D(3,2) | D(3,3) | D(3,4) |
|        |        |        |        |

The second time through the inner loop, R = 1 and C = 2; so the second item is read into D(1,2).

| D(1,1) | D(1,2) | D(1,3) | D(1,4) |
|--------|--------|--------|--------|
| 1000   | 800    |        |        |
| D(2,1) | D(2,2) | D(2,3) | D(2,4) |
|        |        |        |        |
| D(3,1) | D(3,2) | D(3,3) | D(3,4) |
|        |        |        |        |

The third time through the inner loop, R = 1 and C = 3; so the third item is read into D(1,3).

| D(1,1) | D(1,2) | D(1,3) | D(1,4) |
|--------|--------|--------|--------|
| 1000   | 800    | 500    |        |
| D(2,1) | D(2,2) | D(2,3) | D(2,4) |
|        |        |        |        |
| D(3,1) | D(3,2) | D(3,3) | D(3,4) |
|        |        |        |        |

The fourth time through the inner loop, R = 1 and C = 4; so the fourth item is read into D(1,4).

| D(1,1) | D(1,2) | D(1,3) | D(1,4) |
|--------|--------|--------|--------|
| 1000   | 800    | 500    | 1200   |
| D(2,1) | D(2,2) | D(2,3) | D(2,4) |
|        |        |        |        |
| D(3,1) | D(3,2) | D(3,3) | D(3,4) |
|        |        |        |        |

Then, R is incremented to 2 and again the inner loop (C) varies from 1 to 4. This results in the following sequence:

| R | C |            |
|---|---|------------|
| 2 | 1 | READ D(2,1) |
| 2 | 2 | READ D(2,2) |
| 2 | 3 | READ D(2,3) |
| 2 | 4 | READ D(2,4) |

Now the array appears as follows in memory.

| D(1,1) | D(1,2) | D(1,3) | D(1,4) |
|--------|--------|--------|--------|
| 1000   | 800    | 500    | 1200   |
| D(2,1) | D(2,2) | D(2,3) | D(2,4) |
| 500    | 2000   | 2000   | 500    |
| D(3,1) | D(3,2) | D(3,3) | D(3,4) |
|        |        |        |        |

FIGURE 8.1    Nested FOR/NEXT Loops for Read-In

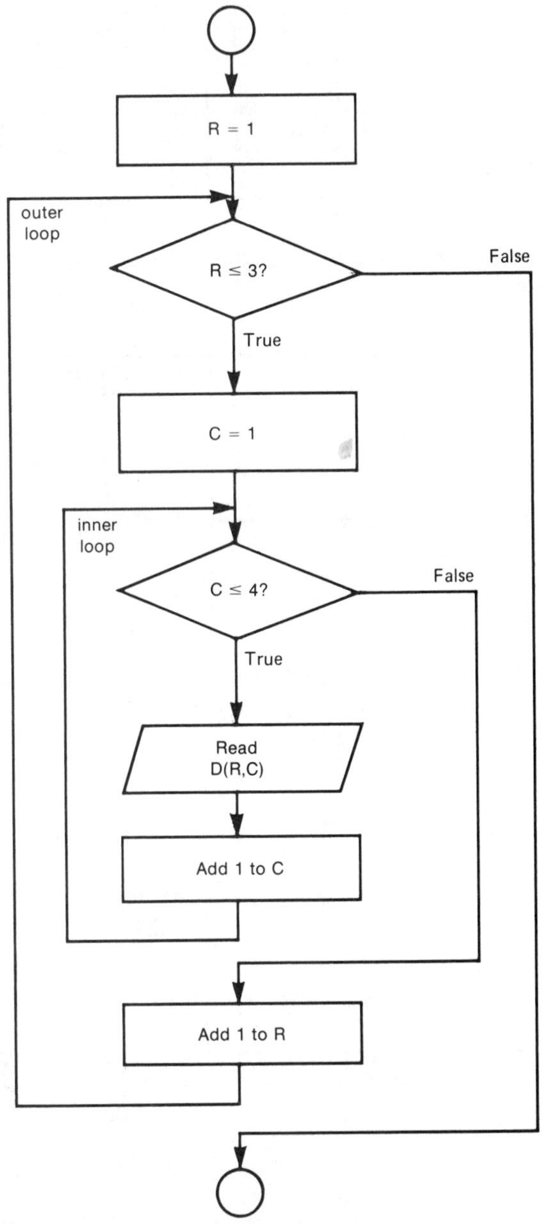

Finally, R is set to 3 and the inner index C varies from 1 to 4. This results in the sequence:

| R | C |   |
|---|---|---|
| 3 | 1 | READ D(3,1) |
| 3 | 2 | READ D(3,2) |
| 3 | 3 | READ D(3,3) |
| 3 | 4 | READ D(3,4) |

At this point, read-in of the array is complete, yielding the following configuration in memory:

| D(1,1) | D(1,2) | D(1,3) | D(1,4) |
|--------|--------|--------|--------|
| 1000   | 800    | 500    | 1200   |
| D(2,1) | D(2,2) | D(2,3) | D(2,4) |
| 500    | 2000   | 2000   | 500    |
| D(3,1) | D(3,2) | D(3,3) | D(3,4) |
| 1500   | 300    | 700    | 1500   |

Note that the READ statement is executed exactly 12 times. Since there is only one variable in the list of the READ statement, this means that 12 data items are required.

Nested loops are likewise used to print two-dimensional arrays. For example, the statements

```
100 FOR R = 1 TO 3
110    FOR C = 1 TO 4
120        PRINT D(R,C)
130    NEXT C
140 NEXT R
```

print the array D as follows:

```
1000
800
500
1200
500
2000
2000
500
1500
300
700
1500
```

To print the two-dimensional array in a table format requires a trailing comma or semicolon and a blank print line.
For example,

```
100 FOR R = 1 TO 3
110    FOR C = 1 TO 4
120        PRINT D(R,C);          Hold the row
130    NEXT C
135    PRINT                      Space down to next row (by filling
140 NEXT R                        the remainder of the current row
                                  with blanks)
```

results in

| | | | |
|---|---|---|---|
| 1000 | 800 | 500 | 1200 |
| 500 | 2000 | 2000 | 500 |
| 1500 | 300 | 700 | 1500 |

We cannot overemphasize the need for you to concentrate on the manner in which the subscripts of D in the READ or PRINT statement change values. Again, *the inner loop must be exhausted (the index must exceed its terminal value) for each iteration (loop) of the outer loop. Once the inner loop is exhausted, then the index of the outer loop is incremented and the index of the inner loop is reset to its initial value.*

## Follow-up Exercises

1.  How would output appear if the PRINT statement in line 135 were omitted?
2.  How would output appear if loop R were the inner loop and loop C were the outer loop (that is, interchange statements 100 and 110, and 130 and 140)?
3.  Suppose the following arrangement of statements is used:

```
500 DATA 1000
510 DATA 800
520 DATA 500
530 DATA 1200
540 DATA 500
      .
      .
      .
610 DATA 1500
```

How does memory appear after execution of lines 10 to 50 on page 229?
4.  Suppose the following program segment is executed using the same data as the example on page 229.

```
10 FOR C = 1 TO 4
20    FOR R = 1 TO 3
30        READ D(R,C)
40    NEXT R
50 NEXT C
```

How would D appear in memory? Does the array in memory get filled in row by row or column by column? How should we place data on the DATA statements so as to store the values in D exactly as they appear on page 233?

5. The array L is to be stored in memory as follows:

| L(1,1) | L(1,2) |
|--------|--------|
| 10 | 50 |
| **L(2,1)** | **L(2,2)** |
| 4 | 320 |
| **L(3,1)** | **L(3,2)** |
| 15 | 8 |

Prepare program segments that could be used to input these six values into the array L in one of two ways:

a. Row-by-row input (that is, in the sequence 10, 50, 4, 320, 15, 8).
b. Column-by-column input (that is, in the sequence 10, 4, 15, 50, 320, 8).

6. Indicate how the output of array L in Exercise 5 would appear for each segment below.

a.
```
100 FOR I = 1 TO 3
110    FOR J = 1 TO 2
120       PRINT L(I,J)
130    NEXT J
140 NEXT I
```

b.
```
100 FOR I = 1 TO 3
110    FOR J = 1 TO 2
120       PRINT L(I,J);
130    NEXT J
140 NEXT I
```

c.
```
100 FOR I = 1 TO 3
110    FOR J = 1 TO 2
120       PRINT L(I,J);
130    NEXT J
135    PRINT
140 NEXT I
```

# 8.5
# MANIPULATING ARRAYS

Processing data stored in two-dimensional arrays normally involves nesting of FOR/NEXT loops. The next example illustrates some common manipulations of two-dimensional arrays.

## EXAMPLE 8.2   Row and Column Totals

One of the more common processing tasks is finding totals of each row or column in an array. The row or column totals can be stored either in one-dimensional arrays or in an extra row or column of the two-dimensional array. For example, to find the annual bank deposits in each branch for the data given on page 229, we need to sum the entries in each row. The following program segment would determine row sums:

```
200 FOR R = 1 TO 3
210    LET S(R) = 0
220    FOR C = 1 TO 4
230       LET S(R) = S(R) + D(R,C)
240    NEXT C
250 NEXT R
```

When R = 1, S(1) is initialized to zero; then, the inner loop sums the values in the first row given by D(1,1), D(1,2), D(1,3), and D(1,4) and stores this sum in the first element of the array S.

| S(1) | D(1,1) | D(1,2) | D(1,3) | D(1,4) |
|------|--------|--------|--------|--------|
| 3500 | 1000 | 800 | 500 | 1200 |
| S(2) | D(2,1) | D(2,2) | D(2,3) | D(2,4) |
|      | 500 | 2000 | 2000 | 500 |
| S(3) | D(3,1) | D(3,2) | D(3,3) | D(3,4) |
|      | 1500 | 300 | 700 | 1500 |

When the outer loop is incremented (R = 2), S(2) is initialized to zero, and the values in row 2 are accumulated and stored in the second element of array S.

| S(1) | D(1,1) | D(1,2) | D(1,3) | D(1,4) |
|------|--------|--------|--------|--------|
| 3500 | 1000 | 800 | 500 | 1200 |
| S(2) | D(2,1) | D(2,2) | D(2,3) | D(2,4) |
| 5000 | 500 | 2000 | 2000 | 500 |
| S(3) | D(3,1) | D(3,2) | D(3,3) | D(3,4) |
|      | 1500 | 300 | 700 | 1500 |

Finally the outer loop is incremented (R = 3) and the values of the third row are added to the third element in the array S.

| S(1) | D(1,1) | D(1,2) | D(1,3) | D(1,4) |
|------|--------|--------|--------|--------|
| 3500 | 1000 | 800 | 500 | 1200 |
| S(2) | D(2,1) | D(2,2) | D(2,3) | D(2,4) |
| 5000 | 500 | 2000 | 2000 | 500 |
| S(3) | D(3,1) | D(3,2) | D(3,3) | D(3,4) |
| 4000 | 1500 | 300 | 700 | 1500 |

## Follow-up Exercises

7. Write a program segment that
   a. Accumulates the bank's total deposits for each quarter. Store these totals in a one-dimensional array called T.
   b. Calculates the grand total (G) of all deposits.

**8. Assume that D has been dimensioned to four rows and five columns. Instead of using the array S as in the example and the array T as in the preceding exercise, use the fourth row of D to store column totals and the fifth column to store row totals. Write program segments which accomplish this. Don't forget to initialize to zero the array elements which accumulate the sums. What does D(4,5) represent?

*9. Write a program segment which calculates for each branch the percentage of each quarter's deposit to the annual number of deposits. Store these percentages in the two-dimensional array P. After processing, P should have the stored values below. Can you fill in the third row? Note that, except for possible rounding error, rows of P sum to 100.

| P(1,1) | P(1,2) | P(1,3) | P(1,4) |
|--------|--------|--------|--------|
| 28.5714 | 22.8571 | 14.2857 | 34.2857 |
| P(2,1) | P(2,2) | P(2,3) | P(2,4) |
| 10.0000 | 40.0000 | 40.0000 | 10.0000 |
| P(3,1) | P(3,2) | P(3,3) | P(3,4) |
|  |  |  |  |

**10.** Suppose the array W has been dimensioned as follows:

15 DIM W(100,50)

Write a program segment that initializes each element in W to 100.

## 8.6
## SELECTED APPLICATIONS

This section illustrates two applications using two-dimensional arrays.

### Financial Report

The sales revenue and cost data for each region and model line of the Effete Automotive Corporation have been collected. The controller needs a report that presents sales, cost, and profit with totals for each region and model line. The program below prepares the desired report.

| Program | Comments |
|---|---|

```
010 REM ---- FINANCIAL REPORT PROGRAM ----
020 REM        VARIABLE KEY
030 REM           R1 = NUMBER OF REGIONS
040 REM           M1 = NUMBER OF MODELS
050 REM           R  = ARRAY FOR SALES REVENUE, WHERE
055 REM                ROWS REPRESENT REGIONS AND
056 REM                COLUMNS REPRESENT MODELS
060 REM           C  = ARRAY FOR COSTS, WHERE
065 REM                ROWS REPRESENT REGIONS AND
066 REM                COLUMNS REPRESENT MODELS
070 REM           P  = ARRAY FOR PROFITS, WHERE
075 REM                ROWS REPRESENT REGIONS AND
080 REM                COLUMNS REPRESENT MODELS
100 DIM R(10,10),C(10,10),P(10,10)        Dimension arrays.
110 READ R1,M1                            Read number of rows and columns to be utilized in array.
115 REM ------------------------------------------------
120 FOR I=1 TO R1
130   FOR J=1 TO M1
140     READ R(I,J)                       Read revenue data.
150   NEXT J
160 NEXT I
165 REM ------------------------------------------------
170 FOR I=1 TO R1
180   FOR J=1 TO M1
190     READ C(I,J)                       Read cost data.
200   NEXT J
210 NEXT I
215 REM ------------------------------------------------
220 FOR I=1 TO R1
230   FOR J=1 TO M1
240     LET P(I,J)=R(I,J)-C(I,J)          Determine profit by region and model.
250   NEXT J
260 NEXT I
265 REM ------------------------------------------------
270 FOR I=1 TO R1
280   LET R(I,M1+1)=0
```

```
290    LET C(I,M1+1)=0
300    LET P(I,M1+1)=0
310    FOR J=1 TO M1
320      LET R(I,M1+1)=R(I,M1+1) + R(I,J)
330      LET C(I,M1+1)=C(I,M1+1) + C(I,J)
340      LET P(I,M1+1)=P(I,M1+1) + P(I,J)
350    NEXT J
360 NEXT I
365 REM ------------------------------------------------
```

Find row (region) sums for each array. Store these in the *first unused (M1 + 1) column* of each array. Note initialization of this column in lines 280 to 300.

```
370 FOR J=1 TO M1
380    LET R(R1+1,J)=0
390    LET C(R1+1,J)=0
400    LET P(R1+1,J)=0
410    FOR I=1 TO R1
420      LET R(R1+1,J)=R(R1+1,J) + R(I,J)
430      LET C(R1+1,J)=C(R1+1,J) + C(I,J)
440      LET P(R1+1,J)=P(R1+1,J) + P(I,J)
450    NEXT I
460 NEXT J
465 REM ------------------------------------------------
```

Find column (model) sums for each array. Store these in the *first unused (R1 + 1) row* of each array. Note initialization of this row in lines 380 to 400. Also note that the I loop is now nested within the J loop.

```
470 PRINT "REVENUES"
480 PRINT ,
490 FOR J=1 TO M1+1
500    PRINT J,
510 NEXT J
515 REM ------------------------------------------------
```

Print label and column numbers for revenue array.

```
520 PRINT
530 FOR I=1 TO R1+1
540    PRINT I,
550    FOR J=1 TO M1+1
560      PRINT R(I,J),
570    NEXT J
580    PRINT
590 NEXT I
600 PRINT
610 PRINT
615 REM ------------------------------------------------
```

Print row number.

Print array element.

```
620 PRINT "COSTS"
630 PRINT ,
640 FOR J=1 TO M1+1
650    PRINT J,
660 NEXT J
665 REM ------------------------------------------------
```

Print label and column numbers for cost array.

```
670 PRINT
680 FOR I=1 TO R1+1
690    PRINT I,
700    FOR J=1 TO M1+1
710      PRINT C(I,J),
720    NEXT J
730    PRINT
740 NEXT I
750 PRINT
760 PRINT
765 REM ------------------------------------------------
```

Print row number.

Print array element.

```
770 PRINT "PROFITS"
780 PRINT ,
790 FOR J=1 TO M1+1
800    PRINT J,
810 NEXT J
815 REM ------------------------------------------------
```

Print label and column numbers for profit array.

```
820 PRINT
830 FOR I=1 TO R1+1
840    PRINT I,
```

Print row number.

```
850     FOR J=1 TO M1+1                    Print array element.
860        PRINT P(I,J),
870     NEXT J
880     PRINT
.900 NEXT I
905 REM  --- --- --- --- --- --- --- --- --- --- --- ---   Number of rows and columns.
910 DATA 3,2                               Revenue data (row by row).
920 DATA 100,150,60,40,30,70              Cost data (row by row).
930 DATA 50,100,40,10,25,75
995 REM  --- --- --- --- --- --- --- --- --- --- --- ---
999 END
```

```
REVENUES
                1               2           3

   1           100             150         250

   2           60              40          100

   3           30              70          100

   4           190             260         0



COSTS
                1               2           3

   1           50              100         150

   2           40              10          50

   3           25              75          100

   4           115             185         0



PROFITS
                1               2           3

   1           50              50          100

   2           20              30          50

   3           5               -5          0

   4           75              75          0


TIME 0.09 SECS.
```

Note that the sums for each region and model line are stored within each of the two-dimensional arrays (R, C, P). For example, the statement

$$320 \text{ LET } R(I, M1 + 1) = R(I, M1 + 1) + R(I, J)$$

stores a row total (region total) in the column immediately after the last model-line column. The statement

420 LET R(R1 + 1,J) = R(R1 + 1,J) + R(I,J)

stores column totals (model-line totals) in the row immediately following the last row which stores revenues.

### Follow-up Exercises

11. Roleplay the computer by processing the given data. In particular, notice how the program stores row and column sums. Confirm the output, paying close attention to spacing and the method of numbering rows and columns.
** 12. The program does not accumulate overall totals for revenue, cost, and profit. (Did you notice the 0 in the fourth row and third column of each table?) Modify the program so these totals are accumulated.
** 13. Modify the program so one additional row and one additional column is used with each array. The new row contains each model's contribution to overall revenue, cost, and profit (each column total as a percentage of the overall total). The new column contains each region's contribution to overall revenue, cost, and profit (each row total as a percentage of the overall total).

## *Income Tax Program*

After taking a tax course, you decide to earn some extra money (so that you can pay more taxes) by opening a computerized tax service for local accountants and individual taxpayers.

Given a taxpayer's wages (W) from form W-2, dividends (D), interest income (I1), income other than wages (O), and adjustments (A1) such as moving expenses, the adjusted gross income (A2) is given by

$$A2 = W + D + I1 + O - A1$$

Taxable income (T2) is determined as adjusted gross income less excess itemized deductions (E2) less the product of number of exemptions (E1) and the allowance per exemption (E3):

$$T2 = A2 - E2 - E1*E3$$

E2 is set to 0 if a single taxpayer's itemized deductions (D1) are less than \$2200; however, if D1 is greater than \$2200, then $E2 = D1 - 2200$. The income tax for single (unmarried) taxpayers is based on the taxable income according to the schedule on page 242.

To illustrate the computations, consider an individual who declares \$19,700 in wages, \$225 in dividends, \$305.20 in interest income, \$3200 in income other than wages, and no adjustments. This gives an A2 of \$23,430.20. If itemized deductions amount to \$4230 and one exemption is claimed at a \$750 allowance per exemption, then E2 is \$2030 and T2 is \$20,650.20. From the above tax schedule, the income tax (T3) is determined as \$4510 + (0.36) × (20,650.20 − 20,200), or \$4672.07. If the taxpayer had paid taxes during the year which amounted to more than T3, then the taxpayer would receive a

*Tax Schedule for Single Taxpayers*

| | | COLUMN | | |
| --- | --- | --- | --- | --- |
| (1) | (2) | (3) | (4) | (5) |
| | | | | OF THE |
| | BUT NOT | | | AMOUNT |
| OVER— | OVER— | INCOME TAX | | OVER— |
| $0 | $2,200 | $0 | + 0% | — |
| $2,200 | $2,700 | $0 | + 14% | $2,200 |
| $2,700 | $3,200 | $70 | + 15% | $2,700 |
| $3,200 | $3,700 | $145 | + 16% | $3,200 |
| $3,700 | $4,200 | $225 | + 17% | $3,700 |
| $4,200 | $6,200 | $310 | + 19% | $4,200 |
| $6,200 | $8,200 | $690 | + 21% | $6,200 |
| $8,200 | $10,200 | $1,110 | + 24% | $8,200 |
| $10,200 | $12,200 | $1,590 | + 25% | $10,200 |
| $12,200 | $14,200 | $2,090 | + 27% | $12,200 |
| $14,200 | $16,200 | $2,630 | + 29% | $14,200 |
| $16,200 | $18,200 | $3,210 | + 31% | $16,200 |
| $18,200 | $20,200 | $3,830 | + 34% | $18,200 |
| $20,200 | $22,200 | $4,510 | + 36% | $20,200 |
| $22,200 | $24,200 | $5,230 | + 38% | $22,200 |
| $24,200 | $28,200 | $5,990 | + 40% | $24,200 |
| $28,200 | $34,200 | $7,590 | + 45% | $28,200 |
| $34,200 | $40,200 | $10,290 | + 50% | $34,200 |
| $40,200 | $46,200 | $13,290 | + 55% | $40,200 |
| $46,200 | $52,200 | $16,590 | + 60% | $46,200 |
| $52,200 | $62,200 | $20,190 | + 62% | $52,200 |
| $62,200 | $72,200 | $26,390 | + 64% | $62,200 |
| $72,200 | $82,200 | $32,790 | + 66% | $72,200 |
| $82,200 | $92,200 | $39,390 | + 68% | $82,200 |
| $92,200 | $102,200 | $46,190 | + 69% | $92,200 |
| $102,200 | — | $53,090 | + 70% | $102,200 |

welcome refund from the IRS; otherwise, a not-so-welcome balance due the IRS would have to be paid.

This is another example of a table look-up, this time using a two-dimensional array to store the table. To solve this problem the data in columns 2, 3, and 4 of the tax schedule are stored in a two-dimensional array named T. The "search key" is the taxpayer's taxable income (T2); the "set of keys" is the upper limits of each income class (column 1 of T, which is column 2 of the tax schedule) and the "function values" are in columns 3 and 4 of the tax schedule (columns 2 and 3 of T).

The flowchart in Figure 8.2 illustrates the design of the income tax program that follows.

FIGURE 8.2  *Flowchart for Income Tax Program*

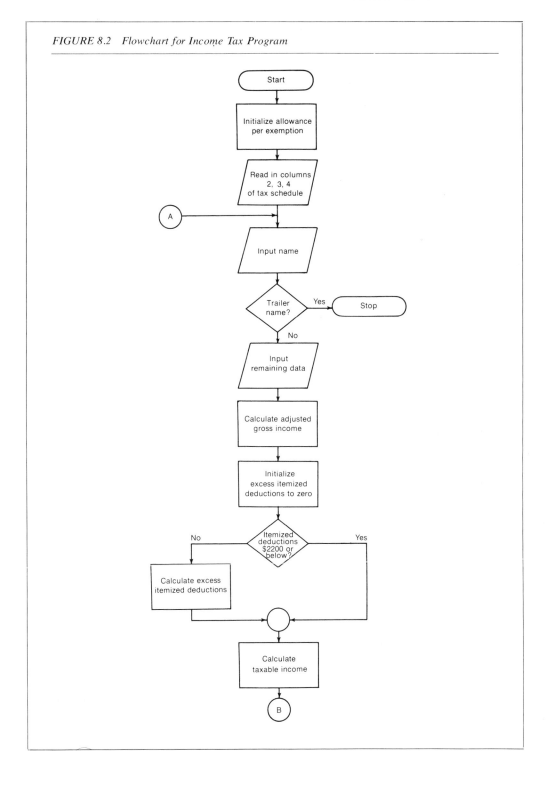

FIGURE 8.2    *Continued*

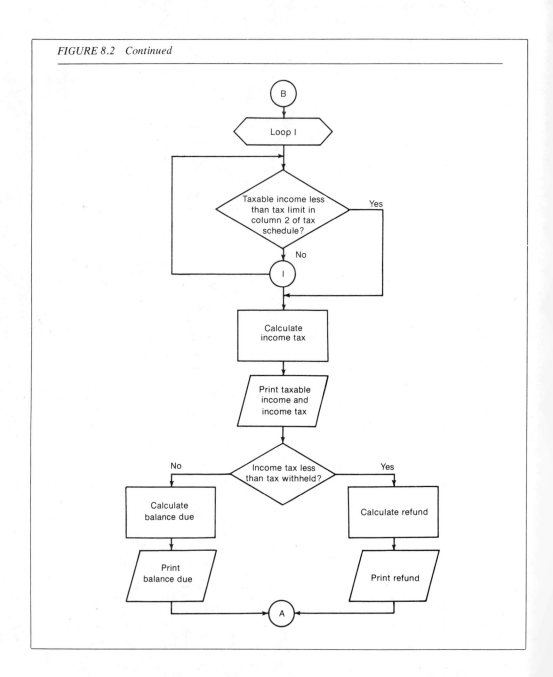

```
005 REM ---INCOME TAX PROGRAM---
010 REM----------------------------------------------------
015 REM        KEY:
020 REM          W = WAGES
025 REM          D = DIVIDENDS
030 REM          I1 = INTEREST INCOME
035 REM          O = INCOME OTHER THAN WAGES
040 REM          A1 = ADJUSTMENTS TO INCOME
045 REM          A2 = ADJUSTED GROSS INCOME
050 REM          E1 = NUMBER OF EXEMPTIONS
055 REM          E2 = EXCESS ITEMIZED DEDUCTIONS
060 REM          E3 = ALLOWANCE PER EXEMPTION
065 REM          T1 = TAX WITHHELD
070 REM          T2 = TAXABLE INCOME
075 REM          T3 = INCOME TAX
080 REM          D1 = ITEMIZED DEDUCTIONS
085 REM          B = BALANCE DUE IRS
090 REM          R = REFUND FROM IRS
092 REM          T = ARRAY THAT STORES COLUMNS 2,3,4
093 REM              OF TAX SCHEDULE
095 REM----------------------------------------------------
100 DIM T(26,3)
110 LET E3=750
120 FOR J=1 TO 3
130    FOR I=1 TO 26
140       READ T(I,J)              Read array T. Remember that columns 1, 2, and 3 of T are
150    NEXT I                      columns 2, 3, and 4 of tax schedule.
160 NEXT J
170 REM ----------------------------------------------------
180 PRINT "ENTER NAME";
190 INPUT N$
200 IF N$="EOD" THEN 999           Input data for individual taxpayer.
210 PRINT "ENTER WAGES";
220 INPUT W
230 PRINT "ENTER DIVIDENDS, INTEREST,"
240 PRINT "OTHER INCOME, ADJUSTMENTS";
250 INPUT D,I1,O,A1
260 PRINT "ENTER DEDUCTIONS AND EXEMPTIONS";
270 INPUT D1,E1
280 PRINT "ENTER TAX WITHHELD";
290 INPUT T1
300 REM ----------------------------------------------------
310 LET A2=W+D+I1+O-A1              Calculate adjusted gross income.
320 REM ----------------------------------------------------
330 LET E2=0                       Logic for extra deduction.
340 IF D1 <= 2200 THEN 370
350 LET E2=D1 - 2200
360 REM ----------------------------------------------------
370 LET T2=A2-E2-E1*E3             Calculate taxable income.
380 REM ----------------------------------------------------
390 FOR I=1 TO 26                  Table look-up logic. Unnatural exit from
400    IF T2 < T(I,1) THEN 420     loop I gives correct row (value of I) in tax table.
410 NEXT I
420 LET T3=T(I,2) + (T2-T(I-1,1)) * T(I,3)/100    Income tax calculation.
430 REM ----------------------------------------------------
440 PRINT
450 PRINT "TAXABLE INCOME $";T2
460 PRINT "TAX LIABILITY  $";T3
470 PRINT
480 IF T3<T1 THEN 530
490 LET B=T3 - T1
```

```
500 PRINT "BALANCE DUE     $";B
510 PRINT
520 GO TO 180
530 LET R=T1 - T3
540 PRINT "REFUND          $";R
550 PRINT
560 GO TO 180
570 DATA 2200,2700,3200,3700,4200,6200,8200,10200,12200,14200,16200
580 DATA 18200,20200,22200,24200,28200,34200,40200,46200,52200,62200
590 DATA 72200,82200,92200,102200,999999
600 DATA 0,0,70,145,225,310,690,1110,1590,2090,2630,3210,3830,4510,5230
610 DATA 5990,7590,10290,13290,16590,20190,26390,32790,39390,46190,53090
620 DATA 0,14,15,16,17,19,21,24,25,27,29,31,34,36,38,40,45,50,55,60,62
630 DATA 64,66,68,69,70
999 END
```

```
ENTER NAME?ADAM SMITH
ENTER WAGES?19700
ENTER DIVIDENDS, INTEREST,
OTHER INCOME, ADJUSTMENTS?225,305.2,3200,0
ENTER DEDUCTIONS AND EXEMPTIONS?4230,1
ENTER TAX WITHHELD?4100

TAXABLE INCOME $ 20650.2
TAX LIABILITY  $ 4672.07

BALANCE DUE    $ 572.07

ENTER NAME?ADAM SMITH JR
ENTER WAGES?12100
ENTER DIVIDENDS, INTEREST,
OTHER INCOME, ADJUSTMENTS?0,0,0,0
ENTER DEDUCTIONS AND EXEMPTIONS?1900,1
ENTER TAX WITHHELD?2530

TAXABLE INCOME $ 11350
TAX LIABILITY  $ 1877.5

REFUND         $ 652.5

ENTER NAME?EOD

TIME 0.07 SECS.
```

## Follow-up Exercises

**14.** Identify what the following variables represent in the program:
- a. T(I,1)
- b. T(I,2)
- c. T(I,3)
- d. T(I − 1,1)

**15.** Describe how the tax schedule is entered and stored. What entry is used for the last item in column 1 of T?

**16.** Describe the stored contents of the following memory locations for the *second* taxpayer when the computer executes line 540: E3, W, D, I1, O, A1, D1, E1, T1, A2, E2, T2, T3, B, R.

**\*17.** As the program stands, it has a bug whenever taxable income (T2) is less than $2200. Can you identify the problem? Modify the program to eliminate this bug.

**\*18.** Array T has 26 rows and 3 columns. The last entry in the first column needs to be a very large number to account for taxable incomes that exceed $102,200. Our data item in line 590 limits this number to $999,999. Thus, the program will not handle taxable incomes of $1 million or more. (Not much to be concerned about, actually.) Incorporate a new statement that calculates T3 for someone who exceeds a taxable income of $102,200.

# 8.7
# COMMON ERRORS

Errors associated with two-dimensional arrays are as likely to occur as errors associated with one-dimensional arrays. So, review once more the common errors discussed on pages 216 to 217 and mentally modify the examples for two-dimensional arrays.

When using nested loops, keep in mind that the inner loop index varies faster than the outer loop index. Typically, we let the inner loop index represent the column subscript and the outer loop index, the row subscript. This gives us row-by-row read/input/output, which is conceptually consistent with the usual way we treat tables.

If you want your printout to look like a table, then you must use a trailing comma or semicolon and an extra PRINT statement, as illustrated in Example 8.1 on page 234.

## Additional Exercises

**19. Mailing List Revisited.** Rewrite the program in part c of Exercise 34 in Chapter 6 on page 175 by storing columns (7) and (8) on the data file in a two-dimensional array. Store columns (1) to (6) in six one-dimensional arrays. Design your program to include a FOR/NEXT loop for processing multiple regions and interest areas. Thus, one run can handle the four separate runs required by the old version.

**20. Computerized Matching Revisited.** Rewrite the program in part b of Exercise 28 in Chapter 5 on page 141 by incorporating a loop to handle the different inquiries. Store the numeric portion of the placement office file in a two-dimensional array. Store name, ID, and address in three one-dimensional arrays.

**21. Crime Data Summary Revisited.** Solve Exercise 22 in Chapter 7 on page 218 using two-dimensional arrays for numeric data.

**22. Interactive Airline Reservation System.** All major airlines have automated their systems for handling seat reservations. A central computer keeps a record in storage of all relevant information describing the services being sold: flight numbers, flight schedules, seats available, prices, and other data.

A reservation clerk can request information on seat availability, can sell seats to passengers (providing they are available), can cancel reservations (which increases available seats), and if a flight is full, can put individuals on a waiting list.

a.  Develop a flowchart and an interactive program to incorporate the following options:

1.  Update the flight information table shown below. For example, if a customer requests one tourist reservation on flight number 4, then the program should check for available tourist seats. Since one is available, it should then adjust the available tourist seats to zero and print a message such as RESERVATION ALLOWED. If the passenger had requested two seats, however, the program should print RESERVATION DISALLOWED. SORRY, OUR HIGH ETHICAL STANDARDS PREVENT OVERBOOKING.
2.  Retrieve status on a particular flight by printing the appropriate row in the flight information table.
3.  Print entire flight information table.
4.  Terminate the run.

Remember to read the flight information data into arrays at the start of the program.

### Current Table of Flight Information

| Flight Number | Departing Airport | Arriving Airport | Time of Departure | Time of Arrival | Available Seats First Class | Available Seats Tourist | Seats Sold First Class | Seats Sold Tourist |
|---|---|---|---|---|---|---|---|---|
| 1 | BOS | CHI | 0730 | 0855 | 20 | 8 | 10 | 75 |
| 2 | BOS | CHI | 1200 | 1357 | 20 | 20 | 10 | 50 |
| 3 | BOS | DEN | 0810 | 1111 | 30 | 10 | 0 | 120 |
| 4 | ATL | SF | 1145 | 1604 | 15 | 1 | 25 | 129 |
| 5 | CHI | BOS | 0645 | 0948 | 30 | 25 | 5 | 90 |
| 6 | CHI | NY | 0945 | 1237 | 30 | 8 | 0 | 120 |
| 7 | CHI | LA | 1530 | 1851 | 20 | 10 | 30 | 60 |
| 8 | CHI | DEN | 1955 | 2114 | 5 | 5 | 25 | 85 |
| 9 | DEN | PIT | 1025 | 1611 | 10 | 6 | 60 | 60 |
| 10 | DEN | SF | 1435 | 1556 | 20 | 10 | 10 | 89 |

Process the following requests in your computer run on an interactive basis:

| Option Request | Flight Number | Seat Type | Number of Tickets | Reservation Request |
|---|---|---|---|---|
| 1 | 4 | Tourist | 1 | Reserve |
| 1 | 6 | Tourist | 4 | Reserve |
| 2 | 3 | — | — | — |
| 1 | 9 | Tourist | 2 | Cancel |
| 1 | 9 | 1st Class | 4 | Cancel |
| 1 | 4 | Tourist | 2 | Reserve |
| 3 | — | — | — | — |

**b. Besides the options in part a, give your program the capability to retrieve and print flight information on all flights between two specified airports. Test your program for flights from Boston to Chicago and from Chicago to Los Angeles. In the first case, you should get a printout of the first two rows; in the second case, the seventh row should be printed.

23. **Poisson-Distributed Electronic Failures.** The likelihoods (probabilities) of failures for many electronic processes can be described by the Poisson probability function

$$f(x) = \frac{\lambda^x \cdot e^{-\lambda}}{x!}$$

where

$f(x)$ = probability of $x$ failures per time period
$\lambda$ = average number of failures per time period (lambda)
$e$ = base of natural logarithm (the irrational number $2.71828 \cdots$)
$x$ = number of failures per time period
$x!$ = $x$ factorial, or the product $1 \cdot 2 \cdot 3 \cdots (x - 1) \cdot (x)$
   (*Note:* 0! is defined as 1.)

For example, suppose that malfunctions of onboard navigation systems for a large squadron of aircraft are Poisson-distributed with a failure rate of 20 per month (that is, $\lambda = 20$). In this case, the probability of 15 failures (that is, $x = 15$) in a month is

$$f(15) = \frac{(20)^{15} \cdot e^{-20}}{15!} = 0.0516$$

or about 5.16 percent.

a. Print a table of Poisson probabilities where rows represent values of $x$ from 0 to 40 in increments of 1 and columns represent values of $\lambda$ from 10 to 20 in increments of 2. Use a two-dimensional array to store probabilities. *Note:* You might want to use the exponential function described in Table 9.1 on page 258.

b. Print a table of cumulative probabilities, where again rows represent the same values of $x$ and columns represent the same values of $\lambda$. The cumulative probability of $x$ for a given $\lambda$ is defined as the probability of $x$ or less failures, or

$$F(x) = f(0) + f(1) + f(2) + \cdots + f(x)$$
$$= \sum_{i=0}^{x} f(i)$$

For example, the probability of three *or less* failures during a month when $\lambda = 10$ is

$$
\begin{aligned}
F(3) = \ & f(0) \ + \ f(1) \ + \ f(2) \ + \ f(3) \\
= \ & 0.0000 + 0.0005 + 0.0023 + 0.0076 \\
= \ & 0.0104
\end{aligned}
$$

or just over 1 percent.

c.  Use your tables to find the following probabilities:

1.  The probability of exactly 20 failures given $\lambda = 20$.
2.  The probability of 20 or less failures given $\lambda = 20$.
3.  The probability of exactly 0 failures given $\lambda = 10$.
4.  The probability of exactly 10 failures given $\lambda = 10$.
5.  The probability of exactly 20 failures given $\lambda = 10$.
6.  The probability of 20 or less failures given $\lambda = 10$.
7.  The probability of 20 or less failures given $\lambda = 16$.
8.  The probability of more than 20 failures given $\lambda = 16$.

24. **Personnel Salary Budget.** The personnel office for a state government agency is in the process of developing a salary budget for the next fiscal year. The personnel file contains the following information on each employee:

1.  Employee name
2.  Social security number
3.  Current annual salary
4.  Union code (1 = clerical, 2 = teachers, 3 = electrical)
5.  Current step in pay schedule (1 through 5)
6.  Year hired

The state agency deals with three labor unions: clerical, teachers, and electrical. Each union has negotiated a separate salary schedule which entitles each employee to an annual step increase. The salary schedules are listed in the table below. Each employee is hired at the lowest step in the salary schedule for their union, and moves up one step each year. The field "current step in pay schedule" indicates the employee's step prior to the new salary for the coming year; that is, "current annual salary" is consistent with this step. The salary for the upcoming year is to be based on the next highest step. Employees who have reached step 5 are at the maximum salary level for that job. Thus, next year's step salary is the same as their current annual salary.

In addition to the salary step increase, employees who have been employed by the state for 10 years or more are entitled to a longevity increase. A longevity increase represents a 5 percent increment added to the employee's *new* step salary.

### Salary Schedules

| Step | Clerical | Teachers | Electrical |
|------|----------|----------|------------|
| 1 | 10176 | 9133 | 12170 |
| 2 | 10592 | 10433 | 14260 |
| 3 | 10956 | 11833 | 16668 |
| 4 | 11320 | 13333 | 19501 |
| 5 | 11921 | 14893 | 22801 |

Personnel File

| | | | | | |
|---|---|---|---|---|---|
| SMYTHIE SMILE | 032166789 | 10956 | 1 | 3 | 71 |
| ALFRED ALFREDO | 123454321 | 13333 | 2 | 4 | 68 |
| MENDAL MICKEY | 987654345 | 22801 | 3 | 5 | 67 |
| FIELD FLORA | 543297541 | 12170 | 3 | 1 | 76 |

| CURRAN CURRENT | 045811222 | 10176 | 1 | 1 | 76 |
| HANDEL HALO | 315791123 | 11320 | 1 | 4 | 70 |
| UNKIND CORA | 129834765 | 9133 | 2 | 1 | 75 |

a. Prepare a flowchart and write a program that prints a budget report for the personnel office. Output from the report includes employee's name, current salary, increase in salary due to step, increase in salary due to longevity, and new salary. Following the output table, print totals for the four numeric columns. Treat the salary schedules as a two-dimensional (5 × 3) array that is to be read in. Data in the personnel file and in the output table need not be treated as arrays.

b. Print a table which summarizes the salary budgets as follows:

SALARY BUDGETS

| CLERICAL | $ | xxxxxx |
| TEACHERS | $ | xxxxxx |
| ELECTRICAL | $ | xxxxxx |
| | $ | xxxxxxx |

** c. Print the table of part b *prior* to the output in part a. *Hint:* Unlike part a, now you must subscript both the variables in the personnel file and the output in the report of part a. Do you see why? Use two-dimensional arrays.

**25. Fortune 500 Sort.** The Fortune 500 list is a listing compiled by *Fortune Magazine* of the top 500 corporations according to sales. The table below provides selected data for the top 20 corporations in 1978.[3]

| Rank | Corporation | Sales (millions) | Assets (millions) | Profits (millions) | Employees (thousands) |
|---|---|---|---|---|---|
| 1 | General Motors | 54961 | 26658 | 3338 | 797 |
| 2 | Exxon | 54126 | 38453 | 2423 | 127 |
| 3 | Ford Motor | 37842 | 19241 | 1673 | 479 |
| 4 | Mobil | 32126 | 20576 | 1005 | 201 |
| 5 | Texaco | 27920 | 18926 | 930 | 71 |
| 6 | Standard Oil (CA) | 20917 | 14822 | 1016 | 38 |
| 7 | IBM | 18133 | 18978 | 2719 | 310 |
| 8 | Gulf Oil | 17840 | 14225 | 752 | 59 |
| 9 | General Electric | 17519 | 13697 | 1088 | 384 |
| 10 | Chrysler | 16708 | 7668 | 163 | 251 |
| 11 | ITT | 13146 | 12286 | 551 | 375 |
| 12 | Standard Oil (IN) | 13020 | 12884 | 1012 | 47 |
| 13 | Atlantic Richfield | 10969 | 11119 | 702 | 52 |
| 14 | Shell Oil | 10112 | 8877 | 735 | 34 |
| 15 | US Steel | 9610 | 9914 | 138 | 166 |
| 16 | DuPont | 9435 | 7431 | 545 | 131 |
| 17 | Continental Oil | 8700 | 6625 | 381 | 43 |
| 18 | Western Electric | 8135 | 5876 | 490 | 162 |
| 19 | Tenneco | 7440 | 8278 | 427 | 93 |
| 20 | Procter & Gamble | 7284 | 4487 | 461 | 54 |

[3] Reprinted by permission from the Fortune Directory; © 1978 Time Inc.

a.  Prepare a flowchart and write a program which sorts the data from high to low according to assets, profits, or employees (as specified by the user). Your output would simply be the above two-dimensional array rearranged according to the requested sort. In your output use the numeric code (rank) for the corporation instead of the name. Conduct three runs for three separate sorts: by assets, by profits, and by employees. *Hint:* You might try a sort by the **pointer method,** which avoids the large number of exchanges required by the bubble sort when dealing with a two-dimensional array.

In this procedure you store your data file in a two-dimensional array and also create a separate one-dimensional array to indicate the relative order of the data in the two-dimensional array. Initially, the sequence in the one-dimensional array is 1, 2, 3, . . . , N where each value points to a row number of the data in the two-dimensional array (look at the example below). When you find two items in the two-dimensional array out of order, you interchange the row numbers in the one-dimensional array. When the sort is complete, the relative order of the file is indicated in the one-dimensional array. The data in the two-dimensional array remain undisturbed.

### Sample Two-Dimensional Array

|  ID  | SALARY |
|------|--------|
| 1012 | 15000  |
| 1007 | 12500  |
| 1003 | 10000  |
| 1011 | 14000  |

Initial and final arrangement of data

### Initial One-Dimensional Array

| 1 |
|---|
| 2 |
| 3 |
| 4 |

### Final One-Dimensional Array

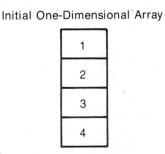

| 3 |
|---|
| 2 |
| 4 |
| 1 |

If sort is to be ID in ascending order

| 1 |
|---|
| 4 |
| 2 |
| 3 |

If sort is to be ID in descending order

b. As part of your output in part a, include the name of the corporation.

c. Include two new columns in the output to part a: profit as a percentage of sales and profit as a percentage of assets.

**d. Include the option of rearranging the output in alphabetic order according to the names. Alphabetic comparisons can be treated in the same manner as numeric comparisons.

**26. Questionnaire Analysis.** A university is conducting a survey to determine its undergraduates' "attitudes toward and experiences with the consumption of alcoholic beverages." The following questionnaire has been designed for this survey:

_____1. What is your sex? 1. male _____ 2. female _____

_____2. Where do you live? 1. on campus _____ 2. off campus with parents _____ 3. off campus alone/with roommates _____

_____3. What is your class standing? 1. freshman _____ 2. sophomore _____ 3. junior _____ 4. senior _____ 5. other _____

_____4. How often on the average do you drink alcoholic beverages? 1. never _____ 2. less than once a week _____ 3. one to three times per week _____ 4. four to five times per week _____ 5. more than five times per week _____ .

_____5. Do you feel other people's drinking has any adverse effects on your life? 1. frequently _____ 2. occasionally _____ 3. rarely _____ 4. never _____

_____6. Do your drinking habits affect your academic life? 1. frequently _____ 2. occasionally _____ 3. rarely _____ 4. never _____

_____7. Do you ever feel guilty about your drinking? 1. frequently _____ 2. occasionally _____ 3. rarely _____ 4. never _____

_____8. Do you feel you drink primarily because of 1. boredom _____ 2. peer pressure _____ 3. tension _____ 4. other _____ (specify)

Before conducting the full survey, it has been decided to pretest the questionnaire on 10 students. The results are shown below.

*Answer to Question No.*

| Student | 1 | 2 | 3 | 4 | 5 | 6 | 7 | 8 |
|---------|---|---|---|---|---|---|---|---|
| 1 | 1 | 1 | 3 | 3 | 4 | 4 | 2 | 3 |
| 2 | 1 | 1 | 3 | 1 | 2 | 2 | 1 | 1 |
| 3 | 2 | 2 | 2 | 2 | 1 | 3 | 3 | 2 |
| 4 | 2 | 3 | 1 | 4 | 3 | 1 | 3 | 3 |
| 5 | 1 | 1 | 4 | 4 | 1 | 1 | 2 | 3 |
| 6 | 1 | 2 | 2 | 2 | 1 | 1 | 2 | 3 |
| 7 | 2 | 3 | 4 | 1 | 3 | 2 | 1 | 2 |
| 8 | 2 | 1 | 1 | 2 | 4 | 4 | 2 | 1 |
| 9 | 1 | 2 | 3 | 3 | 1 | 1 | 1 | 1 |
| 10 | 2 | 2 | 1 | 4 | 2 | 3 | 2 | 1 |

a. Prepare a flowchart and write a program that reads questionnaire data into a two-dimensional array and outputs a frequency distribution for each question. For example, the frequency distribution for the first question and the above data would be

|          | Responses |   |
|----------|-----------|---|
| Question | 1 | 2 |
| 1        | 5 | 5 |

For the second question, we have:

|          | Responses |   |   |
|----------|-----------|---|---|
| Question | 1 | 2 | 3 |
| 2        | 4 | 4 | 2 |

Label your output and try to make it as efficient as possible.

**b. Modify your program to provide cross tabulation of responses for any two questions which are specified by the user. For example, if we wish to assess differences between the drinking frequencies of men and women, then your output might appear as follows:

|              |     | QUESTION 1 |   |
|--------------|-----|------------|---|
|              |     | 1 | 2 |
|              | 1—  | 1 | 1 |
| QUESTION 4   | 2—  | 1 | 2 |
|              | 3—  | 2 | 0 |
|              | 4—  | 1 | 2 |
|              | 5—  | 0 | 0 |

To make sure you understand this cross tabulation, confirm the numbers based on the data.

27. **Cross Tabulations.** Read the problem described in Exercise 27 in Chapter 5 on page 140.

a. Prepare a flowchart and write a program that enters the personnel file into a two-dimensional array in memory and performs cross tabulations on *average salary* between any two variables specified by the user (age vs. sex, age vs. marital status, age vs. education, sex vs. marital status, sex vs. education, and marital status vs. education). For example, the output for age vs. sex might look like this:

|       | Sex |   |
|-------|-----|---|
| Age   | 1 | 2 |
| 21–30 | 24000 | 17250 |
| 31–40 | 22750 | 0 |
| 41–50 | 27000 | 25000 |

For marital status vs. education, the output would appear as:

| Marital | Education | | | |
|---------|---|---|---|---|
| Status | 1 | 2 | 3 | 4 |
| 1 | 0 | 13500 | 0 | 22500 |
| 2 | 0 | 0 | 25500 | 23500 |
| 3 | 0 | 0 | 0 | 21500 |

To make sure you understand the concept of cross tabulation, you should confirm the above cross tabulations by hand.

**b. Design the program such that the number of classes and their upper limits for the age variable are specified by the user. For example, in part a above, three classes were used for the age variable, with the following limits:

| Class | Limits |
|-------|--------|
| 1 | 21 to 30 |
| 2 | 31 to 40 |
| 3 | 41 to 50 |

You should let the user choose the number of classes and the specific limits.

# CHAPTER 9

# *Functions and Subroutines*

A **subprogram** is a set of one or more statements for a specialized purpose that can be "called" or utilized by another program termed the **calling program.** The calling program itself can be either another subprogram or a program of the type you have been writing up to this point, which we now label as **main program.**

Subprograms are the last major feature of the minimal BASIC language that we discuss. Strictly speaking, subprograms are not essential to writing complex programs; rather, subprogramming capability provides certain advantages. For example, their use can reduce programming effort immensely, save primary memory, and permit a "building-block" approach to programming.

The BASIC language allows three classes of subprograms, each with specialized advantages for particular tasks:

1. BASIC-supplied functions
2. User-defined functions
3. Subroutines

* This section can be skipped without loss of continuity.

## 9.1
## BASIC-SUPPLIED FUNCTIONS

Suppose we wish to determine the square root of the arithmetic expression

$$b^2 - 4 \cdot a \cdot c$$

and to store it in the address labeled Y. As you know, we could simply use the assignment statement

    50 LET Y = (B**2 − 4*A*C)**.5

An alternative approach in this case is to use the following:

    50 LET Y = SQR(B**2 − 4*A*C)

The right-hand side of this statement is an example of a **BASIC-supplied function,**[1] which is of the following general type:

> *function name* **(argument)**

A *function name* is identified by a group of three letters, and the **argument** must be a valid arithmetic expression. In the above example, SQR is the function name and B**2 − 4*A*C is the argument. If A = 10, B = 7, and C = 1, then the result of this function is 3. The purpose of this function, of course, is to determine the square root of the argument. The SQR function is preferred to raising an expression to the 0.5 power from the standpoints of programming style and computational efficiency.

The 11 BASIC-supplied functions in minimal BASIC are grouped into the four categories shown in Table 9.1. Generally, only functions in the first three categories are useful to applications in the management and social sciences, particularly EXP, SQR, INT, and RND, whereas the trigonometric functions are used primarily in engineering and the physical sciences.

Briefly study the examples in the table, noting that the function is called by using its name in an arithmetic expression. When this arithmetic expression is translated, the machine-language instructions for evaluating the function are provided by the compiler or interpreter. For example, to find the logarithm of a number, the compiler utilizes a set of prewritten instructions (a subprogram) that calculates logarithms. This saves us much programming effort by not having to "reinvent the wheel" (write these instructions ourselves) each time we wish to evaluate a logarithm or any other function.

In the examples that follow we illustrate some common uses of the INT, EXP, and RND functions.

---

[1] Other commonly used terms are **built-in function, implementation-supplied function,** and **library function.** In actual practice there are technical distinctions among these terms, but we need not be concerned for our purposes.

TABLE 9.1. *Basic-Supplied Functions*

| CATEGORY | FUNCTION† | PURPOSE | ARGUMENT | ALGEBRAIC EXAMPLE | BASIC EXAMPLE |
|---|---|---|---|---|---|
| Algebraic | 1. EXP(X) | Exponential of X, or antilog of X, or base $e$ raised to Xth power | Numeric value | $y = a \cdot e^{-2 \cdot t}$ | LET Y = A*EXP(−2*T) |
| | 2. LOG(X) | Natural (base e) logarithm of X | Positive numeric value | $p = q \cdot \ln 5$ | LET P = Q*LOG(5) |
| | 3. SQR(X) | Square root of X | Positive numeric value | $r = (\sqrt{s}) \cdot (t + 1)^2$ | LET R = SQR(S)*(T + 1)**2 |
| Arithmetic | 4. ABS(X) | Absolute value of X | Numeric value | $z = \|x - y\|$ | LET Z = ABS(X − Y) |
| | 5. INT(X) | Greatest integer less than or equal to X | Numeric value | $k = [a/b]$ | LET K = INT(A/B) |
| | 6. SGN(X) | Algebraic sign of X | Numeric value | $y = \begin{cases} -1 & \text{if } X < 0 \\ 0 & \text{if } X = 0 \\ +1 & \text{if } X > 0 \end{cases}$ | LET Y = SGN(X) |
| Utility | 7. RND or RND(X) | Uniformly distributed random real number between 0.0 and 1.0 | May or may not be required, depending on system | $y = 0 \leq rn < 1$ | LET Y = RND or LET Y = RND(X) |
| Trigonometric | 8. ATN(X) | Arctangent of X | Expression in radians | | |
| | 9. COS(X) | Cosine of X | Expression in radians | | |
| | 10. SIN(X) | Sine of X | Expression in radians | | |
| | 11. TAN(X) | Tangent of X | Expression in radians | | |

† The symbol X refers to any arithmetic expression, including a single numeric variable or single numeric constant.

## EXAMPLE 9.1   Rounding Numbers Using the INT Function

Rounding numbers to a desired number of decimal places is a common use of the INT function. For example, to round a computed dollar amount such as $28.4563 to two decimal places, we could do the following:

1.   Multiply by 100 to obtain 2845.63
2.   Add 0.5 to obtain 2846.13
3.   Take the integer part to obtain 2846
4.   Divide by 100 to obtain 28.46

In BASIC this can be coded as follows:

```
50  LET X = 28.4563
60  LET Y = INT(X*100 + .5)/100
```

## EXAMPLE 9.2   Continuous Compounding Using the EXP Function

The following formula determines the accumulated savings (*A*) in a bank account given the initial amount or principal (*P*), the annual interest rate (*R*), the number of years over which interest is earned (*N*), and the number of times in a year (*M*) the account earns interest (365 for daily, 12 for monthly, and so on):

$$A = P \cdot \left( 1 + \frac{R}{M} \right)^{N \cdot M}$$

For example, if we start with $5000 (*P* = 5000) at an annual interest rate of 6 percent (*R* = 0.06) and the account compounds quarterly (*M* = 4), then after 5 years (*N* = 5) our savings account will grow to

$$A = 5000 \cdot \left( 1 + \frac{0.06}{4} \right)^{5 \cdot 4}$$
$$= 5000 \cdot (1.015)^{20}$$
$$= 5000 \cdot (1.34686)$$
$$= \$6734.28$$

This calculation illustrates what is called *quarterly compounding,* meaning that our money earns interest every (or once a) quarter. It should make sense to you that compounding as often as possible is to our monetary benefit. For example, if our savings were to be compounded monthly (*M* = 12) instead of quarterly, then we would end up with

$$A = 5000 \cdot \left( 1 + \frac{0.06}{12} \right)^{5 \cdot 12} = \$6744.25$$

or $9.97 richer.

In recent years banks have offered what is called *continuous compounding.* In this case the ultimate in compounding is achieved: our money earns interest continuously, even as we sit here thinking about it. The appropriate formula for continuous compounding is

$$A = P \cdot e^{R \cdot N}$$

where $e$ is the base of natural logarithms, or the irrational number 2.71828 $\cdots$ For our sample data, we would end up with

$$
\begin{aligned}
A &= 5000 \cdot e^{(0.06) \cdot (5)} \\
&= 5000 \cdot e^{0.3} \\
&= 5000 \cdot (1.34986) \\
&= \$6749.29
\end{aligned}
$$

which is a not-so-impressive \$15.01 better than under quarterly compounding.

In BASIC, the continuous compounding formula is coded as follows:

```
50 LET A = P*EXP(R*N)
```

## EXAMPLE 9.3   State Lottery Numbers Using the RND Function

The RND function is used to generate a uniform real number between 0.0 and 1.0 (including 0.0 but less than 1.0). By *uniform* we mean that every decimal value between 0.0 and 1.0 has an equal chance of occurring. This function is particularly useful in computer simulation models, which we take up in some detail in Module C.

To illustrate the RND function, consider a state lottery that generates a three-digit winning number each day. To select the winning number, many states use a machine with 10 "whirling" balls numbered 0, 1, 2, 3, 4, 5, 6, 7, 8, 9. These balls are randomly whirled by air streams, so that the machine selection of any one ball is as likely as the selection of any other ball. Thus, digits between 0 and 9 have an equal chance of occurring. To generate a three-digit random number, the lottery commission simply uses three different machines of the type described.

In BASIC we can generate these three "balls" as follows:

```
10 FOR I=1 TO 3
20    LET R=RND
30    LET N=INT(10*R)
40    PRINT R,N
50 NEXT I
60 END

RUN

   7.63242E-06       0
   .250198           2
   .753869           7

TIME 0.01 SECS.
```

In this case N is an integer number between 0 and 9 inclusive, whereby each digit ("ball") has the same likelihood of being generated as any other. We guarantee equal likelihood by basing the evaluation of N on the generation of the random number R. In line 20, R is generated as a uniform random real number in the range 0.0 or greater but less than 1.0; in line 30 this random real number first is scaled to the range 0 or greater but less than 10 and then is "integerized" to a digit between 0 and 9. Thus, for the given run we get the sequence

| R | 10*R | N = INT(10*R) |
| --- | --- | --- |
| $7.63242 \times 10^{-6}$ | 0.000076 | 0 ← first digit |
| 0.250198 | 2.50198 | 2 ← second digit |
| 0.753869 | 7.53869 | 7 ← third digit |

which gives 027 for the three-digit winning lottery number.[2]

Some systems generate a different sequence of random numbers each time the program is run, as the following illustrates:

```
20 FOR J=1 TO 5
30   PRINT RND;
40 NEXT J
50 END

RUN

 2.81636E-03    .323211    .177519    .242841    .563188
TIME 0.00 SECS.

RUN

 4.03755E-03    .354955    .796497    .971444    .899529
TIME 0.01 SECS.
```

Other systems, however, always generate the same sequence of random numbers each time the program is run.

The ability to generate identical sequences of random numbers is useful for debugging and certain other statistical purposes. In other situations, however, it is undesirable. For systems that otherwise would generate identical random number sequences, the statement

> *line no.* **RANDOMIZE**

can be used to generate different sequences from run to run. For example, the program

```
10 RANDOMIZE
20 FOR J = 1 TO 5
30    PRINT RND;
40 NEXT J
50 END
```

would generate different sequences of five random numbers on systems that otherwise would generate identical sequences. Without the randomize statement,

---

[2] On some systems any argument X in RND(X) is required, but may serve no useful purpose. The proposed ANSI standard recommends the elimination of the argument altogether, since current systems differ considerably on the use and meaning of the argument.

these systems would generate the same sequence of five random numbers each time this program is run.[3]

## Follow-up Exercises

1. In Table 9.1 look at the column labeled "BASIC Example" and answer the following:
   a. Example 1. What is stored in Y if 2 is stored in A and 4 is in T?
   b. Example 2. What is stored in P if 10 is stored in Q?
   c. Example 3. What is stored in R if 25 is in S and 3 is in T?
   d. Example 4. What is stored in Z if 5.4 is in X and 2.1 is in Y? If 5.4 is in X and 7.4 is in Y?
   e. Example 5. What is stored in K if 7 is in A and 2 is in B? If 7.6 is in A and 2 is in B? If 6 is in A and 2 is in B? If −7.6 is in A and 2 is in B?
   f. Example 6. What is stored in Y if −73.2 is stored in X? If 105 is in X? If 0 is in X?

2. With respect to Example 9.1,
   a. What would be stored in Y if 28.451 is stored in X?
   b. Explain why we add 0.5?
   c. Modify line 60 to round to the nearest dollar (whole number).
   d. Modify line 60 to round to the nearest $1000.

*3. Write a short program that compares compounding effects based on the formulas in Example 9.2. Specifically, compare values of A for the following data:

| P | R | N | M |
|---|---|---|---|
| $10,000 | 0.06 | 10 | 1 |
| 10,000 | 0.06 | 10 | 4 |
| 10,000 | 0.06 | 10 | 12 |
| 10,000 | 0.06 | 10 | 52 |
| 10,000 | 0.06 | 10 | 365 |
| 10,000 | 0.06 | 10 | Continuous |
| 10,000 | 0.08 | 10 | Continuous |

4. With respect to the first program in Example 9.3:
   a. Combine lines 20 and 30 into 40 and print only the winning lottery number.
   b. Modify the program to generate a four-digit lottery number.
   *c. Modify the program to generate seven three-digit lottery numbers, one for each day of the week. Print the three digits of a lottery number on the same line. Each lottery number is to appear on a separate line. This program is to be used week after week by a lottery commission, so make sure you don't generate the same numbers each week.

[3] Not all systems support the RANDOMIZE statement. The proposed ANSI standard recommends that systems generate identical random number sequences whenever the RANDOMIZE statement is not used.

*5. A ballplayer's batting average can be used to estimate the probability of getting a hit when at bat. For example, if the batting average is 273, then we can say that 0.273 is the probability of a hit (that is, the batter gets a hit 27.3 percent of the time). Write the code which simulates a time at bat. If the batter gets a hit, then the computer prints BATTER GOT A HIT; otherwise, the computer prints BATTER MADE AN OUT.

*6. Write down the code which would generate N real random numbers within the interval A to B, where values for A and B are to be input by the user. Run this program on your system such that
   a. Twenty real random numbers are generated between 10 and 20.
   b. Eight real random numbers are generated between −0.5 and 2.5.

**7. Find our how your system treats the use of arguments in the RND function, how it handles the issue of identical sequences of random numbers, and whether or not it supports the RANDOMIZE statement. For example, IBM's CALL 370 system does not support the RANDOMIZE statement; rather it treats the control of the sequence in the following traditional way:

```
10 PRINT "SEED";
15 INPUT X
20 FOR J=1 TO 5
25    LET R=RND(X)
30    PRINT R;
35    LET X=R
40 NEXT J
50 END

RUN

SEED?0
 7.63242E-06    5.07990E-02    7.75366E-02    .928628    .911499
TIME 0.01 SECS.

RUN

SEED?1016
 .762604    .652015    .491019    .87533    8.66637E-02
TIME 0.01 SECS.

RUN

SEED?0
 7.63242E-06    5.07990E-02    7.75366E-02    .928628    .911499
TIME 0.01 SECS.
```

In this case the initial value of X, called a *seed*, is assigned through the INPUT statement in line 15. In line 35 the sequence is "reseeded" to avoid generating the same random number each time RND(X) is evaluated. Note that the seed 1016 in the second run differs from the seed 0 in the first run, which guarantees a different sequence in the second run from the first run. Using the same seed in the third run gives the same sequence of random numbers as in the first run. Thus, this approach allows the generation of either identical sequences (by using the same seed) or different sequences (by changing the seed). Try this program on your system.

## 9.2
## USER-DEFINED FUNCTIONS*

At times you need access to a function that is not included in the computer's set of library functions, in which case you can define your own function. Functions defined by programmers are called **user-defined functions**,[4] and are identified by the DEF statement. This approach is illustrated in the next example.

---

### EXAMPLE 9.4　Mathematical Functions

A function is a mathematical relation through which the value of a particular variable is determined from the values of one or more other variables. For example, the notation

$$y = f(x)$$

indicates that the variable y is a function of the variable x.

Functions are widely used in the management, engineering, social, and physical sciences to represent real-world phenomena through mathematical modeling. For example, the *second-degree exponential function*

$$y = a \cdot e^x \cdot e^{x^2}$$

has been used in sales forecasting and biological growth prediction, where a is a parameter (numeric constant) and e is the base of natural logarithms.

The programs on page 265 illustrate two ways of printing the following tables of (x,y) values for this function.

```
A= .5
  X                    Y
  1                    3.69453
  2                    201.714
  3                    81377.4
  4                    2.42583E+08
  5                    5.34324E+12


A= 5
  T                    S
  .5                   10.585
  1                    36.9453
  1.5                  212.605
  2                    2017.14


A= 50
  N                    Y
  -5                   2.42583E+10
  -4                   8137739
  -3                   20171.4
  -2                   369.453
  -1                   50.
   0                   50

TIME 0.03 SECS.
```

---

* This section can be skipped without loss of continuity.
[4] Other commonly used names for user-defined functions are **user-supplied statement function** or **arithmetic statement function**.

```
                    Version A                                        Version B

200 READ A
210 DATA .5                              100 DEF FNY(X)=A*EXP(X)*EXP(X**2)
220 PRINT "A=";A                         200 READ A
230 PRINT " X","      Y"                 210 DATA .5
240 FOR X=1 TO 5                         220 PRINT "A=";A
250    LET Y=A * EXP(X) * EXP(X**2)       230 PRINT " X","      Y"
260    PRINT X,Y                         240 FOR X=1 TO 5
270 NEXT X                               250    LET Y=FNY(X)
280 PRINT                                260    PRINT X,Y
300 READ A                               270 NEXT X
310 DATA 5                               280 PRINT
320 PRINT "A=";A                         300 READ A
330 PRINT " T","      S"                 310 DATA 5
340 FOR T=.5 TO 2 STEP .5                320 PRINT "A=";A
350    LET S=A * EXP(T) * EXP(T**2)       330 PRINT " T","      S"
360    PRINT T,S                         340 FOR T= .5 TO 2 STEP .5
370 NEXT T                               350    LET S=FNY(T)
380 PRINT                                360    PRINT T,S
400 READ A                               370 NEXT T
410 DATA 50                              380 PRINT
420 PRINT "A=";A                         400 READ A
430 PRINT " N","      Y"                 410 DATA 50
440 FOR N=-5 TO 0                        420 PRINT "A=";A
450    LET Y=A * EXP(N) * EXP(N**2)       430 PRINT " N","      Y"
460    PRINT N,Y                         440 FOR N= -5 TO 0
470 NEXT N                               450    LET Y=FNY(N)
999 END                                  460    PRINT N,Y
                                         470 NEXT N
                                         999 END
```

The general form of the DEF statement is

*line no.* **DEF** *function name* (*dummy argument*) = *arithmetic expression*

where the keyword **DEF** is a signal to the translator that this line is a user-defined function. The *function name* must begin with the letters FN and must be three letters in length. For example, FNA, FNG and FNY are all legal function names. The **dummy argument** is one simple numeric variable and is usually used in the arithmetic expression that appears to the right of the equal sign.[5] This numeric variable is called a *dummy argument* because its value is assigned only when the function is called or referenced in another part of the program; it is meaningful only within the function itself. The *arithmetic expression* indicates the numeric calculations to be performed. This expression may consist of constants, numeric variables from other parts of the program, the dummy argument, and other functions.

In version B of Example 9.4, the function

```
100 DEF FNY(X) = A*EXP(X)*EXP(X**2)
```

[5] Some versions of BASIC permit more than one dummy argument in the function definition.

is a subprogram that calculates values of Y given values of A and X in a second-degree exponential. In this case, FNY is the function name, X is the dummy argument, and

A*EXP(X)*EXP(X**2)

is the arithmetic expression.

The following points should help you understand how user-defined functions work:

1.  Once a function is defined by its DEF statement the function may be used anywhere in the program in the same manner as BASIC-supplied functions.
2.  These functions are limited to a single statement.
3.  The function definition can be placed anywhere before its use in a program, but it is a good programming practice to place all DEF statements at the beginning of the program.
4.  The function definition (DEF statement) is a nonexecutable statement.
5.  A function definition may reference other BASIC-supplied and user-defined functions. For example, the function FNY references the EXP library function.
6.  If the dummy argument is unnecessary, then it may be omitted.[6] For example,

DEF FNP = 3.14159

defines a function whose value is $\pi$.

The function is evaluated whenever it is referenced (called) elsewhere in the program. It is referenced by using the function name followed by the optional **actual argument** enclosed in parentheses. In Example 9.4 the function is called three separate times by the following statements:

250 LET Y = FNY(X)
350 LET S = FNY(T)
450 LET Y = FNY(N)

When the function is called, "control" of the program goes to the user-defined function, where the arithmetic expression is evaluated using the *actual* argument in place of the *dummy* argument. For example, when the call is made at line 350, the actual argument T is used in place of the dummy argument X in the function of line 100. Thus, the function can be visualized as

A*EXP(T)*EXP(T**2)

If 5 is stored in A and 1.0 is stored in T, then the DEF statement uses these values to evaluate the function. The result 36.94528 is "returned" to the statement which made the call and stored in S.[7]

Note that the name of the actual argument (T) in the function reference FNY(T) is not the same as the dummy argument name (X) in the function definition FNY(X). The dummy argument is a device that generalizes the use of the function for more than one

---

[6] Not all systems allow this option.
[7] In actual practice, since DEF is a nonexecutable statement, control remains at the statement making the call. The compiler simply provides the necessary machine instructions for evaluating the function immediately following the statement that calls the function.

call within the same program. For example, the function is called three times in Example 9.4. In each case the variable in the actual argument is different; that is, X, T, and N are different variables. In the function definition, X represents each of these variables.

Also note that the arithmetic expression in the DEF statement may also contain variables that are used elsewhere in the program. In our example, the A in the DEF statement is the same as the A in lines 200, 300, and 400. The opposite is not necessarily true, however, when it comes to the dummy argument. In our example, the use of the variable X in line 250 is consistent with its use in the dummy argument; however, X could have been used elsewhere in the program for a purpose quite apart from its use in the dummy argument. Do you now see why the argument in the DEF statement is called *dummy?*

As a final point, the dummy argument must be a simple numeric variable. The actual argument, however, may be a constant, simple, or subscripted numeric variable, arithmetic expression, or other function.[8]

In general, the use of a user-defined function is recommended as a convenient device which can save main storage for instructions whenever a complicated arithmetic expression recurs at many points in a program (which is not all that often). Additionally, the use of functions simplifies the appearance of programs and promotes the concept of modularity, as discussed in the next section.

---

**Follow-up Exercises**

8. Describe the output for the following program:
   a. 10 DEF FNC(Y) = Y**3 + Y + 3 − 2*SQR(2*Y − 1)
      20 PRINT FNC(1), FNC(3), FNC(5)
      30 END

   b. Rewrite this program without the DEF statement. Which version is preferable and why?

9. What does the following program output?

    10 DEF FNB(X) = X + 3*ABS(X − 2)
    20 READ A,B,C
    30 PRINT FNB(A), FNB(INT(B)), FNB(C)
    40 DATA 3, 1.25,3.5
    50 END

10. Create a user-defined function for the following expressions. In each case treat $n$ as a dummy variable.

    a. $\dfrac{1}{n^2} + \dfrac{1}{\sqrt{n}}$

    b. $\left| p \cdot (1 + i)^n - e^{i \cdot n} \right|$

11. Indicate what is wrong, if anything, with each of the following:

---

[8] Some systems include the enhancement of allowing more than one argument.

| Function | Calling Statement |
|---|---|
| a.  10  DEF FNE1 = (A + B + C)/3 | 50  LET D = FNE1 |
| b.  15  DEF FNE(A,B,C) = (A + B + C)/3 | 55  LET D = FNE(X,Y,Z) |
| c.  20  DEF FNE(N) = (A + B + C)**N | 10  LET D = 4*FNE(3) + A**2 + 10 |
| d.  25  DEF FNE(A(I)) = A(I)*B | 60  PRINT FNB(B(J)) |
| e.  25  DEF FN5(A) = A*B*C | 65  PRINT FN5(A + 5*X − 7) |

## 9.3
## SUBROUTINES

A subroutine is a uniquely identifiable group of successive statements within a program that accomplishes a specific purpose within that program. Subroutines are useful (1) because they allow a modular or building-block approach to long complicated programs, (2) because they promote shorter programs when the repeated use of a sequence of statements is needed at different points in a program, and (3) because they save programming effort when a code to accomplish a popular task can be used by more than one program.

### Structure of Programs with Subroutines

A subroutine is not used by itself; rather it is embedded within a larger program and can be executed only when called by the main program or another subroutine. A typical structure of programs using one or more subroutines is depicted below.

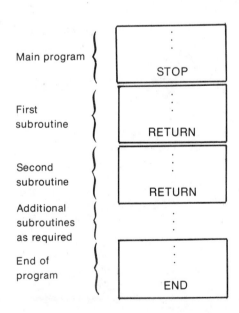

Note how this scheme effectively subdivides a program into blocks or modules, where typically each module performs a specific task within the overall framework of the program. Subroutines in BASIC thus can be used to illustrate simple examples of a programming style called **modular programming.**

## Calling the Subroutine

Each subroutine is accessed (called) with a GOSUB statement of the following general form:

```
line no. GOSUB line number
```

Two actions occur when the GOSUB statement is executed.

1. The computer stores the line number of the statement following the GOSUB statement in a memory location sometimes referred to as the *return location* or *transfer vector.*
2. The computer transfers control to the line number referenced in the GOSUB statement (this is the first statement of the subroutine).

For example, in the statements

```
105 INPUT A,B
110 GOSUB 300
115 PRINT X,Y
120 STOP
```

the computer executes line 110 by transferring control to line 300, which is the first statement in the subroutine, and also stores line number 115 in the return location.

Typically, the last statement in a subroutine is the following:

```
line no. RETURN
```

Execution of the RETURN statement returns control to the line number in the return location associated with the calling statement. For example, in the program segment

Main program
```
105 INPUT A,B
110 GOSUB 300
115 PRINT X,Y
120 STOP
```

Equivalent to

```
110 LET X = A/B
112 LET Y = A*B
```

Subroutine
```
300 LET X = A/B
310 LET Y = A*B
320 RETURN
```

lines 300 through 320 represent a subroutine. At line 110, control is transferred to the subroutine beginning on line 300. The statements within the subroutine are executed until the RETURN statement is encountered, at which point control returns to the statement following the GOSUB (line 115). Thus, for this segment the execution sequence is as follows: lines 105, 110, 300, 310, 320, 115, 120. Note that the effect is equivalent to placing lines 300 and 310 at the place of call in line 110.

## EXAMPLE 9.5   Polynomial Plot

The program and run below illustrate the use of a subroutine that plots the coordinates (X,Y) of any mathematical function, where X runs from 1 to an upper limit U in increments of 1.

```
050 REM ***** POLYNOMIAL PLOT PROGRAM *****
060 REM
100 REM *** MAIN PROGRAM ***
120 REM
130 DIM Y(15)
140 READ B0,B1,U
150 DATA 1,4,8
160 FOR X=1 TO U
170    LET Y(X)=B0 + B1 * X
180 NEXT X
190 GOSUB 400
200 READ B0,B1,B2,U
210 DATA 25,8,-1,10
220 FOR X=1 TO U
230    LET Y(X)=B0 + B1 * X + B2 * X**2
240 NEXT X
250 GOSUB 400
260 STOP
385 REM --------------------------------------------------
390 REM *** SUBROUTINE PLOT ***
395 REM
400 PRINT
410 PRINT TAB(25);"*** GRAPH OF Y-FUNCTION ***"
420 PRINT
430 PRINT TAB(11);"...Y-SCALE..."
440 PRINT
450 PRINT "X-SCALE"
460 FOR X=1 TO U
470    PRINT TAB(6);X;TAB(10+Y(X));"*   ";Y(X)
480 NEXT X
490 RETURN
500 REM--------------------------------------------------
999 END
```

Subroutine called. Equivalent to placing the code in lines 400 to 480 at this point.

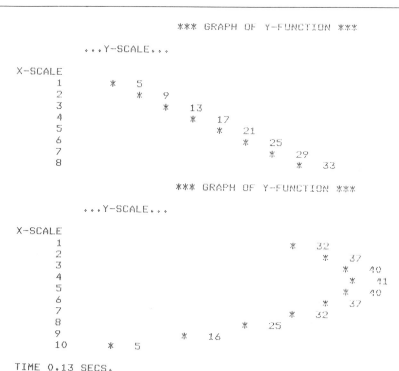

```
                      *** GRAPH OF Y-FUNCTION ***

             ...Y-SCALE...

  X-SCALE
       1         *    5
       2           *    9
       3            *    13
       4           *    17
       5            *    21
       6             *    25
       7              *    29
       8               *    33


                      *** GRAPH OF Y-FUNCTION ***

             ...Y-SCALE...

  X-SCALE
       1                        *    32
       2                         *    37
       3                          *    40
       4                           *    41
       5                          *    40
       6                         *    37
       7                        *    32
       8               *    25
       9          *    16
      10     *    5

TIME 0.13 SECS.
```

In the main program, lines 140 to 180 calculate values of $y$ using the first-degree polynomial function (straight line)

$$y = 1 + 4x$$

where values of $x$ range from 1 to 8. Note that values of $y$ are stored in the one-dimensional array Y. In line 190, the subroutine for plotting this function is called. This subroutine plots the function by placing an asterisk at the appropriate $(x,y)$ coordinate. Values of $x$ are printed along the left margin, and values of the function are printed to the right of the asterisk.

When the first plot is complete, the RETURN statement in line 490 is executed and control returns to line 200 in the main program. Lines 200 to 240 then calculate functional values for the second-degree polynomial

$$y = 25 + 8x - x^2$$

where values of $x$ range from 1 to 10. At line 250 the subroutine is called once again, giving the second plot illustrated above. Thus, the sequence of execution is as follows:

Lines 140 through 180—calculation of first-degree polynomial
Line 190—subroutine called
Lines 400 through 480—plot of first-degree polynomial
Line 490—return to main program

Lines 200 through 240—calculation of second-degree polynomial
Line 250—subroutine called
Lines 400 through 480—plot of second-degree polynomial
Line 490—return to main program
Line 260—stop execution

Note that this program is consistent with the typical structure given in the preceding section on page 268: the main program runs from lines 100 to 260; the subroutine runs from lines 385 to 490 (including the REM statements); lines 500 through 999 represent the ending of the program; and a STOP statement is inserted at the end of the main program to avoid reexecuting the subroutine (alternatively, we could have used the less "clean" 260 GO TO 999).

Finally, you should note that *this program illustrates three advantages of using subroutines.* First, it promotes *modular design* by treating the plotting routine as a module that is utilized at two different points in the program. Second, the use of the same subroutine for two separate plots *reduces the amount of code* compared to a "brute-force" version that twice repeats the code in lines 400 to 480. Third, a plotting routine of this type may be common enough in certain programming environments to be used as a *module in more than one program.* For example, many standardized routines exist for plotting, statistical analyses, and data editing. These can be written up as subroutines, stored separately in libraries, and merged with main routines when required.

## Follow-up Exercises

**12.** The current program in Example 9.5 is 25 lines long (excluding REM statements). How long would be an equivalent program that does not use subroutines? Assume that the code in lines 400 to 480 is placed between lines 180 to 200 and again between lines 240 to 260.

**13.** Some versions of BASIC do not have a TAB statement. If your system is one of these, then redesign the subroutine. *Hint:* Print the required number of blanks using a FOR/NEXT loop.

**14.** Modify the subroutine to "dress up" the *y* scale by printing 50 dashes beginning in column 11 right under the label Y-SCORE, and again along the bottom of the plot.

**15.** Design the new code in the preceding exercise as a second subroutine that is called by the first subroutine. Write down the sequence of execution.

**\*\*16.** The present program would not work if values of *x* are negative or greater than 15. Modify the program so these values of *x* can be graphed.

**\*\*17.** Redesign the main program to accommodate polynomials up to third degree:

$$y = b_0 + b_1 x + b_2 x^2 + b_3 x^3$$

Include an outer loop for processing as many polynomials as required, instead of the two separate segments given by lines 140 to 190 and 200 to 250. Run this version using the same data as the example.

**18.** Same as Exercise 17 except treat the polynomial as a user-defined function.

**19.** The current version of the subroutine does not scale values of $y$, which means for example that a value of 200 for $y$ would exceed the width of a print line. Modify the subroutine to scale the $y$ scale such that the asterisk is always printed between print positions 11 to 60. For example, if the maximum value of $y$ is 200 and the minimum is 7, then the asterisk corresponding to a value of 100 for $y$ gets printed at print position 34, as calculated from the integer part of

$$11 + \left(\frac{100 - 7}{200 - 7}\right) \cdot 49$$

*Hint:* Adapt the code in Example 7.8 as a second subroutine that determines the minimum and maximum values of $y$. The plotting subroutine calls the sort subroutine. *Warning:* Create a second one-dimensional array for purposes of the sort in order to avoid altering the original Y array.

**20.** Are the following programs identical with respect to output?

a.
```
05 READ N
10 FOR J = 1 TO N
15    PRINT J;
20 NEXT J
25 DATA 5
30 END
```

b.
```
05 READ N
10 FOR J = 1 TO N
15    GOSUB 30
20 NEXT J
25 STOP
30 PRINT J;
35 RETURN
40 DATA 5
45 END
```

c.
```
05 READ N
10 GOSUB 20
15 STOP
20 FOR J = 1 TO N
25    PRINT J;
30 NEXT J
35 RETURN
40 DATA 5
45 END
```

In each case identify the main program and the subroutine. Look at the program of Section 8.6 on page 238 and state why a subroutine of the type in part c might be useful.

## Additional Considerations

Study the following additional points regarding subroutines:

1. A subroutine has access to all variables in a program.
2. The calling program can be the main program or another subroutine. The effect of calling the subroutine is identical to placing the set of statements in the subroutine at the point of call in the calling program.
3. A subroutine can be placed anywhere within the program, but it is important that the subroutine not be executed except via a GOSUB statement. It is good programming practice, however, that subroutines follow the main program.
4. An entry to a subroutine does not have to be made at the same initial statement each time the subroutine is called; that is a subroutine can be entered at any point. For example, a technique for providing a variable number of blank lines between headings is illustrated below (the subroutine is defined by lines 200 to 250):

```
100 INPUT O,P$,D$,N$
105 GOSUB 220
110 PRINT,"STEWART NURSERY"
115 GOSUB 230
120 PRINT "TUCKERTOWN RD",,,"WAKEFIELD RI"
130 GOSUB 200
140 PRINT "ORDER NO";O,"PHONE NO ",P$,"DATE ";D$
145 GOSUB 240
150 PRINT "SOLD TO ";N$
160 STOP
200 PRINT
210 PRINT
220 PRINT
230 PRINT
240 PRINT
250 RETURN
260 END
```

```
RUN

?123,783-1798,10-12-80,JUNE JUNIPER



          STEWART NURSERY


TUCKERTOWN RD                                         WAKEFIELD RI




ORDER NO 123            PHONE NO          783-1798          DATE 10-12-80

SOLD TO JUNE JUNIPER

TIME 0.01 SECS.
```

5.  A subroutine may be terminated at more than one statement. Thus you may have several RETURN statements within the subroutine, or one or more STOP statements.

6.  Although it is not necessary to give a subroutine a name, doing so makes reading the program much easier. For example, in the program of Example 9.5 the line

    390 REM ***SUBROUTINE PLOT***

    identifies the subroutine to the reader of the program. Under this procedure each subroutine could be characterized as starting with a REM statement and ending with a RETURN statement.

7.  A call to a subroutine is flowcharted using the **predefined process symbol.** For example, in Example 9.5 on page 270, GOSUB would be flowcharted as

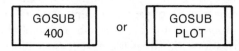

The actual subroutine is flowcharted separately from the main program. Subroutines begin and end with an oval symbol. The first symbol contains the name or line

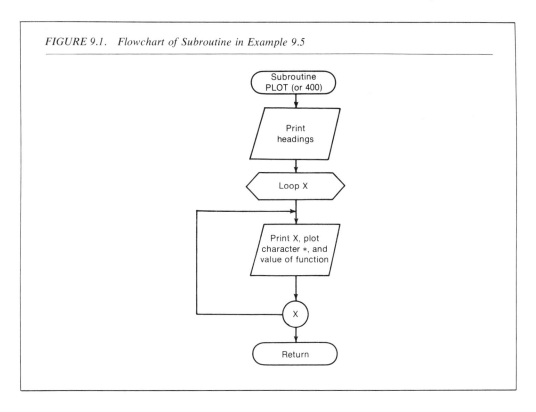

FIGURE 9.1. *Flowchart of Subroutine in Example 9.5*

number of the subroutine, while the last symbol in the flowchart indicates the RETURN to the calling program. The subroutine in Example 9.5 might be flowcharted as in Figure 9.1.

## 9.4
## AUTOMOBILE RENTAL DECISION PROGRAM

In our next program we illustrate how subroutines can be used to structure a program into modules, whereby each module accomplishes a set of related tasks. Additionally, we illustrate **nested subroutines,** that is, the call of one subroutine by another subroutine.

### Step I. Analysis

*1. Problem statement.* Hartz Rent-Some-Wheels, the largest and most progressive car rental company, has decided to improve customer service by designing an interactive computer program that would be used by its agents to quote projected rental fees. Basically, the program computes projected total cost for each of its two rental plans: the daily plan and the weekly plan. A customer who rents a car under the daily plan pays a fixed cost per day plus a charge per mile but does not pay for gasoline expenses. Under the weekly plan, the customer pays both a fixed cost per week and buys gasoline, but does not pay a mileage charge. Which plan is cheaper for a customer depends on factors such as the various costs for the specific type of automobile, the projected number of miles to be driven, the number of days that the car is to be rented, the price of gasoline, the efficiency of the automobile, and (of course) the driving habits of the customer. The table below defines the required variables and illustrates sample data.

| VARIABLE | DESCRIPTION | SAMPLE VALUES CASE I | CASE II |
|---|---|---|---|
| *2. Provided data* | | | |
| D | Daily fixed cost ($/day) | 17.00 | 17.00 |
| M1 | Charge per mile ($/mile) | 0.15 | 0.15 |
| W1 | Weekly fixed cost ($/week) | 145.00 | 145.00 |
| P | Price of gasoline ($/gallon) | 0.75 | 0.75 |
| G | Miles per gallon (EPA rating) | 20 | 20 |
| M2 | Projected miles of driving | 800 | 300 |
| N | Number of days | 12 | 5 |
| *3. Data Output* | | | |
| C1 | Total cost of daily plan ($) | 324.00 | 130.00 |
| C2 | Total cost of weekly plan ($) | 320.00 | 156.25 |
| C3 | Cost difference ($) | 4.00 | −26.25 |
| *4. Algorithm* | | | |

$$C1 = D \cdot N + M1 \cdot M2$$

$$C2 = W1 \cdot \left( \left[ \frac{N - .1}{7} \right] + 1 \right) + \frac{M2 \cdot P}{G}$$

$$C3 = C1 - C2$$

Thus, for the given data, a 12-day rental with 800 projected miles of driving (case I) is best under the weekly plan ($4.00 cheaper); however, for 5 days and 300 miles (case II), all other things being equal, the daily plan is best by $26.25. Before going on, you should confirm these calculations for C1 and C2. Note that the fixed charge under the weekly plan is incurred for any part of a week; that is, the fixed charge for 12 days is the same as for 2 weeks, or $290.00 (2 × 145); the fixed charge for 5 days is the same as for 1 week, or $145.00.

## Steps II and III. *Flowchart and Code*

The primary programing tasks are divided into five modules:

1. The main program, which repeatedly calls modules 2, 3, and 4
2. A subroutine (INITIALIZE) that initializes data which are common to a car plan
3. A subroutine (CUSTOMER DATA) that inputs data for the customer's trip and tests for the end of data
4. A subroutine (COSTS) that calculates relevant costs (*Note:* This subroutine calls the next subroutine.)
5. A subroutine (OUTPUT) that prints the results

Relationships among modules are often depicted by a **hierarchy chart,** as illustrated in Figure 9.2. Thus, a hierarchy chart clearly shows which subroutines are called from the main program and which subroutines are called from other subroutines. In this case, subroutine OUTPUT is said to be *nested* within subroutine COSTS.

The flowchart in Figure 9.3 further illustrates this simplified modular approach to programing. Again, note that the main program and the subroutines each require a separate flowchart.

In the program itself (pages 279–281), the main program and modules break down as follows:

| SEGMENT | Lines (Excluding REM Statements) |
|---|---|
| Main program | 100–140 |
| Subroutine INITIALIZE | 200–250 |
| Subroutine CUSTOMER DATA | 300–390 |
| Subroutine COSTS | 400–450 |
| Subroutine OUTPUT | 500–600 |

The sequence of execution is as follows:

Line 100
Lines 200 to 250
Line 110
Lines 300 to 370 (or lines 300 to 320 and 380 to 385)
Line 120
Lines 400 to 440
Lines 500 to 600
Line 450
Line 130
Line 100
.
.
.

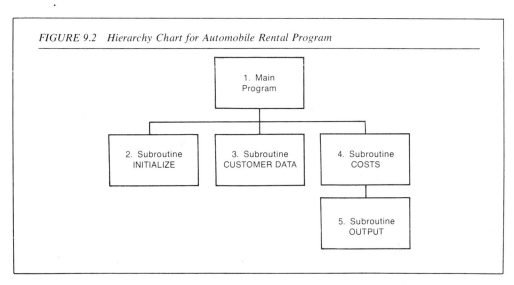

FIGURE 9.2   *Hierarchy Chart for Automobile Rental Program*

FIGURE 9.3    *Flowcharts for Automobile Rental Decision*

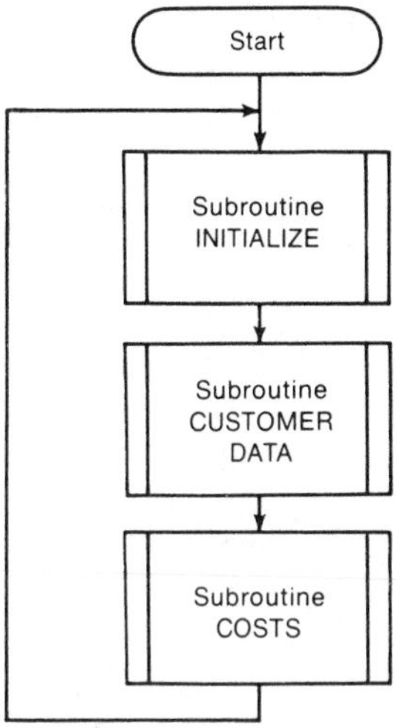

a.  Main Program

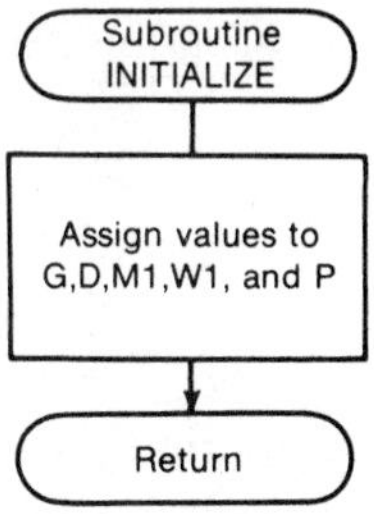

b.  First Subroutine

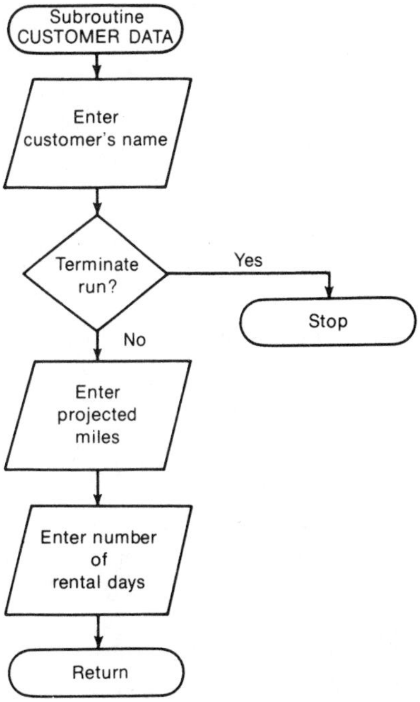

c. Second Subroutine

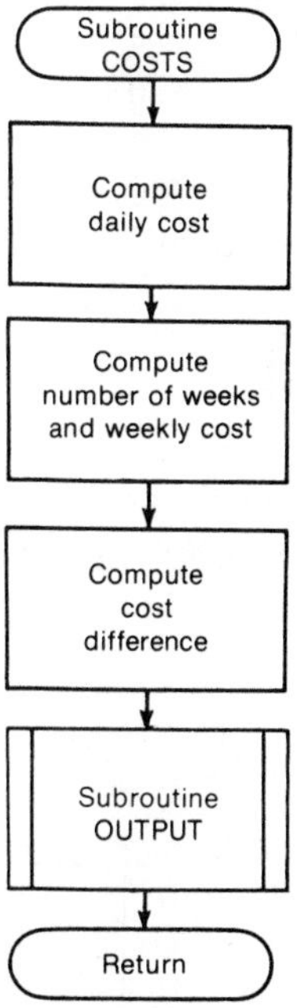

d.  Third Subroutine

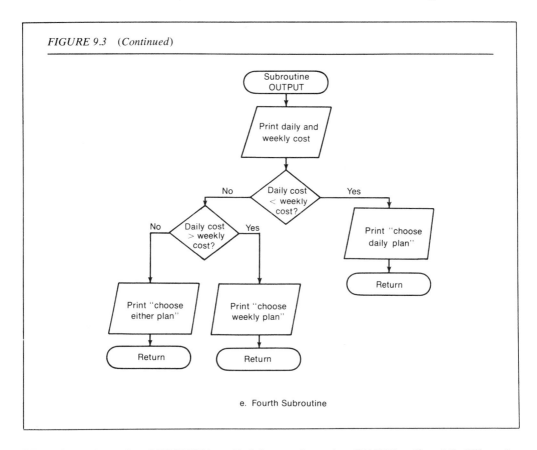

FIGURE 9.3    (*Continued*)

e. Fourth Subroutine

Note that subroutine OUTPUT is called from subroutine COSTS at line 440. When the RETURN statement is executed in subroutine OUTPUT, control returns to a point just below the call in subroutine COSTS (line 450). Since subroutine OUTPUT is nested within subroutine COSTS, execution of a RETURN statement in OUTPUT returns control to COSTS. Control next returns to line 130 in the main program, since subroutine COSTS was originally called by the main program.

```
002 REM---------------------------------------------------------------------
004 REM--AUTOMOBILE RENTAL DECISION PROGRAM
006 REM-
008 REM- PROGRAM COMPUTES COST OF DAILY AND WEEKLY PLAN
010 REM- GIVEN THE INPUTS PROJECTED MILES OF DRIVING AND
012 REM- NUMBER OF DAYS IN RENTAL.
014 REM-
016 REM- VARIABLE KEY:
018 REM-    PROVIDED:
020 REM-       D  = DAILY FIXED COST
022 REM-       M1 = CHARGE ($) PER MILE
024 REM-       W1 = WEEKLY FIXED COST ($)
026 REM-       P  = PRICE ($) PER GALLON OF GASOLINE
028 REM-       G  = MILES PER GALLON (EPA RATING)
030 REM-    INPUT:
032 REM-       C$ = CUSTOMER NAME
```

```
034 REM-      M2 = PROJECTED MILES OF DRIVING
036 REM-      N  = NUMBER OF DAYS IN RENTAL
038 REM-   OUTPUT:
040 REM-      C1 = TOTAL COST DAILY PLAN ($)
042 REM-      C2 = TOTAL COST WEEKLY PLAN ($)
044 REM-      C3 = COST DIFFERENCE (C1-C2)
046 REM-
048 REM-   MODULES IN PROGRAM:
050 REM-      1.  MAIN------------REPEATEDLY CALLS MODULES 2, 3, AND 4
052 REM-      2.  INITIALIZE-----PROVIDES DATA COMMON TO CAR PLANS
054 REM-      3.  CUSTOMER DATA--INPUTS DATA AND TESTS FOR TERMINATION
056 REM-      4.  COSTS----------CALCULATES ALL COSTS AND CALLS OUTPUT MODULE
058 REM-      5.  OUTPUT---------PRINTS RESULTS
060 REM-      NOTE: SEE HIERACHY CHART
062 REM------------------------------------------------------------------
064 REM
095 REM---MAIN PROGRAM
100     GOSUB 200
110       GOSUB 300
120       GOSUB 400
130     GO TO 100
140     STOP
190 REM------------------------------------------------------------------
195 REM---SUBROUTINE INITIALIZE
197 REM-    ASSIGNS VALUES TO D,M1,W1,P,G AND RETURNS TO MAIN
200     LET G=20
210     LET D=17
220     LET M1=.15
230     LET W1=145
240     LET P=.75
250     RETURN
290 REM------------------------------------------------------------------
295 REM---SUBROUTINE CUSTOMER DATA
297 REM-    INPUTS C$,M2,N AND RETURNS TO MAIN
300     FOR J=1 TO 40
301       PRINT "-";
302     NEXT J
303     PRINT
305     PRINT"ENTER CUSTOMER NAME";
310     INPUT C$
320     IF C$="EOD" THEN 380
330     PRINT"ENTER PROJECTED MILES OF DRIVING";
340     INPUT M2
350     PRINT"ENTER NUMBER OF RENTAL DAYS";
360     INPUT N
370     RETURN
380     PRINT "PROGRAM COMPLETED"
385     STOP
390     RETURN
395 REM------------------------------------------------------------------
396 REM---SUBROUTINE COSTS
398 REM-    CALCULATES C1,C2,C3 AND RETURNS TO MAIN
399 REM
400     LET C1=D * N + M1 * M2
402 REM
403 REM-    C1 ROUNDED TO DOLLAR AND CENTS
404 REM
405     LET C1=INT(C1*100 + .5)/100
406 REM
407 REM-    W2 IS NUMBER OF WEEKS IN RENTAL. FRACTION SUBTRACTED FROM
408 REM-    N TO GIVE CORRECT VALUE WHEN N=7,14,21,...
409 REM
410     LET W2=INT((N-.1)/7) + 1
```

```
420     LET C2=W1 * W2 + M2/G * P
422 REM
423 REM-     C2 ROUNDED TO DOLLARS AND CENTS
424 REM
425     LET C2=INT(C2*100 + .5)/100
430     LET C3=C1 - C2
440     GOSUB 500
450     RETURN
490 REM-------------------------------------------------------
495 REM--SUBROUTINE OUTPUT
497 REM-     CALLED BY MODULE COST TO PRINT C1,C2,C3 AND PLAN OF BEST CHOICE
500     PRINT
510     PRINT"TOTAL COST-DAILY PLAN  $";C1
520     PRINT"TOTAL COST-WEEKLY PLAN $";C2
530     IF C1 < C2 THEN 570
540     IF C1 > C2 THEN 590
550     PRINT"CHOOSE EITHER PLAN"
560     RETURN
570     PRINT"CHOOSE DAILY PLAN. YOU SAVE $";ABS(C3)
580     RETURN
590     PRINT "CHOOSE WEEKLY PLAN. YOU SAVE $";C3
600     RETURN
610 REM-------------------------------------------------------
615     END
```

## Step IV. Debugging

```
RUN
-------------------------------------------------------
ENTER CUSTOMER NAME?OJ SAMPSON
ENTER PROJECTED MILES OF DRIVING?800
ENTER NUMBER OF RENTAL DAYS?12

TOTAL COST-DAILY PLAN  $ 324
TOTAL COST-WEEKLY PLAN $ 320
CHOOSE WEEKLY PLAN. YOU SAVE $ 4
-------------------------------------------------------
ENTER CUSTOMER NAME?WIZARD OF AVIS
ENTER PROJECTED MILES OF DRIVING?300
ENTER NUMBER OF RENTAL DAYS?5

TOTAL COST-DAILY PLAN  $ 130
TOTAL COST-WEEKLY PLAN $ 156.25
CHOOSE DAILY PLAN. YOU SAVE $ 26.25
-------------------------------------------------------
ENTER CUSTOMER NAME?EOD
PROGRAM COMPLETED

TIME 0.06 SECS.
```

### Follow-up Exercises

**21.** Test your understanding of the program by answering the following questions:
  a. Do we need the STOP statement in line 140? Explain.
  b. Do we need the RETURN statement in line 390? Explain.
  c. Explain the purpose of the loop in lines 300 to 304.

d. Do you see why we subtracted 0.1 from N in line 410? Does it have to be 0.1, or can we just subtract any fraction?

e. What is the purpose of line 425?

f. Why do we use the ABS function in line 570?

**22.** Modify subroutine INITIALIZE in each of the following ways:

a. Use READ/DATA statements instead of LET statements. What is the advantage of this approach?

b. Use conversational input. What is the advantage of this approach?

## 9.5
## COMMON ERRORS

Certain errors regarding subprograms seem to occur more commonly than others. Make note of these.

*1. Functions.* The following cause fatal execution errors: a zero or negative argument for the LOG function; a zero argument for the SQR function; an incorrect number of arguments in user-defined functions. Overflow or underflow in the evaluation of the EXP function is a nonfatal execution error. Logic errors are common in the use of the RND function because of differences in the treatment of arguments from system to system. Make sure you understand exactly how your RND function works by solving Exercise 7.

*2. Subroutines.* Watch out for the following logic errors: inadvertent entry into a subroutine, as when the main program is not operationally separate from the subroutine that follows (for example, the elimination of the STOP statement in line 260 of the program in Example 9.5 on page 270 not only causes a logic error but also may cause an execution error since a GOSUB was not used to enter the subroutine); failing to logically separate subroutines, as when the RETURN statement is omitted in a subroutine; and *inadvertently changing the value in a variable by using the same variable for different purposes in the main program and in one or more subroutines.*

### Additional Exercises

**23.** Define or explain the following:

subprogram
calling program
main program
BASIC-supplied functions
built-in function
implementation-supplied function
library function
argument
RANDOMIZE
user-defined functions
user-supplied statement function

arithmetic statement function
DEF statement
dummy argument
actual argument
subroutine
modular programming
GOSUB statement
RETURN statement
predefined process symbol
nested subroutines

24. **Automobile Rental Decision Revisited.** Modify the program in Section 9.4 as follows:
    a. The main program calls all subroutines.
    b. Subroutine INITIALIZE is replaced by subroutine TECHNICAL DATA. This subroutine conversationally inputs G, D, M1, W1, and P.
    c. Subroutine CUSTOMER DATA remains unchanged.
    d. Subroutine DAILY calculates and prints total cost of the daily plan.
    e. Subroutine WEEKLY calculates and prints total cost of the weekly plan.
    f. Subroutine HYBRID calculates and prints total cost of the following new plan: The customer pays an extra $1.95 over the daily fixed cost ($18.95 per day for the given data), pays for gasoline expenses, and pays a charge of 25 cents for each mile over an allotment given by 100 times the number of days in the rental.
    g. Eliminate subroutines COSTS and OUTPUT.
  \**h. Subroutines DAILY, WEEKLY, and HYBRID each have nested FOR/NEXT loops, where M (projected miles of driving) is the index of the outer loop and G1 (miles per gallon) is the index of the inner loop. Use the same data as in the example, except let M run from 50 to 150 percent of M2 in steps of 10 percent of M2 (all expressed as integers) and let G1 run from G − 4 to G + 4 in steps of 1. (*Note:* DAILY need not have a loop for G1.) The purpose of each nested loop is to print a cost table, where rows represent projected miles of driving and columns represent miles per gallon. Do a nice job of labeling your output. Conduct four runs so as to vary the number of days in the rental as follows: 2, 5, 12, 23. What factors favor each plan?

25. **Mopups Revisited.** Modify the program in Section 6.6 on page 165 or Exercise 20 in Chapter 7 on page 218 as follows:
    a. The main program reads N$ and S, and tests for the end of the data.
    b. A subroutine determines and prints total price (T).
    c. Store values of T for all dealers in a one-dimensional array which is specified in the main program. Following the last dealer, call subroutine MEAN and output the sum of total prices and the mean (average) total price.
    d. Call subroutine SORT (Example 7.8) to sort and print values of T in descending order.
    Debug your program using the test data in the example. Include flowcharts.

26. **Property Tax Assessment Revisited.** Modify Exercise 23 in Chapter 5 on page 137 or Exercise 21 in Chapter 7 on page 218 as follows:
    a. Main program reads the number of property values (N), lot number, and property value and outputs lot number, property value, and tax charge with appropriate labels. Use a FOR/NEXT loop for processing the N property values.
    b. Develop a subroutine that determines the tax charge.
    c. Store property values and tax charges in two one-dimensional arrays (or one two-dimensional array) which are specified in the main program. Following the last property, call subroutine MEAN and output the sum and mean (average) of property values and tax charges.
    d. Use another subroutine to sort (Example 7.8) and print tax charges in descending order. Include corresponding lot numbers and property values in your output table.

**27. Telephone Company Billing Revisited.** Modify Exercise 35 in Chapter 6 on page 176 as follows:

    a.  Main program reads number of customers to be processed, customer name, phone number, code, and number of extensions; outputs name, phone number, and charge with appropriate labels.

    b.  A subroutine edits the data for errors. Specifically, it ensures that

        1.  Codes are 1, 2, 3, or 4.

        2.  Number of extensions is greater than 0 but less than

            5 for code 1
            10 for code 2
            100 for code 3
            1000 for code 4

        If an error is detected in either the code or the number of extensions, bypass the charge calculation and print an appropriate error message that identifies the phone number and error. Add new customers to the data to debug the program's edit logic for each possible error.

    c.  A second subroutine calculates the appropriate charge for a given customer.

  \**d.  Once all customers have been processed, a third subroutine determines and outputs (with labels) total number and percent number of customers by code category. *Hint:* Use an array to store codes.

  \**e.  Once all customers have been processed, a fourth subroutine computes and outputs (with labels) total charges and percent charges by code category, and overall total charges. *Hint:* Use arrays to store code and number of extensions.

**28. Personnel Benefits Budget Revisited.** Modify Exercise 26 in Chapter 5 on page 139 as follows:

    a.  Main program reads data and prints output data with labels.

    b.  A subroutine edits data for errors. Specifically, it ensures that:

        1.  annual salary is greater than $5000 and less than $50,000

        2.  retirement code is 1, 2, or 3

        If an error is detected in either the salary or the code, bypass the calculations of contributions and print an appropriate error message that identifies the SS number and the error. Add new employees to the data to debug your error logic for each possible error.

    c.  A second subroutine calculates social security, retirement, group life insurance, and total contributions.

  \**d.  Store all contributions in a two-dimensional array in the main program, where rows represent employees and the four columns represent the contributions. Call a subroutine that calculates and prints column totals and averages.

**29. Credit Billing Revisited.** Modify Exercise 29 in Chapter 5 on page 142 as follows:

    a.  The main program reads all data.

    b.  A subroutine edits the data for errors. Specifically, it ensures that

1. Credit limit is $800 or above and $1500 or less.
2. Payment is greater than zero.
3. New purchase amount is greater than zero.

If an error is encountered, then print an appropriate error message that includes the customer's name and address, bypass the calculation and printout for this customer, and go on to the next customer. Add new customers to your data to test each of these three possible read errors.

c.  A second subroutine calculates the new balance.
d.  A third subroutine prints the bill, including the minimum payment due and any warning message. It calls a fourth subroutine that calculates the minimum payment due.

**30.  Checking Account Report Revisited.** Modify Exercise 39 in Chapter 6 on page 181 as follows:

a.  The main program reads all data.
b.  A subroutine edits the data for errors. Specifically, it ensures that

1. The bank account number is greater than 100,000 and less than 900,000.
2. The number of transactions is above zero but less than 100.
3. The beginning balance is positive.

If an error is encountered, then print an appropriate error message that includes the customer's name and account number, bypass the calculations and printout for this customer, and go on to the next customer. Add new customers to your data to test each of these three possible read errors.

c.  A second subroutine performs all calculations.
d.  A third subroutine prints the report.

**31.  Student Fee Bill Revisited.** Modify Exercise 30 in Chapter 5 on page 144 as follows:

a.  The main program reads all data.
b.  A subroutine edits the data for errors according to part d in that exercise.
c.  A second subroutine performs all calculations.
d.  A third subroutine prints the fee bill.
e.  A fourth subroutine prints the summary totals.

**32.  Installment Loan Revisited.** Modify Exercise 38 in Chapter 6 on page 180 as follows:

a.  A subroutine reads all data.
b.  A second subroutine calculates A and the total interest paid over the life of the loan.
c.  A third subroutine calculates and prints the amortization table.

**33.  Crime Data Summary Revisited.** Modify Exercise 22 in Chapter 7 on page 218 or Exercise 21 in Chapter 8 on page 247 as follows:

a.  A subroutine reads all data.
b.  A second subroutine performs necessary calculations and prints the augmented table.
c.  A third subroutine calculates and prints the second table described in part c on page 219.

34. **Exam Grading Revisited.** Modify Exercise 26 in Chapter 7 on page 222 as follows:
    a. The main program reads and outputs all data.
    b. A subroutine grades the exam.
    c. A second subroutine sorts and outputs final grades in descending order. *Hint:* As the first subprogram returns each final grade, the main program stores it in a one-dimensional array. Once this array is filled, the sort subroutine can be called.
    **d. A third subroutine determines and prints the frequency distribution of final grades. This subroutine calls a fourth subroutine that calculates the mean grade.

35. **Personnel Salary Budget Revisited.** Modify Exercise 24 in Chapter 8 on page 250 as follows:
    a. The main program reads all data.
    b. A subroutine edits employee data for errors. Specifically, it ensures that

       1. The current annual salary is below $30,000.
       2. The union code is 1, 2, or 3.
       3. The step code is 1, 2, 3, 4, or 5.
       4. The year hired is less than or equal to the current year.

       If an error is encountered, then print an appropriate error message that includes the employee's name and social security number, bypass the calculations and print line for this employee, and go on to the next employee. Add new data to test each of the possible errors.
    c. A second subroutine performs all calculations.
    d. A third subroutine prints the report.
    e. A fourth subroutine prints totals.
    f. A fifth subroutine summarizes the salary budgets by union.

36. **Questionnaire Analysis Revisited.** Modify Exercise 26 in Chapter 8 on page 253 as follows:
    a. A subroutine reads all data.
    b. A second subroutine calculates and outputs frequency distributions.
    **c. A third subroutine performs cross tabulations.

37. **Craps Simulation.** A front line bet in a game of craps works as follows:

    1. You win what you bet if on the first toss you roll 7 or 11 (a natural).
    2. You lose what you bet if on the first toss you roll a 2, 3, or 12 (a crap).
    3. If you roll a 4, 5, 6, 8, 9, or 10 on the first toss, then this number becomes your *point* for subsequent rolls.
    4. To win, you must roll your point again *before* you roll a 7.
    5. If you roll a 7 while trying to get your point, then you lose.
       a. Design a flowchart and write a modular program that simulates the toss of dice. Note that you need two random numbers for each toss—one for the first die and one for the second die. *Hint:* Uniform digits between 1 and 6 can be simulated using

          INT(RND*6 + 1)

       b. Design a loop that simulates a single game of craps as described in items 1 through 5 above. The outcome of this loop is either "won" or "lost."

c. Add a second loop that simulates N games. Assume $1 is bet on each game. Keep track of wins and losses. Debug your program by simulating five games. In your output for each roll, print the point on the first die, the point on the second die, and the overall point (sum of the two dice). At the end of a game print "won" or "lost." At the end of the five games print the following summaries: number of games won, number of games lost, your total dollar winnings (or losses), and the percent (of the total amount bet) dollar winnings (or losses).

d. Provide an option in the program to suppress the output for each roll and the "won" or "lost" output at the end of each game. For each of the following runs just print the summary statistics:

(1) N = 100
(2) N = 500
(3) N = 1000
(4) N = 5000

Based on your output, estimate the expected (percent) loss by betting the front line in craps.

**38. Electric Bill.** Gotham City Electric Company wishes to redesign the computerized bills that it sends to commercial and residential customers. It has announced a city-wide contest to determine the best flowchart and BASIC program for this purpose.

a. Provided data include the following:
*Initialization data*

1. Month (three letters) and day (two digits) for beginning date of monthly billing cycle
2. Month and day for ending date of monthly billing cycle
3. Year (two digits)
4. Number of customers to be billed (up to four digits)

*Customer data*

5. Previous meter reading in kilowatthours (up to 7 digits)
6. New meter reading in kilowatthours
7. Customer rate code (one digit)
8. Past due amount (dollars and cents)
9. Payment since last bill (dollars and cents)
10. Name of customer (up to 20 characters)
11. Street address of customer (up to 20 characters)
12. City, state, and ZIP (up to 24 characters)
13. Account number of customer (up to eight digits)

Use the following sample data for the computer run:

| Billing Cycle | | | Number of |
| From | To | Year | customers |
| --- | --- | --- | --- |
| SEP 19 | OCT 18 | 1980 | 5 |

Use the following sample data per customer:

| Pre-vious Read-ing | New Read-ing | Rate Code | Past Due Amount | Pay-ment | Name | Street Address | City, State Zip | Account Number |
|---|---|---|---|---|---|---|---|---|
| 27648 | 28648 | 1 | 60.10 | 60.10 | make these up . . . . . . . . . . . . . . . . | | | |
| 42615 | 45115 | 2 | 45.20 | 0.00 | make these up . . . . . . . . . . . . . . . | | | |
| 314625 | 354625 | 3 | 3110.00 | 3110.00 | make these up . . . . . . . . . . . . . . . . | | | |
| 615700 | 695700 | 3 | 8000.00 | 8000.00 | make these up . . . . . . . . . . . . . . . . | | | |
| 800500 | 1025500 | 3 | 3000.00 | 1000.00 | make these up . . . . . . . . . . . . . . . . | | | |

Rate codes and their corresponding rates per kilowatthour (kWh) are explained by the following table:

| Rate Code | Rate Per kWh (cents) | Comment |
|---|---|---|
| 1 | 5.25 | Residential, partly electric home |
| 2 | 4.85 | Residential, all electric home |
| 3 | 8.50 | Commercial, usage under 50,000 kWh |
| 3 | 7.50 | Commercial, usage between 50,000 kWh and 100,000 kWh |
| 3 | 6.50 | Commercial, usage above 100,000 kWh |

If past due amount less payment is above zero, then a 1 percent per month charge on this difference is added to the customer's bill. For example, the last customer in the input data is commercial and used 225,000 kWh (1,025,500 − 800,500). Thus, the customer is charged at 6.5 cents per kWh, which amounts to a current bill of $14,625.00. This customer, however, has a $3000 past due account and payments of only $1000. At an interest rate of 1 percent per month, the interest charge is $20, that is, (3000 − 1000) × 0.01; hence, the total now due from this customer is $16,645.00, that is, (2000 + 20 + 14625).

Output from your program should include the following:

1. Name of customer
2. Street address of customer
3. City, state, and ZIP
4. Account number
5. Billing cycle: from (month,day) to (month,day,year)
6. Kilowatthours
7. Current amount owed
8. Past due amount
9. Interest charge
10. Total amount due

Label your output and design it to fit within a 3- × 5-inch image, since these statements must fit in a standard sized envelope.

b.  Include error detection to ensure that the rate code is 1, 2, or 3 and the new meter reading is greater than the previous meter reading. If an error is encountered, then print an appropriate error message that includes the customer's name, complete address, and account number; bypass the calculations and printout for this customer; space down to the next statement; and go on to the next customer. Add new data to test each of the possible input errors.

Use a modular design for your program. By the way, the winner of the contest gets to ride the Batmobile, which recently was retrofitted with an all-electric power plant.

**39. Comparison of Depreciation Methods.** Read Exercise 32 in Chapter 3 (page 70). In this problem we wish to print a "depreciation schedule" over the life of the asset. For the automobile which costs $4200, lasts 4 years, and has a salvage value of $200, the following output is desired for the straight-line method:

DEPRECIATION SCHEDULE
FOR AUTOMOBILE

STRAIGHT-LINE METHOD

| YEAR | DEPRECIATION EXPENSE | ACCUMULATED DEPRECIATION | BOOK VALUE |
|------|----------------------|--------------------------|------------|
| 1 | 1000 | 1000 | 3200 |
| 2 | 1000 | 2000 | 2200 |
| 3 | 1000 | 3000 | 1200 |
| 4 | 1000 | 4000 | 200 |

The double-declining-balance method would yield the following output:

DEPRECIATION SCHEDULE
FOR AUTOMOBILE

DOUBLE-DECLINING-BALANCE METHOD

| YEAR | DEPRECIATION EXPENSE | ACCUMULATED DEPRECIATION | BOOK VALUE |
|------|----------------------|--------------------------|------------|
| 1 | 2100 | 2100 | 2100 |
| 2 | 1050 | 3150 | 1050 |
| 3 | 525 | 3675 | 525 |
| 4 | 262.5 | 3937.5 | 262.5 |

a. Prepare a flowchart and write a modular program which outputs depreciation schedules for the following assets:

| Asset | Cost ($) | Life (years) | Salvage Value ($) |
|-------|----------|--------------|-------------------|
| Automobile | 4,200 | 4 | 200 |
| Kidney Machine | 200,000 | 10 | 500 |
| Building | 75,000 | 40 | 0 |

Store the above data in DATA statements. Make the program interactive by giving the user the following processing options:

1. Read in data for the next asset.
2. Print schedule by the straight-line-method only.
3. Print schedule by the double-declining-balance method only.
4. Print schedule by both depreciation methods.
5. Stop.

Draw conclusions which compare the effects of these two methods of depreciation. Under what conditions is one method more desirable than the other with respect to the impact on income taxes?

**b. Find an accounting book and study the sum-of-the-years-digit method of depreciation. Include this method as an option. Draw conclusions about the desirability of this method.

40. **Statistical Analysis Program.** Large programs that give options for various statistical analyses are common in commercial applications. For example, IBMs STATPACK, UCLAs BMD, North Carolina State's SAS, and the University of Chicago's SPSS are all widely used packages for implementing a variety of statistical analyses across many disciplines.

a. *Measures of central tendency and dispersion.* Design and write a modular program that calculates and prints the statistics described below for analyzing a set of $n$ data items given by $x_1, x_2, \ldots, x_n$. In the descriptions below, assume the following set of values for $x$: 7, 14, 10, 6, 3.

   1. *Mean,* given by

$$\bar{x} = \frac{x_1 + x_2 + \cdots + x_n}{n} = \frac{\sum_{i=1}^{n} x_i}{n} = \frac{40}{5} = 8$$

   2. *Median,* a value such that one-half of the values are above it and one-half of the values are below it. First sort the data in ascending order, and then find the *position* of the median using the formula $(n + 1)/2$. For example, if the sorted values of $x$ are

$$3 \quad 6 \quad 7 \quad 10 \quad 14$$

   ↑_____ location of median

   then the median is found in position $(5 + 1)/2$, or third position. Thus the median is 7. If $n$ is an even number, however, then the median is defined as halfway between the two adjacent positions in the center. For example, in the six-item sequence

$$3 \quad 6 \quad 7 \quad 10 \quad 14 \quad 16$$

   ↑_____ location of median in position

$$\frac{6 + 1}{2}$$

   the median is in position 3.5, or midway between the third item (7) and the fourth item (10). Thus the median is 8.5.

3. Minimum value of $x$, or 3 for the given data.
4. Maximum value of $x$, or 14 for the given data.
5. *Range,* the difference between max $x$ and min $x$, or 11 for the given data.
6. *Mean absolute deviation (MAD),* given by

$$MAD = \frac{\sum_{i=1}^{n} |x_i - \bar{x}|}{n} = \frac{16}{5} = 3.2$$

7. *Variance,* given by

$$s^2 = \frac{\sum_{i=1}^{n} (x_i - \bar{x})^2}{n-1} = \frac{70}{4} = 17.5$$

8. *Standard deviation,* given by

$$s = \sqrt{s^2} = \sqrt{17.5} = 4.1833$$

b. *Frequency distribution.* Add a second option to the program to print a frequency distribution. Let the user specify two suboptions here: (1) enter number of classes and upper class limits, or (2) just enter number of classes and let the computer determine class limits. For example, in the first suboption we might want to group the data into four classes with upper limits 5, 10, and 15 for the first three classes.

In this case, the frequency distribution is given by

| Class Limits | Frequency |
|---|---|
| under 5 | 1 |
| 5 but under 10 | 2 |
| 10 but under 15 | 2 |
| 15 or above | 0 |
| | 5 |

Thus, of the five data items, one was under 5, two were at least 5 but under 10, two were in the range 10 but under 15, and none were 15 or above. In the second suboption, a four-class frequency distribution would be given by

| | Class Limits | Frequency |
|---|---|---|
| min $x$ → | 3.00 but under 5.75 | 1 |
| Width of each class is 2.75, or range divided by number of classes | 5.75 but under 8.50 | 2 |
| | 8.50 but under 11.25 | 1 |
| | 11.25 but under 14.01 ← max $x$ + .01 | 1 |
| | | 5 |

c. *Bar chart.* Add a third option that prints a bar chart, as illustrated for the second frequency distribution in part b:

```
CLASS +        FREQUENCIES
------------------------------------
    1 +* 1
    2 +** 2
    3 +* 1
    4 +* 1
```

**d. *Histogram.* Instead of the bar chart in part c, print a histogram as follows:

```
              2
    1        ***      1        1
   ***       ***     ***      ***
------------------------------------
  5.75      8.50    11.25    14.01
```

# PART III

# Enhanced BASIC

The next three chapters present some common enhancements to BASIC: formatted (the precise control of) output, the use of data files, and matrix (MAT) operations. The statements in Part III are not included in the subset of the language termed *minimal BASIC* by the proposed ANSI standard; hence, variations do exist from system to system. To distinguish the set of statements in the next three chapters from those statements termed minimal BASIC, we have chosen to label this new set **enhanced BASIC.**

Interestingly, the use of many of these statements is so common in actual practice that the ANSI committee currently working on the standard is proposing six enhancement modules for standardization. Three of these modules deal with the topics covered by the next three chapters.

In the next three chapters you should keep in mind that these enhancements are not yet specified by ANSI, let alone adopted officially. As much as possible, we either have tried to keep the discussion general or have used what appear to be the most universal approaches. Still, your system is likely to differ in its treatment, so it would help if your system's BASIC manual and/or your instructor is handy. *We also advise that you experiment by running our examples and exercises on your system.*

# Formatted Output

Computer results presented in neat and orderly reports often require more control over the output of numeric and character (string) data than is possible by using only PRINT statements. The statements in this chapter allow you to format (precisely control) the output.

## 10.1
## PRINT USING AND IMAGE STATEMENTS

Compare the two sets of output below. The first version is based on the use of PRINT statements; the second version utilizes what are called *PRINT USING* statements. Notice that version B is easier to read and is more attractive than version A.

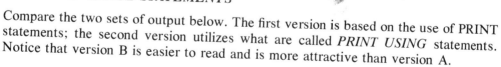

| Version A | | | |
|---|---|---|---|
| ID | HOURS | RATE | PAY |
| 98 | 35 | 3.25 | 113.75 |
| 99 | 32 | 3 | 96 |
| 100 | 40 | 3.5 | 140 |
| 101 | 38 | 3.45 | 131.1 |

| Version B | | | |
|---|---|---|---|
| ID | HOURS | RATE | PAY |
| 98 | 35 | 3.25 | 113.75 |
| 99 | 32 | 3.00 | 96.00 |
| 100 | 40 | 3.50 | 140.00 |
| 101 | 38 | 3.45 | 131.10 |

In general the application of the PRINT USING statement allows us to

1.  Right-justify rather than left-justify the output (align output on the right).
2.  Round numbers to a specified number of decimal places.
3.  Align a column of numbers so that decimal points appear one below the other.
4.  Insert blanks and other characters at precise locations on the line of output.

Three versions of the PRINT USING statement are illustrated in this chapter: IBMs CALL 370, Hewlett Packard's (HP) HP3000, and Digital Equipment Corporation's (DEC) BASIC PLUS II. The general form of the PRINT USING statement is given by one of the following:

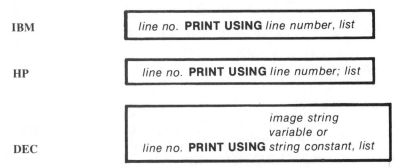

IBM     *line no.* **PRINT USING** *line number, list*

HP      *line no.* **PRINT USING** *line number; list*

DEC     *line no.* **PRINT USING** *image string variable or string constant, list*

This statement specifies the *list* of constants, variables, or expressions whose values are to be output according to an "image" of the line that is either referenced by the line number following the key words PRINT USING (for IBM and HP) or described within the PRINT USING statement (for DEC). An *image* of the output line is written using codes called **image control characters;** its purpose is to describe exactly how the printed output line is to appear.

IBM and HP systems utilize an **image statement** to describe the image of the output line as follows:

IBM     *line no.* :*image control characters*

HP      *line no.* **IMAGE***image control characters*

The image statement is identified by either a colon (:) or the key word IMAGE placed immediately after the line number, and the remainder of the statement describes the information needed by the computer to print the output.

DEC systems incorporate the image of the output line within the PRINT USING statement itself, by specifying image control characters within either a string variable or a string constant.

Table 10.1 (p. 298–299) illustrates PRINT USING and image statements for the version B output shown earlier. At this time don't be concerned about the exact details regarding image control characters such as #, ƀ, X, and D. Simply relate the statements to the output and to the general discussion.

## 10.2
## TYPES OF OUTPUT FIELDS

Image control characters correspond to types of output values based on distinct groupings within the image. These groupings are termed **output fields.**

In the discussion which follows, it is useful to identify five types of fields that can be output through the image:

1. Integer fields
2. Real (decimal) fields
3. Exponential fields
4. String variable fields
5. String constant (literal) fields

### Integer fields

Integer values are printed by using the pound symbol # (IBM and DEC systems) or letter D (HP systems) as an image control character. In this case the symbol is repeated for each numeric digit of the field. For example, the program

| IBM | HP | DEC |
|---|---|---|
| 10 LET B = 500 | 10 LET B = 500 | 10 LET B = 500 |
| 20 LET R = 7000 | 20 LET R = 7000 | 20 LET R = 7000 |
| 30 PRINT USING 40,B,R | 30 PRINT USING 40;B,R | 40 LET A$ = ''###ƀƀƀƀ####'' |
| 40 :###ƀƀƀƀ#### | 40 IMAGEDDDXXXXDDDD | 45 PRINT USING A$,B,R |
| 50 END | 50 END | 50 END |
| Null field　Integer fields | Null field　Integer fields | Integer fields / Null field |

would yield the following output:

```
Print Column
        111
123456789012. . .
500    7000
```

The width of the first numeric field is three (columns 1–3) and the width of the second numeric field is four (columns 8–11). Columns 4 to 7 of the print line represent a **null field,** as specified either by the four blank image control characters in line 40 of the IBM and DEC versions[1] or by the four X's in line 40 of the HP version. As you can see, *null fields are used to control output spacing.*

---

[1] The symbol ƀ is our way of denoting a blank character. As usual, this character is typed by depressing the space bar on the keyboard.

TABLE 10.1   PRINT USING and Image Statement Examples

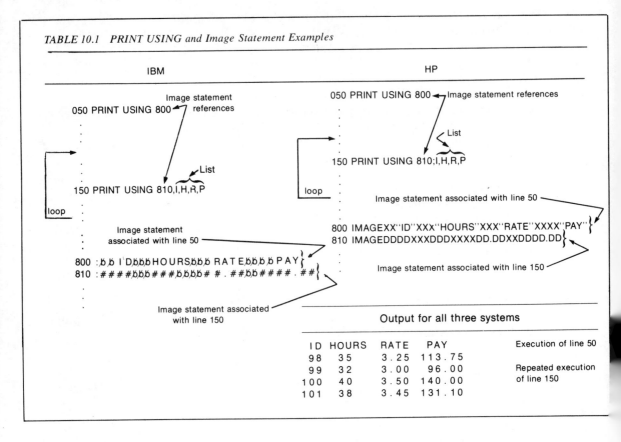

Notice that the width of the first numeric field is five (columns 1–5) and the width of the second numeric field is eight (columns 10–17). In this case the null field is in columns 6 to 9.

---

If the width of the field (number of # or D symbols) is greater than the number of digits stored in the variable, then the numeric value is **right-justified** within (placed at the extreme right of) the field. For example, if the image were changed to

| IBM | HP | DEC | Your System (If different) |
|---|---|---|---|
| 10 LET B = 500 | 10 LET B = 500 | 10 LET B = 500 | |
| 20 LET R = 7000 | 20 LET R = 7000 | 20 LET R = 7000 | |
| 30 PRINT USING 40,B,R | 30 PRINT USING 40;B,R | 40 LET A$ = "#####ƀƀƀƀ#########" | |
| 40 :#####ƀƀƀƀ######### | 40 IMAGEDDDDDXXXXDDDDDDDD | 45 PRINT USING A$,B,R | |
| 50 END | 50 END | 50 END | |

then the output would appear as

```
            Print Column
               1 1 1 1 1 1 1 1 1 2 . . .
      1 2 3 4 5 6 7 8 9 0 1 2 3 4 5 6 7 8 9 0
         5 0 0             7 0 0 0
```

Notice that the width of the first numeric field is five (columns 1–5) and the width of the second numeric field is eight (columns 10–17). In this case the null field is in columns 6 to 9.

TABLE 10.1    *(Continued)*

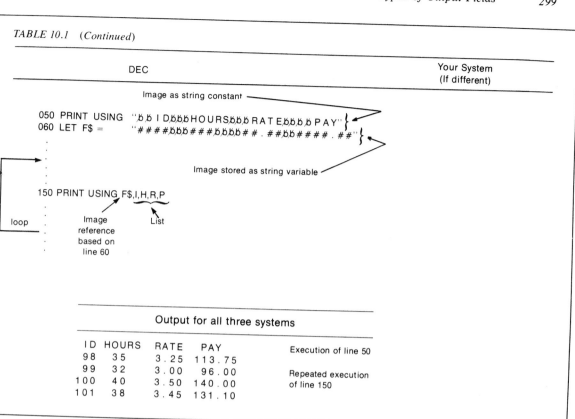

|  DEC  | Your System (If different) |
|-------|-------|

Image as string constant —

```
050 PRINT USING  "ƀ ƀ I Dƀƀƀ HOURSƀƀƀ RATEƀƀƀ ƀ PAY"
060 LET F$ =     "####ƀƀƀ ####ƀƀƀ ## . ##ƀƀ #### . ##"
```

Image stored as string variable —

```
150 PRINT USING F$,I,H,R,P
```

loop   Image reference based on line 60    List

### Output for all three systems

| ID | HOURS | RATE | PAY | |
|----|-------|------|-----|---|
| 98 | 35 | 3.25 | 113.75 | Execution of line 50 |
| 99 | 32 | 3.00 | 96.00 | |
| 100 | 40 | 3.50 | 140.00 | Repeated execution of line 150 |
| 101 | 38 | 3.45 | 131.10 | |

If the width of the field is smaller than the number of digits stored in the variable, then the output will not conform exactly to the image. In this case, each system differs in its "fixup" procedure, as illustrated next.

| IBM | HP | DEC | Your System (If different) |
|-----|-----|-----|-----|

```
10 LET B = 500         10 LET B = 500         10 LET B = 500
20 LET R = 7000        20 LET R = 7000        20 LET R = 7000
30 PRINT USING 40,B,R  30 PRINT USING 40;B,R  40 LET A$ = "##ƀƀƀ ####"
40 :##ƀƀƀ ####         40 IMAGEDDXXXXDDDD     45 PRINT USING A$,B,R
50 END                 50 END                 50 END
```

```
Print Column          Print Column          Print Column
    111                   111                  11111
123456789012...       123456789012...       1234567890123 4...
**    7000            $$    7000            %  500    7000
```

Asterisks printed since 500 doesn't fit in field of width 2

Dollar signs printed since 500 doesn't fit in a field width of 2

% sign indicates that 500 would not fit in the given field of width 2

## Decimal fields

Decimal or real values are printed by using the # or D symbol and a single decimal point as image control characters. The placement of the decimal point indicates its precise location, and the number of # or D symbols to its right specifies the number of decimal places to be output. For example, the program

| IBM | HP | DEC | Your System (If different) |
|---|---|---|---|
| 10 LET P = 3.1453 <br> 20 PRINT USING 30,P <br> 30 :bb##.## <br><br> 40 END   Decimal field | 10 LET P = 3.1453 <br> 20 PRINT USING 30;P <br> 30 IMAGEXXDD.DD <br><br> 40 END   Decimal field | 10 LET P = 3.1453  Decimal field <br> 20 LET F$ = "bb##.##" <br> 30 PRINT USING F$,P <br><br> 40 END | |

would yield the output

```
Print Column

123456789...
    3.15
```

*Notice that the image in this example rounds the number to two decimal places.* Further note that the decimal point is placed in print column 5 since it is the fifth image control character in the image.

## Exponential fields

The output of very large or small numbers can be printed in exponential (scientific) form. For example, the value 9,100,000 can be expressed in E-notation as 9.1 E + 06. Exponential output is indicated by supplying four exclamation marks (!!!! on IBM systems) or four upward arrows (↑↑↑↑ on DEC systems) or the letter E (on HP systems) as image control characters for a decimal number. The system fits as much of the number as it can within the decimal image and then determines the appropriate exponent, as the following example illustrates.

| IBM | HP | DEC | Your System (If different) |
|---|---|---|---|
| 10 LET B = 9100000 <br> 20 PRINT USING 30,B <br> 30 :##.#!!!! <br> 40 END | 10 LET B = 9100000 <br> 20 PRINT USING 30;B <br> 30 IMAGEDD.DE <br> 40 END | 10 LET B = 9100000 <br> 20 LET I$ = "##.#↑↑↑↑" <br> 30 PRINT USING I$,B <br> 40 END | |

In this case the output would appear as

```
Print Column

123456789...
  9.1E 06
```

Note that the decimal point is aligned in print column 3 since it is the third image control character in the image.

## String variable fields

Data stored in string variables also can be output with the PRINT USING statement. The following image control characters are used to output character data:

| SYSTEM | CHARACTER |
|--------|-----------|
| IBM    | #         |
| HP     | A         |
| DEC    | \         |

For example, the program

| IBM | HP | DEC | Your System (If different) |
|-----|-----|-----|-----|
| 10 LET N$ = ''HELP'' | 10 LET N$ = ''HELP'' | 10 LET N$ = ''HELP'' | |
| 20 PRINT USING 30,N$ | 20 PRINT USING 30;N$ | 20 LET I$ = ''ƀ\\\\\'' | |
| 30 ;ƀ#### | 30 IMAGEXAAAA | 30 PRINT USING I$,N$ | |
| 40 END | 40 END | 40 END | |

would provide the output

```
Print Column

1 2 3 4 5 6 7 8 9 . . .
HELP
```

## String constant (literal) fields

Messages, headings, and labeled output also can be printed with the PRINT USING statement. A literal field is a set of characters other than image control characters that is to be transmitted to the terminal exactly (literally) as it appears in the line image. The following example illustrates literal fields.

| IBM | HP | DEC | Your System (If different) |
|-----|-----|-----|-----|
| 05 PRINT USING 40 | 05 PRINT USING 40 | 05 LET A$ = ''FI NANCI ALƀREPORT '' | |
| 10 READ R,C | 10 READ R,C | 10 LET B$ = ''REVENUE:ƀƀ$ ##. ##'' | |
| 15 DATA 40.05,45.20 | 15 DATA 40.05,45.20 | 15 LET C$ = ''COST: ƀ,ƀƀƀƀ$ ##. ##'' | |
| 20 LET P = R − C | 20 LET P = R − C | 20 LET D$ = ''PROFI T: ƀƀƀ$ ##. ##'' | |
| 25 PRINT USING 45,R | 25 PRINT USING 45;R | 25 PRINT USING A$ | |
| 30 PRINT USING 50,C | 30 PRINT USING 50;C | 30 READ R,C | |
| 35 PRINT USING 55,P | 35 PRINT USING 55;P | 35 DATA 40.05,45.20 | |
| 40 :FI NANCI ALƀREPORT | 40 IMAGE''FI NANCI ALƀREPORT '' | 40 LET P = R − C | |
| 45 :REVENUE:ƀƀ$ ##. ## | 45 IMAGE''REVENUE: ƀƀ$ ''DD. DD | 45 PRINT USING B$,R | |
| 50 :COST: ƀ,ƀƀƀƀ$ ##. ## | 50 IMAGE''COST: ƀ,ƀƀƀ$ ''DD. DD | 50 PRINT USING C$,C | |
| 55 :PROFI T: ƀƀƀ$ ##. ## | 55 IMAGE''PROFI T: ƀƀƀ$ ''DD. DD | 55 PRINT USING D$,P | |
| 60 END | 60 END | 60 END | |

```
Print Column
                   11111111112. .
1 2 3 4 5 6 7 8 9 0 1 2 3 4 5 6 7 8 9 0
FI NANCI AL REPORT
REVENUE:    $40 . 05
COST:       $45 . 20
PROFI T:    $−5 . 15
```

You should notice several items in this last example. First, *we placed the image statements in a group in order to facilitate alignment of the output.* Moreover, the image lines were placed either at the beginning or end of the program so as to visually get them "out of the way" of the execution logic. Second, PRINT USING statements can ensure the alignment of decimal points in the output when desirable.[2] Finally, *the decimal field width should account for the possibility of a negative numeric value.* In the example, the −5.15 takes up the entire field width of five. A number such as −12.50 could not be printed using the decimal field referenced for the output of P.[3]

### Follow-up Exercises

1. Confirm each example in Section 10.2 on your system. If you use a system other than IBM, HP, or DEC, then make appropriate modifications to our examples before running.

2. Make the following changes for the indicated examples and run these on your system.

   a. In the integer field example, output the 500 in columns 7 to 9 and the 7000 in columns 11 to 14.

   b. In the integer field example, output as follows:

   ```
            Print Column
          1 2 3 4 5 6 7 8 9. . .
          ─────────────────────
          B =    5 0 0
          R =  7 0 0 0
   ```

   c. In the decimal field example, make successive changes to output P right-justified in column 9. First output P to zero decimal places without using a decimal point; then output P to zero decimal places using a decimal point; then to one decimal place; then to three decimal places; then to four decimal places; and finally to five decimal places.

   d. In the exponential field example, make successive changes to output B with the decimal point in column 6 and two decimal places; the decimal point in column 4 and three decimal places; and the decimal point in column 4 and zero decimal places.

   e. In the string variable field example, successively change the storage contents of N$ to GO; to GOOF; and to GOOFUS. (Leave the image line as is.)

   f. In the string constant example, print a dashed line immediately following the report heading and immediately after the output line for profit. Also, change the value of C to 52.55.

3. Assume the following values are stored:

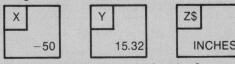

What would the output look like in each situation?

---

[2] Compare this example to Example 3.9 on page 57.

[3] Some systems treat the $ character as an image control character that packs the dollar symbol against the leftmost digit of the number.

| IBM | HP | DEC |
|---|---|---|
| a. 10 PRINT USING 20,X,Y<br>   20 :###bb##.# | 10 PRINT USING 20;X,Y<br>20 IMAGEDDDXXDD.D | 10 LET A$ = "###bb##.#"<br>20 PRINT USING A$,X,Y |
| b. 10 PRINT USING 20,X<br>   20 :bbNUMBERb = b#### | 10 PRINT USING 20;X<br>20 IMAGEXX"NUMBERb=b"DDDD | 10 LET A$ = "bbNUMBERb=b####"<br>20 PRINT USING A$,X |
| c. 10 PRINT USING 20,Y,Z$<br>   20 :###.##b######### | 10 PRINT USING 20;Y,Z$<br>20 IMAGEDDD.DDDXAAAAAAAAAA | 10 LET A$ = "###.###b¦¦¦¦¦¦¦"<br>20 PRINT USING A$,Y,Z$ |
| d. 10 PRINT USING 20<br>   20 :bbbbbbbbbbbENROLLMENT | 10 PRINT USING 20<br>20 IMAGEXXXXXXXXXX"ENROLLMENT" | 10 PRINT USING"bbbbbbbbbbbENROLLMENT" |

Run appropriate versions on your system to confirm your expectations.

4. Specify PRINT USING/image statements to output:

a. The integer values of the variables A and B and the real value of C in scientific notation. The value of A ranges from 0 to 9999, the value of B ranges from $-100$ to 999, and the value of C ranges from $-1.00$ to $9.99 \times 10^{35}$.

b. The label and the value of the variable B, whose value ranges from 0.00 to 999.99.

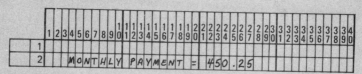

c. The heading

d. The column headings and the values of variables N$ (15 characters or less), S(nine-digit positive integer numbers), R(positive real numbers less than 10 to two decimal places), and P(positive real numbers less than 1000 to two decimal places).

| | EMPLOYEE | SOCIAL | PAY | |
| | NAME | SEC. NO. | RATE | GROSS PAY |
| | | | | |
| SMITH ADAM | | 199310716 | $5.72 | $275.23 |

## 10.3
## SALES COMMISSIONS REVISITED

The following program demonstrates the use of column headings and detail print lines within a loop, as initially illustrated in Example 5.4 on page 119. *This program was run using IBM's CALL version of BASIC.* Notice that, in our system, the # symbol is used for the output of character strings. Also note that the body of the table is printed by repeatedly referencing the image statement in line 303 through the PRINT USING statement in line 200. Finally, note that we reference the image in line 302 twice, at lines 120 and 220.

```
005 REM---SALES COMMISSIONS REVISITED
010 REM
015 REM--KEY:
020 REM     S$ = SOCIAL SECURITY NUMBER
025 REM     N$ = NAME
030 REM     S  = SALES
035 REM     C  = COMMISSIONS
040 REM     B  = BASE SALARY
045 REM     T  = TOTAL PAY
050 REM
100 LET B=150
110 PRINT USING 301
120 PRINT USING 302
130 READ N
140 FOR I= 1 TO N
150    LET C=0
160    READ S$,N$,S
170    IF S <= 5000 THEN 190
180    LET C=.02 * S
190    LET T=B + C
200    PRINT USING 303,N$,S$,T
210 NEXT I
220 PRINT USING 302
300 REM ***************************************
301:EMPLOYEE NAME     SS NUMBER     TOTAL PAY
302:-----------------------------------------
303:#############   ###########   $###.##
305 REM ***************************************
900 DATA 3
910 DATA "266-62-9431","B. FLINTSTONE",4150
920 DATA "375-41-6216","P. RABBIT",6000
930 DATA "154-25-1298","B. B. BABBLE",2020
999 END
```

```
EMPLOYEE NAME     SS NUMBER     TOTAL PAY

B. FLINTSTONE     266-62-9431     $150.00
P. RABBIT         375-41-6216     $270.00
B. B. BABBLE      154-25-1298     $150.00


TIME 0.02 SECS.
```

## Follow-up Exercises

5. Answer the following questions regarding the sales commission example:
   a. What would happen if the field for the output of SS number in line 303 had a width of 9?
   b. What would happen if the field for total pay in line 303 were expressed as ##.##?
   c. Is the dollar sign ($) part of the decimal field in line 303?
   d. Would the output differ if the three image statements in lines 301 to 303 were inserted between lines 200 and 210?
   e. Why do we recommend not generally placing image lines immediately after corresponding PRINT USING statements?
*6. Design and run a program that reproduces the output in Table 10.1 on page 298. Read in I, H, and R and make improvements in the output format. For example, include a report heading, dashed lines, etc.

## 10.4
## COMMON ERRORS

A common error in the use of PRINT USING/image lines is unaligned output, as when related labeled output does not align visually. In the sales commission example, we placed the four image lines together in order to simplify the alignment of output. Additionally, *it helps if you first design your output on a sheet of paper.*

A more vexing error is called **field overflow.** In this case the width of the field is smaller than the value to be printed. On some systems asterisks are printed instead of the value, while on other systems the field is widened to accommodate the value. For example, see page 299. As another example, the program

```
10 READ A$
15 DATA "TOYS-R-US"
20 PRINT USING 50,A$
30 READ B
35 DATA 1000
40 PRINT USING 50,B
50 :###
60 END
```

yields the following output on our IBM CALL system:

```
    Print Columns
 1 2 3 4 5 6 7 8 9 . . .
 ────────────────────────
 T O Y
 * * *
```

In the first case, the leftmost three characters (TOY) of the character string are fitted into the field of width 3. In the second case, the field overflow of numeric data is indicated by asterisks (*). *What happens on your system?* In general, you should take care that your field widths are sufficiently large to handle the data you need to process.

## Additional Exercises

7.  Define or explain the following terms:
    PRINT USING statement          null field
    image control characters       right-justified
    image statement                field overflow
    output fields
8.  Apply the PRINT USING statement instead of the PRINT statement to prepare output for one of the following programs:
    a. Credit billing (Chapter 5, Exercise 29, page 142)
    b. Student fee bill (Chapter 5, Exercise 30, page 144)
    c. Aging customer accounts (Chapter 6, Exercise 36, page 177)
    d. Installment loan (Chapter 6, Exercise 38, page 180)
    e. Checking account report (Chapter 6, Exercise 39, page 181)
    f. Revenue sharing (Chapter 7, Exercise 24, page 220)
    g. Electric bill (Chapter 9, Exercise 38, page 287)
    h. Comparison of depreciation methods (Chapter 9, Exercise 39, page 289).

# CHAPTER 11

# Data Files

In earlier chapters we entered a data item into a storage location in one of three ways: by using a LET statement while coding the program; by using READ/DATA statements while coding the program; by using an INPUT statement while the program was executing. LET statements are desirable when data do not change from run to run, whereas the latter two methods are efficient for entering small amounts of data but are cumbersome when large amounts of data are involved. In addition, all three methods have the limitation of making data available to only one program and must be retyped to be used by other programs. Moreover, up until now, results from a program could be printed only on paper or video screen. In many applications it is desirable to store the output from a program on some medium for later use.

   BASIC provides a vehicle called a **file (data file or external file)** whereby data may be stored and made available to any number of programs. Files store data separate from the program on a secondary storage medium such as magnetic disk, diskette, or cassette. The file is assigned a name, and by referencing the name we can either retrieve data from the file or place data on the file. Since the data are stored in a medium that is separate from the program, it follows that any number of programs can access these data.

TABLE 11.1.   *Opening a Data File*

| IBM | HP |
|---|---|
| line no. **OPEN** file number, file name, **INPUT** or **OUTPUT** | line no. **ASSIGN** file specifier **TO #** file number |

**IBM**

where

*file number* is an integer number that links the file and the program (other statements in the program reference this file by using this integer number); *file name* is either a string constant or a string variable that identifies a file; **INPUT** opens an existing file to allow input of data from the file; **OUTPUT** opens an existing file to allow output of data onto the file.†

*Examples:*

10 OPEN 1, N$,OUTPUT

The file whose name is stored under N$ is to be treated as output file number 1.

20 OPEN 4, "GRADES",INPUT

The file named GRADES is an input file that is to be referenced as file number 4.

**HP**

where

*file specifier* is either a string constant or a string variable that identifies a file by name; *file number* is an integer number that links the file and the program (other statements in the program reference this file by using this integer number).‡

*Examples:*

10 ASSIGN N$ TO #1

The file whose name is stored under N$ is to be referenced as file number 1.

20 ASSIGN "GRADES" TO #4

The file named GRADES is to be referenced as file number 4.

† All files, whether to be used as input or output, must be created by a system command before running the program. In the second example

FILE GRADES

must be typed to allocate disk space for a file named GRADES.

‡ All files must be created by a system command before running the program. In the second example

CREATE GRADES

must be typed to allocate disk space for a file named GRADES.

## 11.1
## FILE INSTRUCTIONS

The instructions necessary to read, write, and modify file data vary from one system to another. In this section we illustrate the following operations for Digital Equipment Corporation's BASIC PLUS II, IBMs CALL, and Hewlett-Packard's 3000 systems:

1. Opening a data file
2. Output to a data file
3. Input from a data file
4. Closing a data file

*TABLE 11.1*    (*Continued*)

| DEC | YOUR SYSTEM (IF DIFFERENT) |
|---|---|

```
line            FOR INPUT            file
no. OPEN string      or       AS FILE number
            FOR OUTPUT
```

where

*string* is either a string constant or a string variable
that names a new or existing file; **FOR INPUT**
opens an existing file to allow input of data from
the file; **FOR OUTPUT** creates a new file to allow
output of data onto the file; *File number* is an
integer number that links the file and the program
(other statements in the program reference this file
by using the integer number).

*Examples:*

10  OPEN N$ FOR OUTPUT AS FILE 1

The file whose name is stored under N$ is to
be treated as output file number 1.

20  OPEN "GRADES.001" FOR INPUT AS FILE 4

The file named GRADES.001 is an input file
that is to be referenced as file number 4.

If your system is not illustrated, then you should focus on the principles of file processing and make necessary changes in our examples based on your systems manual or
instructor.

## Opening a Data File

A program must first inform the computer that a certain file is to be used in a particular
manner. The **OPEN** or **ASSIGN** statement "opens" the file to be used; it usually
identifies the name of the file, designates the operation to be performed (*input* from the
file or *output* to the file), and assigns a number to the file. The general form of this
statement for three different systems is illustrated in Table 11.1.

---

TABLE 11.2.   *Output to a Data File*

| IBM | HP |
|---|---|

<table>
<tr><td>

> line      file
> no. **PUT** number : list

</td><td>

> line        file
> no. **PRINT** # number ; list

</td></tr>
</table>

where

*file number* references the file on which output is to be placed (this number is the same as that used in the OPEN statement);

*list* is the variables whose values are to be placed on the file.

*Example:*

50 PUT 1 : S$,G1,G2,G3

Place the contents in S$, G1, G2, G3 on file number 1.

where

*file number* references the file on which output is to be placed (this number is the same as that used in the ASSIGN statement);

*list* is the variables whose values are to be placed on the file.

*Example:*

50 PRINT #1;S$,G1,G2,G3

Place the contents in S$, G1, G2, G3 on file number 1.

---

### Output to a Data File

Up until now, output from a program was placed at the terminal through the execution of PRINT statements, as illustrated in Figure 11.1(a). When utilizing data files, output from the program also may be placed on the data file, as depicted in Figure 11.1(b) (notice the arrow) and illustrated in Table 11.2. Generally, output to a terminal is meant for immediate human "consumption," whereas output to a secondary storage medium such as magnetic disk is meant to be used at a later time by another program. We illustrate these ideas more fully in Example 11.2 and Section 11.2.

### Input From a Data File

Parts (a) and (b) of Figure 11.2 illustrate the usual methods, up until now, of entering data into storage locations in the CPU. READ/DATA statements are used in Figure 11.2(a) to enter data that are provided within the program itself (as shown by the arrow); INPUT statements are used in Figure 11.2(b) to enter data that are provided from the terminal (as shown by the arrow). Figure 11.2(c) shows the input of data from a file to storage locations in the CPU through statements illustrated in Table 11.3.

### Closing a Data File

All files that have been opened during the execution of a program should be closed before the program terminates, as some systems allow a maximum number of files to be opened at any one time and other systems may lose data from files not closed. Also, if a particular file is to be used first as an input file and then as an output file (or vice versa) within the same program, then the file must be closed before it is reopened. The statements in Table 11.4 illustrate this operation.

TABLE 11.2    *(Continued)*

| DEC | YOUR SYSTEM (IF DIFFERENT) |
| --- | --- |

> line            file
> no. **PRINT** # number , list

where

*file number* reference the file on which output is to be placed (this number is the same as that used in the OPEN statement);

*list* is the variables whose values are to be placed on the file.

*Example:*

50  PRINT  #1,S$,G1,G2,G3

Place the contents in S$, G1, G2, G3 on file number 1.

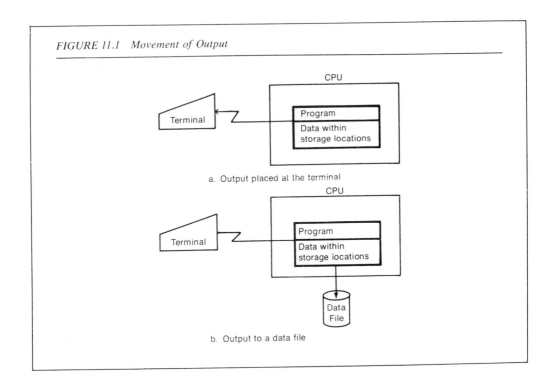

FIGURE 11.1    *Movement of Output*

a. Output placed at the terminal

b. Output to a data file

TABLE 11.3.　*Input from a Data File*

| IBM | HP |
|---|---|

| line            file | line            file |
|---|---|
| no.  **GET** number : list | no.  **READ** # number ; list |

| where | where |
|---|---|
| *file number* references the file from which data are to be input (this number is the same as that used in the OPEN statement); | *file number* references the file from which data are to be input (this number is the same as that used in the ASSIGN statement); |
| *list* is the variables whose values are to be entered into memory from the file. | *list* is the variables whose values are to be entered into memory from the file. |

*Example:*

60 GET 4:S$,G1,G2,G3

Take the next four values from file number 4 and store them in the CPU storage locations named S$, G1, G2, and G3.

*Example:*

60 READ #4; S$,G1,G2,G3

Take the next four values from file number 4 and store them in the CPU storage locations named S$, G1, G2, and G3.

---

TABLE 11.4.　*Closing a Data File*

| IBM | HP |
|---|---|

| line            file | line            file |
|---|---|
| no.  **CLOSE** numbers | no.  **ASSIGN** * **TO** # number |

| where | where |
|---|---|
| *file numbers* indicate the files that are to be closed. You can close as many files as you want by separating each file number with a comma. | *file number* indicates the file that is to be closed. |

*Example:*

100 CLOSE 1,4

*Examples:*

100 ASSIGN * TO #1
110 ASSIGN * TO #4

TABLE 11.3    (*Continued*)

| DEC | YOUR SYSTEM (IF DIFFERENT) |
|---|---|

> line                    file
> no. **INPUT** # *number* , *list*

where

*file number* references the file from which data are
to be input (this number is the same as that used in
the OPEN statement);

*list* is the variables whose values are to be entered
into memory from the file.

*Example:*

60  INPUT  #4,S$,G1,G2,G3

Take the next four values from file number 4 and
store them in the CPU storage locations named S$,
G1, G2, and G3.

TABLE 11.4    (*Continued*)

| DEC | YOUR SYSTEM (IF DIFFERENT) |
|---|---|

> line
> no.  **CLOSE** *file numbers*

where

*file numbers* indicate the files
that are to be closed. You can
close as many files as you want
by separating each file number
with a comma.

*Example:*

100  CLOSE  1,4

FIGURE 11.2   *Methods of Data Entry.*

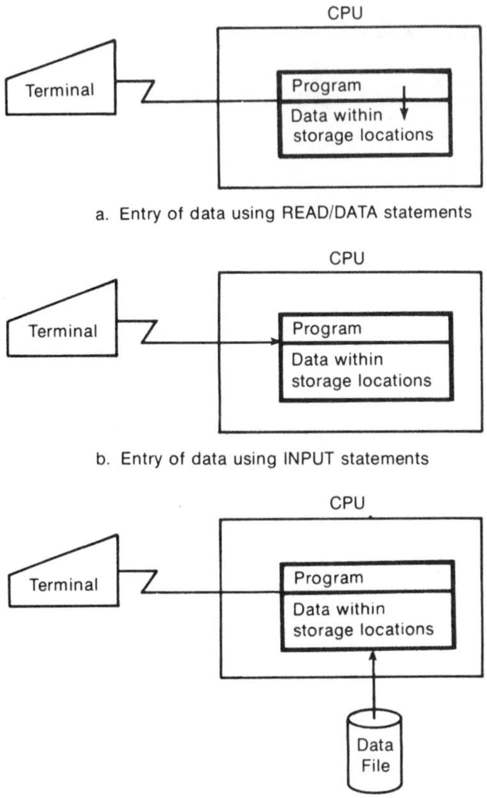

a. Entry of data using READ/DATA statements

b. Entry of data using INPUT statements

c. Entry of data as input from a file

## EXAMPLE 11.1   Class Grades Using Data Files

A faculty member has decided to computerize the exam grades for a course. The data to be stored consist of student names and three exam scores for each student.

The first program on page 315 accepts terminal input of names and grades and outputs these data on a file named GRADES.[1]

The second program uses GRADES as an input file, calculates the average grade for each student, and outputs name, grades, and average grade at the terminal.

[1] Many systems (for example, IBM and HP as footnoted in Table 11.1) require the use of a system command to reserve storage space for the file *before* the program is run. Check with your instructor regarding your system.

*Program 1:*

**IBM**

```
010 PRINT "ENTER FILE NAME";
020 INPUT N$
030 OPEN 1,N$,OUTPUT
040 PRINT "ENTER NUMBER OF STUDENTS";
050 INPUT K
060 PUT 1:K
070 FOR J = 1 TO K
080    PRINT "ENTER NAME AND GRADES"
090    INPUT S$,G1,G2,G3
100    PUT 1: S$,G1,G2,G3
120 NEXT J
130 CLOSE 1
999 END
```

*Sample Run:*

```
ENTER FILE NAME?GRADES
ENTER NUMBER OF STUDENTS?2

ENTER NAME AND GRADES
?MUMPS,75,67,68

ENTER NAME AND GRADES
?MCGUEE,93,88,89
STOP
```

**HP**

*Program 1:*

```
010 PRINT "ENTER FILE NAME";
020 INPUT N$
030 ASSIGN 1,N$,OUTPUT
040 PRINT "ENTER NUMBER OF STUDENTS";
050 INPUT K
060 PRINT #1;K
070 FOR J = 1 TO K
080    PRINT "ENTER NAME AND GRADES"
100    INPUT S$,G1,G2,G3
110    PRINT #1;S$,G1,G2,G3
120 NEXT J
130 ASSIGN * TO #1
999 END
```

*Sample Run:*

```
ENTER FILE NAME? GRADES
ENTER NUMBER OF STUDENTS?2

ENTER NAME AND GRADES
?MUMPS,75,67,68

ENTER NAME AND GRADES
?MCGUEE,93,88,89
STOP
```

**DEC**

*Program 1:*

```
010 PRINT "ENTER FILE NAME";
020 INPUT N$
030 OPEN N$ FOR OUTPUT AS FILE 1
040 PRINT "ENTER NUMBER OF STUDENTS";
050 INPUT K
060 PRINT #1;K
070 FOR J = 1 TO K
080    PRINT
090    PRINT "ENTER NAME AND GRADES"
100    INPUT S$,G1,G2,G3
110    PRINT #1;S$,G1,G2,G3
120 NEXT J
130 CLOSE 1
999 END
```

*Sample Run:*

```
ENTER FILE NAME? GRADES.001
ENTER NUMBER OF STUDENTS?2

ENTER NAME AND GRADES
?MUMPS,75,67,68

ENTER NAME AND GRADES
?MCGUEE,93,88,89
STOP
```

---

Structure of file GRADES following execution of program 1:

| 2 | MUMPS | 75 | 67 | 68 | MCGUEE | 93 | 88 | 89 |

Note that data are placed sequentially on the file.

---

*Program 2:*

**IBM**

```
10 PRINT "ENTER FILE NAME";
20 INPUT F$
30 OPEN 4,F$,INPUT
40 GET 4:K
50 FOR J = 1 TO K
60    GET 4:S$,G1,G2,G3
70    LET A=(G1+G2+G3)/3
75    PRINT
80    PRINT S$,G1,G2,G3;A
90 NEXT J
95 CLOSE 4
99 END
```

*Sample Run:*

```
ENTER FILE NAME? GRADES

MUMPS      75  67  68  70

MCGUEE     93  88  89  90
STOP
```

**HP**

*Program 2:*

```
10 PRINT "ENTER FILE NAME";
20 INPUT F$
30 ASSIGN F$ TO #4
40 READ #4:K
50 FOR J = 1 TO K
60    READ #4:S$,G1,G2,G3
70    LET A = (G1 + G2 + G3)/3
75    PRINT
80    PRINT S$,G1;G2;G3;A
90 NEXT J
95 ASSIGN * TO #4
99 END
```

*Sample Run:*

```
ENTER FILE NAME? GRADES

MUMPS      75  67  68  70

MCGUEE     93  88  89  90
STOP
```

**DEC**

*Program 2:*

```
10 PRINT "ENTER FILE NAME";
20 INPUT F$
30 OPEN F$ FOR INPUT AS FILE 4
40 INPUT #4;K
50 FOR J = 1 TO K
60    INPUT #4,S$,G1,G2,G3
70    LET A = (G1 + G2 + G3)/3
75    PRINT
80    PRINT S$,G1;G2;G3;A
90 NEXT J
95 CLOSE 4
99 END
```

*Sample Run:*

```
ENTER FILE NAME? GRADES .001

MUMPS      75  67  68  70

MCGUEE     93  88  89  90
STOP
```

**Follow-up Exercises**

1. Run programs 1 and 2 of Example 11.1 on your system. Make any necessary changes to conform to your system.

2. Did you notice that we changed the file number and the string variable for file name from program 1 to program 2 in Example 11.1? Could we have used N$ and file number 1 again in program 2? Explain.

3. Why is it best to use a string variable for file name rather than a specific string constant such as GRADES?

4. Describe programs 1 and 2 in Example 11.1 in terms of Figures 11.1 and 11.2.

\* 5. Assume a second file already has been created named ADDRESS, which contains the name (N$), address (A$), city (C$), state (T$) and zip code (Z$) corresponding to each student in file GRADES. Modify program 2 in Example 11.1 so that the program prints only the students' name, city, state, and average grade. Print an error message each time corresponding student names between the two files do not match.

\*\* 6. Suppose a file named GRADE1 already has been created which contains the exact data as the file named GRADES in Example 11.1, except that immediately after the 2 (number of students) it has a 3 (number of grades per student). Write a new program which updates the grade file as follows: Read into memory a student's name and grades from file GRADE1; read into memory from the terminal this student's fourth grade; place onto file GRADE2 this student's name and four grades. By the time the program terminates execution, GRADE2 contains the name and four grades for each student. Describe this program using the approach of Figures 11.1 and 11.2. Describe the structure (as in Example 11.1) of file GRADE2.

## 11.2
## DATA PROCESSING APPLICATIONS

Many data processing applications such as payroll, inventory, and accounts receivable make use of files to process large amounts of data. In these applications data are organized in a logical manner for more efficient processing. The following classification scheme is typically used in data processing applications:

**Field.** A data item (fact or attribute) about some entity such as a person, place, thing or event. For example, an employer might maintain data on employees' name, social security number, rate of pay, number of deductions, and other items. Each of these attributes is considered a field.

**Record.** A collection of related fields grouped together and retrievable as a unit. For example, all of the data items relating to a single employee represent a record.

**File.** A collection of related records. Each record is a logical part of the file because it contains the same data items as all the other records in the file. For example, an "employee file" contains the data on each employee.

The following scheme illustrates this relationship among fields, records, and files:

Fields

| | Name | ID Number | Salary | Sex Code |
|---|---|---|---|---|
| Record 1 → | ABATAR | 099342101 | 20000 | F |
| File Record 2 → | BOMBERG | 881211113 | 15800 | M |
| Record 3 → | DRURY | 125718112 | 18000 | M |

As another illustration, program 1 of Example 11.1 created a file named GRADES having two records each with four fields. Note that the first entry in the file, the data item 2, indicates the number of records that follow.

Several different types of files are used in data processing applications. Two commonly used file types are the master file and the transaction file. A **master file** contains data items that are central to continued operation of the organization. These files are relatively permanent collections of records containing informational, historical, and current-status items. For example, the master file for bank checking accounts might contain a record for each customer account which includes the customer's name, account number, address, telephone, and last month's ending balance.

A **transaction file** is a relatively temporary collection of records containing data about transactions that have occurred during the most recent operating period of time. This type of file is used to process data against the master file. For example, a transaction file for bank checking accounts might contain data on all checks processed during the current month. At the end of the current month, data from both the transaction file and the master file are processed into a new master file which updates the current status of ending balance for each account.

---

**EXAMPLE 11.2   Computerized Inventory Control System**

Controlling inventory is a very important function for most organizations. Poor inventory control can lead to unnecessarily high levels of inventory, resulting in high rates of spoilage and obsolescence, and high costs for storing, maintaining, and insuring goods. At the other extreme, poor inventory control can lead to frequent shortages, resulting in customer's ill will and lost sales. Good inventory control means that management is able to provide a desired level of service to its customers (by delivering goods from inventory) at the least expense to the organization. For most organizations, good inventory control generally dictates a computerized inventory control system.

In a computerized inventory control system every addition and deletion in stock is recorded in a transaction file. Periodically, data in the transaction file are used to update (change) an inventory master file which maintains, among other things, the current balance of each inventory item.

To illustrate an inventory control system, consider the "blood bank" (inventory of blood) at a hospital. To simplify the discussion, suppose that only two types of blood are carried in inventory, A-negative (ANEG) and A-positive (APOS), and three actions against inventory are possible: action code 1 means that inventory has been depleted by some amount (number of units) for use by a patient; action code 2 means that inventory has been depleted by the number of units in storage that have exceeded the maximum legal life of blood (21 days); and action code 3 means that inventory has been augmented by new blood.

The process of updating inventory is illustrated by the system flowchart in Figure 11.3. A **system flowchart** presents a general overview of an entire system, the sequence of major processing operations, and the data flow to and from files. The type of flowchart you have been drawing is technically called a **program flowchart.**

*FIGURE 11.3   System Flowchart for Inventory Control System*

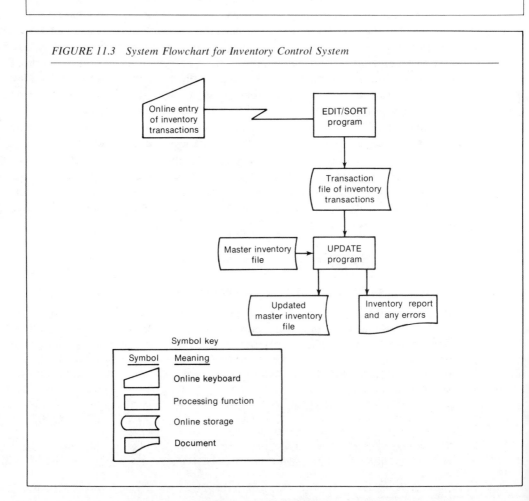

In our blood bank illustration, each inventory transaction (type of blood, action code, and number of units of blood) is entered at the terminal interactively under the control of an EDIT/SORT program. For example, at the end of a given day the following transactions might be entered:

| Blood Type | Action Code | Amount (pints) |
|---|---|---|
| APOS | 1 | 3 |
| APOS | 1 | 4 |
| ANEG | 2 | 15 |
| APOS | 3 | 50 |
| ANEG | 1 | 5 |
| APOS | 75 | 2 | ←—Incorrect entries |
| END | 0 | 0 | ←—End-of-file record |

The EDIT/SORT program in Figure 11.3 checks the validity of action codes (note the mistake in the last entry), sorts the data alphabetically according to blood type, and places the data on the transaction file as follows:

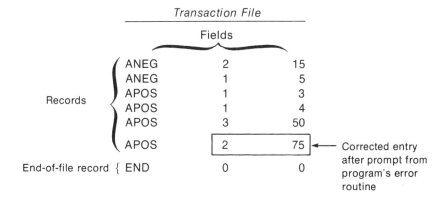

*Transaction File*

Fields

| | | |
|---|---|---|
| ANEG | 2 | 15 |
| ANEG | 1 | 5 |
| APOS | 1 | 3 |
| APOS | 1 | 4 |
| APOS | 3 | 50 |
| APOS | 2 | 75 | ←— Corrected entry after prompt from program's error routine |

Records

End-of-file record { END    0    0

The UPDATE program next utilizes the transaction file and the master file to create an updated master file. Additionally, the UPDATE program prints a report showing the date and a table of blood type and current inventory balance (as described in Exercise 10). If the master file contains the data shown below,

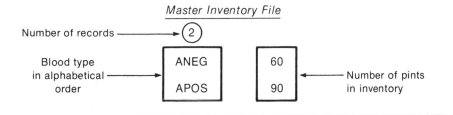

*Master Inventory File*

Number of records ——→ (2)

Blood type in alphabetical order ——→ | ANEG | 60 |
| APOS | 90 | ←—— Number of pints in inventory

then the processing of the transaction file against the master file would result in the following updated master file:

*Updated (New) Master Inventory File*

| 2 | |
|---|---|
| ANEG | 40 |
| APOS | 58 |

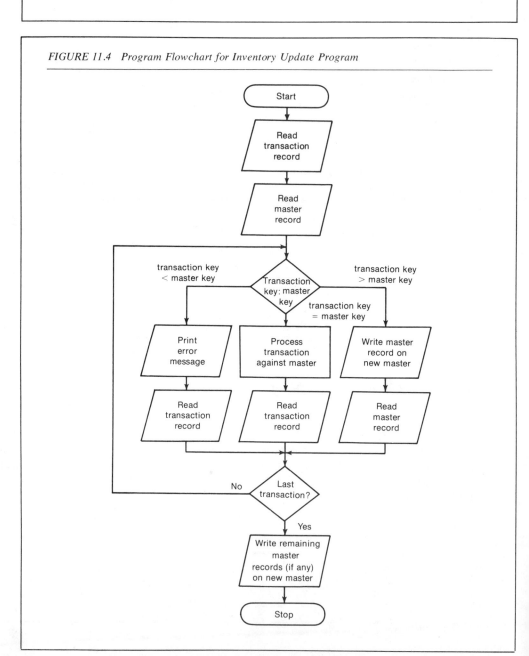

FIGURE 11.4   *Program Flowchart for Inventory Update Program*

A program flowchart for the UPDATE program is illustrated in Figure 11.4. The "transaction key" is the blood type (ANEG or APOS) read from a record of the transaction file and the "master key" is the blood type read from a record of the master file. In the discussion that follows keep in mind that records in both the transaction and master files are in alphabetical order according to blood type.

The update program compares the key of the transaction record with the corresponding data item (key) in the master record. If a match occurs (keys of both files are equal) the transaction data are used to update the number of pints in inventory for that master record (the inventory would increase or decrease based on the transaction amount), as illustrated by the middle branch in Figure 11.4.

When the transaction key tests greater than the master key, it follows that processing of the current blood type on the master file has been completed. Thus, the updated record for this blood type now can be written onto the new master file. For example, when the third record in the transaction file on page 319 is processed, the transaction key will test greater than the master key (APOS > ANEG). At this time the updated record for ANEG on the new master file can be written, as depicted in the third branch of Figure 11.4.

A transaction key greater than the master key may also indicate that no transaction (activity) occurred for that record. This is particularly common when master files have many records. In such cases, the master record is copied unchanged onto the new master file. Depending on the situation, however, an error may be indicated by the mismatch of keys. In this case, an error message is printed, as illustrated by the first branch in Figure 11.4.

## 11.3
## COMMON ERRORS

When using files, students sometimes forget to

1. Use the system command necessary to reserve storage space for the file. If your system requires this command and you forget to use it before you run your program, then you will encounter an execution error when the computer attempts to open or use a nonexistent file. (See footnote 1 on page 314).
2. Open the file. If you forget this instruction, then the computer prints an execution error message when it attempts to read from or print to a file.
3. Assign a file number to the READ or PRINT statement. If you forget to specify a file number, then you have caused a syntax error.

### Additional Exercises

**7.** Define or explain each of the following:

| | |
|---|---|
| data file | master file |
| external file | transaction file |
| field | system flowchart |
| record | program flowchart |
| file | |

**8. Affirmative Action Search Revisited.** Design the program of Exercise 27 in Chapter 5 on page 140 so that the personnel file is stored in a data file. *Note:* You may need to write an additional program that places the data on the file.

9. **Computerized Matching—A File Search Revisited.** Design the program of Exercise 28 in Chapter 5 on page 141 so that the placement office file is stored in a data file. *Note:* You may need to write an additional program that places the data on the file.

10. **Blood Bank Inventory System.** Write and run the following programs for the system described in Example 11.2:

    a. EDIT/SORT. Don't forget to design the error routine for action codes.

    b. UPDATE. Modify Figure 11.4 and the program to read or input the current date and output an inventory report that includes a table of new inventory balances for each blood type.

    ** c. Add other useful features. For example, UPDATE could include an option to echo print all records in the transaction and master files, summaries following the inventory table, etc.

11. **Credit Billing Revisited.** Design the program of Exercise 29 in Chapter 5 on page 142 so that master and transaction files are used. The master file contains name, address, credit limit, and last billing period's ending (previous) balance for each customer. The transaction file contains name, payments, and new purchases. Arrange records in the files alphabetically by name.

    a. Run your program for the data given in the problem such that bills are printed and the master file is updated.

    ** b. Include the following action codes in the transaction file and program logic:

        1. Change in address
        2. Change in credit limit
        3. Delete customer from master file
        4. Add customer to master file

Make up data to test each of these action codes.

12. **Electric Bill Revisited.** Design the program of Exercise 38 in Chapter 9 on page 287 so that master and transaction files are used. The master file contains previous reading, rate code, past due amount, name, street address, city, state, zip code, and account number for each customer. In addition to dates, the transaction file contains account number, name, new meter reading, and payments since last bill.

    a. Run your program for the data given in the problem such that bills are printed and the master file is updated.

    ** b. Include the following action codes in the transaction file and program logic:

        1. Change of address
        2. Delete customer from master file
        3. Add customer to master file

Make up data to test each of these action codes.

13. **Payroll.** Each week a small firm processes its weekly payroll for hourly employees. The following input is necessary to process the payroll.

### Master Employee File

Employee ID
Name
Hourly rate of pay
Number of dependents
Cumulative gross pay thus far this year
Cumulative FICA tax thus far this year
Cumulative withholding (income) tax thus far this year
Cumulative group health contribution thus far this year

### Transaction File

Date
Employee ID
Number of hours worked

Develop a program which

a.  Generates a "wage summary report" consisting of a line for each employee; the line contains employee name, employee number, hourly rate, hours worked, gross pay, FICA, income tax, group health, and net pay. After individual figures are printed, the program is to print totals for gross pay, each deduction, and net pay. Include appropriate report and column headings.

b.  Updates cumulative gross pay, cumulative FICA tax, cumulative withholding tax, and cumulative group health contribution for each employee in the master file.

To determine the pay for each employee, the following facts must be included in your program:

1.  Gross pay is defined as pay for regular time plus pay for overtime. Overtime pay is 1.5 times the regular rate for each hour above 40.
2.  Social security tax (FICA) is 6.65 percent of gross pay. The deduction is made until the employee's cumulative earnings are above $29,700 after which there is no deduction.
3.  Deduction for withholding tax and group health plan are tied to the number of dependents as follows:

| Dependents | Income Tax (% of gross pay) | Group Health ($ per week) |
|---|---|---|
| 1 | 22 | 2.50 |
| 2 | 20 | 3.60 |
| 3 | 18 | 5.10 |
| 4 | 16 | 6.00 |
| 5 or more | 13 | 6.50 |

4.  Net pay is defined as gross pay less FICA deduction less income tax deduction less group health deduction. Use the data below to test your program.

## Master File

| 1940 | Bella Bitta, Al | 2.50 | 4 | 1500.00 | 99.75 | 240.00 | 180.00 |
|------|-----------------|------|---|----------|---------|---------|--------|
| 1942 | Budget, Frank | 8.25 | 5 | 30000.00 | 1975.05 | 3900.00 | 195.00 |
| 2001 | Manicotti, Diane | 6.00 | 1 | 12300.00 | 817.95 | 2706.00 | 75.00 |
| 2542 | Saintvi, Arun | 8.00 | 3 | 29600.00 | 1968.40 | 5328.00 | 153.00 |

### Transaction file for (date which you supply)

```
1940 60
1942 40
2001 45
2542 35
```

c.  Run parts a and b again for the next week using the data below.

### Transaction file for (date one week after preceding transaction file)

```
1940 32
1942 45
2001 35
2542 42
```

** d.  Design your program to include the processing of the following action codes in the transaction file:

1.  Change in hourly rate of pay
2.  Change in number of dependents
3.  Delete employee from master file
4.  Add employee to master file

Make up data to test each of these action codes.

# Matrix Operations

---

12.1  MAT READ, INPUT, AND PRINT STATEMENTS

12.2  MATRIX FUNCTIONS

12.3  ALGEBRAIC OPERATIONS

12.4  COMMON ERRORS

ADDITIONAL EXERCISES

---

A **matrix** is a rectangular array of numbers. For example, the matrices

$$\mathbf{A} = \begin{pmatrix} 10 & 15 \\ 20 & 25 \\ 30 & 35 \end{pmatrix} \quad \mathbf{B} = \begin{pmatrix} 1 & 2 & 3 & 4 \\ 5 & 6 & 7 & 8 \end{pmatrix} \quad \mathbf{C} = \begin{pmatrix} 100 \\ 200 \\ 300 \\ 400 \\ 500 \end{pmatrix} \quad \mathbf{D} = (6 \quad 5 \quad 4 \quad 3 \quad 2 \quad 1)$$

identify **A** as a 3 by 2 matrix (3 rows and 2 columns of elements, or 6 elements), **B** as a 2 by 4 matrix, **C** as a 5 by 1 matrix, and **D** as a 1 by 6 matrix. Alternatively, **C** may be called a **column vector** and **D** a **row vector.**

As you can see, a matrix is equivalent to our use of one- and two-dimensional numeric arrays, when as usual the first subscript refers to the number of rows and the second subscript refers to the number of columns.[1]

Many systems include the option of using **MAT statements,** a set of BASIC instructions that greatly facilitate read, input, print, algebraic, and other matrix operations. Unfortunately, MAT statements include variations from system to system, since they are not part of the proposed ANSI standard. Necessarily, this puts the burden on you to confirm the matrix features on your system. In general, it would be a good idea for you to try out our examples and exercises on your system. Note any differences and consult with your instructor and/or systems manual.

---

[1] Systems that include row 0 or column 0 in one- and two-dimensional arrays ignore this row or column when applying the statements in this chapter.

## *12.1*
## *MAT READ, INPUT, AND PRINT STATEMENTS*

Matrices are named in the same manner as numeric arrays by selecting an appropriate alphabetic character.[2] Likewise, they must be dimensioned by using a DIM statement. For example, the four matrices illustrated earlier could be dimensioned as follows:

    10  DIM A(3,2), B(2,4), C(5,1), D(1,6)

Read, input, and print operations of arrays are much less tedious with the use of the following MAT statements:

---

*line no.* **MAT READ** *list of matrix names with or without explicit dimensions*
*line no.* **MAT INPUT** *list of matrix names with or without explicit dimensions*
*line no.* **MAT PRINT** *list of matrix names without explicit dimensions*

---

These statements could have been used in any of the examples of Chapters 7 and 8. The examples that follow illustrate their use.[3]

---

### EXAMPLE 12.1   FOR/NEXT and MAT READ/PRINT Equivalence

Study the following two equivalent versions for reading and printing the matrices

$$A = \begin{pmatrix} 10 & 15 \\ 20 & 25 \\ 30 & 35 \end{pmatrix} \quad \text{and} \quad C = \begin{pmatrix} 100 \\ 200 \\ 300 \\ 400 \\ 500 \end{pmatrix}$$

| Version A | Version B |
| --- | --- |

```
010 DIM A(3,2),C(5,1)          10 DIM A(3,2),C(5,1)
020 FOR I = 1 TO 3
030    FOR J = 1 TO 2
040       READ A(I,J)          20 MAT READ A
050    NEXT J
060 NEXT I
070 FOR I = 1 TO 3
080    FOR J = 1 TO 2
090       PRINT A(I,J);        30 MAT PRINT A;
100    NEXT J
110    PRINT
120 NEXT I
```

---

[2] Some systems allow an optional numeric character following the alphabetic character. Some systems also allow string matrices (letter followed by a dollar sign).

[3] Some systems do not allow explicit dimensions in the INPUT statement. Other systems do not allow more than one name in the PRINT list. We might also note that some systems include MAT READ/PRINT for data files and MAT PRINT USING for formatted output.

| Version A | Version B |
|---|---|

```
130 FOR I = 1 TO 5
140    READ C(I,1)          40 MAT READ C
150 NEXT I
160 FOR I = 1 TO 5
170    PRINT C(I,1)         50 MAT PRINT C
180 NEXT I
190 DATA 10,15,20,25,30,35  60 DATA 10,15,20,25,30,35
200 DATA 100,200,300,400,500 70 DATA 100,200,300,400,500
210 END                     80 END
```

Output for either version would appear as follows:

```
10  15
20  25
30  35

100
200
300
400
500
```

You should make note of the following:

1. The MAT READ statement in line 20 of version B replaces lines 20 through 60 in version A. Notice that *the MAT READ processes the matrix row by row* (first row is read, then the second row, then the third row). The DATA statement in line 60, therefore, is consistent with row-by-row read in.

2. The MAT PRINT statement in line 30 of version B replaces lines 70 through 120 in version A. Note that a trailing semicolon in the MAT PRINT gives packed output. Also note that output is *row by row*.

3. The MAT READ statement in line 40 of version B replaces lines 130 through 150 in version A. Note that C is a *column* vector. If C had been dimensioned using

        10 DIM A(3,2),C(1,5)

   then it would have been treated as a *row* vector, which is equivalent on most systems to a one-dimensional array using

        10 DIM A(3,2),C(5)

4. The MAT PRINT statement in line 50 of version B replaces lines 160 through 180 in version A. Note that C is printed as a column of numbers, since it is a column vector. If C had been dimensioned as a row vector, then its output would have been a row of numbers.

5. Most systems double space between the rows of a given matrix and print additional blank lines between the output of successive matrices.

6. More than one array name can be used in the print list on most systems. For example, if in version B we eliminate line 30 and rewrite line 50 as

        50 MAT PRINT A;C

then we would get the same output as before. Note that the semicolon packs the output of A. If we were to use

    50  MAT PRINT A,C

then this would be equivalent to

    50  MAT PRINT A
    55  MAT PRINT C

## Follow-up Exercises

1. Make the following *successive* changes in version B of Example 12.1. In each part first indicate the expected output on paper and then run the program on your system.

   a. Change line 50 to

          50  MAT PRINT C;

   b. Eliminate line 30 and change line 50 to

          50  MAT PRINT A,C

   c. Change line 50 to

          50  MAT PRINT A;C

   d. Eliminate line 40 and change line 20 to

          20  MAT READ A,C

   e. Change line 20 to

          20  MAT READ C,A

   f. Eliminate lines 60 and 70 and type

          20  MAT INPUT A
          30  MAT INPUT C

   g. Eliminate line 30 and type

          20  MAT INPUT A,C

2. First indicate the output from this program and then run it on your system.

       10  DIM R(1,4),S(4,1),T(4)
       20  MAT READ R
       30  RESTORE
       40  MAT READ S
       50  RESTORE
       60  MAT READ T
       70  MAT PRINT R;S;T;
       80  DATA 10,20,30,40
       90  END

   Is T processed by the MAT statements on your system? If yes, then is T treated as a row vector or a column vector?

## EXAMPLE 12.2  Redimensioning the Matrix during Execution

As demonstrated in Chapters 7 and 8, many applications programs conveniently "overdimension" an array in order to accommodate data having a different number of rows and columns from run to run. The following program illustrates this approach.

Our purpose is to define the matrix

$$X = \begin{pmatrix} 10 & 1 & -2 \\ 20 & 2 & -1 \\ 30 & 3 & 1 \\ 40 & 4 & 2 \end{pmatrix}$$

then calculate the average of each column and store these in

$$A = (25 \quad 2.5 \quad 0)$$

and finally to print X and A; however, we want our programs to process matrices up to 100 rows and 10 columns, depending on the data.

```
010 DIM X(100,10),A(1,10)
015 REM   READ NUMBER OF ROWS (M) AND COLUMNS (N) IN X
020 READ M,N
025 REM   READ AND REDIMENSION X
030 MAT READ X(M,N)
035 REM   READ/INITIALIZE AND REDIMENSION A
040 MAT READ A(1,N)
045 REM   FIND COLUMN SUMS
050 FOR J = 1 TO N
060    FOR I = 1 TO M
070       LET A(1,J) = A(1,J) + X(I,J)
080    NEXT I
090 NEXT J
095 REM   FIND COLUMN AVERAGES
100 FOR J = 1 TO N
110    LET A(1,J) = A(1,J)/M
120 NEXT J
125 REM   PRINT X AND A
130 MAT PRINT X,A
900 DATA 4,3
901 DATA 10,1,-2
902 DATA 20,2,-1
903 DATA 30,3,1
904 DATA 40,4,2
905 DATA 0,0,0
999 END
```

The output for this program would appear as follows:

| | | |
|---|---|---|
| 10 | 1 | -2 |
| 20 | 2 | -1 |
| 30 | 3 | 1 |
| 40 | 4 | 2 |
| 25 | 2.5 | 0 |

Note that the execution of

    30 MAT READ X(M,N)

effectively redimensions matrix X to 4 rows (value in M) by 3 columns (value in N). Thus, 12 items of data are read in from the DATA statements in lines 901 to 904. Also note that when X is printed in line 130, it is treated as a 4 by 3 matrix rather than a 100 by 10 matrix. In general, this program can process matrices up to 100 rows and 10 columns simply by changing the DATA statements. Finally, note that line 40 simultaneously initializes and redimensions A.

### Follow-up Exercises

3. Make the following changes in Example 12.2.
   a. Eliminate lines 900 through 905 and arrange the DATA statements to process the following array:

$$X = \begin{pmatrix} 10 & 1 \\ 20 & 2 \\ 30 & 3 \end{pmatrix}$$

   Run this version on your system. (Don't bother with REM statements).
   b. Eliminate all DATA statements, enter M and N through an INPUT statement, enter X and A through a MAT INPUT statement, pack the output of X and A, and process the data given in part a.
*4. Run Example 7.6 on page 205 after the following modifications: treat the premium schedule as a 6 by 2 matrix called S and read it into memory using the MAT READ statement.
*5. Use a MAT READ statement for the one-dimensional string array D$ in Example 7.5 on page 202. Also include an echo print immediately following the read in of D$. Run this program on your system. Does it work?

## 12.2
## MATRIX FUNCTIONS

Table 12.1 describes and illustrates five common functions using MAT statements. The first two functions (ZER and CON) are discussed in the table and used in Exercise 6. The next three functions (IDN, TRN, and INV) are extensively utilized in **matrix (linear) algebra,** a field of study that manipulates matrices for solving systems of linear equations (Example 12.5) and for describing certain real-world phenomena through mathematical modeling (Example 12.4).

## 12.3
## ALGEBRAIC OPERATIONS

The five MAT commands in Table 12.2 are used to perform certain algebraic operations in matrix algebra. Study this table before going on to the next three examples.

TABLE 12.1  *Matrix Functions*

| FUNCTION | PURPOSE | EXAMPLE |
|---|---|---|
| *line no.* **MAT** *matrix name* = **ZER**<br><br>or<br><br>*line no.* **MAT** *matrix name* = **ZER**(*rows, columns*) | Stores a zero (0) in each element of the matrix. The alternative version redimensions the matrix during execution. Useful for initializing a matrix that is to store sums (see Exercise 6). | The program segment<br><br>10 DIM X(3,4),Y(50,5)<br>20 MAT X = ZER<br>30 MAT Y = ZER(2,2)<br>40 MAT PRINT X;Y;<br><br>would print:<br><br>$$X\begin{cases}0 & 0 & 0 & 0 \\ 0 & 0 & 0 & 0 \\ 0 & 0 & 0 & 0\end{cases}$$<br><br>Redimensioned $Y\begin{cases}0 & 0 \\ 0 & 0\end{cases}$ |
| *line no.* **MAT** *matrix name* = **CON**<br><br>or<br><br>*line no.* **MAT** *matrix name* = **CON**(*rows, columns*) | Stores a one (1) in each element of the matrix. The matrix can be redimensioned with this function. Useful for initializing a matrix whose elements represent counters or switches (on-off states), and for certain operations in matrix algebra (see Exercise 19). | The program segment<br><br>10 DIM K(100,50)<br>20 READ R,C<br>30 DATA 3,2<br>40 MAT K = CON(R,C)<br>50 MAT PRINT K;<br><br>would print:<br><br>1  1<br>1  1<br>1  1 |

*TABLE 12.1  (Continued)*

| FUNCTION | PURPOSE | EXAMPLE |
|---|---|---|
| *line no.* **MAT** *matrix name* = **IDN**<br><br>or<br><br>*line no.* **MAT** *matrix name* = **IDN**(*rows, columns*) | The matrix is set to the **identity matrix**: Each element along the main diagonal stores a one (1) and all other elements store a zero (0). The matrix can be redimensioned with this function. Useful in matrix algebra. See Table 12.2, Exercise 8, and Example 12.5. | The program segment<br><br>10 DIM A(3,3)<br>20 MAT A = IDN<br>30 MAT PRINT A;<br><br>would print:<br><br>1 0 0<br>0 1 0<br>0 0 1 |
| *first*<br>*line no.* **MAT** *matrix name* = **TRN** $\left(\begin{array}{c}\textit{second}\\ \textit{matrix}\\ \textit{name}\end{array}\right)$ | The first matrix is the **transpose of the second** matrix, that is, the rows in the first matrix are set to the columns in the second matrix. Dimensions of the two matrices must be *compatible* (number of rows in the first equals number of columns in the second and number of columns in the first equals number of rows in the second). Useful in matrix algebra. See Exercise 22. | The program segment<br><br>10 DIM A(4,2),B(2,4)<br>20 MAT READ B<br>30 DATA 1,2,3,4<br>40 DATA 5,6,7,8<br>50 MAT A = TRN(B)<br>60 MAT PRINT A;B;<br><br>would print:<br><br>$A\begin{Bmatrix}1 & 5\\ 2 & 6\\ 3 & 7\\ 4 & 8\end{Bmatrix}$<br><br>$B\begin{Bmatrix}1 & 2 & 3 & 4\\ 5 & 6 & 7 & 8\end{Bmatrix}$ |

$$\text{line no. } \textbf{MAT}\,\overset{first}{matrix}_{name} = \textbf{INV}\left(\overset{second}{matrix}_{name}\right)$$

The first matrix is the **inverse** of the second matrix (when the inverse exists). Both matrices must be *square* (number of rows equals number of columns) and the same size. Useful in matrix algebra. Similar to the inverse in scalar algebra whereby the scalar inverse $1/x$ times $x$ gives 1. See Table 12.2 and Example 12.5.

The program segment

```
10 DIM C(2,2),D(2,2)
20 MAT READ C
30 DATA 2,1,5,3
40 MAT D = INV(C)
50 MAT PRINT C;D;
```

would print:

$$C \quad \begin{Bmatrix} 2 & 1 \\ 5 & 3 \end{Bmatrix}$$

$$\begin{matrix} D, \\ \text{the inverse} \\ \text{of } C \end{matrix} \quad \begin{Bmatrix} 3 & -1 \\ -5 & 2 \end{Bmatrix}$$

## Follow-up Exercise

6. Use an appropriate MAT function to simplify the initialization of A in Example 12.2.

*TABLE 12.2  Algebraic Operations*

| OPERATION | PURPOSE | EXAMPLE |
|---|---|---|
| **MAT** $\begin{array}{l}first\\matrix\end{array} = \begin{array}{l}second\\matrix\end{array}$ | **Assignment.** Set each element in the first matrix equal to the corresponding element in the second matrix. Both matrices must have the same dimensions. | The program segment<br><br>10  DIM A(1,4),B(1,4)<br>20  MAT READ A<br>30  DATA 10,15,20,25<br>40  MAT B = A<br>50  MAT PRINT A;B;<br><br>would print:<br><br>A {10  15   20   25<br><br>B {10  15   20   25 |
| **MAT** $\begin{array}{l}first\\matrix\end{array} = \begin{array}{l}second\\matrix\end{array} + \begin{array}{l}third\\matrix\end{array}$<br><br>**MAT** $\begin{array}{l}first\\matrix\end{array} = \begin{array}{l}second\\matrix\end{array} - \begin{array}{l}third\\matrix\end{array}$ | **Addition/subtraction.** Set each element in the first matrix equal to the sum/difference of corresponding elements in the second and third matrices. All matrices must have the same dimensions. The same matrix may appear on both sides of the equal sign. | The program segment<br><br>10  DIM A(2,3),B(2,3),C(2,3)<br>20  MAT A = CON<br>30  MAT B = CON<br>40  MAT C = A + B<br>50  MAT B = B − C<br>60  MAT PRINT C;B;<br><br>would print:<br><br>C $\left\{\begin{array}{ccc}2&2&2\\2&2&2\end{array}\right.$<br><br>B $\left\{\begin{array}{ccc}-1&-1&-1\\-1&-1&-1\end{array}\right.$ |
| **MAT** $\begin{array}{l}first\\matrix\end{array} = \left(\begin{array}{l}arithmetic\\expression\end{array}\right) * \begin{array}{l}second\\matrix\end{array}$ | **Scalar multiplication.** Set each element in the first matrix equal to the value of the arithmetic expression | The program segment<br><br>10  DIM X(2,4),Y(2,4) |

times the corresponding element in the second matrix. Both matrices must have the same dimensions. The same matrix may appear on both sides of the equal sign. The parentheses must be used.

```
20 MAT X = CON
30 MAT Y = (5)*X
40 MAT PRINT X;Y;
```

would print:

$$X \begin{cases} 1 & 1 & 1 & 1 \\ 1 & 1 & 1 & 1 \end{cases}$$

$$Y \begin{cases} 5 & 5 & 5 & 5 \\ 5 & 5 & 5 & 5 \end{cases}$$

**Matrix multiplication.** The first matrix is set to the matrix product of the second and third matrices. The second and third matrices must be *compatible* (the number of columns in the second matrix must equal the number of rows in the third matrix). The same matrix may not appear on both sides of the equal sign.

$$\text{MAT} \quad \begin{array}{c} \textit{first} \\ \textit{matrix} \end{array} = \begin{array}{c} \textit{second} \\ \textit{matrix} \end{array} * \begin{array}{c} \textit{third} \\ \textit{matrix} \end{array}$$

The program segment

```
10 DIM A(3,3),B(3,3),C(3,3)
20 MAT READ A
30 DATA 2,2,3,0,1,1,1,1,1
40 MAT B = INV(A)
50 MAT C = A*B
60 MAT PRINT A;B;C
```

would print:

$$A \begin{cases} 2 & 2 & 3 \\ 0 & 1 & 1 \\ 1 & 1 & 1 \end{cases}$$

$$\begin{array}{c} B, \text{ the} \\ \text{inverse} \\ \text{of } A \end{array} \begin{cases} 0 & -1 & 1 \\ -1 & 1 & 2 \\ 1 & 0 & -2 \end{cases}$$

$$\begin{array}{c} C, \text{ the product of} \\ \text{a matrix (A) and} \\ \text{its inverse yields} \\ \text{the identity matrix} \end{array} \begin{cases} 1 & 0 & 0 \\ 0 & 1 & 0 \\ 0 & 0 & 1 \end{cases}$$

**Follow-up Exercises**

7. Indicate printed output when the following program is executed:

```
010 DIM A(50,50),B(50,50),C(50,50)
020 READ M
030 MAT READ A(M,M)
040 MAT B = IDN(M,M)
050 MAT C = ZER(M,M)
060 MAT C = A − B
070 MAT A = (4*M − 1)*A
080 MAT B = TRN(C)
090 MAT PRINT A;C;B;
100 DATA 3
110 DATA 1,2,3,4,5,6,7,8,9
120 END
```

What would you say is the purpose of line 50?

8. In matrix algebra, the identity matrix plays a role that is analogous to the number 1 in scalar arithmetic. Thus, if we have a matrix **A** that's multiplied by a compatible identity matrix **I**, the result is the matrix **A**. In other words,

$$IA = A \quad \text{or} \quad AI = A$$

Modify the last example in Table 12.2 as follows:

```
65 DIM D(3,3)
70 MAT D = A*C
75 MAT PRINT D;
```

What should be printed for D? Run this program on your system to confirm the expected results. Change line 70 to

```
70 MAT D = C * A
```

Same result?

---

**EXAMPLE 12.3  Financial Report Revisited**

The financial report program on page 238 can be shortened considerably by using MAT statements. For example, the 10 executable statements in lines 120 through 210 would be replaced by the following read in of revenue and cost data.

```
120 MAT READ R(R1 + 1,M1 + 1),C(R1 + 1,M1 + 1)
```

Note that it is necessary at this time to augment each matrix by one row and one column; these eventually will store column and row sums, respectively. This means that we can initialize the last row and last column to zero using the DATA statements. These now change to

    920  DATA 100,150,0,60,40,0,30,70,0,0,0,0
    930  DATA 50,100,0,40,10,0,25,75,0,0,0,0

The calculation of the profit matrix P is illustrated in the five statements of lines 220 through 260 of the original program. Two MAT commands are needed to replace these:

    130  MAT P = ZER(R1 + 1,M1 + 1)
    140  MAT P = R − C

The ZER function in this case accomplishes two purposes. First, it redimensions the matrix properly; second, it stores a 0 for each element in the array, which conveniently includes the proper initialization for the row and column that stores sums. Line 140 accomplishes the required matrix subtraction, namely profit is revenue minus cost.

Finally, since the proper elements of R, C, and P have been initialized to 0, it follows that we do not have need for lines 280, 290, 300, 380, 390, and 400 in the original program.

## Follow-up Exercise

9. Answer the following questions with respect to Example 12.3.
   a. Can you explain why we could have used the CON or IDN function instead of the ZER function in the new line 130?
   b. Where could we place the statement

         MAT P = R − C

      such that we eliminate the need for lines 340 and 440?
   c. Specify other statements that eliminate the need for lines 480 to 610, 630 to 760, and 780 to 900. Assume we need not print column numbers and row numbers as in the original version.
   d. Run the revised financial report program based on the simplifications in this example and parts b and c in this exercise. Do you get the same results as on page 240? How many lines of executable code have you saved by exploiting MAT statements?

## **EXAMPLE 12.4   Brand Switching Problem

Brand switching behavior in the marketplace is a process that has been studied intensively by marketing analysts. The data given in Table 12.3 illustrate a popular analytic approach for describing this behavior. These data summarize consumer brand purchase behavior for three brands from one week to the next. For example, the first row states that 90 percent of the consumers who purchased Brand 1 in a given week repurchased Brand 1 the next week, 7 percent switched from Brand 1 to Brand 2, and 3 percent switched from Brand 1 to Brand 3. These proportions are termed *transition probabilities* because they express the likelihoods that consumers switch (make a transition) from one brand to another.

The transition probabilities suggest certain changes over time in the overall purchasing behavior. For example, Brand 1 customers appear to be the most "loyal," since this brand has the highest probability of retaining its own customers from one week to the next (0.90 is higher than 0.82 for Brand 2 and 0.68 for Brand 3). Brand 3 has the least loyal customers, since only 68 percent of the consumers repurchase this brand from one week to the next. The third row, first column entry of 0.20 in the table further suggests that Brand 3 is losing 20 percent of its customers to Brand 1 from one week to the next.

Based on certain assumptions[4] the behavior of this process can be described for a specified number of weeks into the future. For example, if we define the matrix of transition probabilities by

$$\mathbf{P} = \begin{pmatrix} 0.90 & 0.07 & 0.03 \\ 0.02 & 0.82 & 0.16 \\ 0.20 & 0.12 & 0.68 \end{pmatrix}$$

*TABLE 12.3   Proportion of Consumers Switching from Brand i in One Week to Brand j in the Next Week*

| BRAND i \ BRAND j | 1 | 2 | 3 |
|---|---|---|---|
| 1 | 0.90 | 0.07 | 0.03 |
| 2 | 0.02 | 0.82 | 0.16 |
| 3 | 0.20 | 0.12 | 0.68 |

[4] See, for example, F. Budnick, R. Mojena, and T. Vollmann, *Principles of Operations Research for Management,* Homewood, Ill.: Irwin, 1977, Chapter 15.

then the matrix product

$$\mathbf{P}^2 = \mathbf{P} \cdot \mathbf{P} = \begin{pmatrix} 0.8174 & 0.1240 & 0.0586 \\ 0.0664 & 0.6930 & 0.2406 \\ 0.3184 & 0.1940 & 0.4876 \end{pmatrix}$$

defines transition probabilities 2 weeks into the future.[5] For example, 0.8174 means that 81.74 percent of the customers who purchase Brand 1 this week repurchase Brand 1 in 2 weeks. Similarly, purchase behavior 3 weeks into the future can be predicted by the product

$$\mathbf{P}^3 = \mathbf{P}^2 \cdot \mathbf{P}$$

Moreover, if we define the row vector

$$\mathbf{U} = (0.25 \quad 0.46 \quad 0.29)$$

as current market shares (Brand 1 currently has 25 percent of the customers, Brand 2 has 46 percent, and Brand 3 has 29 percent), then the product

$$\mathbf{U}^2 = \mathbf{U} \cdot \mathbf{P}^2 = (0.32723 \quad 0.40604 \quad 0.26673)$$

predicts market shares 2 weeks hence. Thus, it would appear that Brand 1 is gaining at the expense of both Brand 2 and Brand 3, since over a 2-week period the expected market share of Brand 1 will increase by about 8 percentage points (from 0.25 to 0.32723).

The program and runs below illustrate these calculations. You should note the following points.

1. The output from the first run confirms the $\mathbf{P}^2$ and $\mathbf{U}^2$ results given earlier.
2. Matrices **A** and **B** in the program are used for computational purposes. Matrix **A** is initialized to the identity matrix in line 130 so that the first time line 190 is executed, the result is $\mathbf{B} = \mathbf{P}$ (see Exercise 8 for this result). Thereafter, the replacement in line 200 and the matrix product in line 190 ensure that **P** gets successively multiplied by itself. Thus, using matrix notation, the successive calculations in line 190 give the following for **B**:

$$\mathbf{B} = \mathbf{I} \cdot \mathbf{P} = \mathbf{P} \qquad \text{when } L = 1 \text{ (\textbf{I} is the identity matrix)}$$
$$\mathbf{B} = \mathbf{P} \cdot \mathbf{P} = \mathbf{P}^2 \qquad \text{when } L = 2$$
$$\mathbf{B} = \mathbf{P}^2 \cdot \mathbf{P} = \mathbf{P}^3 \qquad \text{when } L = 3$$
$$\vdots$$
$$\mathbf{B} = \mathbf{P}^{K-1} \cdot \mathbf{P} = \mathbf{P}^K \qquad \text{when } L = K$$

In other words, when the FOR/NEXT loop is completed, **B** is equivalent to $\mathbf{P}^K$, which is the transition probability matrix $K$ weeks into the future.
3. The vector C in line 250 is equivalent to $\mathbf{U}^K$ in the matrix product

$$\mathbf{U}^K = \mathbf{U} \cdot \mathbf{P}^K$$

For example, when $K = 2$, C is equivalent to $\mathbf{U}^2$.

[5] You need not be concerned at this time how we calculated this product. The program on page 340 and Exercise 13 illustrate the mechanics of calculating matrix products. Just focus on the meaning of this product for now.

```
list

100 DIM P(6,6),U(1,6),A(6,6),B(6,6),C(1,6)
110 READ M
120 MAT READ P(M,M)
130 MAT A=IDN(M,M)
140 MAT B=ZER(M,M)
150 MAT C=ZER(1,M)
160 PRINT "ENTER NUMBER OF WEEKS INTO FUTURE";
170 INPUT K
180 FOR L=1 TO K
190    MAT B=A*P
200    MAT A=B
210 NEXT L
218 PRINT
219 PRINT
220 PRINT "TRANSITION PROBABILITIES";K;"WEEKS INTO FUTURE"
230 MAT PRINT B;
240 MAT READ U(1,M)
250 MAT C=U*B
260 PRINT "MARKET SHARES";K;"WEEKS INTO FUTURE"
270 MAT PRINT C;
400 DATA 3
410 DATA .9,.07,.03,.02,.82,.16,.2,.12,.68
420 DATA .25,.46,.29
999 END

RUN

ENTER NUMBER OF WEEKS INTO FUTURE?2

TRANSITION PROBABILITIES 2     WEEKS INTO FUTURE

 .8174      .124      5.86000E-02

 6.64000E-02     .693      .2406

 .3184      .194      .4876

MARKET SHARES 2     WEEKS INTO FUTURE

 .32723    .40604    .26673

TIME 0.03 SECS.

RUN

ENTER NUMBER OF WEEKS INTO FUTURE?4

TRANSITION PROBABILITIES 4     WEEKS INTO FUTURE

 .695034       .198658      .106307

 .176897       .535159      .287943

 .428393       .268518      .303088

MARKET SHARES 4     WEEKS INTO FUTURE

 .379365       .373707      .246926

TIME 0.02 SECS.
```

```
RUN

ENTER NUMBER OF WEEKS INTO FUTURE?52

TRANSITION PROBABILITIES 52    WEEKS INTO FUTURE

    .474072        .320982        .204934

    .474062        .320987        .204938

    .474069        .320983        .204935


MARKET SHARES 52    WEEKS INTO FUTURE

    .474066        .320984        .204936


TIME 0.05 SECS.
```

## Follow-up Exercises

10. With respect to the output:
    a. Compare expected market shares 2, 4, and 52 weeks into the future, and comment on what the future holds for changes in market share conditions. Are Brand 2 and Brand 3 in trouble? Explain.
    b. Look at the matrix of transition probabilities 52 weeks into the future. Notice anything interesting? Explain what this means by relating it to the expected market shares at that time.
*11. Modify the program such that transition probabilities and market shares get printed for 1, 2, 3, . . ., and $K$ weeks into the future.
*12. Modify the program as follows:
    a. Define R as a revenue vector. Its elements equal expected total market revenue times corresponding market shares. Current total market revenue is $75 million. This market revenue, however, is expected to increase at the rate of half a million dollars per week.
    b. Define S as a cost vector. Its elements represent the total costs of each brand. It costs $20 million for Brand 1, $18 million for Brand 2, and $17 million for Brand 3.
    c. Define T as a profit vector. Its elements represent revenue less cost for each brand.
    d. Print R, S, and T following the market share output.
    e. Run this revised program on your system.

**\*\*13.** If you're curious about the mechanics of matrix multiplication, then read on. If **A** has dimensions $m_1$ by $n_1$ and **B** has dimensions $m_2$ by $n_2$, then the matrix product $\mathbf{A} \cdot \mathbf{B}$ is defined if and only if $n_1 = m_2$. The result of this multiplication is a matrix **C** with dimensions $m_1$ by $n_2$. Element $c_{ij}$ in **C** is calculated by multiplying the elements in *row i* of **A** times the corresponding elements in *column j* of **B.** For example, if

$$\mathbf{A} = \begin{pmatrix} 1 & 4 \\ 5 & -3 \end{pmatrix} \quad \text{and} \quad \mathbf{B} = \begin{pmatrix} 1 \\ 4 \end{pmatrix}$$

then

$$\mathbf{C} = \mathbf{A} \cdot \mathbf{B}$$
$$= \begin{pmatrix} 1 & 4 \\ 5 & -3 \end{pmatrix} \cdot \begin{pmatrix} 1 \\ 4 \end{pmatrix}$$
$$= \begin{pmatrix} 1 \times 1 + 4 \times 4 \\ 5 \times 1 - 3 \times 4 \end{pmatrix} = \begin{pmatrix} 17 \\ -7 \end{pmatrix}$$

Notice that the (2,1) element in **C**, or $-7$, is calculated by the product of row 2 in **A**, $(5 \quad -3)$, and column 1 in **B**, $\begin{pmatrix} 1 \\ 4 \end{pmatrix}$. Thus,

$$c_{21} = (5 \quad -3) \cdot \begin{pmatrix} 1 \\ 4 \end{pmatrix} = (5) \cdot (1) + (-3) \cdot (4) = -7$$

Also notice that attaching dimensions to

clearly shows that the "inner" dimensions are equal, thereby defining the validity of the matrix product. Moreover, the result **C** will have dimensions equivalent to the "outer" dimensions; that is, **C** will be a 2 by 1 matrix.

a. Calculate the product $\mathbf{B} \cdot \mathbf{A}$, where **A** and **B** are defined above.

b. Confirm the last result in Table 12.2; that is, show that

$$\mathbf{C} = \mathbf{A} \cdot \mathbf{B}$$

gives the identity matrix, where **A** and **B** are defined in Table 12.2.

c. Confirm that a matrix multiplied by the identity matrix gives the matrix itself; that is, show that if

$$\mathbf{A} = \begin{pmatrix} 2 & 2 & 3 \\ 0 & 1 & 1 \\ 1 & 1 & 1 \end{pmatrix} \quad \text{and} \quad \mathbf{I} = \begin{pmatrix} 1 & 0 & 0 \\ 0 & 1 & 0 \\ 0 & 0 & 1 \end{pmatrix}$$

then

$$\mathbf{A} \cdot \mathbf{I} = \mathbf{A} \quad \text{or} \quad \mathbf{I} \cdot \mathbf{A} = \mathbf{A}$$

Is this result consistent with Exercise 8?

d. Confirm the result we got for $\mathbf{P}^2$ in Example 12.4.

e. Confirm the result we got for $\mathbf{U}^2$ in Example 12.4.

f. Show by example that $\mathbf{A} \cdot \mathbf{B}$ does not equal $\mathbf{B} \cdot \mathbf{A}$, where $\mathbf{A}$ and $\mathbf{B}$ are square.

## **EXAMPLE 12.5   Solving Systems of Simultaneous Linear Equations

The need to solve systems of simultaneous linear equations is very common in applications in mathematics, hard sciences, social sciences, and management. In precomputer days large systems involving hundreds of equations were quite costly to solve by "hand." Today, however, computer codes are readily available for efficiently solving simultaneous equations. The MAT statements in BASIC are especially convenient for carrying out this task.

Suppose we have the system of equations

$$
\begin{aligned}
x_1 + x_2 + x_3 &= 3 \qquad &(1)\\
5x_1 - x_2 + 2x_3 &= 3 \qquad &(2)\\
2x_1 - 3x_2 + x_3 &= -4 \qquad &(3)
\end{aligned}
$$

and we wish to solve for the values of $x_1$, $x_2$, and $x_3$ that satisfy this system. In other words, we wish to determine values of $x_1$, $x_2$, and $x_3$ that make each expression on the left-hand side equal to the corresponding right-hand-side constant. Using matrix algebra we would proceed as follows.

Represent the coefficients on the left side by the matrix

$$
\mathbf{A} = \begin{pmatrix} 1 & 1 & 1 \\ 5 & -1 & 2 \\ 2 & -3 & 1 \end{pmatrix}
$$

define the column vector for the unknown variables by

$$
\mathbf{x} = \begin{pmatrix} x_1 \\ x_2 \\ x_3 \end{pmatrix}
$$

and represent the right-hand constants by the column vector

$$
\mathbf{b} = \begin{pmatrix} 3 \\ 3 \\ -4 \end{pmatrix}
$$

The system of equations given by (1), (2), and (3) now can be described by the matrix equation

$$
\mathbf{A} \cdot \mathbf{x} = \mathbf{b}
$$

To solve for $\mathbf{x}$, we premultiply both sides of this equation by the inverse of $\mathbf{A}$, which we label $A^{-1}$. Thus,

$$A^{-1} \cdot A \cdot x = A^{-1} \cdot b$$

Since $A^{-1} \cdot A$ yields the identity matrix (see Table 12.2 on page 334 and Exercise 13b on page 342), we have

$$I \cdot x = A^{-1} \cdot b$$

But we know that $I \cdot x$ simply gives $x$ (see Exercises 8 and 13c on pages 336 and 342); so we end up with

$$x = A^{-1} \cdot b$$

Thus, we can solve a system of linear simultaneous equations by premultiplying the vector of right-hand constants by the inverse of the matrix of left-hand coefficients, as illustrated by the program below.

```
100 DIM A(50,50),X(50,1),B(50,1),C(50,50)
110 READ M
120 MAT READ A(M,M),B(M,1)
130 MAT X=CON(M,1)
135 MAT C=CON(M,M)
140 MAT C=INV(A)
150 MAT X=C*B
155 PRINT "X-VALUES:"
160 MAT PRINT X
900 DATA 3
910 DATA 1,1,1,5,-1,2,2,-3,1
920 DATA 3,3,-4
999 END

X-VALUES:

 .999999

 2.

-9.53674E-07



TIME 0.02 SECS.
```

The actual solution is $x_1 = 1$, $x_2 = 2$, and $x_3 = 0$. Comparing this to the output shows that the computer introduced slight rounding error.

## Follow-up Exercises

14. Confirm that the solution for $x$ satisfies the system of equations on page 343.
15. Why is the CON function used in lines 130 and 135? What does C represent in the program?
*16. Modify the program as follows:

a. Print the elements in **x** as a row rather than a column. *Hint:* You need to use a function from Table 12.1.
b. Redesign the program to process N sets of M simultaneous equations each.

To debug your program process the additional set of simultaneous equations below.

$$3x_1 + 2x_2 = 16 \tag{1}$$
$$x_1 + 5x_2 = 27 \tag{2}$$

Confirm the solution by plugging it into these two equations.

## 12.4
## COMMON ERRORS

Certain errors in the use of MAT statements occur commonly, which we now summarize.

1. *Forgetting dimensions.* If you forget to dimension an array using the DIM statement, then the first use of the array in a MAT statement may provoke a syntax error. In some cases this may not be a problem since many systems implicitly dimension arrays to 10 rows and 10 columns when the DIM statement is omitted. As before, we recommend the use of DIM statements regardless of the system.

2. *Redimensioning.* You can redimension the size of a matrix during execution using the READ and INPUT statements and the functions ZER, CON, and IDN.[6] An attempt to redimension using any other statement results in a syntax error. An execution error occurs when you attempt to redimension a matrix beyond the size defined in the DIM statement. For example,

```
10 DIM A(20,10)
20 READ M,N
30 MAT READ A(M,N)
 .
 .
 .
70 DATA 50,5
```

would not be allowed since line 30 attempts to redimension A as a matrix of 50 rows, which exceeds the 20 rows specified in line 10.

3. *Nonconformity.* The functions TRN and INV and all operations require conformity in matrix dimensions, as follows:

---

[6] Some systems do not have this option with the INPUT statement.

| | |
|---|---|
| 10 MAT B = TRN(A) | The number of rows in B must equal the number of columns in A; the number of columns in B must equal the number of rows in A. |
| 20 MAT B = INV(A) | A and B must be square (the number of rows equals the number of columns) and of the same dimensions. |
| 30 MAT B = A | A and B must have identical dimensions. |
| 40 MAT C = A ± B | A, B, and C must have identical dimensions. |
| 50 MAT B = (75)*A | A and B must have identical dimensions. |
| 60 MAT C = A*B | The number of columns in A must equal the number of rows in B; the number of rows in C must equal the number of rows in A; the number of columns in C must equal the number of columns in B. |

Any violation of these conformity rules results in an execution error. Thus make sure your DIM statements reflect conformity. If you redimension during execution, then make sure these reflect conformity.

4. *Other violations.* In certain functions and operations the same matrix may not appear on both sides of the equal sign. For example, the following are not allowed:

```
70 MAT A = TRN(A)
80 MAT A = INV(A)
90 MAT A = A*B
```

Also, multiple operations are not allowed. For example,

```
100 MAT D = A + B - C
110 MAT D = A*B*C
```

provoke syntax errors. Line 100 could be rewritten as

```
100 MAT D = A + B
105 MAT D = D - C
```

and line 110 as

```
110 MAT E = A*B
115 MAT D = E*C
```

## Additional Exercises

**17.** Define or explain the following terms:

| | |
|---|---|
| matrix | TRN function |
| column vector | INV function |
| row vector | identity matrix |
| MAT statements | transpose |
| MAT READ statement | inverse |
| MAT INPUT statement | matrix assignment |
| MAT PRINT statement | matrix addition |
| matrix algebra | matrix subtraction |
| ZER function | scalar multiplication |
| CON function | matrix multiplication |
| IDN function | |

18. Use MAT statements where possible in one of the following exercises from Chapter 8:
    a. Exercise 21    b. Exercise 22
    c. Exercise 23    d. Exercise 24
    e. Exercise 25

19. **Row and Column Totals.** The sums of rows and columns in a matrix can be calculated by matrix multiplication.
    a. Use MAT statements to replace lines 50 to 120 in Example 12.2. Run the revised program.
    b. Rewrite the financial report program on page 238 by including the features in Exercise 9 on page 337. In addition, include the use of MAT statements for calculating row and column totals; that is, replace lines 270 through 460 in the original program using operations in matrix algebra. *Hint:* If we premultiply an $M \times N$ matrix by a $1 \times M$ vector having 1s for each element, then we end up with a $1 \times N$ vector whose elements are the column sums of the $M \times N$ matrix. Similar logic can be used to calculate and store row sums.

20. **Stock Portfolio Valuation.** Companies, universities, banks, pension funds, and other organizations routinely invest funds in the stock market. The set of stocks in which the organization invests its funds is called a *stock portfolio.* Table 12.4 illustrates a sample stock portfolio, including the number of shares owned of each stock, the purchase price per share, and the latest price per share quoted by the stock exchange.
    a. Design and run a program that uses MAT statements to calculate the initial (purchase) value of the portfolio, the current value of the portfolio, and the net change in the value. Store number of shares, purchase prices, and current prices in separate vectors. Number of shares and purchase prices are to be read in using the MAT READ statement, but current prices are to be input interactively. *Hint:* The value of the portfolio is found by multiplying shares by corresponding prices and summing, which is equivalent to multiplication of two vectors.
    b. Include a FOR/NEXT loop in the program for processing more than one portfolio. Find two copies of a newspaper, where one copy is at least 2

---

TABLE 12.4   *Stock Portfolio*

| STOCK | NUMBER OF SHARES | PURCHASE PRICE ($/SHARE) | CURRENT PRICE ($/SHARE) |
|---|---|---|---|
| Allegh Airls | 40,000 | $5\frac{7}{8}$ | $7\frac{1}{4}$ |
| Boeing | 5,000 | $61\frac{1}{2}$ | 56 |
| EastmKo | 10,000 | 60 | $64\frac{1}{2}$ |
| Hewlett P | 15,000 | 80 | $100\frac{1}{8}$ |
| IBM | 2,500 | $77\frac{1}{8}$ | $80\frac{3}{4}$ |
| Texaco | 8,000 | $23\frac{1}{2}$ | 19 |
| Tex Inst | 12,000 | 80 | $85\frac{7}{8}$ |

weeks apart from the other. Select a portfolio, make up shares owned, and use the two sets of prices for purchase and current prices. Process the Table 12.4 portfolio and the new portfolio in one run, and include the output of combined value of all portfolios.

**\*\*21. Faculty Flow Model.** The current distribution of faculty at State University is given in Table 12.5.

The transition probability data in Table 12.6 illustrate the typical "flow" behavior of faculty from one year to the next. The administration wishes to utilize these data in a planning and budget model that generates future faculty needs and budgets. Your program should

a. Determine the number of faculty in each rank for each of the next 5 years. Assume a policy of attrition, whereby no new faculty are hired during this period.

b. Assume the administration wants to maintain the current number of faculty positions of 300. Determine the number of faculty that need to be hired for each of the next 5 years. Include the calculation of number of faculty in each rank. Assume that all new faculty hirings are at the rank of Assistant Professor.

c. The average faculty salary for each rank is listed in Table 12.7. Develop salary budgets for each of the next 5 years, first under the hiring policy in part a and then under the hiring policy in part b. Build in a 6 percent inflation rate into average faculty salaries.

TABLE 12.5     *Distribution of Faculty by Rank*

| RANK | NUMBER OF FACULTY |
|------|-------------------|
| Full Professor | 50 |
| Associate Professor | 100 |
| Assistant Professor | 100 |
| Instructor | 50 |

TABLE 12.6     *Year-to-Year Changes by Rank*

| STATUS AT START OF YEAR \ STATUS AT END OF YEAR | FULL | ASSO-CIATE | ASSIST-ANT | INSTRUC-TOR | LEAVE OR RETIRE |
|------|------|------|------|------|------|
| Full | 0.80 | 0.00 | 0.00 | 0.00 | 0.20 |
| Associate | 0.10 | 0.80 | 0.00 | 0.00 | 0.10 |
| Assistant | 0.00 | 0.20 | 0.65 | 0.00 | 0.15 |
| Instructor | 0.00 | 0.00 | 0.25 | 0.50 | 0.25 |

TABLE 12.7   *Average Faculty Salaries by Rank*

| RANK | SALARY($) |
|------|-----------|
| Full Professor | 28,000 |
| Associate Professor | 23,000 |
| Assistant Professor | 17,000 |
| Instructor | 12,000 |

**\*\*22.  Multiple Linear Regression Analysis.** The data in Table 12.8 are based on actual residential sales in 1974 of 50 single-family residences in Eugene, Oregon. Real estate analysts use data of this type to study the relationship between the sale price of a house and characteristics of the house such as size, number of bedrooms, number of bathrooms, total rooms, age, whether there is an attached garage (0 = no; 1 = yes), and whether there is a view (0 = no; 1 = yes).

TABLE 12.8   *Real Estate Data*

| RESI-DENCE, $i$ | SALES PRICE, $y(\times \$1000)$ | SQUARE FEET, $x_1(\times 100)$ | BED-ROOMS, $x_2$ | BATH-ROOMS, $x_3$ | TOTAL ROOMS, $x_4$ | AGE, $x_5$ | ATTACHED GARAGE, $x_6$ | VIEW, $x_7$ |
|---|---|---|---|---|---|---|---|---|
| 1 | 10.2 | 8.0 | 2 | 1 | 5 | 5 | 0 | 0 |
| 2 | 10.5 | 9.5 | 2 | 1 | 5 | 8 | 0 | 0 |
| 3 | 11.1 | 9.1 | 3 | 1 | 6 | 2 | 0 | 0 |
| 4 | 15.3 | 9.5 | 3 | 1 | 6 | 6 | 0 | 0 |
| 5 | 15.8 | 12.0 | 3 | 2 | 7 | 5 | 0 | 0 |
| 6 | 16.3 | 10.0 | 3 | 1 | 6 | 11 | 0 | 0 |
| 7 | 17.2 | 11.8 | 3 | 2 | 7 | 8 | 0 | 0 |
| 8 | 17.7 | 10.0 | 2 | 1 | 7 | 15 | 1 | 0 |
| 9 | 18.0 | 13.8 | 3 | 2 | 7 | 10 | 0 | 0 |
| 10 | 18.1 | 12.5 | 3 | 2 | 7 | 11 | 0 | 0 |
| 11 | 18.4 | 15.0 | 3 | 2 | 7 | 12 | 0 | 0 |
| 12 | 18.4 | 12.0 | 3 | 2 | 7 | 8 | 0 | 0 |
| 13 | 18.9 | 16.0 | 3 | 2 | 7 | 9 | 1 | 1 |
| 14 | 19.3 | 16.5 | 3 | 2 | 7 | 15 | 0 | 0 |
| 15 | 19.5 | 16.0 | 3 | 2 | 7 | 11 | 1 | 0 |
| 16 | 19.9 | 16.8 | 2 | 2 | 7 | 12 | 0 | 0 |
| 17 | 20.3 | 15.0 | 3 | 1 | 7 | 8 | 1 | 0 |
| 18 | 20.3 | 17.8 | 3 | 2 | 8 | 13 | 1 | 0 |
| 19 | 20.8 | 17.9 | 3 | 2 | 7 | 18 | 1 | 0 |
| 20 | 21.0 | 19.0 | 2 | 2 | 7 | 22 | 0 | 0 |

TABLE 12.8 *Real Estate Data (Continued)*

| RESI-DENCE, $i$ | SALES PRICE, $y(\times \$1000)$ | SQUARE FEET, $x_1(\times 100)$ | BED-ROOMS, $x_2$ | BATH-ROOMS, $x_3$ | TOTAL ROOMS, $x_4$ | AGE, $x_5$ | ATTACHED GARAGE, $x_6$ | VIEW, $x_7$ |
|---|---|---|---|---|---|---|---|---|
| 21 | 21.5 | 17.6 | 3 | 1 | 6 | 17 | 0 | 0 |
| 22 | 22.0 | 18.5 | 3 | 2 | 8 | 11 | 1 | 0 |
| 23 | 22.1 | 18.0 | 3 | 2 | 7 | 5 | 0 | 0 |
| 24 | 22.5 | 17.0 | 2 | 3 | 8 | 2 | 1 | 0 |
| 25 | 22.8 | 18.7 | 3 | 1 | 6 | 6 | 0 | 0 |
| 26 | 22.8 | 20.0 | 3 | 2 | 7 | 16 | 0 | 0 |
| 27 | 22.9 | 20.0 | 3 | 2 | 7 | 12 | 0 | 0 |
| 28 | 23.2 | 21.0 | 3 | 2 | 7 | 10 | 1 | 0 |
| 29 | 23.5 | 20.5 | 2 | 2 | 7 | 11 | 1 | 0 |
| 30 | 24.9 | 19.9 | 3 | 1 | 7 | 13 | 1 | 1 |
| 31 | 25.0 | 21.5 | 2 | 2 | 7 | 8 | 0 | 0 |
| 32 | 25.1 | 20.5 | 3 | 1 | 7 | 9 | 1 | 0 |
| 33 | 26.6 | 22.0 | 3 | 2 | 7 | 10 | 0 | 0 |
| 34 | 26.9 | 22.0 | 3 | 2 | 7 | 6 | 1 | 1 |
| 35 | 26.9 | 21.8 | 2 | 1 | 6 | 15 | 1 | 0 |
| 36 | 27.8 | 22.5 | 3 | 2 | 7 | 11 | 1 | 0 |
| 37 | 28.0 | 24.0 | 3 | 2 | 7 | 17 | 0 | 0 |
| 38 | 28.7 | 23.5 | 3 | 2 | 8 | 12 | 0 | 0 |
| 39 | 29.0 | 25.0 | 3 | 2 | 7 | 11 | 1 | 0 |
| 40 | 30.1 | 25.6 | 3 | 2 | 7 | 15 | 1 | 0 |
| 41 | 32.0 | 25.0 | 4 | 2 | 8 | 12 | 1 | 0 |
| 42 | 33.8 | 25.0 | 2 | 2 | 8 | 8 | 0 | 1 |
| 43 | 35.3 | 26.8 | 3 | 2 | 7 | 6 | 1 | 0 |
| 44 | 37.1 | 22.1 | 3 | 2 | 8 | 18 | 1 | 0 |
| 45 | 37.5 | 27.5 | 3 | 2 | 8 | 12 | 1 | 0 |
| 46 | 38.0 | 25.0 | 4 | 2 | 8 | 10 | 1 | 0 |
| 47 | 38.4 | 24.0 | 3 | 2 | 8 | 13 | 1 | 1 |
| 48 | 39.0 | 31.0 | 4 | 3 | 9 | 25 | 1 | 0 |
| 49 | 43.0 | 21.0 | 4 | 2 | 9 | 18 | 1 | 0 |
| 50 | 55.0 | 40.0 | 5 | 3 | 12 | 22 | 1 | 0 |

Source: W. Mendenhall and J. E. Reinmuth, *Statistics for Management and Economics,*
3d ed., Duxbury Press, California, 1978, p. 428.

A statistical methodology called *multiple linear regression analysis* directly assesses the relationship between $y$ (sale price) and the set of variables, $x_1, x_2, \ldots, x_7$ (as defined in the table) by fitting the linear function (model)

$$y = b_0 + b_1 x_1 + b_2 x_2 + \cdots + b_7 x_7$$

to the given data. The symbols $b_0, b_1, \ldots, b_7$, called *regression coefficients*, are calculated by a procedure called the *least-squares technique*. Applying this procedure to the given data yields the model

$$y = -13.46 + 1.02x_1 + 1.63x_2 - 3.85x_3 + 2.89x_4 - 0.02x_5 + 1.25x_6 - 1.29x_7$$

The regression coefficient of 1.02, for example, means that an increase of 1 unit in the variable $x_1$ (an additional 100 square feet) increases $y$ by 1.02 units (the average price of a house increases by $1020), all other variables being held constant; an increase of 1 unit in $x_2$ (one additional bedroom) increases the average price of a house by $1630. Can you interpret the other $b$-values?

A model of this type can be used not only to study the relationships between variables (for example, what is the effect on price of an extra bedroom?) but also to predict the values of similar homes. For example, realtors are interested in predicting the potential sales price of a given home and tax assessors are interested in assessing the value of homes to establish "fair" taxes.

a.  Write a program that uses the data in Table 12.8 to fit a linear model (that is, find the values of $b_0, b_1, \ldots, b_7$) by the least-squares method. If we define the matrices

$$\mathbf{y} = \begin{pmatrix} 10.2 \\ 10.5 \\ \cdot \\ \cdot \\ \cdot \\ 55.0 \end{pmatrix}_{50 \times 1} \qquad \mathbf{x} = \begin{pmatrix} 1 & 8.0 & 2 & 1 & 5 & 5 & 0 & 0 \\ 1 & 9.5 & 2 & 1 & 5 & 8 & 0 & 0 \\ \cdot & & \cdot & & \cdot & \cdot & & \cdot \\ 1 & 40.0 & 5 & 3 & 12 & 22 & 1 & 0 \end{pmatrix}_{50 \times 8}$$

and

$$\mathbf{b} = \begin{pmatrix} b_0 \\ b_1 \\ \cdot \\ \cdot \\ \cdot \\ b_7 \end{pmatrix}_{8 \times 1}$$

then the least-squares method calculates regression coefficients by the formula

$$\mathbf{b} = (\mathbf{X}' \cdot \mathbf{X})^{-1} \cdot \mathbf{X}' \cdot \mathbf{y}$$

where $\mathbf{X}'$ is the transpose of $\mathbf{X}$ and $(\mathbf{X}' \cdot \mathbf{X})^{-1}$ is the inverse of the matrix product $\mathbf{X}' \cdot \mathbf{X}$. In your program represent the number of rows in the data by the variable $n$ (50 in the example) and the number of columns in $\mathbf{X}$ or rows in $\mathbf{b}$ by the variable $k$ (8 in the example).

b.  The model derived in part a can be used to predict the sale prices of similar homes. For example, a home having 2000 square feet ($x_1 = 20$), three bedrooms ($x_2 = 3$), two bathrooms ($x_3 = 2$), eight total rooms ($x_4 = 8$), that was built 10 years ago ($x_5 = 10$), that has an attached garage ($x_6 = 1$), and that has no view ($x_7 = 0$) can be expected to sell for

$$y = -13.46 + 1.02(20) + 1.63(3) - 3.85(2) + 2.89(8) - 0.02(10)$$
$$+ 1.25(1) - 1.29(0) = 28.3$$

or \$28,300 (this sample obviously was taken in "pre-inflation" days). If we let **p** represent a $k \times 1$ vector of predictor values given by

$$\mathbf{p} = \begin{pmatrix} 1 \\ x_1 \\ x_2 \\ \cdot \\ \cdot \\ \cdot \\ \cdot \\ x_7 \end{pmatrix}_{k \times 1}$$

then the product $\mathbf{b}' \cdot \mathbf{p}$ calculates the predicted value of $y$.

Add an interactive feature to the program that requests predictor values and calculates the corresponding $y$ value. Loop as often as the user desires and process the following data:

| $x_1$ | $x_2$ | $x_3$ | $x_4$ | $x_5$ | $x_6$ | $x_7$ |
|-------|-------|-------|-------|-------|-------|-------|
| 17.0  | 2     | 3     | 8     | 2     | 1     | 0     |
| 25.6  | 3     | 2     | 7     | 15    | 1     | 0     |
| 20.0  | 3     | 2     | 8     | 10    | 1     | 0     |
| 40.0  | 4     | 2.5   | 10    | 4     | 1     | 1     |

# PART IV

## Modules

Modules A. Debugging Programs
             B. Structured Programming and Other Topics
             C. Selected Case Studies

# MODULE A

# *Debugging Programs*

---

A.1  ERROR DETECTION AND CORRECTION

A.2  ILLUSTRATION

EXERCISES

---

**Debugging** is the process of detecting and correcting errors. Much of your time, in fact, will be spent on this process. To help you along, we now define general types of errors, illustrate each in actual computer runs, and indicate how you go about debugging such errors.

## *A.1*
## *ERROR DETECTION AND CORRECTION*

Any programming error can be classified into one of the following three categories:

1. Syntax error
2. Execution error
3. Logic error

A **syntax error** occurs when a BASIC statement violates a rule of the BASIC language. When you make this type of error, your program will fail to run, and the translator (compiler/interpreter) will identify the incorrect instruction by an appropriate diagnostic message. Thus, syntax errors are detected by the translator during the translation of the program.

Any error that aborts execution of the program is said to be a **fatal error.** Virtually all syntax errors are fatal; that is, the program never enters the execution phase of a run.

Common syntax errors at this point in your programming development include the following:

1. Typing error, as when PRINT is typed as PRENT.
2. Incorrectly naming a variable. *Note:* A separate error message will be printed for each statement which contains the incorrect variable name.

3. Forgetting to type a line number. Technically, this is not a syntax error because the system rejects (does not understand) the line immediately after you depress the carriage return key.

4. Forgetting to include an END statement as the highest-numbered line of your program. On some systems, this error is not fatal.

5. Imbalance between the number of left parentheses and the number of right parentheses in an arithmetic expression.

6. Missing equal sign (=) in a LET statement.

7. Arithmetic expression to the left of the equal sign in a LET statement.

8. Forgetting to use * for multiplication.

9. Forgetting the key word LET in a LET statement. *Note:* Some systems allow this.

10. Omitting required commas, semicolons, or quotes in the list of PRINT statements. See Exercise 17 in Chapter 3 on page 63.

11. Omitting the key word REM in a REM statement. All remarks or comments in a program must begin with a line number followed by the key word REM.

12. **Treatment of spaces.** Have you wondered about the use of spaces within BASIC statements? According to the proposed ANSI standard, spaces must not be inserted at
    a. The beginning of a line
    b. Within line numbers
    c. Within key words (exception: GO TO and GO SUB as described in later chapters)
    d. Within numeric constants
    e. Within variables or function names
    f. Within multicharacter relation symbols (Chapter 5)

Moreover, it is proposed that all key words shall be preceded by at least one space and, unless it is at the end of a line, shall be followed by at least one space. Otherwise, spaces can occur anywhere in a program without affecting the execution of the program. *Most systems are more "permissive" than this standard; they simply ignore blanks except within quoted strings. In general, you should use spaces to improve the readability and visual appeal of your programs.* For example, most systems will allow

        100 PRINT"YES"

but

        100 PRINT "YES"

is slightly more visually appealing. Finally, you should realize that *spaces within string constants are significant.* For example,

        100 PRINT "YES"

is not identical in its effect to

        100 PRINT "  YES"

The latter prints the word YES three spaces to the right of the former.

Once you determine the exact nature of your syntax error (with the help of error messages printed by the system), you simply replace the incorrect instruction with a syntactically correct instruction.

Your program begins executing only after it is free of syntax errors. Unfortunately, a second type of error can occur after the compilation phase; an **execution error** is one that takes place during the execution of your program. Typically, when an execution error is encountered, an error message or code is printed and the computer terminates execution (the error proves fatal). Common execution errors relating to the material in Chapter 3 include the following.

1. **Improper numeric condition during the evaluation of an arithmetic expression.** For example, you might attempt to divide by a variable which has the value zero in its storage location, or you might attempt to raise a negative number to a noninteger power, or the evaluation might exceed the range of values allowed. If a computed value is larger than that allowed by the system, then an "overflow" error occurs; if smaller, then an "underflow" error message is printed. Most systems continue execution by assigning machine infinity (largest possible value) to the value that overflows and machine zero to the value that underflows.

2. **Initialization of variables.** *Initialization* is a term that refers to the initial value taken on by a variable. Just prior to execution, some systems assign arbitrary values to all variables, while other systems initialize all variables to zero. To illustrate the possible difficulties you might encounter, consider the following statement:

   50 LET N = N + 1

   Now, suppose that prior to this statement you have not *explicitly* assigned a value to N. One of three things will happen when the system executes this statement.
   a. An arbitrary (wrong) value is used for the N to the right of the equal sign.
   b. A value of zero is used for the N to the right of the equal sign.
   c. The system treats the initial contents of N as undefined and aborts execution.
   Thus, whenever a variable is used in an arithmetic expression, it needs to have been previously defined (explicitly assigned a value) either through a LET statement or through input/read statements (Chapter 4). For example, if we want N to have an initial value of zero prior to the execution of line 50 above, then earlier in the program we should write

   10 LET N = 0

Generally, it is more difficult to determine the exact location and nature of an execution error than of a syntax error, for several reasons: execution errors tend to be system-dependent; execution error messages may be more ambiguous than syntax error messages in locating and diagnosing errors; the cause of an execution error may be due to faulty program logic, which is related to the third category of errors.

If your program runs but gives you unexpected, unwanted, or erroneous output, then you may assume that a **logic error** exists. Common logic errors include the following:

1. No output. Did you forget to include PRINT statements?
2. Wrong numeric results.
   a. Are the provided data correct?
   b. Are the arithmetic expressions and LET statements correct? In particular,

check the sequence of arithmetic calculations within arithmetic expressions based on hierarchy rules.

c.  Is the program logic correct? For example, are the statements in proper sequence?

d.  Have any statements been omitted?

3.  Unintentional, displeasing, or unaligned output. Output from a program should be labeled, easy to read, and visually appealing. Prior to writing down your PRINT statements, you should map out your output on a sheet of paper or special paper called **print chart**. First, of course, you need to know the following for your system: maximum number of print columns in a print line, number of print columns in a print zone, number of print zones, and treatment of numeric output that is packed. You might be surprised at how much effort will be saved by this practice of laying out your output prior to designing your PRINT statements.

Here is some emphatic advice: *Just because your program runs (that is, you get results) does not mean your program is correct—check your results for logic errors against a set of known results.* We cannot overemphasize the importance of this advice. In Step IV of the four-step procedure, *always* validate your program under varying conditions using a set of test data for which you already know the correct results.

In your efforts to debug execution and logic errors, you might try the following classic debugging techniques:

1.  **Roleplaying** *the computer.* Pretend that you're the computer and begin "executing" your program line by line. As you do this, enter data into boxes that represent storage locations. You will be surprised at how many errors you can find this way. (Really.) You should do this with every program you write.

2.  **Diagnostic PRINT (trace) statements.** Place temporary PRINT statements at strategic points in your program. These should print the values of important variables as the calculating sequence evolves. In other words, these PRINT statements provide you intermediate results which may be helpful in tracing what, where, and when something went wrong. When the error is corrected, remove these trace statements.

3.  *Programming technique.* You will avoid many errors if you carefully develop the first three steps of our four-step procedure. Get in the habit now.

4.  *Experience.* Learn by your mistakes. Experience is a classic teacher.

5.  *Attitude.* Debugging can be fun. Finding errors and correcting them can be a very satisfying experience. Perhaps you will become the greatest debugging sleuth in computer history.

## A.2
## ILLUSTRATION

In this section we run the tuition revenue program once more, with the exceptions that syntax, execution, and logic errors are purposely included. *Keep in mind that the specifics in this illustration relate to IBM's CALL System. If your system is different,* just pay attention to the general procedures and concepts, and then duplicate our run on your system.

To distinguish clearly between matter printed by the computer and matter typed by the user, we shade computer matter.

```
ON AT 11:30 TUE  01 MAY 79  LINE 147

USER NUMBER,PASSWORD--
saw101,bbbsbxbb
READY

ENTER BASIC
READY
```

As before.

```
10 LET 80=C
20 LET B=15**C+250
30 LET REV=B*S
40 PRINT "REVENUE = $";REV
```

Entry of program with syntax errors in lines 10, 30, and 40; execution error in line 20; and logic error by failing to explicitly initialize S.

```
RUN

        11:35   TUE  01 MAY 79

LINE 10: SYNTAX ERROR IN STATEMENT
LINE 30: SYNTAX ERROR IN STATEMENT
LINE 40: SYNTAX ERROR IN STATEMENT
LINE 40: END SUPPLIED

TIME 0.01 SECS.
```

Execution aborted and lines with syntax errors identified. We realize that C is on wrong side of the = in line 10 and that REV is an incorrect variable name. Note that this single error in naming a variable caused an error message for each line (30 and 40) containing this variable. The last error message indicates a nonfatal error due to missing END statement. *Note:* This system uses a compiler; systems using an interpreter identify a syntax error immediately after the line is entered

```
10 LET C=80
30 LET R=B*S
40 PRINT "REVENUE = $";R
50 END
```

Syntax errors corrected by retyping incorrect lines. The new lines replace the old lines in the work area.

```
RUN
        11:36   TUE  01 MAY 79

LINE  20:    OVERFLOW
REVENUE = $ 0

TIME 0.01 SECS.
```

No syntax errors exist; however, wrong arithmetic expression in line 20 causes an overflow execution error (value of B exceeds $10^{78}$, the maximum allowed for this system). The error is not fatal, as B is set to the maximum value and execution continues.

```
20 LET B=15*C+250
```

Correction of execution error: New line 20 replaces old line 20 in work area.

```
RUN
                11:37   TUE   01 MAY 79

REVENUE = $ 0

TIME 0.00 SECS.
```

By hand calculation, the answer for R is $8700000. The computer, however, prints $ 0. It follows that a logic error must exist within the program.

```
LIST
                11:37   TUE   01 MAY 79


10 LET C=80
20 LET B=15*C+250
30 LET R=B*S
40 PRINT "REVENUE = $";R
50 END
```

A "fresh" copy of the program is listed in order to better study the logic.

```
25 PRINT B,S
```

A trace statement (diagnostic PRINT) is inserted so as to "view" the storage contents of B and S.

```
RUN
                11:38   TUE   01 MAY 79

 1450                    0
REVENUE = $ 0

TIME 0.01 SECS.
```

Value of B is correct but S should be 6000, not zero. We forgot to explicitly initialize S.

```
15 LET S=6000
25
```

Correction of logic error: New line 15 is inserted between lines 10 and 20. Diagnostic PRINT is eliminated by typing 25 followed by carriage return.

```
LIST
                11:38   TUE   01 MAY 79


10 LET C=80
15 LET S=6000
20 LET B=15*C+250
30 LET R=B*S
40 PRINT "REVENUE = $";R
50 END
```

Confirmation that program stands corrected.

```
RUN
                11:39   TUE   01 MAY 79

REVENUE = $ 8700000

TIME 0.01 SECS.
```

Correct answer as before.

Our system uses a compiler; hence, syntax errors appear all in one place following the RUN command. If your system uses an interpreter, then a syntax error message is printed immediately following the entry of a syntactically incorrect line.

Note that the compiler or interpreter will identify syntax errors and the operating system will print execution error messages, but you must identify any logic errors by checking the correctness of the output.

In our examples, all errors are corrected by simply retyping the entire lines of instruction. All time-sharing systems, however, include specific system commands which greatly facilitate the process of editing programs. Also, all terminals have specific keys for correcting a line while still on that line. Ask your instructor about your system.

One final note: *Any time you replace an old line with a new line, the replacement is made in the work area, not in your library.* So if you wish to use your corrected program at a later date, you must type the system command that stores or replaces the program in your library (or, first delete the old copy, then save the new one).

## Exercises

1. Define or explain each of the following:

   syntax error        logic error
   fatal error          print chart
   execution error   roleplaying
   initialization     diagnostic PRINT statements
                    trace statements

2. Duplicate our debugging illustration on your system, noting any differences.

*3. Modify Figure 2.2 on page 32 to account for the process of detecting and correcting logic and execution errors. Distinguish between computer and user actions by identifying symbols in the figure that indicate action primarily initiated by the computer.

*4. **Debugging Problem.** Run the program below on your system *exactly* as shown. On the first run, let the compiler or interpreter identify syntax errors, and then you make the necessary corrections. On the second run, let the operating system identify execution errors, and then you make the necessary corrections. Finish with an error-free run. Use the following data: first try 4.2 for X and 0 for Y as shown; next try $-4.2$ for X and 0.1 for Y; finally, try 4.2 for X and 0.1 for Y.

```
010 REM PROGRAM WHICH ADDS, SUBTRACTS, MULTIPLIES, DIVIDES,
020      AND EXPONENTIATES TWO NUMBERS
030 LET X = 4.2
040 LET Y = 0
050 LET SUM = X + Y
060 S2 = X - Y
070 LET X*Y = M
080 LET D + X/Y
090 LET E = X**Y
100 PRINT SUM,S2,M,D,E
```

## MODULE B

# *Structured Programming and Other Topics*

---

---

By now you have studied and put into practice the key features of the BASIC language. As you probably realize, the act of writing good programs for solving specific problems requires not only knowledge of BASIC and an understanding of the problem, but also practice, skill, judgment, thought, and art. In this module we illustrate some principles and techniques for improving the design of programs.

## B.1
## ON DESIGNING BETTER PROGRAMS

Most computer applications in business, government, education, and other organizations require complex programs. For instance, an application such as a company's payroll may include dozens of programs with hundreds of instructions within each program.

A programmer's ability to organize and develop a program becomes considerably more important as the complexity of the task increases. Unfortunately, many applications programs have been planned inadequately, which makes them difficult to follow, hard to debug, and time consuming to modify. The result is low software productivity and higher costs. In fact, *industry estimates now place the total cost of software above the total cost of hardware.*

In an effort to control software costs, a number of guidelines and new techniques have evolved for improving the design of programs. In all cases their aim is to produce readable, well-organized, easy-to-debug, reliable, easy-to-update programs. These guidelines and techniques include the following, many of which you will recognize.

*1. Indentation.* The indentation of statements within loops improves the readability of programs by clearly identifying loops. Unfortunately, some versions of BASIC do not allow indentation. For these versions, a hand-drawn bracket to the left of the loop helps to identify the loop. In Section B.5 we illustrate another type of indentation which helps to improve readability.

*2. Selecting Variable Names.* The restriction of using a single letter in naming BASIC variables is a weakness that hinders readability and severely limits the ability to select meaningful variable names. For this reason, programs should include keys that define variables. Still, you should pay attention to the meaning of a variable when selecting its name. If names reflect what they represent, then a reader can follow programming logic without constantly referring to a key that defines variables. For example, the variable C has more meaning than the variable X if we wish to represent the cost of an item.

*3. Data Structures.* Carefully consider the structure of data before designing the algorithm. For example, a table of numbers is usually best represented by a two-dimensional subscripted variable than by a series of one-dimensional subscripted variables or by an "army" of unsubscripted variables. In other situations, the use of subscripted variables promotes shorter programs. For instance, the program in Example 7.7 on page 209 would be much longer without the use of arrays.

*4. Use of GO TO Statements.* For better readability and reliability GO TO statements should be used sparingly. For example, the program segment on the left is preferred to the program segment on the right.

```
10  LET X = 0              10  IF C <= D THEN 40
20  IF C > D THEN 40       20  LET X = 0
30  LET X = 10             30  GO TO 50
40  PRINT X                40  LET X = 10
                           50  PRINT X
```

For the same reasons, many loops are best designed with FOR/NEXT statements than with IF's paired with GO TO statements, as the following illustrates:

```
10  READ N                    10  READ N
15  FOR I = 1 TO N            15  LET I = 1
20     READ M                 20  READ M
25     LET S = 0              25     LET S = 0
30     FOR J = 1 TO M         30     LET J = 1
35        READ A              35     READ A
40        LET S = S + A       40        LET S = S + A
45     NEXT J                 45        LET J = J + 1
50     PRINT I,S              50     IF J <= M THEN 35
55  NEXT I                    55     PRINT I,S
 .                            60     LET I = I + 1
 .                            65  IF I <= N THEN 20
 .                             .
                              .
                              .
```

See what we mean? The segment on the right has a "jumbled" appearance which is more difficult to follow and more likely to make incorrect line-number transfers than the segment on the left. In designing complicated algorithms, inattention to the unrestricted use of GO TO's results in programs having a "spaghetti-line" appearance (for example, see Exercises 17 and 18 on pages B-24–B-25).

In general, it is desirable to *design programs that simplify transfers of control, since this tends to promote readability and reduces the likelihood of incorrectly transferring control to a wrong line number.* In fact, some would go so far as to eliminate the use of the GO TO statement altogether. We discuss the theoretical basis for this philosophy in Section B.5.

5. *General versus Specific Programs.* A general program requires less upkeep than a specific program for applications where certain data items may change. To illustrate what we mean, consider a program that calculates the mean (average) of a set of numbers or items. A general program would treat the number of items as an input/read variable (say, N), whereas a specific program would calculate the mean for, say, 100 items. Thus, the general program can calculate the mean for any number of items, whereas the specific program is restricted to 100 items. If the number of items is likely to change from one application to the next, then the general program is better, since the specific program would require frequent changes.

Since estimates now place the cost of designing and maintaining software above the cost of purchasing or leasing hardware, *it is good programming practice to treat all required data as variables rather than constants.* This practice reduces the cost of updating programs in situations where data may change. See pages 77, 81, and 119 to review earlier discussions of these issues.

6. *Documentation.* Programs that are to be *actually* used for information and scientific processing should be carefully documented. This facilitates the evolutionary process of updating (changing) programs to reflect improvements or new circumstances. In other words, well-documented programs are easier to understand and change than poorly documented programs.

While documentation requirements vary from project to project, a well-documented program might include

a.  A short narrative summary describing the scope and purpose of the program (see, for example, page 65)
b.  A description of read, input, and output (see, for example, page 279)
c.  A **system flowchart** showing the overall relationships in the processing system, for example, the flow and interactions of documents, reports, input/output media, and major processing requirements such as sorts and data file updates (see page 318 in Chapter 11 and page C-7 in Module C)
d.  A **program flowchart** of the type you have been writing describing detailed programming logic (see Section B.2 for an alternative to the program flowchart)
e.  A liberal use of comment lines within the program which define variables, describe modules, explain computations and complicated logic, and otherwise improve the appearance and facilitate the readability of the program (see, for example, page 280)
f.  A description of the read/input/output data used to test the program (see, for example, the sample run on page 281)
g.  An **operator's manual** which gives instructions to operators on running the program, for example, the program and data files that are needed and responses to console error messages
h.  A **user's manual** which gives instructions to users on how to prepare input, make data corrections, use output, and actions to take in the event of program error messages

7.  *Efficiency.*    A good program, in addition to being readable, is one that accomplishes its objective efficiently with respect to computer time. Here are a few suggestions to help you write more efficient programs.

a.  BASIC-supplied functions are usually faster and more accurate than using alternative code. For example,

    50 LET B = SQR(A)

is more efficient than

    50 LET B = A**.5

and

    70 LET C = ABS(X − Y)

is more efficient than

    70 LET C = X − Y
    72 IF C > 0 THEN 80
    74 LET C = −C
    80 . . .
      ⋮

b.  Avoid excessive nesting of IF/THEN statements if possible. For example, the segment

```
350 ON K GO TO 400,500,600
400 ...
    :
    :
500 ...
    :
    :
600 ...
    :
```

is a more efficient design than

```
350 IF K = 1 THEN 400
360 IF K = 2 THEN 500
370 IF K = 3 THEN 600
400 ...
    :
    :
500 ...
    :
    :
600 ...
    :
```

c.  When possible, avoid unnecessary loops since time is spent in incrementing and testing loop termination. For example, the segment

```
50 LET S = 0
55 FOR I = 1 TO N
60     READ A(I)
65     LET S = S + A(I)
70 NEXT I
```

is more efficient than

```
50 FOR I = 1 TO N
55     READ A(I)
60 NEXT I
65 LET S = 0
70 FOR I = 1 TO N
75     LET S = S + A(I)
80 NEXT I
```

d.  Poor data structures, poorly designed algorithms, and excessive read/input/output are primary factors that contribute to excessive computer time. For example, if large amounts of data need to be processed, the first program on page 189 doubles the time-consuming read-in of data and the second program on page 189 illustrates a grossly inefficient algorithmic design, whereas the program on page 190 illustrates the efficiency of good data structures through the appropriate use of an array.

In general, programmers should *look for economies that make a significant difference, but without degrading the readability of the program.* In commercial applications, an esoteric, obscure code that saves CPU time is generally not preferred to a less efficient version that is readable, understandable, and easy to change.

8.  *Transportability.*  A **transportable program** is one that can be used by different installations with little or no modification. If a particular program either is to be run on

different computer systems or the system on which it is to be used is likely to change in the future, then software costs will be reduced if the program is designed with transportability in mind. Thus, as much as possible, transportable programs maximize the use of statements in the proposed ANSI standard and simultaneously minimize the use of statements based on local enhancements.

*9. Debugging.* The process of testing and correcting programs for errors is time-consuming and costly. In fact, an industry rule of thumb states that *debugging consumes on the average between one third and one half of the total project time.* The incorporation of good design principles as discussed in this chapter, the use of classic debugging techniques as discussed in Module A, and familiarity with common programming errors as discussed at the end of Chapters 4 through 12 all serve to promote an efficient debugging phase. In particular great care must be exercised in designing test data to ensure that all branches, combinations of branches, and boundary values of data are tested, as discussed on page 171.

*10. Reliability.* A program should reliably operate as intended once it is implemented on an on-going basis. A process called **defensive programming** means that the design of a program should anticipate "unforeseen circumstances" as much as feasible. For example, good commercial programs anticipate errors in the input data through programmed error routines, as emphasized in Chapters 6 and 9. Generally, programmers should anticipate what might go wrong operationally, thereby designing their programs to react accordingly. At the same time the temptation to make programs "over-reliable" must be tempered by judgments regarding the benefits versus the costs. In other words, reliable program design requires assessments regarding the nature of potential difficulties, their likelihood of occurrences, the costs of incorporating programmed reactions to these difficulties, and the benefits (or cost savings) realized when these difficulties are avoided through program design.

*11. Other Techniques.* Recent trends point to a growing use of certain approaches, techniques, and new statements for improving the documentation, readability, design, and reliability of programs. Among these, we discuss pseudocode, modular programming, top down design, and structured programming in the next several sections.

# B.2
# PSEUDOCODE

A flowchart is one way of diagramming the logic of a program. Many professional programmers and systems analysts use them regularly; others do not. One reason for their not using flowcharts is the difficulty in revising the flowchart once a program has been modified.

In the past few years, a program design tool called **pseudocode** has been gaining acceptance among professional programmers. Two key reasons for the growing acceptance of pseudocode are its compatibility with the thinking processes of the programmer and its ease of revision. Unfortunately, pseudocode has not been standardized, because there are many variations. The example which follows, however, should give you a good idea of its syntax and structure.

## EXAMPLE B.1    Student Billing Program

Consider a simple student billing problem whereby tuition for full-time students (enrolled in 12 or more credits during the term) is $1200 and tuition for part-time students (less than 12 credits) is $100 per credit. The balance due the university is tuition plus fees of $250.

    Before coding the actual program we might map out its structure by using a "false" (pseudo) code, as follows:

```
READ credit cutoff, full-time tuition, cost/credit, fees
READ no. students
Start loop
   READ student id and no. credits
   IF no. credits ≥ credit cutoff THEN
      Tuition = full-time tuition
   ELSE
      Tuition = no. credits × cost per credit
   END IF
   Balance due = tuition + fees
   PRINT id and balance due
End loop
Stop
```

```
0005 REM *** STUDENT BILLING PROGRAM ***
0010 REM
0015 REM PURPOSE: CALCULATES BALANCE DUE UNIVERSITY BASED
0018 REM              ON TUITION AND FEES
0020 REM
0025 REM
0030 REM KEY:      C1 = CREDIT CUTOFF
0035 REM           T1 = FULL-TIME TUITION
0040 REM           C2 = COST PER CREDIT
0045 REM           F  = FEES
0050 REM           N  = NUMBER OF STUDENTS
0055 REM           I  = STUDENT ID
0060 REM           C  = CREDITS TAKEN
0065 REM           T  = TUITION
0070 REM           B  = BALANCE DUE UNIVERSITY
0075 REM
0080 REM ---------------------------------------------------------------------------------
0100 READ C1,T1,C2,F
0110 READ N
0200 FOR J = 1 TO N
0210    READ I,C
0220    LET T = T1
0230    IF C >= C1 THEN 250
0240    LET T = C*C2
0250    LET B = T + F
0260    PRINT I,B
0300 NEXT J
```

```
0900  DATA 12,1200,100,250
1000  DATA 3
1001  DATA 901,9
1002  DATA 902,12
1003  DATA 903,15
9999  END
```

In general, a program written in pseudocode is similar to a program written in a higher-level language such as BASIC. The major difference is the emphasis placed on structure versus syntax. Pseudocode primarily concentrates on mapping out the structure of a program, with little regard for the syntax of the actual programming language to be used. Thus, we are free to concentrate on the design of the program by expressing its structure using ordinary English, including abbreviations, symbols, and formulas.

Either flowcharts or pseudocode can be used to design and document programs. The simplicity and compactness of pseudocode, however, may tip the balance in its favor, particularly for documenting programs that are likely to undergo frequent modification. In particular, note that pseudocode can be included within a program as part of its documentation, thereby facilitating changes by using the system's edit commands.

## B.3
## MODULAR PROGRAMMING

Another approach to the organization and development of complex programs is **modular programming.** This approach divides a program into groups of related instructions called **modules.** Each module within a program typically performs one function related to the overall purpose of the program. For example, in a telephone billing program separate modules might be developed for the following purposes.

1. Data input and error routine
2. Calculation of bills
3. Printing of bills
4. Management report which includes statistical summaries of billing information, for example, sums, averages, frequency distributions (Exercise 26 in Chapter 7), aging of accounts receivables (Exercise 36 in Chapter 6)
5. Bills sorted by ZIP codes (for the purpose of simplifying mailings)

Generally, two characteristics identify a module. First, *a module has a single entry point and a single exit point.* In essence a module is like a "black box" that is uniquely activated (entered at a specific point); it performs some assigned function, and it is uniquely deactivated (exited at a specific point). Second, *a module is "independent" from other modules.* Essentially, this means that we should be able to change or modify a module without affecting other modules. In reality absolute independence may not be achievable in many cases; however, modules should at least exhibit the type of *functional* independence described in the five modules of the telephone billing example.

If you have read Chapter 9, then you might recall that subroutines are one way of representing modules in BASIC. Typically, a main program, called the **control module,** directs the entire program by calling modules (subroutines) as required. Another way of conceptualizing modules is discussed in Section B.5.

A **hierarchy chart** is a useful way to express the relationships among modules. This chart is similar in appearance to an organization chart, with each box representing a module. For example, the telephone billing modules might be related as shown in Figure B.1. In this case, the control module (main program) not only calls modules (subroutines) 1, 2, and 3 as required but also might perform certain "housekeeping" chores such as documentation (features of programs, definition of variables, and so forth) and initializations. Notice that module 2 successively calls modules 4 and 5.

A hierarchy chart, together with a description of each module, is an early step in good program design. In effect, the hierarchy chart allows the programmer to focus on defining *what* needs to be done before deciding *how* it is to be done.

The use of modular programming concepts results in several advantages when writing long, complicated programs:

1.  *Facilitates design and improves readability and comprehension of programs.* For example, the hierarchy chart in Figure B.1 gives the "big picture" and shows interrelationships among programming tasks. Moreover, a modular design promotes independence among parts of a program. This means, for example, that errors in one module have no effect on the proper functioning of another module. Consequently, the cost or time of debugging is reduced.

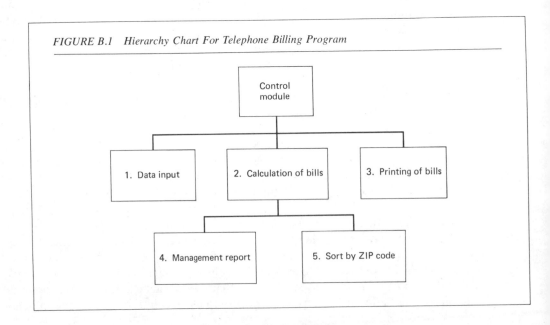

FIGURE B.1   *Hierarchy Chart For Telephone Billing Program*

2. *Provides flexibility in a dynamic environment.* Most applications programs evolve over time, which means that they are changed either to reflect new conditions or to incorporate improvements. The use of modules simplifies this evolutionary process by minimizing the required effort in making changes; that is, modules can be changed, added, or deleted with greater independence and ease. Additionally, general-purpose modules (for example, statistical routines) can be written for use in more than one program, thereby reducing overall programming effort.

3. *Allows specialization and division of labor.* Specific modules can be assigned to specific programmers, which can promote greater productivity and more effective programs. For example, programmer A might be better at designing I/O features than programmer B, but the latter is better at designing efficient calculating procedures. The assignment of modules, therefore, should reflect these specializations.

## B.4
## TOP DOWN DESIGN

The term **top down design** refers to a process for simplifying and systematizing the design and development of complex programs. Strictly speaking, it is not a specific technique, but rather a philosophy which translates into a personalized process for writing programs. As such, the manner of implementing top down design will vary from programmer to programmer or organization to organization.

Top down design starts with an overall "look" at the entire problem, that is, a look from the "top." Subsequently the problem is refined further by working "down" through successive levels of greater detail. To illustrate what we mean, consider the process of writing a textbook. First we decide the topic of the book. This is the least level of detail and the highest level of abstraction. Next we write down the titles of chapters, which gives us the next level of detail. Next we specify the main headings within each chapter, which represents a further refinement in the level of detail. Next we state the subheadings within each main heading. Finally, we provide the greatest level of detail: each word in the body of the text.

To illustrate the *implementation* of top down design in programming by a process called **stepwise refinement,** consider the student billing problem first introduced in Example B.1. Step 1, the first level of detail, might be to specify the nature of the program as follows:

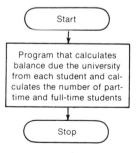

Step 2, the next level of detail, might specify the following sequence of processing tasks:

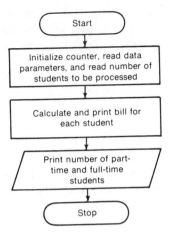

The next step might specify the sequence of tasks within the loop indicated by the second box in the above sequence:

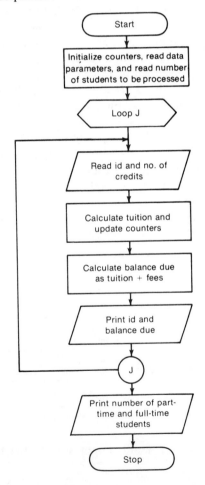

The final step isolates the tasks in the first box and replaces the box labeled "Calculate tuition and update counters" with the decision logic shown in Figure B.2.

Exploding the pseudocode is an alternative approach to the clumsy use of flowcharts, as illustrated in Table B.1.

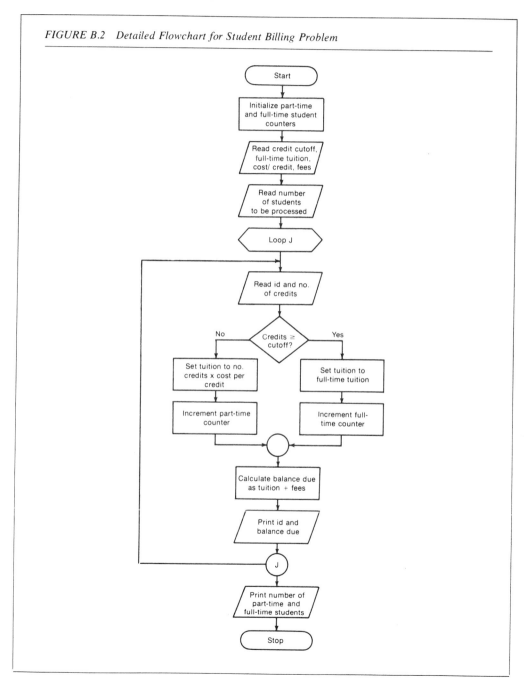

FIGURE B.2   *Detailed Flowchart for Student Billing Problem*

TABLE B.1  *Stepwise Refinement by Exploding the Pseudocode*

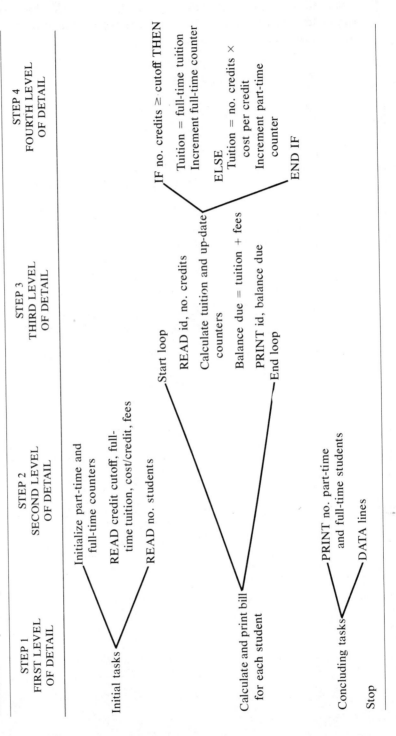

| STEP 1 FIRST LEVEL OF DETAIL | STEP 2 SECOND LEVEL OF DETAIL | STEP 3 THIRD LEVEL OF DETAIL | STEP 4 FOURTH LEVEL OF DETAIL |
|---|---|---|---|
| Initial tasks | Initialize part-time and full-time counters | | |
| | READ credit cutoff, full-time tuition, cost/credit, fees | | |
| | READ no. students | | |
| | | Start loop | |
| | | READ id, no. credits | |
| | | Calculate tuition and up-date counters | IF no. credits ≥ cutoff THEN |
| | | | Tuition = full-time tuition |
| | | | Increment full-time counter |
| | | | ELSE |
| | | | Tuition = no. credits × cost per credit |
| | | | Increment part-time counter |
| | | | END IF |
| | | Balance due = tuition + fees | |
| Calculate and print bill for each student | | PRINT id, balance due | |
| | | End loop | |
| Concluding tasks | PRINT no. part-time and full-time students | | |
| | DATA lines | | |
| Stop | | | |

Another aspect of top down design relates to the method of testing or debugging a modular program of the type described in Figure B.1 on page B-9. One popular way of implementing **top down testing** is to first code and test the control module before coding the other modules. In this case, "dummy" modules (also called program stubs) are used in place of modules 1–5. For example, these dummy modules might be nothing more than a PRINT statement for tracing execution and a RETURN statement. Once the control module is debugged, we proceed to the next level of detail (modules 1, 2, and 3) and repeat the coding and testing procedure. Now modules 4 and 5 are the dummy modules. Finally, we code and test modules 4 and 5.

Variations on this modular, top down procedure are common, depending on the programmer and the problem. For example, we could: first, code and test the control module and module 2, with modules 1, 3, 4, and 5 as dummies; second, code and test modules 4 and 5, with modules 1 and 3 remaining as dummies; and third, code and test modules 1 and 3.

The four-step procedure first introduced in Chapter 2 also utilizes top down design ideas. Part 1 of "Step I, Analyzing the Problem" is the first level of detail. Once the nature of the problem is fully defined in words, then the process can be refined further by working "down" through successive levels of greater detail. For example, in parts 2 (specification of inputs), 3 (specification of outputs), and 4 (algorithm) of Step I, the problem is expressed at a greater level of detail than in part 1.

Relatively complex programs may require an additional level of detail between parts 3 and 4 of Step I: the specification and description of modules. Also, it may be best to describe the algorithm in part 4 by using pseudocode.

The preparation of the flowchart (or pseudocode) in Step II of the procedure is one way of representing the next level of detail, which then can be followed by the final level of detail, the program itself (Step III).

# B.5
# STRUCTURED PROGRAMMING

**Structured programming** is an approach to organizing and writing programs based on a body of principles that promotes readable code and reliable execution. The basic foundation of structured programming consists of three types of structures:

1. Sequence structure
2. Decision structure
3. Loop structure

These so-called **control structures** can be used to describe the logic of any program completely.

## Sequence Structure

The **sequence structure** consists of a sequence of instructions that occur one after the other without any transfer of control statements. Figure B.3 illustrates the concept of the sequence structure for the student billing program.

FIGURE B.3    *Sample Sequence Structure*

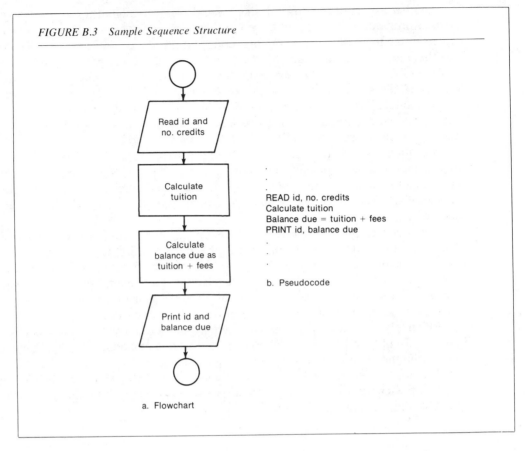

```
READ id, no. credits
Calculate tuition
Balance due = tuition + fees
PRINT id, balance due
```

b.  Pseudocode

a.  Flowchart

FIGURE B.4    *Sample Two-Choice Decision Structure*

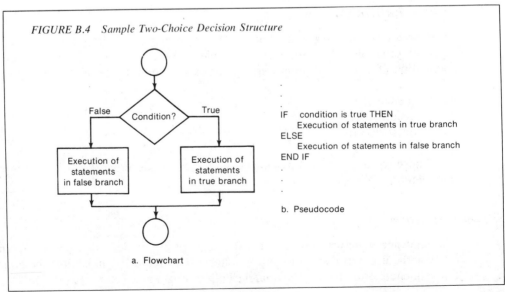

```
IF    condition is true THEN
         Execution of statements in true branch
ELSE
         Execution of statements in false branch
END IF
```

b.  Pseudocode

a.  Flowchart

## Decision Structure

The **decision structure** consists of a choice between two or more alternatives. In the two-alternative case, either a sequence of one or more statements is to be executed if the condition is true, or a sequence of one or more statements is to be executed if the condition is false. Figure B.4 illustrates this two-choice structure, which is also called an IF/THEN/ELSE structure.

One example of the decision structure is the calculation of tuition based on part-time (less than the cutoff of 12 credits) versus full-time (12 credits or more) student status, as illustrated in Figure B.5. Note that *the minimal BASIC version in Figure B.5(c)*

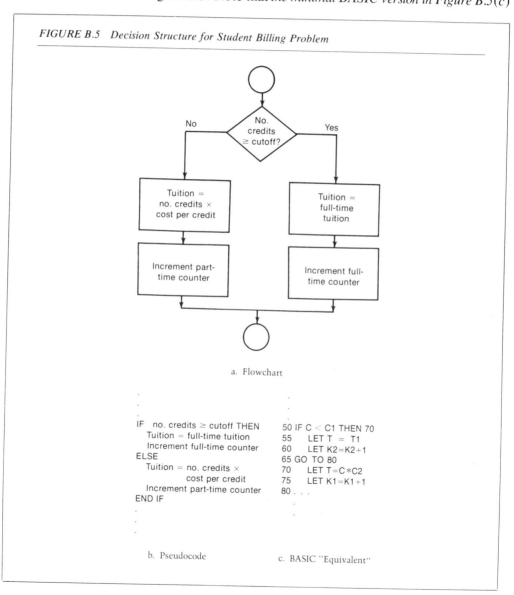

**FIGURE B.5   Decision Structure for Student Billing Problem**

a. Flowchart

```
IF  no. credits ≥ cutoff THEN
    Tuition = full-time tuition
    Increment full-time counter
ELSE
    Tuition = no. credits ×
              cost per credit
    Increment part-time counter
END IF
```

```
50 IF C < C1 THEN 70
55    LET T = T1
60    LET K2=K2+1
65 GO TO 80
70    LET T=C*C2
75    LET K1=K1+1
80 . . .
```

b. Pseudocode                    c. BASIC "Equivalent"

*is an effective but not an exact equivalent of the IF/THEN/ELSE structure.* We reversed the sense of the inequality from "greater than or equal to" in part b to its *complement* "less than" in part c. This allowed us to place the full-time student logic immediately after the IF/THEN statement for consistency with the true branch in the pseudocode version. Unlike the structured pseudocode version, however, the BASIC version enters the full-time segment when the result of the test is false.[1] Further note that *both the pseudocode and BASIC versions indent the logic within each branch, for better readability.*

When more than two choices need to be made, IF/THEN/ELSE structures can be *nested* within other IF/THEN/ELSE structures, as illustrated in Figure B.6. It should be evident that readability is inversely related to degree of nesting. For this reason, the **CASE structure** illustrated in Figure B.7 is preferred to nested IF/THEN/ELSE structures. Note that the BASIC codes in Figures B.6 and B.7 exactly reproduce the flow-chart and pseudocode versions, unlike the BASIC version in Figure B.5.

## Loop Structure

The **loop structure** refers to the repeated execution of a sequence of instructions. This structure consists of two parts:

1. A *loop body,* which represents the sequence of steps that are to be repeated.
2. A *loop control,* which specifies either the number of times a loop must be executed or the condition under which the loop is to be terminated.

Figure B.8 represents the logic of the loop structure. Part a specifically represents the **DO WHILE structure.** In this structure, the first action is to test whether or not the body of the loop is to be executed. If the condition is true, then control passes to the body of the loop. After the statements within the body have been executed, control goes back to the test statement preceding the loop body. When the test indicates a false condition, then looping is finished and control passes to the next statement outside the loop. Thus, looping continues WHILE the condition is true.

A variation of the loop structure is the **DO UNTIL structure** first introduced in Chapter 6. This structure ensures that the body of the loop is executed at least once. In this case, the test for the end of the loop is made after the loop body is executed. Thus, looping continues UNTIL the condition is true.

*The major difference between these two loop structures is that the test precedes the body in a DO WHILE loop whereas the body precedes the test in a DO UNTIL loop.* A more subtle difference is that the former gives a loop exit when the condition is false, whereas the latter results in a loop exit when the condition is true.

The FOR/NEXT loop first introduced in Chapter 5 is an example of a DO WHILE structure.[2] The LRC loop first introduced in Chapter 6, however, does not fit neatly into either a DO WHILE or DO UNTIL structure. Figure B.9 illustrates the necessary modifications to incorporate a last record check into a DO WHILE structure. Note that the loop structure needs to be preceded by an extra READ statement.

---

[1] We defer an exact BASIC equivalent to Exercise 1b on page B-22.
[2] Compare Figure 5.1 on page 118 to Figure B.8a.

**FIGURE B.6**   *Nested IF/THEN/ELSE Structures*

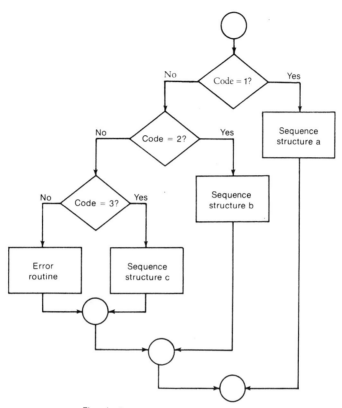

a. Flowchart

```
.
.
.
IF   Code=1 THEN
     Sequence structure a
ELSE
    IF   Code=2 THEN
       Sequence structure b
    ELSE
        IF  Code=3 THEN
            Sequence structure c
        ELSE
            Error routine
        END IF
    END IF
END IF
.
.
```

```
050 IF K=1 THEN 100
060 IF K=2 THEN 200
070 IF K=3 THEN 300
090 GO TO 395
100 .  .  .
      .
      .
190 GO TO 400
200 .  .  .
      .
      .
290 GO TO 400
300 .  .  .
      .
      .
390 GO TO 400
395     PRINT "CODE ERROR"
400 .  .  .
      .
      .
```

b. Pseudocode          c. BASIC Equivalent

FIGURE B.7   *CASE Structure*

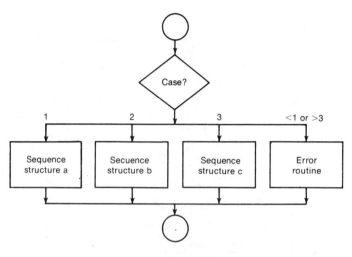

a. Flowchart

```
CASE START code
    CASE 1
        Sequence structure a
    CASE 2
        Sequence structure b
    CASE 3
        Sequence structure c
    CASE wrong code
        Error routine
END CASE
```

b. Pseudocode

```
050 IF K>=1 THEN 60
055    LET K=4
060 IF K<=3 THEN 70
065    LET K=4
070 ON K GO TO 100,200,300,395
100 . .

190 GO TO 400
200 . . .

290 GO TO 400
300 . . .

390 GO TO 400
395    PRINT "CODE ERROR"
400 . . .
```

c. BASIC Equivalent

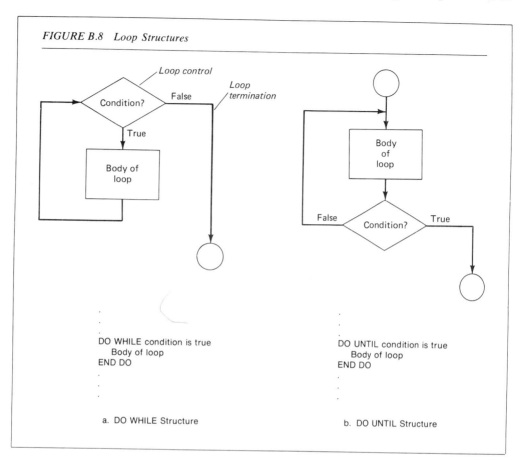

FIGURE B.8   Loop Structures

a. DO WHILE Structure                                    b. DO UNTIL Structure

## The Top Down, Modular Connection

A program that is written strictly in terms of sequence, decision, and loop structures is said to be a **structured program,** and its corresponding flowchart is said to be a **structured flowchart.** Pseudocode itself reflects a structured design when it is based strictly on sequence, decision (IF/THEN/ELSE or CASE), and loop (DO WHILE or DO UNTIL) structures.

If you look back at Figures B.3 through B.8, you should realize that each control structure has a single entry point and a single exit point, as denoted by the ○ symbol. In effect a structured program is simply a set of these control structures put together in some meaningful fashion. For example, the flowchart in Figure B.9 is actually a sequence structure, followed by a DO WHILE structure, followed by another sequence structure. The DO WHILE structure itself contains an IF/THEN/ELSE structure followed by (in sequence with!) a sequence structure. Finally, the IF/THEN/ELSE structure contains a sequence structure within each of its logical branches.

In essence, control structures can be viewed as *blocks* or *modules* which together make up the whole. *Thus, structured programs utilize the modular programming concept.*

*FIGURE B.9  Student Billing Program with LRC Loop as a DO WHILE Structure*

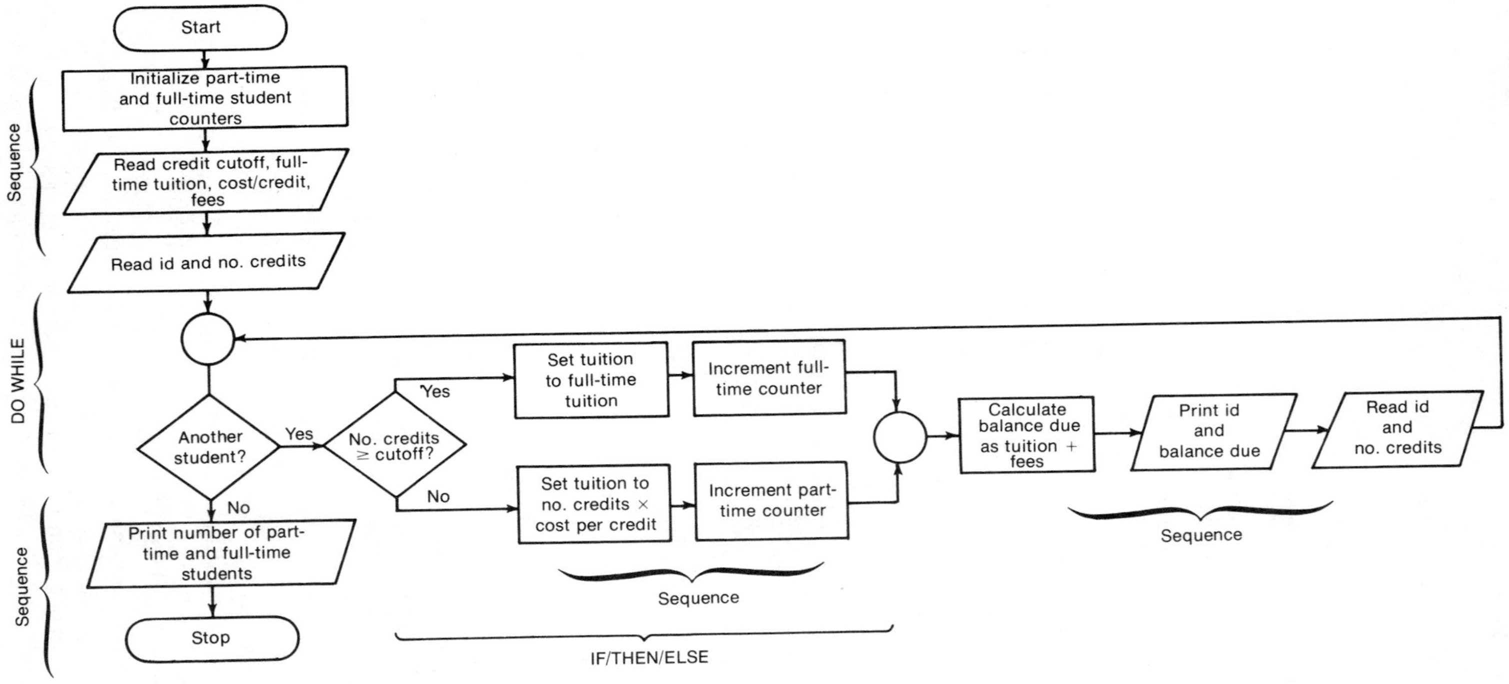

You should also realize that *structured programming is related to the stepwise refinement process in top down design.* The student billing problem illustrated on page B-10 begins with a one block sequence structure and successively builds into the design additional sequence, loop, and decision structures. This approach to designing programs is often called **top down, structured programming.** Moreover, the execution of structured programs proceeds from the top down to the bottom; that is, transfers of control to upper parts of the program are not possible (except for the loop structure, of course).

Unfortunately, the proposed ANSI standard falls short of including statements that directly incorporate IF/THEN/ELSE, CASE, DO WHILE, and DO UNTIL structures. Still, statements in minimal BASIC can be used to functionally reproduce (simulate) structures, as illustrated by the code that simulates the CASE structure in Figure B.7(c). This has the advantage of creating structured programs for processing on BASIC compilers/interpreters that do not support structured statements. The simulation of structures, however, sacrifices some clarity and efficiency, since it takes "gymnastics" to use minimal BASIC code to exactly simulate structure (see Exercises 1, 4, 13, and 14, for example). Additionally, reliability is somewhat degraded because of the necessity to use extra GO TO's which increases the likelihood of incorrect transfers.

For these reasons *we disagree with programmers that would "force" structure without exception on all parts of a program written in an inherently unstructured language such as minimal BASIC.* It seems to us that this "pure" approach defeats the argument for and philosophical underpinning of structured programming: increased clarity and reliability. Exercise 1 clearly illustrates our argument.

Fortunately, some BASIC implementations include structured BASIC statements that greatly facilitate the design and implementation of structured programs.[3] In years to come, we expect (hope) that all BASIC implementations will include a full complement of structured BASIC statements. Moreover, we expect that ANSI will incorporate structure in the BASIC standard so as to facilitate the portability of structured programs.

**Follow-up Exercises**

1.  With respect to simulating the IF/THEN/ELSE structure:
    a.  Did you notice that the program in Example B.1 on page B-7 is not exactly consistent with the IF/THEN/ELSE pseudocode representation of the two-choice decision structure? (If not, go back to sleep.) Flowchart the decision structure in this program to show that it is not exactly consistent with Figure B-4 on page B-15.
    b.  Is it possible to exactly duplicate an IF/THEN/ELSE structure using the IF/THEN and GO TO statements? If so, rewrite the code in Figure B.5(c) and comment on clarity, efficiency, and reliability.

---

[3] For example, Digital Equipment Corporation's BASIC-PLUS and BASIC-PLUS-2, Radio Shack's Level II BASIC for the TRS-80 microcomputer, Sperry Univac's UBASIC, and Dartmouth College's SBASIC.

2. Completely describe Figure B.2 in terms of sequence, decision, and loop structures.
3. Write down the pseudocode that corresponds to Figure B.9.
4. Write down BASIC code for the program described by Figure B.9. Is your DO WHILE loop *exactly* consistent with the flowchart or pseudocode version? Explain.
5. Describe the changes you would make in Figure B.9 to incorporate the LRC method into a DO UNTIL loop? Why is this approach an example of poor design?
**\*\*6.** If your system has structured BASIC statements, then incorporate these in
   a. The BASIC code of Example B.1.
   b. The BASIC code of Figure B.6(c).
   c. The BASIC code of Figure B.7(c).
   d. The program described by Figure B.9.

### Additional Exercises

7. Define or explain each of the following:

| | |
|---|---|
| system flowchart | top down testing |
| program flowchart | structured programming |
| operator's manual | control structures |
| user's manual | sequence structure |
| transportable program | decision structure |
| defensive programming | loop structure |
| pseudocode | IF/THEN/ELSE structure |
| modular programming | CASE structure |
| modules | DO WHILE structure |
| control module | DO UNTIL structure |
| hierarchy chart | structured program |
| top down design | structured flowchart |
| stepwise refinement | top down, structured programming |

8. What are the two key characteristics of modules? Do control structures have the same characteristics?
9. How is modular programming related to top down design?
10. How is modular programming related to structured programming?
11. How is top down design related to structured programming?
12. **Traffic Court Fines with Error Routine.** Is the program of Example 6.5 on page 164 a structured program? Why or why not? If not, make necessary modifications to make it structured. Include pseudocode.
13. **Table Look-up.** Is the program of Example 7.6 on page 205 a structured program? Why or why not? If not, make necessary modifications to make it structured. *Hint:* See Exercise 14 in Chapter 7 on page 209. Include pseudocode.
14. **Income Tax Program.** Is the program of Section 8.6 on page 241 a structured program? Why or why not? If not, make necessary modifications to make it structured. Include pseudocode.
15. **Automobile Rental Decision Program.** Is the program of Section 9.4 on page 275 a structured program? Why or why not? If not, make necessary modifications to make it structured. Include pseudocode.

**16.** Select one of the programs that you have completed from an earlier chapter and do the following:

   a. Improve its style by taking into consideration indentation, selection of meaningful variable names, minimal use of GO TO statements, generality, more thorough documentation, and defensive programming.

   b. Improve its efficiency without degrading its readability.

   c. Select a better set of test data.

   d. Redesign it by specifying modules and drawing a hierarchy chart. Include the description of modules within the program's documentation. In describing a module, state its data needs, its function, and its results.

   e. Develop a pseudocode version before setting down your new BASIC code. Include this as part of your program's documentation. Why is it advantageous to include pseudocode within a program's documentation?

   f. Rewrite your program's code to conform to the pseudocode version. Use structured BASIC statements if these are featured on your system (now it's possible to eliminate *all* GO TO statements).

   Is your program a "structured" program?

**17. Electric Bill Revisited.** The following poorly written program is a technically correct solution to Exercise 38a in Chapter 9 on page 287.

```
01 LET K = 0
02 LET K = K + 1
03 IF K > 5 THEN 38
04 READ A,B,C,D,E,F$,G$,H$,I$,J$,K$,L
05 IF C <> 1 THEN 13
06 LET M1 = B*.0525 − A*.0525
07 LET N1 = 1.01*D − 1.01*E + M1
08 PRINT F$;G$;H$;I$
09 PRINT J$;K$;L
10 PRINT "FROM SEP 19 TO OCT 18, 1980"
11 PRINT B − A;M1;D − E;(D − E)*.01;D − E + (D − E)*.01 + M1
12 GO TO 2
13 IF C <> 2 THEN 21
14 LET M2 = B*.0485 − A*.0485
15 LET N2 = 1.01*D − 1.01*E + M2
16 PRINT F$;G$;H$;I$
17 PRINT J$;K$;L
18 PRINT "FROM SEP 19 TO OCT 18, 1980"
19 PRINT B − A;M2;D − E;(D − E)*.01;D − E + (D − E)*.01 + M2
20 GO TO 2
21 IF C = 3 THEN 27
22 PRINT F$;G$;H$;I$
23 PRINT J$;K$;L
24 PRINT "FROM SEP 19 TO OCT 18, 1980"
25 PRINT B − A;M3;D − E;(D − E)*.01;D − E + (D − E)*.01 + M3
26 GO TO 2
27 IF B − A >= 50000 THEN 31
28 LET M3 = B*.085 − A*.085
29 LET N3 = 1.01*D − 1.01*E + M3
30 GO TO 22
31 IF B − A <= 100000 THEN 35
32 LET M3 = B*.065 − A*.065
33 LET N3 = 1.01*D − 1.01*E + M3
34 GO TO 22
35 LET M3 = B*.075 − A*.075
36 LET N3 = 1.01*D − 1.01*E + M3
37 GO TO 22
38 END
```

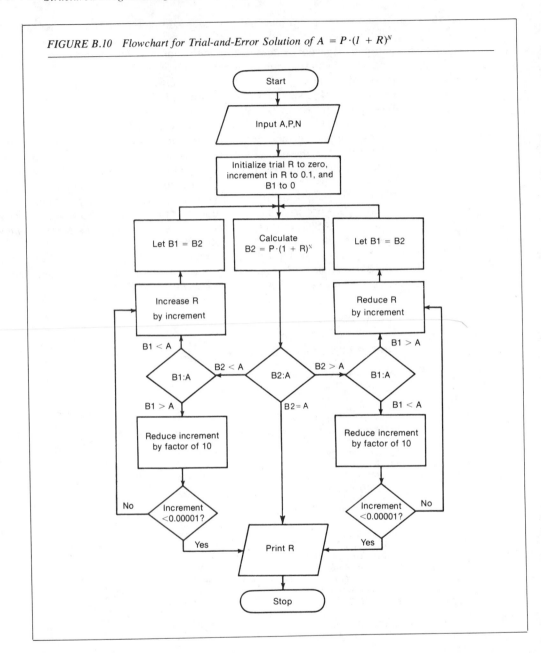

FIGURE B.10    *Flowchart for Trial-and-Error Solution of* $A = P \cdot (1 + R)^N$

a. Briefly describe aspects of this program that illustrate poor style and design. Flowchart this program. Do you see what we mean by a spaghetti-like appearance?

b. Redesign the program (from scratch) by following the steps described in Exercise 16.

c. Incorporate part b of Exercise 38 in Chapter 9.

18. **Bracket Search Algorithm Revisited.** Do you like spaghetti? Try understanding the flowchart of Figure B.10, which is algorithmically correct for Exercise 41 in Chapter 6 on page 185, but a reader's nightmare.

a. Draw a structured flowchart for this algorithm.

b. Write down pseudocode.

c. Write down BASIC code.

d. Select a thorough set of test data and test your program.

*MODULE C*

# *Selected Case Studies*

---

C.1  CASE I: REPLACEMENT CONSULTANTS, INC.

C.2  CASE II: AUTOMATED REPAIR AND MAINTENANCE SYSTEM (ARMS)

C.3  CASE III: INVENTORY SIMULATION ASSOCIATES, INC.

---

The **case method** of study pioneered by Harvard Business School is a widely used approach to study real problems. A **case** is a written description of a realistic problem that requires a solution. The problem scenario is usually based on actual events, although certain aspects might be fictionalized (to protect the innocent, of course).

Typically, the instructor assigns the case either to individuals or to teams of individuals. The latter is more common because large-scale, real-world management problems are usually best solved by groups or teams made up of individuals having expertise in different areas.

The solution of a case generally includes an oral presentation summarizing a typewritten report that outlines the problem, describes solutions or analyses, and recommends courses of action to be taken by management. This closely parallels the approach taken by large governmental agencies, corporations, and consultants.

In short, the case method of study gives the student an opportunity to actively participate in the creative solution of a "meaty" problem in an environment that effectively simulates real-world conditions.

## C.1
## CASE I: REPLACEMENT
## CONSULTANTS, INC.

The **replacement problem** is concerned with determining the best time period (week, month, year) in which to replace a capital asset (automobile, machine, bus, ship). As you might know from owning a car, these types of assets typically are characterized by *operating costs* which increase over time and *salvage values* (resale prices) which decrease over time. As the car gets older, the increases in operating costs, which include the costs of maintenance, repair, and regular operation, tend to favor a short ownership period. As time goes on, however, the resale price of a car tends to decrease more slowly than previously. This means that the *capital* or *depreciation cost,* which is the difference between the price you paid and the price you get on resale, decreases from year to year, on the average. For example, a car that costs $5000 when new might resell for $4000 one year later, which gives a capital cost of $1000 for the first year. Now, if it can be sold for $2800 at the end of three years and for $2400 at the end of four years, then the capital cost in the fourth year is $400. Annual capital costs, therefore, tend to decrease as the years go by, which favors a long ownership period, all other things equal (such as styling, prestige, and so on).

This dilemma now raises an interesting question: Since operating costs favor a short ownership period and capital costs favor a long ownership period, what is the best period to replace the asset? One way of resolving this tradeoff is to define total cost per time period as the sum of capital costs and operating costs divided by the number of time periods and to replace the asset in the time period for which this cost is a minimum. In the scenario which follows, we present only one replacement model of the many that are available.

Suppose that, once you get your degree, you are hired as a consultant by Replacement Consultants, Inc., one of the many management consulting firms that operate nationally. You have been assigned to advise the administrator of a very large urban hospital. Specifically, you are to recommend how many years the hospital is to keep its fleet of ambulances before replacing them.

Fortunately, detailed records have been kept on the costs of operating each ambulance. On the average, it costs $2800 to operate an ambulance in its first year, which includes the costs of insurance, gasoline, regular maintenance, and repairs. Each year thereafter, it is estimated that the cost increases by $300 per year on the average.

A new ambulance of this type costs $15,000. Experience shows that the used ambulance price decreases by a *depreciation factor* of 20 percent each year on the average. Thus, after one year, the ambulance can be sold for $12,000 (or 0.8 × 15,000). This gives a capital cost in the first year of $3000 (or $15,000 − $12,000).

It follows that the total cost in the first year is $5800, or $2800 for operating cost and $3000 for capital cost. Sample calculations of total cost per year for each of the first three years are shown in Table C.1. Note that column 3 is a running sum of column 2; each entry in column 4 is 80 percent of the preceding entry in that column; each entry in column 5 is the new ambulance price ($15,000) minus the corresponding entry in column 4; column 6 is the sum of corresponding elements in columns 3 and 5; and column 7 is column 6 divided by column 1.

As you can see from this table, it would cost $5,800 per year to replace an ambulance every year. If each ambulance were replaced every 2 years, then the cost per year would drop to $5,650 per ambulance. This cost further drops to $5540 per year per ambulance when the ambulances are replaced every 3 years. The best replacement cycle, that which yields minimum total cost per year, is yet to be found.

In addition to the analysis of the current ambulance, called the Deluxe Model, the administrator wants you to analyze costs and replacement cycles for the Economy Model, costing $10,000. After some effort, you have located a hospital that has been using this particular model. Luckily, this hospital also is a client of Replacement Consultants, Inc., and so they cooperated in providing the following estimates: $2500 to

TABLE C.1   *Cost Calculations for Ambulance Replacement Problem*

| 1<br>REPLACE-<br>MENT<br>PERIOD<br>(END OF<br>YEAR) | 2<br>OPERATING<br>COST<br>FOR<br>PERIOD<br>($) | 3<br>CUMULA-<br>TIVE<br>OPERATING<br>COST<br>($) | 4<br><br><br>SALVAGE<br>PRICE<br>($) | 5<br>CUMULA-<br>TIVE<br>CAPITAL<br>COST<br>($) | 6<br>CUMULA-<br>TIVE<br>TOTAL<br>COST<br>($) | 7<br>TOTAL<br>COST<br>PER<br>YEAR<br>($) |
|---|---|---|---|---|---|---|
| 1 | 2,800 | 2,800 | 12,000 | 3,000 | 5,800 | 5,800 |
| 2 | 3,100 | 5,900 | 9,600 | 5,400 | 11,300 | 5,650 |
| 3 | 3,400 | 9,300 | 7,680 | 7,320 | 16,620 | 5,540 |

operate the ambulance in the first year, thereafter increasing by approximately $500 per year; average decrease of 30 percent per year in the used ambulance price.

Within 2 weeks, the administrator would like you to present your analyses for each ambulance and to make recommendations as to which model to purchase and how long it should be kept.

Trudging home one night with your briefcase full of facts and figures, the following thoughts occurred to you: "I would be insane to analyze this problem by hand. It makes more sense to program it for our computer. In fact, if I make the program general enough, we could use it for any ambulance and hospital in the city, the country, even the world! Besides, I would not only pass myself off as an ambulance expert but also as an applications programmer of the first magnitude."

The following suggestions might be helpful in designing your program:

1. Design your program using the principles discussed in Module B.
2. If your compiler supports it, use structured BASIC commands.
3. Design your program to include the following output options:
   a. Print the entire Table C.1.
   b. Terminate the printing of Table C.1 as soon as the total cost per period begins to increase.
   c. Omit the printing of Table C.1 and just print the best replacement period and its associated total cost per period.
4. The figures given for operating cost in the first year, increase in operating cost, and percent depreciation factor are *estimates* of actual values. In reality, these estimates can be in error. Design your program to perform and output **sensitivity analysis** based on ±20-percent errors as shown in Table C.2. Three tables of this type should be printed for each model: the first for a −20-percent error in the depreciation factor; the second for the expected depreciation factor; and the third for a +20-percent error in the depreciation factor. This means that depreciation factors of 16 percent, 20 percent, and 24 percent would be considered for the $15,000 ambulance. Better yet, let the user specify through data input just what ±

TABLE C.2   *Best Replacement Cycle and Associated Total Cost per Year*

|  | −20% ERROR IN OPERAT- ING COST INCREASE | EXPECTED OPERAT- ING COST INCREASE | +20% ERROR IN OPERAT- ING COST INCREASE |
|---|---|---|---|
| −20% ERROR IN FIRST YEAR OPERATING COST | XX YEARS $XXXXX | XX YEARS $XXXXX | XX YEARS $XXXXX |
| EXPECTED FIRST YEAR OPERATING | XX YEARS $XXXXX | XX YEARS $XXXXX | XX YEARS $XXXXX |
| +20% ERROR IN FIRST YEAR OPERATING COST | XX YEARS $XXXXX | XX YEARS $XXXXX | XX YEARS $XXXXX |

percent error is to be considered. Note that each cell in Table C.2 contains the best replacement cycle and its associated total cost per year (based on column 7 in Table C.1) given the operating cost parameters for that cell.

5.  Write a short report to answer the following questions:
    a.  How often should the $15,000 ambulance be replaced?
    b.  On the average, how much would such a replacement policy cost per year?
    c.  Compared to the best cost in part b, how much more would it cost per year to replace the ambulance every 4 years? every 10 years?
    d.  How would you characterize the $10,000 ambulance compared to the $15,000 ambulance?
    e.  How often and at what average cost per year should you replace the $10,000 ambulance?
    f.  Which ambulance do you recommend? Should you consider factors or criteria other than financial?
    g.  Which ambulance would you recommend if the administrator's policy was to replace an ambulance every 8 years? Every 5 years?
6.  You might try using the same computer program to analyze replacement periods and costs for some popular automobiles. Try to get good estimates for input data by asking around, class discussion, and personal experience. Don't forget to include the effects of differences in gas mileage. Any surprises?

# C.2
# CASE II: AUTOMATED REPAIR AND MAINTENANCE SYSTEM (ARMS)

A municipality maintains a fleet of vehicles, including automobiles, vans, trucks, buses, pay loaders, and others. Because of energy problems, rising prices, and wages, the costs of running this fleet continue to rise.

Ms. Sterlina Moss, the newly hired manager of the physical plant, has the responsibility of reviewing the condition of all assets within the municipality, including the fleet. For the fleet, she must formulate a replacement policy on these vehicles as well as evaluate lease versus buy financial alternatives.

Currently the municipality has its own maintenance and repair facility. When a vehicle needs maintenance, a work order is filled out specifying the problem. When work is completed, the parts cost and labor cost are listed on this form so the department owning the vehicle can be billed.

Unfortunately, Ms. Moss has quite a task because records to date have been maintained manually. Worse yet, these records are incomplete: an inventory of each vehicle is not available and no history of operating costs for each vehicle can be determined.

Luckily, she remembered an article in the newspaper about college students helping local businesses find solutions to some of their management problems. So she contacted Professor Harvey Core, who teaches a systems analysis course, and arranged to have a team of students investigate the maintenance facility. Ms. Moss, however, placed two constraints on the team:

1.  Although the municipality does have a computer, no funds would be available for additional hardware.
2.  A minimum amount of time should be required of the maintenance supervisor in providing data for any automated system.

During the previous school term, a team of Professor Core's students studied the problem and submitted the accompanying report, entitled Automated Repair and Maintenance System (ARMS). This school term Professor Core has instructed you (or your team) to write the necessary BASIC program(s).

## Automated Repair and Maintenance System (ARMS)

I.   Objectives
   A.   Produce a monthly report of vehicles owned by the municipality.
   B.   Produce a cumulative record of maintenance cost incurred for each vehicle.
II.  System Flowchart. The design of the new maintenance reporting system is shown pictorially in the system flowchart of Figure C.1.
III. Reports (see print charts)
   A.   Edit run. Lists all transactions to be processed within the month
   B.   Vehicle inventory. Lists all vehicles within municipality
   C.   Vehicle by department. Lists vehicles owned by each department
IV.  Files
   A.   Vehicle Master File

| FIELD | DESCRIPTION |
|-------|-------------|
| 1 | Vehicle number |
| 2 | Department number |
| 3 | Type of vehicle (code) |
| 4 | Manufacturer (code) |
| 5 | Year made |
| 6 | Year acquired |

|    |    |
|----|----|
| 7  | Purchase cost |
| 8  | Odometer reading at date of purchase |
| 9  | Odometer reading at start of year |
| 10 | Current odometer reading |
| 11 | Cumulative parts cost, previous year (including no cost from current year) |
| 12 | Cumulative labor cost, previous year (including no cost from current year) |
| 13 | Year to date part cost |
| 14 | Year to date labor cost |
| 15 | Current period, part cost |
| 16 | Current period, labor cost |

B. Transaction File. Monthly Maintenance Transactions

| RECORD TYPE | FIELD | DESCRIPTION |
|-------------|-------|-------------|
| New vehicle (add record to file) | 1 | Vehicle number |
|  | 2 | Action code = 1 |
|  | 3 | Department number |
|  | 4 | Type of vehicle (code) |
|  | 5 | Manufacturer (code) |
|  | 6 | Year made |
|  | 7 | Year acquired |
|  | 8 | Purchase cost |
|  | 9 | Original odometer reading |
|  | 10 | Odometer reading at start of year |
|  | 11 | Current odometer reading |
| Sold vehicle (delete record from file) | 1 | Vehicle number |
|  | 2 | Action code = 2 |
| Maintained vehicle (update cost information in existing record) | 1 | Vehicle number |
|  | 2 | Action code = 3 |
|  | 3 | Current odometer reading |
|  | 4 | Current cost, parts |
|  | 5 | Current cost, labor |

V. Program Specifications
   A. Edit and Sort Phase
      *Input.* Transaction file
      *Process*
      1. Sort record into vehicle number sequence
      2. Edit checks
         a. Vehicle number must be in ascending order sequence
         b. No vehicle number is greater than 975
         c. Valid action codes are 1, 2, and 3 only
         d. If action code = 3, the current cost of parts should not be greater than $500 nor the current cost of labor greater than $250
      *Printed Output.* Edit report (see print layout). All transactions are listed; however, place an asterisk in front of any record that has an error
      *Other Output.* Valid transaction file (see layout of input file). Any record with error is not to be placed on this file

FIGURE C.1    *System Flowchart*

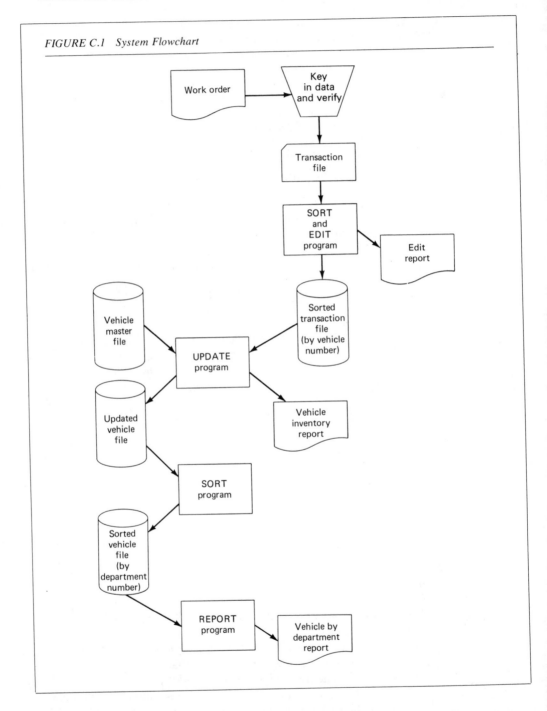

B.  Update Phase
    *Input*
    1.  Transaction file
    2.  Vehicle master file
    3.  Code tables
    *Process*
    1.  Action code 1. Add record to file; set cost fields to zero
    2.  Action code 2. Remove entire record from vehicle file
    3.  Action code 3.
        a.  Add current cost of parts in the transaction file to year-to-date cost of parts in the master file.
        b.  Replace current cost of parts in the master file by the current cost of parts in the transaction file.
        c.  Add current cost of labor in the transaction file to year-to-date cost of labor in the master file.
        d.  Replace current cost of labor in the master file by the current cost of labor in the transaction file.
        e.  Replace current odometer reading field in master file with current odometer reading from transaction file.
    *Printed Output.* Printed vehicle inventory report (see print layout)
    *Other Output.* Update master file
C.  Sort Phase
    *Input.* Vehicle master file (vehicle number sequence)
    *Process.* Sort on department number
    *Other Output.* Vehicle master file (department number sequence)
D.  Report Phase
    *Input*
    1.  Vehicle master file
    2.  Code table
    *Process*
    1.  Cost field in output report. Includes total of parts and labor
    2.  Cost per mile. Represents total costs (parts and labor) since acquisition divided by total miles since acquisition
    *Printed Output.* Vehicle by department report (see print chart)
        For all printed output, the following descriptions should be used in place of code numbers.

| TYPE OF VEHICLE | | MANUFACTURER | | DEPARTMENT | |
| --- | --- | --- | --- | --- | --- |
| CODE | DESCRIPTION | CODE | NAME | CODE | NAME |
| 1 | Pickup | 1 | Ford | 1 | Land and grounds |
| 2 | Sedan | 2 | Plymouth | 2 | Administration |
| 3 | Jeep | 3 | International | 3 | Recreation |
| 4 | Forklift | 4 | Willys | | |
| 5 | Van | 5 | Chevrolet | | |
| 6 | Trailer | 6 | Baker | | |
| 7 | Tractor | | | | |

PROGRAM TITLE _ARMS_

PROGRAMMER OR DOCUMENTALIST _____

CHART TITLE _EDIT RUN_

|  |  |
|---|---|
| 1 | EDIT RUN |
| 2 |  |
| 3 | Input record image → { XXXXXXXXXXXXXXXXXX |
| 4 | XXXXXXXXXXXXXXXXXX |
| 5 | XXXXXXXXXXXXXXXXXX |
| 6 |  |
| 7 | END OF RUN SUMMARY |
| 8 |  |
| 9 |  |
| 10 | NUMBER OF RECORDS    XXXXX |
| 11 | VALID    XXXXX |
| 12 | INVALID    XXXXX |
| 13 |  |
| 14 |  |
| 15 |  |

PROGRAM TITLE _____ ARMS

PROGRAMMER OR DOCUMENTALIST _____

CHART TITLE _____ VEHICLE INVENTORY

|  |  |
|---|---|
| 1 | VEHICLE INVENTORY |
| 2 | REPORTING PERIOD |
| 3 | XX/XX/XX TO XX/XX/XX |
| 4 |  |
| 5 | VEHICLE  VEHICLE    MANUFACTURER    DEPARTMENT    CURRENT COSTS   YEAR TO DATE COSTS   COST SINCE PURCHASE |
| 6 | NUMBER   TYPE |
| 7 |                                                          XXXX   XXX   XXXX |
| 8 | XXXX   AAAAAAAA   AAAAAAAAAAAAA   AAAAAAAAAAAAAAAA   XXXX   XXXX   XXXX |
| 9 | XXXX   AAAAAAAA |
| 10 |  |
| 11 | .   .                  .   .   . |
| 12 | .   . |
| 13 | .   . |
| 14 |                                   TOTALS  XXXXX   XXXXX   XXXXX |
| 15 |  |
| 16 |  |
| 17 |  |
| 18 |  |
| 19 | END OF RUN SUMMARY |
| 20 |  |
| 21 | RECORDS IN-MASTER   XXX |
| 22 |  |
| 23 | TRANSACTIONS PROCESSED |
| 24 | ADDS   XXX |
| 25 | DELETES   XXX |
| 26 | UPDATES (XXX) |
| 27 |  |
| 28 | RECORDS OUT-MASTER   XXX |
| 29 |  |
| 30 |  |

PROGRAM TITLE _____ ARMS

PROGRAMMER OR DOCUMENTALIST _____

CHART TITLE _____ VEHICLE BY DEPARTMENT

|  |  |
|---|---|
| 1 | VEHICLE BY DEPARTMENT REPORT |
| 2 | PERIOD XX/XX/XX TO XX/XX/XX |
| 3 | Note: New page for |
| 4 | each department |
| 5 | DEPARTMENT  AAAAAAAAAAAAAAAA |
| 6 |  |
| 7 |  |
| 8 |                          C O S T S |
| 9 | VEHICLE    VEHICLE    CURRENT    YEAR TO    SINCE |
| 10 | NUMBER     TYPE       MONTH      DATE       PURCHASE |
| 11 |  |
| 12 | XXXX   AAAAAAAA   XXXX   XXXX   XXXX |
| 13 | XXXX   AAAAAAAA   XXXX   XXXX   XXXX |
| 14 |  |
| 15 |     ↓         ↓         ↓        ↓        ↓ |
| 16 | DEPARTMENT TOTALS   XXXXX   XXXXX   XXXXX |
| 17 |  |
| 18 |  |

MASTER FILE DATA

Fields

| 1 | 2 | 3 | 4 | 5 | 6 | 7 | 8 | 9 | 10 | 11 | 12 | 13 | 14 | 15 | 16 |
|---|---|---|---|---|---|---|---|---|----|----|----|----|----|----|----|
| 593 | 1 | 2 | 1 | 78 | 78 | 4000 | 00000 | 15000 | 15000 | 0000 | 0000 | 0000 | 0000 | 0000 | 0000 |
| 613 | 3 | 7 | 3 | 74 | 76 | 10000 | 06000 | 06000 | 06000 | 0000 | 0000 | 0000 | 0000 | 0000 | 0000 |
| 645 | 3 | 3 | 3 | 70 | 70 | 3500 | 00000 | 40000 | 40000 | 0000 | 0000 | 0000 | 0000 | 0000 | 0000 |
| 659 | 2 | 2 | 2 | 79 | 79 | 5000 | 00000 | 00000 | 00000 | | | | | | |
| 667 | 2 | 2 | 5 | 75 | 77 | 2500 | 22000 | 22000 | 22000 | | | | | | |
| 668 | 3 | 2 | 5 | 76 | 76 | 4200 | 00000 | 30000 | 30000 | | | | | | |
| 674 | 1 | 4 | 6 | 77 | 77 | 8000 | 00000 | 01200 | 01200 | | | | | | |
| 676 | 1 | 2 | 1 | 78 | 78 | 4500 | 00000 | 15000 | 15000 | | | | | | |
| 677 | 3 | 2 | 5 | 78 | 78 | 4500 | 00000 | 12000 | 12000 | | | | | | |
| 678 | 3 | 6 | 3 | 69 | 69 | 6200 | 00000 | 65000 | 65000 | | | | | | |
| 679 | 1 | 3 | 4 | 65 | 65 | 2900 | 00000 | 85000 | 85000 | | | | | | |
| 688 | 2 | 1 | 1 | 70 | 75 | 3600 | 45000 | 45000 | 45000 | | | | | | |
| 689 | 2 | 5 | 5 | 72 | 76 | 3000 | 33000 | 33000 | 33000 | | | | | | |
| 692 | 3 | 1 | 3 | 75 | 77 | 3200 | 21000 | 21000 | 21000 | | | | | | |
| 695 | 1 | 7 | 3 | 76 | 76 | 10150 | 00000 | 03100 | 03100 | | | | | | |
| 696 | 2 | 2 | 2 | 79 | 79 | 4800 | 00000 | 00000 | 00000 | | | | | | |
| 699 | 1 | 1 | 5 | 61 | 61 | 2600 | 00000 | 78000 | 78000 | | | | | | |
| 798 | 1 | 3 | 4 | 70 | 72 | 2900 | 48000 | 48000 | 48000 | | | | | | |
| 804 | 1 | 4 | 4 | 73 | 74 | 2500 | 06000 | 06000 | 06000 | | | | | | |
| 805 | 3 | 2 | 1 | 75 | 75 | 2300 | 00000 | 52000 | 52000 | | | | | | |
| 806 | 1 | 6 | 6 | 78 | 78 | 8000 | 00650 | 00650 | 00650 | | | | | | |
| 807 | 2 | 2 | 5 | 77 | 78 | 3950 | 17000 | 17000 | 17000 | | | | | | |
| 838 | 1 | 5 | 5 | 77 | 79 | 4000 | 09000 | 09000 | 09000 | | | | | | |
| 841 | 3 | 1 | 1 | 76 | 79 | 3700 | 26000 | 26000 | 26000 | 0000 | 0000 | 0000 | 0000 | 0000 | 0000 |

TRANSACTION FILE DATA—MONTH 1

Fields

| 1 | 2 | 3 | 4 | 5 | 6 | 7 | 8 | 9 | 10 | 11 |
|---|---|---|---|---|---|---|---|---|----|----|
| 699 | 2 |       |     |     |    |    |      |   |   |   |
| 842 | 1 | 2     | 2   | 1   | 80 | 80 | 5000 | 0 | 0 | 0 |
| 844 | 1 | 3     | 1   | 5   | 80 | 80 | 6000 | 0 | 0 | 0 |
| 645 | 3 | 42000 | 52  | 75  |    |    |      |   |   |   |
| 806 | 3 | 775   | 10  | 10  |    |    |      |   |   |   |
| 659 | 3 | 3275  | 150 | 60  |    |    |      |   |   |   |
| 692 | 3 | 25788 | 40  | 25  |    |    |      |   |   |   |
| 613 | 3 | 6250  | 35  | 50  |    |    |      |   |   |   |
| 798 | 3 | 52000 | 95  | 125 |    |    |      |   |   |   |
| 841 | 4 | 27500 | 14  | 45  |    |    |      |   |   |   |
| 979 | 3 | 85400 | 37  | 350 |    |    |      |   |   |   |
| 674 | 3 | 1200  | 625 | 125 |    |    |      |   |   |   |

TRANSACTION FILE DATA—MONTH 2

Fields

| 1 | 2 | 3 | 4 | 5 | 6 | 7 | 8 | 9 | 10 | 11 |
|---|---|---|---|---|---|---|---|---|----|----|
| 678 | 2 |       |     |    |   |   |   |   |   |   |
| 677 | 3 | 13900 | 150 | 75 |   |   |   |   |   |   |
| 688 | 3 | 48375 | 25  | 50 |   |   |   |   |   |   |
| 593 | 3 | 17275 | 175 | 70 |   |   |   |   |   |   |
| 667 | 3 | 22500 | 45  | 50 |   |   |   |   |   |   |
| 804 | 3 | 6700  | 15  | 10 |   |   |   |   |   |   |

## C.3
## CASE III: INVENTORY SIMULATION ASSOCIATES, INC.

Fresh out of college, you have been hired by a dynamic management consulting firm called Inventory Simulation Associates, Inc., otherwise known as ISA. As the name of the firm suggests, it specializes in performing inventory simulations for clients in government, nonprofit institutions, industry, and other organizations willing to pay stiff consulting fees.

In your job interview with ISA you passed yourself off as an expert in inventory theory and simulation, among other things, based on the strength of a course in each area. So, in their infinite wisdom, the management of ISA has assigned you to study the inventory policies of Gotham City Hospital's (GCH) blood bank. Your first act in tackling this problem was to review your class notes on inventory theory and simulation, portions of which follow.

An **inventory** may be thought of as a stock of an item (material, machine, spare part, money, consumable product, and so on) that gets "added to" and "depleted from" over time. In retail and nonprofit environments, inventories improve the degree of customer service by absorbing variabilities in customer demands and replenishment times. For example, the inventory of blood in a hospital serves to satisfy a critical need whenever patients require (demand) blood. In manufacturing environments, inventories smooth the variability in work force levels. For example, the same number of workers can be used during slow periods of demand as during busy periods of demand by building up inventories during slow periods and depleting inventories during busy periods.

Inventories are pervasive and expensive to maintain. The U.S. business investment in physical materials inventory amounts to more than $200 billion. For General Motors Corporation alone, this investment runs over $4 billion. For the reasons mentioned, procedures to best manage inventories are topics of great interest to organizations.

In managing an inventory, two decisions need to be made: (1) When should an order be placed to replenish inventory? (2) What should be the size of this order?

In recent years, mathematical approaches to answering these questions have been very successful. One such approach, the **economic order quantity (EOQ) inventory model,** specifies the *order quantity* (Q) and *reorder point* (R, the inventory level below which a replenishment order is placed) that minimizes total inventory cost per time period.

*Total inventory cost* is defined as the sum of ordering cost, carrying cost, and shortage cost. *Ordering cost* is the cost associated with placing a replenishment order. It includes the clerical and administrative costs associated with processing, expediting, receiving, inspecting, and storing the order. *Carrying costs* are made up of the explicit and implicit costs of maintaining and owning the inventory. Explicit costs include the cost of storage space, handling costs, insurance, taxes, utility costs, and costs of administering inventory and maintaining records. A significant implicit component of carrying cost is called the *opportunity cost*. This cost reflects the rate of return that a company might expect to earn on the money tied up in inventory. For example, if General Motors could invest its $4 billion inventory in Treasury Notes yielding 9-percent interest per year, then it could earn $360 million in one year. This $360 million represents their opportunity cost (lost income). *Shortage cost* includes the costs of running out of stock when items are requested. These costs are difficult to estimate, but include costs relating to backorders, lost sales, ill will, and so on.

**Simulation** is a methodology for conducting experiments using a mathematical model of the real system. It is primarily concerned with describing or predicting the behavior of a real system. Its usual purpose is either to design a new system or to modify behavior in an existing system. Simulation is particularly useful either as a low-cost substitute for actual experimentation on the real system or as the only approach for studying the behavior of a proposed system. For example, computer programs have been designed to simulate traffic flow systems in cities for the purpose of establishing the best configuration of computer-controlled traffic signals.

A type of simulation called **Monte Carlo simulation** is used to reconstruct the behavior of phenomena that can be described according to rules of probability. For example, suppose that the number of days between the placement and receipt of an inventory order (called *lead time*) is described by the following:

| Lead Time (Number of Days) | Relative Frequency (Probability) |
|:---:|:---:|
| 1 | 0.2 |
| 2 | 0.5 |
| 3 | 0.3 |
|   | 1.0 |

This says that the probability of receiving an order one day after placing it is 0.2, or that this occurs 20 percent of the time. Similarly, a lead time of 2 days occurs 50 percent of the time; a lead time of 3 days occurs the remaining 30 percent of the time.

One way to simulate this process is to mark 10 poker chips as follows: write the digit 1 on two chips, the digit 2 on five chips, and the digit 3 on three chips. Mix these up and select a poker chip without looking. Chances are 2 in 10 (probability = 0.2) that you select a chip marked with a 1; 5 in 10 that you select a chip marked with a 2; and 3 in 10 that you select a chip marked with a 3. Since these probabilities are identical to the probabilities describing the real process, it follows that we can use the poker chips to reconstruct or simulate the lead times.

"Poker chips" in BASIC programming are created by using the RND function introduced in Section 9.1. Its use can generate a uniformly distributed integer random number between 0 and 99 inclusive.

By a uniformly distributed integer random number between 0 and 99 we mean that the likelihood (probability) that any one number is generated is the same as any other number. To illustrate the simulation of lead times by this approach, consider the following:

| Lead Time | Random Number Range | |
|:---:|:---:|:---|
| 1 | 0–19 | ←——— 20-percent probability |
| 2 | 20–69 | ←——— 50-percent probability |
| 3 | 70–99 | ←——— 30-percent probability |

Thus, we assign 20 random numbers to a lead time of 1 day, the next 50 random numbers to a lead time of 2 days, and the last 30 random numbers to a lead time of 3 days. If the computer generates, say, the random number 32, then we say that a lead time of 2 days has been simulated, since the probability of getting a random number in the interval 20–69 is 50 percent, the same as the probability of a 2-day lead time. You should confirm that the five random numbers below correspond to the simulated lead times that are indicated. (It's like having 100 poker chips.)

| Sample Random Numbers Generated by Computer | Simulated Days of Lead Time |
|:---:|:---:|
| 90 | 3 |
| 15 | 1 |
| 60 | 2 |
| 70 | 3 |
| 81 | 3 |

Alternatively, instead of converting the *real* random number in the range 0 to 1 to an *integer* random number between 0 and 99 inclusive, we can work with the real random number itself. In this case, we express the lead time probabilities as follows:

| Lead Time | Probability | Cumulative Probability |
|:---:|:---:|:---:|
| 1 | 0.2 | 0.2 |
| 2 | 0.5 | 0.7 |
| 3 | 0.3 | 1.0 |

Now, if the generated random number is less than 0.2, we say that a lead time of 1 day has occurred; if the random number is 0.2 or greater but less than 0.7, then a lead time of 2 days has been simulated; and if the random number is 0.7 or above, then we have a 3-day lead time.

After studying these notes, you made an appointment with the head administrator at GCH. After lengthy talks with the administrator and staff, you came away with the following facts:

1. The management of blood by blood banks is an important function of health care delivery systems. A *blood bank* within the hospital performs the functions of procurement, storage, processing, and distribution of blood. The hospital's blood bank places replenishment orders with a regional blood bank that serves member hospitals.
2. Inventory costs have been estimated as follows:

Ordering cost: $50 per order
Carrying cost: $0.10 per unit per day
Shortage cost: $2 per unit backordered

The shortage cost reflects a loan arrangement with the regional blood bank in Gotham City whereby if GCH incurs a temporary shortage of blood, it can *immediately* borrow units at a cost of $2.00 per unit. The agreement also specifies the replacement of the borrowed blood units when GCH receives its next replenishment supply.

3. GCH places replenishment orders with the regional blood bank for 400 units whenever its inventory level drops below 300 units. A study of the records shows that the ordered blood always arrives 2 days after the order. Thus, lead time is 2 days and, according to hospital inventory policy, R = 300 and Q = 400.

4. A study of daily demand (requirements by patients) for units of blood over a recent 200-day period shows the following:

| Number of Units Demanded Daily | Midpoint Demand | Number of Days in Which Specified Demand Occurred | Corresponding Relative Frequency (Probability) | Random Number Range |
|---|---|---|---|---|
| 0 but under 50 | | 0 | | |
| 50 but under 70 | 60 | 14 | 0.07 | 0–6 |
| 70 but under 90 | 80 | 28 | 0.14 | 7–20 |
| 90 but under 110 | 100 | 36 | 0.18 | 21–38 |
| 110 but under 130 | 120 | 58 | 0.29 | 39–67 |
| 130 but under 150 | 140 | 32 | 0.16 | 68–83 |
| 150 but under 170 | 160 | 22 | 0.11 | 84–94 |
| 170 but under 190 | 180 | 10 | 0.05 | 95–99 |
| 190 or over | | 0 | | |
| | | 200 | 1.00 | |

Thus 7 percent (14/200) of the days demand was between 50 and 70 units, 14 percent (28/200) of the days demand was between 70 and 90 units, and so on. For simulation purposes we can say that 7 percent is the probability of 60 units, 14 percent the probability of 80 units, 18 percent the probability of 100 units, and so on. Note that the random number ranges are consistent with these probabilities.

Based on the above information, it seemed like a good idea to get a better feel for the process by "hand" simulating a 20-day period. This is shown in Table C.3.

Based on this 20-day simulation, certain characteristics about the process came to light:

1. To simulate Day 1, we arbitrarily set the beginning inventory level to some "reasonable" figure (500 in this case). Then we generate a random number to simulate demand for that day. The random number 17 translates into a demand of 80 units. This gives us an ending inventory of 420 for Day 1. The carrying cost of $42 is based on the *physical ending* inventory (420 × 0.10). Since ending inventory is above the reorder point given by R = 300, we do not place an order in Day 1. Thus, order cost is zero. No shortages were incurred in Day 1; so shortage cost also is zero. This gives a total cost of $42 for Day 1.

2. The beginning inventory for the next day is based on the ending inventory for the previous day; however, when the ending inventory is negative (units have been backordered), then the beginning physical inventory for the next day is zero. (See Days 9, 11, 12.)

TABLE C.3  *Inventory Hand Simulation*

| DAY | UNITS OF BEGINNING INVENTORY | UNITS RECEIVED | RANDOM NUMBER FOR DEMAND | UNITS OF DEMAND | UNITS OF ENDING INVENTORY | CARRYING COST IN $ | ORDERING COST IN $ | SHORTAGE COST IN $ | TOTAL COST IN $ |
|---|---|---|---|---|---|---|---|---|---|
| 1 | 500 | 0 | 17 | 80 | 420 | 42 | 0 | 0 | 42 |
| 2 | 420 | 0 | 25 | 100 | 320 | 32 | 0 | 0 | 32 |
| 3 | 320 | 0 | 37 | 100 | 220 | 22 | 50 | 0 | 72 |
| 4 | 220 | 0 | 65 | 120 | 100 | 10 | 0 | 0 | 10 |
| 5 | 100 | 0 | 23 | 100 | 0 | 0 | 0 | 0 | 0 |
| 6 | 0 | 400 | 72 | 140 | 260 | 26 | 50 | 0 | 76 |
| 7 | 260 | 0 | 98 | 180 | 80 | 8 | 0 | 0 | 8 |
| 8 | 80 | 0 | 96 | 180 | -100 | 0 | 0 | 200 | 200 |
| 9 | 0 | 300 | 88 | 160 | 140 | 14 | 50 | 0 | 64 |
| 10 | 140 | 0 | 92 | 160 | -20 | 0 | 0 | 40 | 40 |
| 11 | 0 | 0 | 30 | 100 | -120 | 0 | 0 | 200 | 200 |
| 12 | 0 | 280 | 28 | 100 | 180 | 18 | 50 | 0 | 68 |
| 13 | 180 | 0 | 9 | 80 | 100 | 10 | 0 | 0 | 10 |
| 14 | 100 | 0 | 15 | 80 | 20 | 2 | 0 | 0 | 2 |
| 15 | 20 | 400 | 12 | 80 | 340 | 34 | 0 | 0 | 34 |
| 16 | 340 | 0 | 55 | 120 | 220 | 22 | 50 | 0 | 72 |
| 17 | 220 | 0 | 5 | 60 | 160 | 16 | 0 | 0 | 16 |
| 18 | 160 | 0 | 2 | 60 | 100 | 10 | 0 | 0 | 10 |
| 19 | 100 | 400 | 50 | 120 | 380 | 38 | 0 | 0 | 38 |
| 20 | 380 | 0 | 20 | 80 | 300 | 30 | 0 | 0 | 30 |
| Total | 3540 | — | — | 2200 | — | 334 | 250 | 440 | 1024 |
| Average | 177 | — | — | 110 | — | 16.70 | 12.50 | 22.00 | 51.20 |

3. An order is triggered whenever ending inventory drops below R = 300, providing no order is currently outstanding. In other words, *by policy a maximum of one outstanding order is allowed at any one time.* When an order is launched, a $50 cost is incurred. (See Days 3, 6, 9, 12, 16.) The order for Q = 400 is placed at the end of the day. It takes two days for the order to arrive, so it is available by the beginning of the third day following the order. For example, an order for 400 units is placed at the end of Day 3, it arrives at the end of Day 5, and can be utilized in Day 6. Thus, Day 6 has an entry of 400 in the column labeled ''Units Received.''

4. A shortage cost of $2 per unit is incurred whenever ending inventory is negative. (See Days 8, 10, 11.) Note that backordered units must be replaced as soon as replenishment arrives. For example, the 100 units backordered in Day 8 were ''returned'' to the regional blood bank in Day 9. Thus only 300 units (400 − 100) were received in Day 9. Take care not to double count the cost of backordered units. For example, we were 100 units short in Day 11, which gives a shortage cost of $200 for that day. A common error here is to compute this cost as $240 based on the cumulative number of backorders at the end of this day (120). This would double count the cost of 20 units short in Day 10.

5. Based on this short simulation, the hospital's current inventory policy of R = 300 and Q = 400 results in the following average cost estimates:

Carrying cost per day = $16.70
Ordering cost per day =   12.50
Shortage cost per day =   22.00
Total cost per day        $51.20

At this time, certain realizations came to mind: First, to get a better cost per day estimate, I should simulate many more days than 20. This would give me more confidence that my estimates are accurate. It's kind of like estimating whether a coin is balanced by flipping it 20 times versus, say, 1000 times. A simulation of 1000 days would be preferable; so I'd better computerize this process if I don't want to be a glutton for punishment. Second, it makes sense to try different R − Q combinations. Maybe I can suggest a better inventory policy?

Further thought resulted in the following additional programming suggestions:

1. Incorporate the principles discussed in Module B.
2. Use structured BASIC commands if possible.
3. Input the ranges and increments for R and Q.
4. Reset the random number seed for each new R − Q combination. This ensures the same set of demands for each policy, thereby isolating the effect that a new R − Q has on total cost per day. (See Exercise 5 in Chapter 9.)
5. Store total cost per day in a two-dimensional array, where rows represent reorder points and columns represent order quantities.
6. Output of the inventory simulation table as in Table C.3 should be optional. It is primarily used to debug the program.
7. It might be of interest to vary the cost input data by, say, ±20 percent. This allows us to assess the sensitivity of the best inventory policy to errors in estimating the cost data.
**8. Modify the simulation to include probabilistic lead times. Use the lead time data on page C-13.

# Answers to Selected
# Follow-up Exercises

## Chapter 3

1. **(a)** Incorrect. First character must be a letter. **(b)** Depends on system. The proposed ANSI standard does not permit a space within a variable name. Most systems, however, would ignore this space. We recommend not using a space within a variable name, as it hinders readability. **(c)** Correct. **(d)** Incorrect. This is a numeric constant. **(e)** Correct. **(f)** Incorrect. No special characters permitted. **(g)** Incorrect. Too many characters. **(h)** Incorrect. First character must be a letter. **(i)** Incorrect. Numeric variable consists of a letter and optional digit. **(j)** Correct. **(k)** Incorrect. First character must be a letter; special characters not allowed.

2. **(a)** Incorrect. No commas permitted. **(b)** Correct. **(c)** Correct. **(d)** Normally the plus sign is not printed with a positive number. **(e)** Correct. **(f)** Incorrect. Minus sign is misplaced. **(g)** Correct. **(h)** Depends on system. The proposed ANSI standard does not permit a space within a numeric constant. Most systems, however, would ignore this space. We recommend not using a space within a numeric constant, as it hinders readability. **(i)** Incorrect. Asterisk doesn't belong. This describes multiplication of 5 and 7. **(j)** Incorrect. Exponent is too large. **(k)** Incorrect. Exponent should be an integer. **(l)** Incorrect. Quote after T is missing. **(m)** Correct, but not recommended. **(n)** Incorrect. $ is not allowed. **(o)** Incorrect. Number is too large in this format. Use 6.57890E10. **(p)** Incorrect. Number has too many digits to be represented as is. Use 154.613; otherwise the computer may truncate to 154.612.

3. **(a)** $-6.142E15$ **(b)** $-6142E12$ **(c)** $7E - 5$ **(d)** $7E - 5$

4. **(a)** 123000000000 **(b)** 123000000000 **(c)** 0.0456 **(d)** 0.0456

5. **(a)** Only one variable to left of equal symbol. Use 5 LET A = B + C
   **(b)** Two arithmetic operation symbols can not be together.
   **(c)** Variable must appear on left side of equal symbol. Use 15 LET A = 5
   **(d)** Allowed on some systems but not by the proposed ANSI standard. Use

   ```
   20 LET X = 5.3
   22 LET Y = 5.3
   ```

   **(e)** Cannot raise a negative value to a non-integral power.
   **(f)** Correct.

(g) Not allowed by proposed ANSI standard, but many systems allow omission of keyword LET.

6.  A = 7.4
    B = 9
    C = 5
    D = 81

7.  K = 3
    S = 15
    X = 5

8.  V = 5000
    C = 25000
    P = 10000

9.  85.7778

10. (a) 116 (b) 28 (c) 28 (d) 8.5 (e) 4 (f) 4 (g) 10.5

11. (a) X**(I + 1)
    (b) X**I + 1
    (c) S**2/(P − 1)
    (d) (X − A)**2/(P − 1)
    (e) (Y − 3**(X − 1) + 2)**5
    (f) (7 − X)**(1/2) or (7 − X)**.5 or SQR(7 − X) as described in Chapter 9 on page 258.
    (g) ((X − A)**2/(P − 1))**.5 or *SQR*((X − A)**2/(P − 1)) as described in Chapter 9 on page 258.

12. Eliminate line 30 and change line 40 to

          40 LET R = (15*C + 250)*S

13. Unique to each system.

14. Unique to each system.

15. Unique to each system.

16. Unique to each system.

17. (a) PRINT "A=";A
    (b) PRINT "B=";B
    (c) PRINT "QUANTITY   PRICE   REVENUE"
    (d) PRINT A,B,C
    (e) PRINT "MY NAME IS"

19  (a) $a = \dfrac{i}{12} \cdot (p - d - t) \cdot \left( \dfrac{(1 + i/12)^m}{(1 + i/12)^m - 1} \right)$

*Chapter 4*

1. (a) 10 PRINT "ENTER SOCIAL SECURITY NUMBER AND AGE"
      20 INPUT S,A
   (b) 10 PRINT "ENTER PRINCIPAL";
      20 INPUT P
      30 PRINT "ENTER NUMBER OF YEARS";
      40 INPUT N
      50 PRINT "ENTER INTEREST RATE";
      60 INPUT I

2. Unique to system.

3. 7220000, a logic error given by incorrect data input.

4. 05 PRINT "COST PER CREDIT";
   10 INPUT C
   15 PRINT "ENROLLMENT";
   18 INPUT S
      :
      :

5. 05 PRINT "PLEASE ENTER COST PER CREDIT, ENROLLMENT,"
   07 PRINT "FEES, AND AVERAGE CREDITS";
   10 INPUT C,S,F,A
   20 LET R = (A*C + F)*S
      :
      :

7. Eliminate lines 10 and 20 and replace line 10 with

      010 READ E1, E2, E3

   No, although placing all these data items in one DATA statement is more efficient.

8. "OUT OF DATA" error message would be printed when line 30 is executed. Run would terminate at that point.

9. Eliminate lines 5 and 7; change line 10 to

   10 READ C,S,F,A
   12 DATA 80,6000,250,15
      :
      :

11. a, b, d, e

12.  →10        10        10
        20        20        20
        30        30        30
        40       →40        40
        50        50        50
                   →

**13.** A = 100   B = 150

(OUT OF DATA error message)

**14.** **(a)** 10 READ M$,D,4
  20 DATA JULY,4,1976
 **(b)** READ F$,R$,S
  DATA NEWMAN,"INSTRUCTOR-1",14000

**15.** **(a)** INPUT M$,D,Y   ?JULY,4,1976
 **(b)** INPUT F$,R$,S   ?NEWMAN,"INSTRUCTOR–1",14000

note

**16.** 60 PRINT "ƀƀƀƀNAME:ƀ";N$
 70 PRINT "ƀƀƀHOURS:";H
 80 PRINT "PAY RATE:ƀ$";R

**17.** **(a)** Logic error—numeric value (10) read into string variable (B$). Execution error— attempt to read string value (FALSE) into numeric variable (C). **(b)** Logic error—only COS-MIC is stored in A$. **(c)** Unique to system.

**18.** Unique to system.

**19.** 05 PRINT "COLLEGE NAME, COST PER CREDIT AND ENROLLMENT";
 10 INPUT N$,C,S
 20 LET R = (15*C + 250)*S
 30 PRINT "REVENUE FOR ";N$;" IS PROJECTED AT $";R
 40 END

**21.** **(a)** 25 PRINT TAB(24);"($)";TAB(37);"($)"
 **(b)** 20 PRINT "CODE";TAB(10); . . .
  30 READ A$,C,S,C$
  ⋮
  70 PRINT C$,TAB(10); . . .
  80 DATA "SACRAMENTO",30,12000,"SC105"
  90 END

In the printed output, the label CODE now appears in columns 1 to 4 of print line 2 and the code SC105 appears in columns 1 to 5 of print line 4.

**22.**

| | 1 | 2 | 3 | 4 | 5 | 6 | 7 | 8 | 9 | 10 | 11 | 12 | 13 | 14 | 15 | 16 | 17 | 18 | 19 | 20 | 21 | 22 | 23 | 24 | 25 | 26 | 27 | 28 | 29 | 30 |
|---|---|---|---|---|---|---|---|---|---|---|---|---|---|---|---|---|---|---|---|---|---|---|---|---|---|---|---|---|---|---|
| 1 | 5 | 0 | | | | | | | | | | | | | | | | | | | | | | | -1 | 0 | 0 | | | |
| 2 | 5 | 0 | | | | | | | | | | | | | | | | | | | | | | | -1 | 0 | 0 | | | |
| 3 | 5 | 0 | | | | | | | | | | | | | | | | | | | | | | | - | 0 | 0 | | | |
| 4 | | | | | | | | | | | | | | | | | 5 | . | 7 | | | | | | | | | | | |
| 5 | | | | | | | | | | | | | | | | -1 | 0 | 0 | | | | | | | | | | | | |
| 6 | | | | | | | | | | | | | | | R | E | 0 | | | | | | | | | | | | | |
| 7 | | | R | E | 0 | | | | | | | | | | | | | | | | | | | | | | | | | |
| 8 | | | | | | | | R | E | 0 | | | | | | | | | | | | | | | | | | | | |
| 9 | R | E | 0 | | | | | | | | | | | | | | | | | | | | | | | | | | | |

24. Data values change each time a different person comes up to a teller. An interactive program thus avoids having to change LET or DATA statements for each new person.

25. Eliminate lines 250 and 260.
    *First alternative:*

    > 295 LET R = .015

    *Second alternative:*

    > 295 READ R
    > 297 DATA .015

    *Third alternative:*

    > 300 LET A = P*(1.015)**N

    If the bank is likely to change the interest rate once or twice a year, then the first or second alternative is easier than the third alternative.

# Chapter 5

1. (a) True. (b) False. (c) True. (d) True. (e) False. (f) True.

2. Flowchart for Example 5.1 (see next page).

3. Delete line 200, replace line 240 by

    > 240 READ S$,N$,S,B

    and replace line 901 by

    > 901 DATA "266-62-8431","B. FLINTSTONE",4150,150

4. (a) 10 IF C >= 12 THEN 500
   (b) 20 IF P$ = "WRENCH" THEN 750
   (c) 25 IF F+V<P THEN 100
   (d) 30 IF M$ = A$ THEN 50
       40 IF M$ <> B$ THEN 80 ⎫
       50 ...                  ⎬ Note how GO TO's are
        :                      ⎭ suppressed.
       80 ...
        :

   (e) 40 IF A < 25 THEN 75 ⎫ Note how GO TO's are
       45 IF A > 35 THEN 75 ⎭ suppressed.
       50 ...
        :
       75 ...
        :

*Flowchart for Example 5.1*

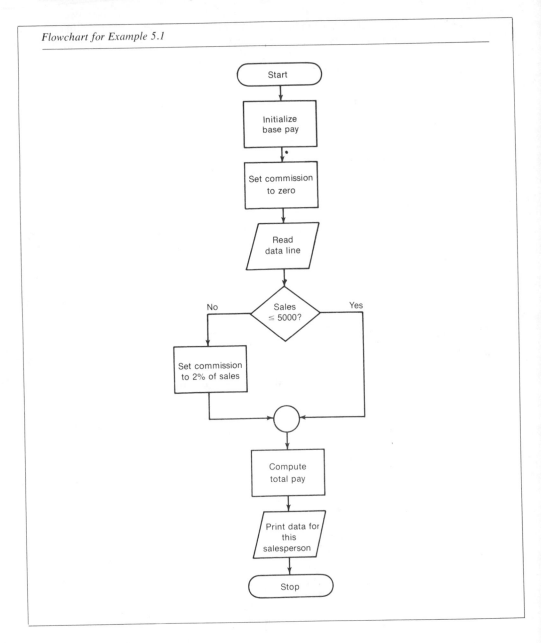

5.  (a) 10 IF E > 25900 THEN 25
        15 LET F = .0613*S
        20 GO TO 30
        25 LET F = 0
        30 . . .
          :

(b)  10  LET F = 0
      15  IF E > 25900 THEN 30
      20  LET F = .0613∗S
      30  ...
          ⋮

The version in part b is shorter and eliminates the use of a GO TO.

(c)  050  IF A > C THEN 100
      060    LET X = X + 3
      070    LET Y = Y + 2
      080    LET A = A + 1
      090  GO TO 50
      100  ...
          ⋮

(d)  10  IF A∗C < B/D THEN 50
      20  LET X = A + B
      30  LET D = B − A
      40  GO TO 75
      50  LET C = D/E
      60  LET F = F − 1
      75  ...
          ⋮

(e)  10  IF A > 50 THEN 40
      20  LET L = L + 3
      30  GO TO 99
      40  IF B >= 40 THEN 80
      50  LET K = K + 2
      60  LET D = D + C
      70  GO TO 99
      80  LET J = J + 1
      99  ...
          ⋮

7.  (a)  In Example 5.3, change line 215 to

      215 FOR I = 1 TO 325 STEP 1

insert 322 more DATA statements, and relabel the END statement to a higher number. In Example 5.4, simply change line 900 to

      900 DATA 325

insert 322 more DATA statements, and relabel the END statement to a higher number. The simplicity of this data change is what makes this version superior to that in Example 5.3.

(b)  208  FOR J = 1 TO 39
      209    PRINT "−";
      210  NEXT J
      211  PRINT ⟵ If this PRINT statement is omitted, then the data line for B. FLINTSTONE will appear immediately to the right of the last dash.

**8. (a)** 1
    2
    3     The loop iterates 10 times.
    4
    5
    6
    7
    8
    9
    10

**(b)** 1     The loop iterates five times.
    3
    5
    7
    9

**(c)** 2     The loop iterates four times.
    3
    4
    5

**(d)** 5     The loop iterates once.
**(e)** Nothing is printed. The loop is inactive (not entered) and execution proceeds to the first executable statement following NEXT L.

**10.** See flowchart on facing page.

| J | C | I | I1 | C1 | N |
|---|------|------|------|-----|---|
| 1 | 147 | 5165 | 5165 | 147 | 5 |
| 2 | 56 | 7860 | 5165 | 147 | 5 |
| 3 | 75 | 6350 | 5165 | 147 | 5 |
| 4 | 41 | 4293 | 4293 | 41 | 5 |
| 5 | 105 | 5415 | 4293 | 41 | 5 |

*Output:*

SMSA NUMBER 41
HAS THE MINIMUM PER CAPITA INCOME OF 4293

**11. (a)** J is the index of the loop, which should not be redefined. We would have an exit from the loop after one iteration.
**(b)** Infinite loop.
**(c)** Branching into the body of a FOR/NEXT loop may not be permissible. Changing line 197 to

    197 GO TO 100

would reactivate the loop when line 120 is executed. In this case, the printed output would be repeated ad infinitum, which of course would have no useful purpose.

Flowchart for Exercise 10

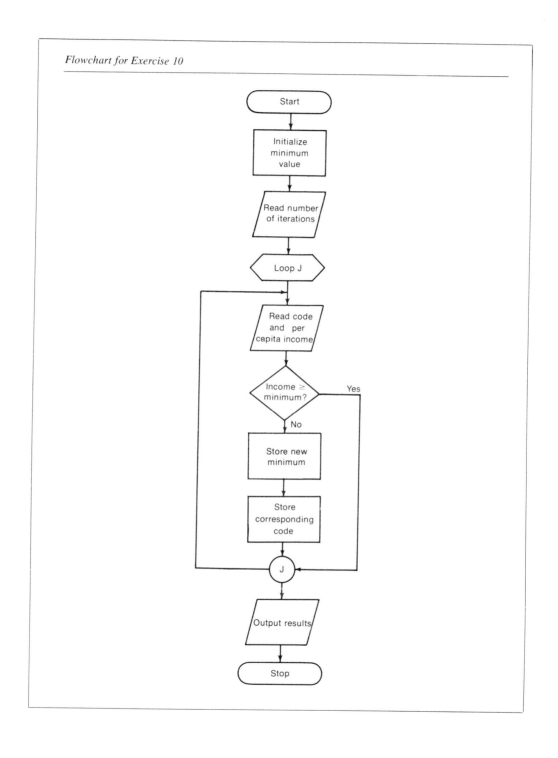

**13.** **(a)** 10        The loop iterates 11 times.
         9
         8
         7
         6
         5
         4
         3
         2
         1
         0

   **(b)** 10        The loop iterates four times.
         7
         4
         1

   **(c)** .05        The loop iterates 21 times.
         .06
         .07
         .08
          :
          :
         .25

   **(d)** .05        The loop iterates five times.
         .10
         .15
         .20
         .25

   **(e)** 1.0        The loop iterates nine times.
         1.5
         2.0
         2.5
         3.0
         3.5
         4.0
         4.5
         5.0

   **(f)** 1.0        The loop iterates nine times.
         1.5
         2.0
         2.5
         3.0
         3.5
         4.0
         4.5
         5.0
         5.0        or 5.5 or undefined (depending on system)

(g) 1.0     The loop iterates five times.
    1.5
    2.0
    2.5
    3.0
    3.0

(h) 4     21     The loop iterates four times.

(i)  4     The loop iterates five times.
    6
    8
   10
   12

14. (a) Valid.
    (b) Invalid. K will never exceed terminal value. Either eliminate negative step or change to

      60 FOR K = 5 TO 1 STEP −1

    (c) Invalid. Line 20 branches into body of loop, line 60 redefines control variable, line 80 causes infinite loop, and control variables do not match in lines 40 and 90.

15. (a) No. (b) Yes, either the incorrect sum 420 would be printed (if the system initializes T to zero) or an execution error would result the first time LET A = A + T is executed (if the system treats T as undefined). (c) The words "TOTAL PAYROLL:" and a running sum (the value of A) would be printed immediately following *each* employee's output line. (d) The headings would appear just before each employee's output line. (e) Some systems initialize all variables to zero; others do not. Those that do not will print an execution error message the first time line 310 is executed. It is good programming practice to always initialize variables that count or sum.

16. Insert the following:

    335 LET M = A/N
       :
       :
    360 PRINT "AVERAGE PAY:",,M

# *Chapter 6*

1. (a) R$ = the name of the region.
    (b) Data line 899: number of regions to process.
        Data lines 900 and 910: region names and number of employees in each region.
    (c) Change the 2 in line 899 to 6; add DATA statements for the other four regions following line 912.

(d)

| J | R$ | N | I | B | S | C | T |
|---|------|---|---|-----|-------|-----|-----|
| 1 | EAST | 3 | 1 | 150 | 4150  | 0   | 150 |
| 1 | EAST | 3 | 2 | 200 | 6000  | 120 | 320 |
| 1 | EAST | 3 | 3 | 175 | 2020  | 0   | 175 |
| 2 | WEST | 2 | 1 | 125 | 3000  | 0   | 125 |
| 2 | WEST | 2 | 2 | 250 | 10500 | 210 | 460 |

3.  (a)

| | | |
|---|---|---|
| 1 | 1 | Loop K iterates eight times. |
| 1 | 2 | Loop J iterates four times. |
| 2 | 1 | |
| 2 | 2 | |
| 3 | 1 | |
| 3 | 2 | |
| 4 | 1 | |
| 4 | 2 | |

(b)

| | | |
|---|-----|---|
| 1 | 1.0 | Loop K iterates 24 times. |
| 1 | 1.2 | Loop J iterates four times. |
| 1 | 1.4 | |
| · | · | |
| · | · | |
| 1 | 2.0 | |
| 2 | 1.0 | |
| 2 | 1.2 | |
| · | · | |
| · | · | |
| 2 | 2.0 | |
| · | · | |
| 4 | 1.0 | |
| · | · | |
| 4 | 2.0 | |

(c)  1

|   |   |   |   |
|---|---|---|---|
| 1 |   |   | Loop K iterates 24 times. |
|   | 1 |   | Loop J iterates six times. |
|   | 2 |   | Loop I iterates two times. |
|   | 3 |   | |
|   | 4 |   | |
| 2 |   |   | |
|   | 1 |   | |
|   | 2 |   | |
|   | 3 |   | |
|   | 4 |   | |
| 3 |   |   | |
|   | 1 |   | |
|   | 2 |   | |
|   | 3 |   | |
|   | 4 |   | |

```
2
  1
      1
      2
      3
      4
  2
      1
      2
      3
      4
  3
      1
      2
      3
      4
```

**4.** **(a)** Mismatch of control variables in FOR/NEXT statements. Switch lines 25 and 30. **(b)** The control variable I is used twice within nested FOR/NEXT loops. Change I to some other variable either in lines 35 and 65 or in lines 45 and 55. Also, most programmers prefer to indent the loops.

**5.**

| J | C | R | F |
|---|---|---|---|
| 1 | 60000 | .1 | 66000 |
| 2 | 60000 | .1 | 72600 |
| 3 | 60000 | .1 | 79860 |
| 4 | 60000 | .1 | 87846 |
| 5 | 60000 | .1 | 96630.6 |
| 6 | 60000 | .1 | 106294 |
| 7 | 60000 | .1 | 116923 |
| 8 | 60000 | .1 | 128615 |

(a) F would be zero or undefined, depending on system. In the latter case, there would be an execution error at line 70.

(b) F would always be 66000, thereby giving an infinite loop (line 90 tests false each time).

**6.** It is not likely that F will ever be exactly equal to 2*C; hence an infinite loop would occur.

**7.** Replace line 90 with

    90 IF F < 2*C THEN 60

and delete line 100. Many programmers prefer this, since it eliminates the GO TO statement. Technically, however, this is not a DO UNTIL loop since exit from the loop is based on a "false" rather than "true" condition.

**8.**  20  PRINT "ENTER C,R AND M";
30  INPUT C,R,M
&#8942;
90  IF F >= M*C THEN 999
&#8942;

**10.**  Replace lines 250 and 904 with

250  IF S = 0 THEN 999
904  DATA " ", " ",0

A salesperson might have sales of zero; thus the loop would terminate before all data were processed.

**11.**  Yes. The trailer data would be processed and output.

**12.**  Yes. The data line must contain a value for each variable in the READ statement. Otherwise, an "END OF DATA" error message would be output. Any values for S$ and N$ can be used in the trailer line.

**13.**  Replace lines 250 and 904 with

250  IF S$ = "NO MORE DATA" THEN 999
904  DATA "NO MORE DATA", " ",0

If " ",0 were omitted we would get an "END OF DATA" error message.

**14.**  The table heading would be output just before each line of output for salespeople.

**15.**  This is a popular interactive variation of an LRC loop. In this case, the trailer number test is based on a "yes" or "no" response at the end of the loop. The loop itself calculates the sum of arithmetic values which are input by the user.

**17.**

| J | T | F | M1 | M2 | S1 | S2 | W2 |
|---|---|----|-----|----|----|----|----|
| 1 | 1 | 50 | 50  | 1  | 0  | 0  | 0  |
| 2 | 2 | 15 | 50  | 1  | 15 | 1  | 0  |
| 3 | 2 | 20 | 50  | 1  | 35 | 2  | 0  |
| 4 | 1 | 75 | 125 | 2  | 35 | 2  | 0  |
| 5 | 3 | 0  | 125 | 2  | 35 | 2  | 1  |
| 6 | 2 | 10 | 125 | 2  | 45 | 3  | 1  |
| 7 | 2 | 15 | 125 | 2  | 60 | 4  | 1  |

| TYPE | NUMBER | AMOUNT |
|------|--------|--------|
| MOVING | 2 | 1 2 5 |
| STANDING | 4 | 6 0 |
| WARNING | 1 | |

The numbering of lines more clearly identifies functional parts.

**18.**  (a) ON F GO TO 100,150,200,250
(b) ON C GO TO 100,100,200,300,300,300
(c) Nineteen IF/THEN statements

*Flowchart for Exercise 21*

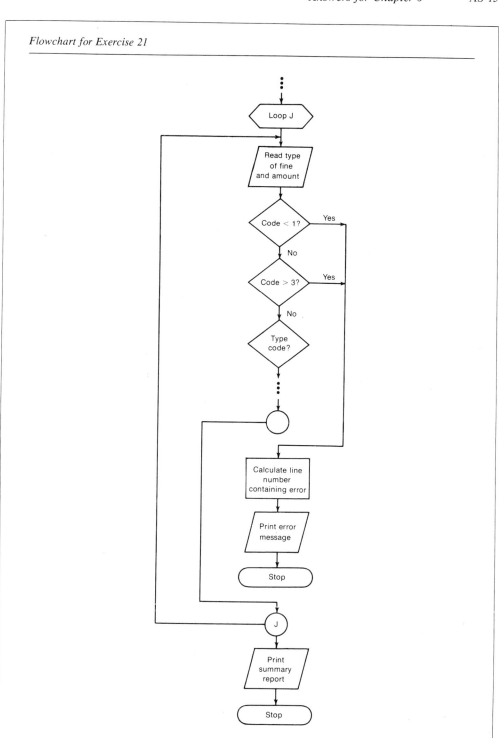

19. (a) Line 10. (b) Line 50. (c) Line 40. (d) Line 40 or execution error. (e) Line 40 or execution error.

20. (a) If T is $<1$ or $>3$. (b) Line number where the code value for T is incorrect. (c) DATA ERROR IN LINE xxx T = xxx Yes. Line 902 contains an error. (d) The program stops execution. (e) If not arranged as shown, then the value of L indicates the wrong data line.

21. See flowchart on previous page. Also, see Exercise 22 for a "cleaner" design.

24. $2250 = 9 \times 250$
    $4650 = (10 \times 240) + 2250$
    $6900 = (10 \times 225) + 4650$

    | N$ | S | T |
    |---|---|---|
    | RENT-A-BIKE | 25 | 6000 |
    | BIKE-A-GO GO | 12 | 2970 |
    | FEET LAST | 29 | 6900 |
    | IBM | 55 | 12230 |
    | MOM and POP | 6 | 1500 |
    | EOD | | |

25. Total price (T) would always be calculated in line 330.

26. 165 LET C = 0
    ⋮
    215 LET C = C + 1
    ⋮
    ⋮
    350 PRINT "PRICE: $";T;TAB(31);C
    ⋮

# Chapter 7

1. The compiler needs to know the number of locations to reserve for the array before execution begins.

2. (a) Variable number of locations reserved for X in line 20; the DIM statement must precede the READ statement. (b) A has not been dimensioned; the subscript in line 50 (M − 2*N) has a value of −11, which is not permitted; the subscript 0 in line 30 is not permitted on some systems. (c) The subscripts in D and E will exceed the upper limits specified in the DIM statement when I = 11 in line 30 and when I = 10 in line 60. E(3) = 36.

4. (a) Change lines 10, 20, and 60 to

    10 DIM D(100)
    20 FOR I = 1 TO 100
    ⋮
    ⋮
    60 FOR I = 1 TO 100

and add more DATA statements. Ninety-seven more LET statements and 97 more PRINT statements would be needed in the second program of page 189. The expression on line 20 would contain 100 variables, as would the list in line 10.

**(b)** 10 DIM D(500)
  :
  :
17 READ N
20 FOR I = 1 TO N
  :
  :
60 FOR I = 1 TO N
  :
  :
99 DATA 3
  :
  :

**5.** 100 DIM M(50)
110 FOR I = 1 TO 50
120    INPUT M(I)
130 NEXT I

**6.** **(a)** 10  20  50
       15  20  75
       10  40  25
       20  50  40

**(b)** 10  20  50  15  20  75  10  40  25  20  50  40

**(c)**   :
          :
160 FOR K = 1 TO M
170    PRINT A(K);
180 NEXT K
190 PRINT
200 FOR K = 1 TO M
210    PRINT B(K);
220 NEXT K
230 PRINT
240 FOR K = 1 TO M
250    PRINT C(K);
260 NEXT K
  :
  :

**8.** C and W remain the same.

        B

| |
|---|
| 150.30 |
| 850.75 |

**9.** T(K) = 0 doesn't initialize 200 positions; T(K) must be within a loop. If K is undefined for the system, then an execution error results; otherwise, T(0) is initialized to 0. T = 0 initializes a simple numeric variable to 0.

```
20 FOR K = 1 TO 200
30     LET T(K) = 0
40 NEXT K
```

**10.** **(a)**

| N | I | M | S | X(1) | X(2) | X(3) | X(4) · · · |
|---|---|---|---|------|------|------|------------|
| 3 | 1 | 5 | — | 5 | — | — | — |
| 3 | 2 | 9 | — | 5 | 4 | — | — |
| 3 | 3 | 12 | — | 5 | 4 | 3 | — |
| 3 | — | 4 | 0 | 5 | 4 | 3 | — |
| 3 | 1 | 4 | 1 | 5 | 4 | 3 | — |
| 3 | 2 | 4 | 1 | 5 | 4 | 3 | — |
| 3 | 3 | 4 | 2 | 5 | 4 | 3 | — |
| 3 | — | 4 | 1 | 5 | 4 | 3 | — |

**(b)** 4    1

**(c)** First M accumulates the sum of the values in X as line 150 is repeatedly executed. Then it's converted to a mean in line 170. Since we have no further use for the sum, this technique saves a storage location. **(d)** First S stores the sum of the deviations squared, as line 200 is repeatedly executed. Then it's converted to a standard deviation in line 220. This saves a storage location. *Note:* Line 220 could be written as

```
220 LET  S = SQR(S/(N − 1))
```

(see Section 9.1 on page 258). **(e)** They are used to accumulate sums. **(f)** Limits the program's generality. 1000 data values. This would waste too much storage if we assume that the number of data items is never anywhere near 100,000. In fact, this many storage locations will exceed the user's primary memory allocation in most time-sharing installations.

**11.** **(a)**            D$

| MONDAY |
|---|
| TUESDAY |
| WEDNESDAY |
| THURSDAY |
| FRIDAY |
| SATURDAY |
| SUNDAY |

(b) TUESDAY
SATURDAY
THURSDAY

(c)
```
100 DIM M$(12)
110 FOR J = 1 TO 12
120    READ M$(J)
130 NEXT J
140 INPUT M,D,Y
150    IF K < 1 THEN 999
160    IF K > 12 THEN 999
170    PRINT M$(M);D;",";Y
180 GO TO 140
901 DATA "JANUARY","FEBRUARY", . . .
    :
    :
999 END
```

**12.** (a) Depends on what the system does with the value in I following a natural exit from the FOR/NEXT loop. For a system that retains the value 5, we would get

PREMIUM IS $357

For a system that stores 6 in I, we would get an execution error as a result of a subscript out of bounds; that is, P(6) was not allocated in the DIM statement. In either case, the program's logic is incorrect.

(b) The bug in part a is corrected by adding

```
425 PRINT "OVER 65—UNINSURABLE"
426 GO TO 300
```

**13.** A RESTORE statement would be needed following loop I in order to reset the pointer to the beginning of the data block for the next policyholder. This would be a poor program design due to the inefficiency of re-reading the premium schedule for each policyholder.

**15.** (a)

| K | S1 | S2 | S | C(1) | C(2) | C(3) | C(4) | T(1) | T(2) | T(3) | T(4) |
|---|-----|-----|------|------|------|------|------|------|------|------|------|
| 2 | 580 | 640 | 1220 | 0 | 1 | 0 | 0 | 0 | 1220 | 0 | 0 |
| 3 | 720 | 680 | 1400 | 0 | 1 | 1 | 0 | 0 | 1220 | 1400 | 0 |
| 2 | 610 | 560 | 1170 | 0 | 2 | 1 | 0 | 0 | 2390 | 1400 | 0 |
| 4 | 415 | 563 | 978 | 0 | 2 | 1 | 1 | 0 | 2390 | 1400 | 978 |
| 1 | 560 | 590 | 1150 | 1 | 2 | 1 | 1 | 1150 | 2390 | 1400 | 978 |

(b) Line 510. Insert

505 LET A(K) = T(K)/C(K)

and change line 510 to

510 PRINT K, A(K), C(K)

There's really no need to create array A since it's not used elsewhere in the program.

**16.**

| I | T | L(1) | L(2) | L(3) | L(4) | S |
|---|---|------|------|------|------|---|
| 2 | 3076 | 3076 | 8321 | 2501 | 7771 | 1 |
| 3 | 2501 | 3076 | 2501 | 8321 | 7771 | 1 |
| 4 | 7771 | 3076 | 2501 | 7771 | 8321 | 1 |
| 2 | 2501 | 2501 | 3076 | 7771 | 8321 | 1 |
| 3 | 2501 | 2501 | 3076 | 7771 | 8321 | 1 |
| 4 | 2501 | 2501 | 3076 | 7771 | 8321 | 1 |
| 2 | 2501 | 2501 | 3076 | 7771 | 8321 | 0 |
| 3 | 2501 | 2501 | 3076 | 7771 | 8321 | 0 |
| 4 | 2501 | 2501 | 3076 | 7771 | 8321 | 0 |

Two passes. Three passes.

## Chapter 8

**1.**   1000   800   500   1200   500   2000   2000   500   1500   300   700   1500

**2.**   1000   500   1500
   800   2000   300
   500   2000   700
   1200   500   1500

**3.**   Same as before:

D

| 1000 | 800 | 500 | 1200 |
|------|-----|-----|------|
| 500 | 2000 | 2000 | 500 |
| 1500 | 300 | 700 | 1500 |

D

**4.**

| 1000 | 1200 | 2000 | 300 |
|------|------|------|-----|
| 800 | 500 | 500 | 700 |
| 500 | 2000 | 1500 | 1500 |

The array in memory gets filled in column by column. In this case values are stored incorrectly if correct storage is assumed to be that given on page 229. If loop R is to be inside loop C, then data should be placed as follows:

```
500  DATA 1000,500,1500
510  DATA 800,2000,300
520  DATA 500,2000,700
530  DATA 1200,500,1500
```

**5.** **(a)** 
```
10  FOR I = 1 TO 3
20      FOR J = 1 TO 2
30          INPUT L(I,J)
40      NEXT J
50  NEXT I
```

**(b)** 
```
10  FOR J = 1 TO 2
20      FOR I = 1 TO 3
30          READ L(I,J)
40      NEXT I
50  NEXT J
```

**6.** **(a)** 
```
10
50
4
320
15
8
```

**(b)** 10   50   4   320   15   8

**(c)** 
```
10   50
4   320
15   8
```

**7.** **(a)** 
```
300  FOR C = 1 TO 4
310      LET T(C) = 0
320      FOR R = 1 TO 3
330          LET T(C) = T(C) + D(R,C)
340      NEXT R
350  NEXT C
```

**(b)** In part a insert:

```
295  LET G = 0
335          LET G = G + D(R,C)
```

Alternatively, instead of line 335 we could use

```
345      LET G = G + T(C)
```

**10.** 
```
20  FOR I = 1 TO 100
30      FOR J = 1 TO 50
40          LET W(I,J) = 100
50      NEXT J
60  NEXT I
```

**14.** **(a)** $T(I,1)$ = upper limit of taxable income (column 2 in Tax Schedule).
**(b)** $T(I,2)$ = fixed amount of tax within a class (column 3 in Tax Schedule)
**(c)** $T(I,3)$ = variable percent amount of tax within a class (column 4 in Tax Schedule).
**(d)** $T(I - 1,1)$ = upper limit of taxable income for previous class, which is the same as lower limit in class I (column 1 in Tax Schedule).

**15.** Column-by-column read in of columns 2, 3, and 4 of Tax Schedule. The data entry for T(26,1) needs to be a large number. In this case we used 999999, although a switch to E-notation would have been preferable. For example, if we had used 1E30, then the bug described in Exercise 18 would not be a problem.

**16.**

| E3 | W | D | I1 | O | A1 | D1 | E1 | T1 | A2 | E2 | T2 | T3 | B | R |
|---|---|---|---|---|---|---|---|---|---|---|---|---|---|---|
| 750 | 12100 | 0 | 0 | 0 | 0 | 1900 | 1 | 2530 | 12100 | 0 | 11350 | 1877.5 | 572.07 | 652.50 |

# Chapter 9

**1.** (a) 6.70925E-04
   (b) 16.0944
   (c) 80
   (d) 3.3
       2
   (e)  3
        3
        3
       −3
   (f) −1
        1
        0

**2.** (a) 28.45. (b) So any fraction above 0.5 can be rounded to the next highest integer.
   (c) 60 LET Y = INT (X + .5)
   (d) 60 LET Y = INT (X/1000 + .5)*1000

**4.** (a) 40 PRINT INT (10*RND)

   (b) 10 FOR I = 1 TO 4
       20    PRINT INT (10*RND)
       30 NEXT I
       40 END

**8.** (a) 3        28.5279        127

   (b) 10 PRINT 1**3+1+3−2*SQR(2*1−1),3**3+3+3−2*SQR(2*3−1),5**3+5+
                                                          3−2*SQR(2*5−1)

       20 END

   The version in part a has 14 characters less code than the version in part b (excluding blanks), and is more aesthetically appealing.

**9.** 6       4       8

**10.** (a) FNA(N) = 1/N**2 + 1/SQR(N)
    (b) FNB(N) = ABS(P*(1 + I)**N − EXP(I*N))

11. **(a)** Function name is too long; missing dummy argument not allowed on some systems.
**(b)** Too many dummy arguments (some systems allow more than one dummy argument).
**(c)** The calling statement (line 10) precedes the DEF statement (line 20). **(d)** Dummy argument cannot be subscripted; function name in calling statement (FNB) does not match function name in DEF statement (FNE). **(e)** FN5 is not allowed as a function name.

12. 31 lines

13.
```
400 PRINT
405 FOR I = 1 TO 24
406     PRINT "b̸";
407 NEXT I
410 PRINT "*** POLYNOMIAL PLOT ***"
420 PRINT
425 FOR I = 1 TO 10
426     PRINT "b̸";
427 NEXT I
430 PRINT ". . . Y-SCALE . . ."
440 PRINT
450 PRINT "X-SCALE"
460 FOR X = 1 TO U
464     PRINT "b̸b̸b̸b̸b̸";X;
466     FOR I = 1 TO 2 + Y(X)
468         PRINT "b̸";
470     NEXT I
472     PRINT "*b̸b̸";Y(X)
480 NEXT X
490 RETURN
```

*Note:* Line 466 assumes that the value of X printed by line 464 is a single digit (integer values 1–9) printed in column 7 of the print line. Thus, for example, if X = 3 and Y(3) = 4, then a 3 gets printed in column 7 (according to line 464), followed by six blank characters (according to the loop in lines 466–470), followed by an asterisk in column 14 and a 4 in column 18 (according to line 472). If the upper limit of X (that is, U) is allowed in the range from 10 to 99, then we must use the following:

```
466 FOR I = 1 TO 2 + Y(X) − INT(X/100 + .905)
```

This preserves the proper scaling of Y. For example, it ensures that the asterisk gets printed in column 51 when X = 10 and Y(X) = 41.

14. Note that print column 11 represents a value of 1 on the Y scale. This is ensured by using a 10 in the argument of the second TAB in line 470.

```
432 PRINT TAB(11);
434 FOR I = 1 TO 50
435     PRINT "−";
438 NEXT I
    :
    :
482 PRINT TAB(11);
484 FOR I = 1 TO 50
486     PRINT "−";
488 NEXT I
```

**15.**  435  GOSUB 500

     ⋮

485  GOSUB 500

     ⋮

494  REM
495  REM *** SUBROUTINE DASHES ***
496  REM
500  PRINT TAB(11);
510  FOR I = 1 TO 50
520     PRINT "−";
530  NEXT I
540  RETURN

Now, at line 435 execution branches to lines 500 through 540, then back to 440 to 480, 485, 500 to 540, 490, and back to the main program. Subroutine DASHES is said to be *nested* within subroutine PLOT.

<table>
<tr><td></td><td></td><td colspan="5" align="center">Output</td></tr>
<tr><td>**20.**</td><td>(a) No subroutine present</td><td>1</td><td>2</td><td>3</td><td>4</td><td>5</td></tr>
<tr><td></td><td>(b) Main:      Lines 5 to 25</td><td></td><td></td><td></td><td></td><td></td></tr>
<tr><td></td><td>    Subroutine: Lines 30 to 35</td><td>1</td><td>2</td><td>3</td><td>4</td><td>5</td></tr>
<tr><td></td><td>(c) Main:      Lines 5 to 15</td><td></td><td></td><td></td><td></td><td></td></tr>
<tr><td></td><td>    Subroutine: Lines 20 to 35</td><td>1</td><td>2</td><td>3</td><td>4</td><td>5</td></tr>
</table>

The use of the subroutine in part c would save code for a program that repeatedly numbers columns in a table, as done on page 239.

**21.**  (a) No. Execution never gets to line 140. We include it for style. (b) No. Line 390 would never be executed. We include it for style. (c) Prints dashes to visually separate each transaction. (d) To correctly calculate the number of weeks when the number of days is 7, 14, 21, . . . . Any fraction less than 1 could be used. (e) To round the value of C2 to two decimal places. (f) C3 is negative whenever line 570 is executed. This would ensure the printout of a positive value.

**22.**  (a) Delete lines 200 to 240 and add:

       200  READ G,D,M1,W1,P
       900  DATA 20,17,.15,145,.75

This version is more convenient if these data values change periodically.

  (b)  200  PRINT "ENTER MILES PER GALLON";
       205  INPUT G
       210  PRINT "ENTER DAILY FIXED COSTS AND WEEKLY FIXED COSTS";
       215  INPUT D,W1
       220  PRINT "ENTER CHARGE PER MILE";
       225  INPUT M1
       230  PRINT "ENTER PRICE PER GALLON";
       240  INPUT P
       250  RETURN

This version is best if these data values are likely to change from customer to customer, as when many different types of cars are available.

## Chapter 10

1. Terminal assignment.

2.

---

IBM

(a) 40 :b̸b̸b̸b̸b̸b̸###b̸####

(b) 30 PRINT USING 40,B
   35 PRINT USING 45,R
   40 :B= $\boxed{\#\#}$ $\boxed{\#\#\#}$ or b̸b̸
   45 :R= $\boxed{\#}$ $\boxed{\#\#\#\#}$ or b̸

(c) 30 :b̸b̸b̸b̸b̸b̸b̸#
   30 :b̸b̸b̸b̸b̸b̸#.
   30 :b̸b̸b̸b̸b̸#.#
   30 :b̸b̸b̸b̸#.###
   30 :b̸b̸b̸#.####
   30 :b̸b̸#.#####

   *Note:* One or more of the rightmost b̸'s can be replaced by #'s. For example, the third line above can be replaced by

   30 :b̸b̸b̸b̸###.#

(d) 30 :b̸b̸b̸##.##!!!!
   30 :b̸##.###!!!!
   30 :b̸##.!!!!

   *Note:* See note in part c.

(e) Note how your system responds to the cases characters less than field width (GO) and characters greater than field width (GOOFUS).

(f) 07 PRINT USING 42
   15 DATA 40.05,52.55
   37 PRINT USING 42
   42 :----------------

   Note what happens when the output of −12.50 for P is attempted.

HP

---

(a) 40 XXXXXXDDDXDDDD

(b) 30 PRINT USING 40;B
   35 PRINT USING 45;R
   40 IMAGE"B=" $\boxed{DD}$ $\boxed{DDD}$ or XX
   45 IMAGE"R=" $\boxed{D}$ $\boxed{DDDD}$ or X

(c) 30 IMAGEXXXXXXXXD
   30 IMAGEXXXXXXXD.

    30  IMAGEXXXXXXD.D
    30  IMAGEXXXXD.DDD
    30  IMAGEXXXD.DDDD
    30  IMAGEXXD.DDDDD

*Note:* One or more of the rightmost X's can be replaced by D's. For example, the third line above can be replaced by

    30  IMAGEXXXDDD.D

**(d)** 30  IMAGEXXXDD.DDE
    30  IMAGEXDD.DDDE
    30  IMAGEXDD.E

*Note:* See note in part c.

**(e)** Note how your system responds to the cases characters less than field width (GO) and characters greater than field width (GOOFUS).

**(f)** 07  PRINT  USING  42
    15  DATA  40.05,52.55
    37  PRINT  USING  42
    42  IMAGE  "---------------"

Note what happens when the output of −12.50 for P is attempted.

## DEC

**(a)** 40  LET  A$="ƀƀƀƀƀƀ###ƀ####"

**(b)** 35  LET  A$="B= | ## | ### "  ⟩or ƀƀ
    40  LET  B$="R= | # | #### "  ⟩or ƀ
    45  PRINT  USING  A$,B
    47  PRINT  USING  B$,R

**(c)** 20  LET  F$="ƀƀƀƀƀƀƀƀ#"
    20  LET  F$="ƀƀƀƀƀƀƀ#."
    20  LET  F$="ƀƀƀƀƀƀ#.#"
    20  LET  F$="ƀƀƀƀ#.###"
    20  LET  F$="ƀƀƀ#.####"
    20  LET  F$="ƀƀ#.#####"

*Note:* One or more of the rightmost ƀ's can be replaced by #'s. For example, the third line above can be replaced by

    20  LET  F$="ƀƀƀƀ###.#"

**(d)** 20  LET  I$="ƀƀƀ##.##↑↑↑↑"
    20  LET  I$="ƀ##.###↑↑↑↑"
    20  LET  I$="ƀ##.↑↑↑↑"

*Note:* See note in part c

**(e)** Note how your system responds to the cases characters less than field width (GO) and characters greater than field width (GOOFUS).

**(f)** 22  LET  E$ = "---------------"
    27  PRINT  USING  E$
    35  DATA  40.05,52.55
    57  PRINT  USING  E$

**3.**
```
              Print Column
                11111111112 ...
       1 2 3 4 5 6 7 8 9 0 1 2 3 4 5 6 7 8 9 0
      ─────────────────────────────────────────
```
(a)  − 5 0      1 5 . 3
(b)     N U M B E R  =    − 5 0
(c)   1 5 . 3 2 0   INCHES
(d)                 ENROLLMENT

**4.**
                                    IBM
───────────────────────────────────────────────────────

(a) 10  PRINT  USING  20,A,B,C
    20  :ƀ # # # #ƀƀƀƀ # # # #ƀƀƀ # #.# #!!!

(b) 10  PRINT  USING  20,B
    20  :ƀƀƀMONTHLYƀPAYMENTƀ=ƀ # # #.# #

(c) 10  PRINT  USING  20
    15  PRINT  USING  25
    20  :ƀƀƀ ∗∗ƀ THERMALƀREPORTƀ∗∗
    25  :ƀƀƀƀƀ ∗ ∗ ∗ ∗ ∗ ∗ ∗ ∗ ∗ ∗ ∗ ∗ ∗

(d) 10  PRINT  USING  25
    15  PRINT  USING  30
    20  PRINT  USING  35,N$,S,R,P
    25  :ƀ ƀ ƀ ƀ E M P L O Y E E ƀ ƀ ƀ ƀ S O C I A L ƀ ƀ ƀ ƀ ƀ PAY
    30  :ƀ ƀ ƀ ƀ N A M E ƀ ƀ ƀ ƀ ƀ ƀ ƀ SEC . ƀNO . ƀƀƀƀƀ RATEƀƀƀƀƀGROSSƀPAY
    35  :# # # # # # # # # # # # # # # #ƀƀ # # # # # # # # #ƀƀ$ # . # #ƀƀƀƀƀ$ # # # . # #

                                    HP
───────────────────────────────────────────────────────

(a) 10  PRINT  USING  20;A,B,C
    20  IMAGEXDDDDXXXXXDDDDXXXXDD.DDE

(b) 10  PRINT  USING  20;B
    20  IMAGE''ƀƀƀMONTHLYƀPAYMENTƀ=ƀ''DDD.DD

(c) 10  PRINT  USING  20
    15  PRINT  USING  25
    20  IMAGE''ƀƀƀƀ∗∗ƀTHERMALƀREPORTƀ∗∗''
    25  IMAGE''ƀƀƀƀƀƀ∗ ∗ ∗ ∗ ∗ ∗ ∗ ∗ ∗ ∗ ∗ ∗∗''

(d) 10  PRINT  USING  25
    15  PRINT  USING  30
    20  PRINT  USING  35;N$,S,R,P
    25  IMAGE''ƀƀƀƀEMPLOYEEƀƀƀƀ SOCIALƀƀƀƀƀƀ PAY''
    30  IMAGE''ƀƀƀƀNAMEƀƀƀƀƀƀƀƀƀSEC.ƀNO.ƀƀƀƀƀƀRATEƀƀƀƀƀƀGROSSƀPAY''
    35  IMAGEAAAAAAAAAAAAAAAAAXXDDDDDDDDDXXX''$''D.DDXXXXXXX''$''DDD.DD

                                    DEC
───────────────────────────────────────────────────────

(a) 10  LET A$ = ''ƀ # # # #ƀƀƀƀ # # # #ƀƀƀ # #.# #↑↑↑↑''
    20  PRINT  USING  A$

**(b)** 10  LET A$ = "b̸b̸b̸MONTHLYb̸PAYMENTb̸ = b̸###.##"
20  PRINT USING A$

**(c)** 10  LET A$ = "b̸b̸b̸b̸**b̸ THERMALb̸REPORTb̸**"
15  LET B$ = "b̸b̸b̸b̸b̸b̸b̸ ** ** * ** ** ** ** **
20  PRINT USING A$
25  PRINT USING B$

**(d)** 10  LET A$ = "b̸b̸b̸b̸EMPLOYEEb̸b̸b̸b̸b̸ SOCIALb̸b̸b̸b̸b̸b̸ PAY"
15  LET B$ = "b̸b̸b̸b̸NAMEb̸b̸b̸b̸b̸b̸b̸b̸ SEC.b̸NO.b̸b̸b̸b̸b̸ RATEb̸b̸b̸b̸b̸b̸GROSSb̸PAY"
20  LET C$ ="\\\\\\\\\\\ \\\\\\\\b̸b̸ ##########b̸b̸b̸$ #.##b̸b̸b̸b̸b̸b̸ $###.##"
25  PRINT USING A$
30  PRINT USING B$
35  PRINT USING C$,N$,S,R,P

5.  **(a)** Depends on system, since field width of nine not large enough to fit the 11 characters in SS number. **(b)** Depends on system, since two digits to the left of the decimal not large enough to fit the total pay output. **(c)** No, it's a literal field. **(d)** No, image statements are nonexecutable. **(e)** In order to group image lines, which facilitates the alignment of output.

# Chapter 11

1.  Terminal assignment.

2.  Yes. The string variable and file number need only be consistent within the same program. In general, different programs may access the same file. The ability to use different string variables for file name and different file numbers facilitate the general use of a file by various programs.

3.  This allows the program to access any file without having to make changes in the program itself. For example, programs 1 and 2 can be used as they are to process a file named MGS1072, as long as this file has the same structure as GRADES.

4.  Program 1 relates to Figure 11.1(b). The user inputs data through the terminal to the CPU, and the computer then outputs the data to the file named GRADES. Program 2 relates to Figure 11.2(c). The user inputs the file name through the terminal, the computer opens (accesses) the file, inputs the file's data into the CPU, and finally outputs the data at the terminal.

# Chapter 12

1.  **(a)** Same output as Example 12.1.
    **(b)**  10      15
         20      25
         30      35

         100
         200
         300
         400
         500

(c) and (d) Same as Example 12.1. (e) If data lines 60 and 70 are not interchanged, then we would get

```
35   100
200  300
400  500

10
15
20
25
30
```

(f) and (g)

```
?10,15
?20,25
?30,35
?100
?200
?300
?400
?500
```

Output same as Example 12.1.

**2.**    10    20    30    40

```
10
20
30
40
```

10    20    30    40

T is treated as a row vector above.

**3.**  (a) DATA statements now appear as follows:

```
900 DATA 3,2
901 DATA 10,1
902 DATA 20,2
903 DATA 30,3
904 DATA 0,0
```

(b) Eliminate lines 900 to 905 and change lines 20, 30, 40, and 130 to

```
18 PRINT "ENTER ROWS,COLUMNS";
20 INPUT M,N
28 PRINT "ENTER X ROW-BY-ROW";
30 MAT INPUT X(M,N)
38 PRINT "ENTER INITIAL VALUES OF A ON ONE LINE";
40 MAT INPUT A(1,N)
130 MAT PRINT X;A;
```

**6.** Delete line 30 and change line 40 to

    40 MAT A = ZER(1,N)

**7.**   11  22  33
      44  55  66
      77  88  99

      0  2  3
      4  4  6
      7  8  8

      0  4  7
      2  4  8
      3  6  8

Line 50 sets array C to same dimensions as A and B so that subtraction can take place in line 60.

**8.** Both runs should give the following output for D:

    2  2  3
    0  1  1
    1  1  1

**9.** **(a)** The primary purpose of line 130 is to redimension P, which just as well could have been done with the CON or IDN functions. The ZER function is not really needed to initialize sums to zero since R and C have zeros in the appropriate locations based on the DATA statements.
    **(b)** The row and column sums of P are identical to differences of corresponding row and column sums of R − C. Thus, it's simpler and more efficient to place this statement at

        462 MAT P = R − C

  **(c)** 480 MAT PRINT R,C,P

  **(d)** In the example, we eliminate 21 lines of executable code and add 3 lines, for a net savings of 18 lines; in part b, we save 2 lines of code; in part c, we eliminate 42 lines of code and add 1, for a net savings of 41 lines. Total savings: 61 lines of executable code.

**10.** **(a)** The market share of brand 1 is gaining at the expense of brands 2 and 3. **(b)** Rows of the transition matrix are nearly identical to one another and to the market share vector. The market shares beyond period 52 will remain essentially the same, a condition called *steady state*.

**14.**   $1(1) + 1(2) + 1(0) = 3$
      $5(1) - 1(2) + 2(0) = 3$
      $2(1) - 3(2) + 1(0) = -4$

**15.** Line 130 redimensions X for consistency with B and line 135 redimensions C for conformity with A. The matrix C is the inverse of A, or $A^{-1}$.

## Module B

**1.** **(a)** The pseudocode version describes the following IF/THEN/ELSE structure

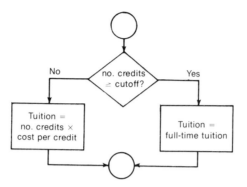

whereas the BASIC program accomplishes the same end by

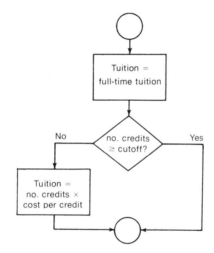

**(b)** Yes. The code in Figure B.5(c) *effectively* reproduces the flowchart and pseudocode versions by testing the *complementary* condition $C < C1$ rather than $C \geq C1$, since when $C < C1$ tests false, it follows that $C \geq C1$ is true. Thus, the program does execute the THEN branch (the full-time tuition statements in lines 55 and 60) when $C \geq C1$ is true, which is consistent with the logic in parts (a) and (b) of the figure. An *exact* reproduction, however, would directly test the $C \geq C1$ condition as follows:

```
  ⋮
50 IF C >= C1 THEN 57
55 GO TO 72
57 REM THEN
60     LET T = T1
65     LET K2 = K2 + 1
```

```
70  GO TO 82
72  REM ELSE
75     LET T = C*C2
80     LET K1 = K1 + 1
82  REM ENDIF
    ⋮
```

Although this is a faithful reproduction of the IF/THEN/ELSE structure, we prefer the approaches in Figure B.5(c) and Example B.1. The extra GO TO in line 55 slightly impairs clarity and efficiency. Moreover, the greater the number of GO TO's the greater the likelihood of unreliable execution due to an incorrect line number transfer.

**2.**  Sequence followed by DO WHILE followed by sequence. The DO WHILE itself contains a sequence followed by IF/THEN/ELSE followed by sequence. The IF/THEN/ELSE itself contains a sequence in each branch.

**3.**
```
Initialize part-time and full-time student counters
READ credit cutoff, full-time tuition, cost/credit, fees
READ id, no. credits
DO WHILE another student needs to be processed
    IF no. credits ≥ cutoff THEN
        Tuition = full-time tuition
        Increment full-time counter
    ELSE
        Tuition = no. credits X cost per credit
        Increment part-time counter
    END IF
    Balance due = tuition + fees
    PRINT id, balance due
    READ id, no. credits
END DO
PRINT no. part-time and full-time students
Stop
```

**4.**  See variable definitions on page B-7.
```
05  LET K1 = 0
10  LET K2 = 0
15  READ C1,T1,C2,F
20  READ I,C
22  REM DO WHILE TRAILER NUMBER NOT ENCOUNTERED
25  IF I = −99 THEN 77
30     IF C < C1 THEN 47
32     REM THEN
35        LET T = T1
40        LET K2 = K2 + 1
45     GO TO 57
47     REM ELSE
50        LET T = C*C2
55        LET K1 = K1 + 1
```

```
57      REM ENDIF
60      LET B = T + F
65      PRINT I,B
70      READ I,C
75 GO TO 25
77 REM ENDDO
80 PRINT K1,K2
91 DATA 901,9
92 DATA 902,12
93 DATA 903,15
94 DATA -99,0
99 END
```

The above code *effectively* reproduces a DO WHILE structure, that is, the loop is processed *while* the trailer number is not encountered, and the test in line 25 precedes the body of the loop in lines 30 to 70.

The effective reproduction was accomplished in line 25 by testing the *complement* of the condition "Another student" in Figure B.9; that is, a false response to "I = -99?" is equivalent to a true response to "another student?" Note, however, that exit from the loop in the program is accomplished by a *true* condition (when the trailer number is encountered in line 25). In this sense, the DO WHILE loop in the program is not an *exact* reproduction of the structure in Figure B.8(a) on page B-20; that is, an exact reproduction requires exit from the loop when the condition is *false*.

An exact reproduction can be accomplished by the following design:

```
  ⋮
22 REM DO WHILE WE HAVE A STUDENT
25 IF I <> -99 THEN 30
28 GO TO 77
30      IF C < C1 THEN 47
  ⋮      ⋮
77 REM END DO
  ⋮
```

Notice that now the loop continues *while* the condition in line 25 tests true and terminates when the condition tests false, which is consistent with Figure B.8(a).

As in our discussion of Exercise 1b, we prefer the *effective* reproduction to the *exact* reproduction, since this last version decreases clarity, efficiency, and reliability.

5. In a DO UNTIL loop the body precedes the test. In this case, the body would contain the sequence

```
READ id, no. credits
Calculate tuition
Calculate balance due
PRINT id, balance due
```

followed by the test for loop termination. This means that when the trailer line is read in it would be processed as if it were a legitimate student.

# INDEX